Encyclopedia
of
ILLINOIS

ABRAHAM LINCOLN

Encyclopedia
of
ILLINOIS

-a volume of
ENCYCLOPEDIA OF THE UNITED STATES

◆

SECOND EDITION

SOMERSET PUBLISHERS, INC.
521 Fifth Ave., 17th Floor
New York, N.Y. 10175

ISBN 0-403-09965-X

Library of Congress Cataloging-in-Publication Data

Encyclopedia of Illinois. -- 2nd ed.
     p.   cm. -- (Encyclopedia of the United States)
   Includes bibliographical references and index.
   ISBN 0-403-09965-X
   1. Illinois--Encyclopedias.   I. Somerset Publishers.   II. Series.
F539.E52   1994
977.3'003--dc20   94-6756
                                                                CIP

iv

FOREWORD

Information on this state is available from many other sources. Histories and geographies abound; there are place-name books, guidebooks and biographical references; many excellent atlases provide map detail; government registers contain in-depth coverage of the political organization.

It is the existance of so many varied sources of information that makes a systematic, encyclopedic reference necessary - a single source for the most useful information about the state.

A secondary purpose of this volume is to play a part in a national reference on all of the states, a systematic approach to referencing the entire nation - an *Encyclopedia of the United States,* with each volume following a planned outline that matches each other volume in the series - with exceptions in the format made only when necessary.

This goal was partly achieved during the Great Depression years with the publication of the WPA Federal Writers' Project State and City Guidebooks, which we are proud to have republished in recent years in their original form. While containing a wealth of interesting and still useful information they are essentially *tour-guides* rather than general reference books. They were, however, very useful in the planning of this new work.

It is our hope that this Encyclopedia series will have a permanence through the issuance of revised editions at intervals to be determined by a careful watch on the availability of new material. Undoubtedly, changes in the concept will be reflected in later editions as a result of feedback from users and the observations and introspection of our editors.

We wish to acknowledge with great appreciation the cooperation of the many state and local government offices that have furnished or reviewed material.

We are further grateful to the many librarians who have made their facilities so available during the years that this project has been in progress.

LIBRARIANS WHO CONTRIBUTED
MATERIAL FOR THIS EDITION

ALLEN, ROBERTA – Danville

BLIETZ, CYNTHIA – Alsip

CARNEY, SHIRLEY – Orion

DAKE, MARY C. – Hartford

DIXON, CHARLENE – Mt. Sterling

DOBBERSTEIN, REV. PAUL M. – Broadview

DUDEK, EDWARD F. – Summit

FORD, ALICE – White Hall

FOSS, MARIE – Walnut

GABRIEL, MICHAEL – Bellwood

GRAFTON, MONA R. – Mattoon

HAHNE, MARY S. – Peru

HANKS, ENID – Galesburg

HICKERSON, MARGARET – Avon

HOORNBEEK, LYNDA C. – Glen Ellyn

HUNTINGTON, STAN D. – Maywood

KUHN, CHRISTINE – Lisle

MCCORMICK, MILDRED B. – Golconda

MCKENZIE, MARY – Norris City

MELLEN, THOMAS – Gurnee

MIEL, DEBRA M. – Roselle

MILLER, JANET – Forrest

MOMA, NANCY M. – Stonington

NITZ-WEISS, JULIE ANNE – Lincolnwood

STITT, SHIRLEY – Hinsdale

WEBER, MAYRETA – Chenoa

WEST, AUDREY L. – Farmer City

WOOD, LOIS – Bloomington

ZNENEK, KATE – LaGrange Park

ZOELLE, ANDREA – Lockport

CONTENTS

INTRODUCTION

THE PRAIRIE STATE.

Illinois became the 21st state to enter the Union on December 3, 1818. It was discovered in 1673 by explorer Louis Jolliet and Jesuit Father Jacques Marquette when they floated down the great Mississippi, returned up the Illinois River, and then crossed the portage to Lake Michigan where Chicago now stands.

Illinois is located at the heart of the great interior river system of the continent. The Mississippi, Ohio, and Wabash rivers form its western, southern, and eastern boundaries. Across it flows the Illinois, the Kaskaskia, the Sangamon, the Spoon, the Rock, the Embarrass, the Kankakee and the Des Plaines; each was, in its day, a highway of trade.

Illinois is a level land of fertile prairies and numerous groves. Beneath its surface are deposits of lead, vast beds of bituminous coal, and known and unknown pools of oil.

Illinois land area and water areas are approximately 58,000 miles. It measures 385 miles long and 218 miles wide. The highest point is 1,241 feet, located at Charles Mound in Jo Daviess County; the lowest point is 279 feet, at the Mississippi River.

STATE SYMBOLS

THE NAME

LaSalle, having sailed along the Illinois River from its mouth in 1679, named it after the tribe of Indians which he found dwelling along its banks.

The Territory of Illinois, having been organized on February 3, 1809, was admitted into the Union as the State of Illinois on December 3, 1818.

1

Both the river and the State were called Illinois, a native name, "given by the French to a confederate tribe of Indians and (to) the country which they inhabited" along the Mississippi Valley.

The name *Illinois* is derived from "the Algonquian Indian word Inini, which the French pronounced Illini," signifying *the men, perfect and accomplished.* "The suffix *ois* is purely French, and denotes tribe." Thus the word *Illinois* in its original meaning signifies *a tribe of men, men perfect and accomplished,* or as it is often given, *a tribe of superior men.*

This combination of Indian and French elements used to form a new word "is a symbol of how the two races--the French and the Indians--were intermixed during the early history of the country."

NICKNAMES

The State of Illinois has five sobriquets: the *Corn State, Egypt,* the *Garden of the West,* the *Prairie State,* and the *Sucker State.*

Illinois is called the *Corn State* because it is one of the most important states in the corn belt.

The sobriquet *Egypt* was given to the State of Illinois, in all probability, both on account of the fertility of the soil in and around Cairo, Illinois, which resembles that around Cairo, Egypt, after the Nile has flooded, and on account of the fact that the people of southern Illinois were dark- complexioned, thus resembling the inhabitants of Egypt. The similarity of the names of the two cities as Cairo probably had something to do with fixing the State nickname.

The State is nicknamed the *Garden of the West,* doubtless, from the appearance of its rolling prairies and its vast cultivated fields.

Illinois is designated as the *Prairie State* because so much of its area is composed of prairie lands. The nickname, the *Sucker State,* is generally applied to Illinois. There is much conjecture as to the origin of this sobriquet. Townsend stated that the term originated at the Galena Lead Mines in 1822, at which time there was a great exodus of Illinois men returning home from the mines. An old miner said to them: "Ye put me in (the) mind of suckers, they do go up the river in the spring, spawn, and all return dow ag'in in the fall."

Townsend gave another possible origin in the fact that many places in the western prairies were filled with crawfish holes out of which the early travelers, by means of long reeds, would suck up the pure water from beneath. When a traveler would find one of the crawfish holes, he would call out "a sucker! a sucker!" meaning thereby a reed; and in this way the name probably originated.

The inhabitants of Illinois are given the sobriquets *Egyptians, Sand-hillers,* and *Suckers.* The people of the southern part of the State are nicknamed *Egyptians* for the reason that the State was called Egypt, as explained in the text previously. The sobriquet *Sand-hillers* was probably first attributed to those citizens who lived on the gradually sloping hills or the broken sandy plains of the State. The name *Suckers* was applied "throughout the West to a native of Illinois," from the facts given as the source of the sobriquet *Sucker State*, explained in the text above.

THE STATE FLAG

The flag of Illinois, which consists of a white field upon which is a reproduction of the emblem of the Great Seal of the State in black or in national colors, was adopted by action of the legislature on July 6, 1915.

In 1969, the legislature amended the 1915 action to include the name of the state on the flag, and to standardize production of the flag. The amended act reads as follows:

"The reproduction of the emblem only on the 'great seal of the State of Illinois' is authorized and permitted when reproduced in black or in the national colors upon a white sheet or background and bearing an actual reproduction of the great seal except for the outer ring thereof for use as a State banner or insignia under the conditions and subject to the restrictions provided by the laws of the United States and the State of Illinois as to the United States or State flag or ensign."

THE STATE MOTTO

The State motto of Illinois as used on the seal of the State, is *State Sovereignty, National Union.* It reads as given, upward, and thus would seem to emphasize national union, as it is the last and uppermost on the seal. In designing the State seal of Illinois, those planning it took the United States Seal, "erasing the image of the federal caesar" and its suprescription, "then they proudly wrote in its stead '*State Sovereignty, National Union.*'" This motto seems to have been inspired by the fact that on the escutcheon of the United States Seal, "the pieces ... represent the several states all joined in one compact entire, supporting a Chief which unites the whole and represents Congress." Brand Whitlock states that "the Motto alludes to the Union."

THE STATE FLOWER

The State legislature on February 21, 1903, declared the native violet (probably the wood violet, or the Bird-foot violet, *Viola pedate*) to be the State flower of Illinois. This law went into effect on July 1, 1908.

THE STATE BIRD

Illinois, by an act of her legislature, approved June 4, 1929, designated the cardinal (*Cardinalis cardinalis*) as her State bird.

The cardinal is from seven and three quarters to nine inches in length. This bird is generally found from the Middle States southward. However, it is occasionally seen in many other parts of the United States. The cardinals, except during the mating season, usually are gregarious in their habits. They eat insects, larvae, bugs, flies, fruits, and seeds. The throat and a narrow ring around the bill of the cardinal are black, the bill is red, and a crest of feathers crowns the head. Most of the plumage of the male is a deep rich red; the crest, wings, and tail are deeper in color, and the back has a greyish tinge. The female is duller in color than the male. Both the male and the female have a pleasing song, that of the female being even more charming in quality than her mate's. This bird is usually found in thickets or in undergrowth.

Introduction

THE STATE SONG

An act establishing a State Song, by the 54th General Assembly:

Be it enacted by the People of the State of Illinois represented in the General Assembly:

Section 1. The song "Illinois," having words written by C. H. Chamberlain and music composed by Archibald Johnston, is established as the official State Song of Illinois. Words of the song follow:

ILLINOIS

By thy gently flowing. Illinois. Illinois.

O'er thy prairies verdant growing. Illinois. Illinois.

Comes an echo on the breeze.

Rustling through the leafy trees, and its mellow tones are these

Illinois. Illinois.

From a wilderness of prairies. Illinois. Illinois.

Straight thy way and never varies. Illinois. Illinois.

Till upon the inland sea.

Stands thy great commercial tree, turning all the world to thee.

Illinois. Illinois.

Turning all the world to thee. Illinois.

When you heard your country calling. Illinois. Illinois.

Where the shot and shell were falling. Illinois. Illinois.

When the Southern host withdrew.

Pitting Gray against the Blue.

There were none more brave than you.

Illinois. Illinois.

There were none more brave than you. Illinois.

Not without they wondrous story. Illinois. Illinois.

Can be writ the nation's glory. Illinois. Illinois.

On the record of thy years.

Abraham Lincoln's name appears. Grant and Logan, and our tears.
Illinois. Illinois.

Grant and Logan, and our tears. Illinois.

THE STATE CAPITOL

On February 25, 1837, the Assembly passed a bill providing that the Capitol be moved from Vandalia to some place nearer the center of the State. Three days later, Springfield was chosen as the new Capital city. Because of the Act of the Genei 1 Assembly in 1820, Vandalia was to continue as the Capital until December 1, 1840, but on June 20, 1839, Governor Thomas Carlin issued a proclamation that all State records be moved to Springfield by July 4, 1839. State government did not actually function in Springfield until December 1839.

The eleventh General Assembly returned the Vandalia Capitol to the county of Fayette and the city of Vandalia, and the old State house still stands, though it is again State property.

The cornerstone of the State's fifth Capitol building was laid in Springfield on July 4, 1837. After many delays, the building was finally completed in 1853, at a cost of $260,000, double its original estimate.

The Enabling Act was passed by the 25th General Assembly on February 24, 1867, and ground was broken for the present Capitol on March 11, 1868. Formal laying of the cornerstone took place on October 5th of the same year. Still unfinished, the building was first occupied in 1876. Twenty-one years after the Legislature first authorized its construction, the building was finally completed. Originally, construction costs were limited to $3,000,000, but before completion, expenditures amounted to more than $4,500,000.

The present Capitol, situated on a nine acre plot, is in the form of a Latin Cross. The circular foundation, 92.5 feet in diameter, upon which the vast dome rests, is 25.5 feet below the grade line, set on solid rock. The walls supporting the dome are 17 feet thick from the foundation to the first story. They are built of granular magnesian limestone from the quarries of Hancock County. The outer walls are of Niagara limestone, those of the lower stories from the quarries of Joliet; those of the upper stories are 379 feet, and from east to west are 268 feet. The height from the ground line to the top of the dome is 361 feet, and to the tip of the flagstaff 405 feet.

THE GREAT SEAL

The present Great Seal of the State of Illinois was authorized by the Assembly on March 7, 1867, but was not used until October 26, 1868. An interesting series of incidents is involved in its history.

The first of all the seals used for official documents in what is now Illinois was that of 1788. It was known as "The Seal of the Territory of the U.S.N.W. of the Ohio River." The words were within two concentric circles. The center of the seal showed a river, on which were two canoes, with woodland showing beyond the river.

In 1800 when Indiana Territory, which included Illinois, was created, a new seal was needed. This situation was met by duplicating the seal of the Northwest Territory, the only change being the substitution of the words "Indiana Territory" within the circles.

When Illinois Territory came into existence in 1809, still another seal was required. So the fathers made an almost exact copy of the Great Seal of the United States, merely eliminating the "E Pluribus Unum." This seal was first used on February 4, 1810.

When Illinois gained statehodd in 1818, the second session of the First General Assembly decreed on February 19, 1819 that it was the duty of the Secretary of State to procure a permanent State seal, as was to be agreed upon by the Governor, Shadrach Bond, and the Justices of the Supreme Court, Thomas C. Browne, William P. Foster, Joseph Phillips, John Reynolds, and William Wilson.

The new seal was another duplicate of the United States seal, but differed from the preceding seal of the Territory in that the eagle held a scroll in its beak on which were the words of the State motto, "State Sovereignty--

7

National Union." As previously, the eagle held a bunch of arrows in one talon, an olive branch in the other, with the escutcheon on its chest.

This seal remained in use until late October 1868, when unexplained activities by Sharon Tyndale, Secretary of State, brought about the creation of the seal which exists today.

Tyndale, in January 1867, told Senator Allen C. Fuller that the old seal had outlived its usefulness, that a new one was necessary, and asked Fuller to sponsor a bill to renew it. The bill was presented to the Senate on January 7, 1867, and passed without comment. It went to the House, and when read there on January 10th, Assemblyman Dinsmore from Whiteside County suggested an amendment to provide that the new seal was to be "an exact facsimile of the present seal."

The amendment was defeated 46 to 31.

Dinsmore's beaten amendment created immediate suspicion of the bill. It was recalled to the Senate. The vote that approved was reconsidered. It was discovered that Tyndale planned in the new seal to reverse the wording on the scroll, changing it from "State Sovereignty, National Union" to "National Union, State Sovereignty." Why he wished the change was never publicly explained. But the change that he contemplated was thwarted by a Senate amendment which ruled that the words on the scroll of the renewed seal were to correspond with the old seal in every particular.

The bill was passed March 7, 1867 in its amended form.

The old seal continued in use until its last official imprint on October 24, 1868, and the final impressions were sharp and clear, indicating it was not "badly out of order" as had been claimed by Tyndale.

The new seal, which is the present one and which was designed by Tyndale, is a radical departure from the old. When it first appeared, and all through the years since, the reasons for the inside design, made at Tyndale's direction, have puzzled many.

The shield no longer adorns the eagle's breast, but is in a tilted position on the grounds; the arrows are gone; the ɔranch bears little resemblance to an olive branch; the eagle is sitting on a boulder in a prairie; and a rising sun shines on a distant horizon. The only thing unchanged was the scroll and the wording on the scroll, and this change was denied to Tyndale only by an innocent sounding and defeated amendment offered by Dinsmore, which started the action that kept the arrangement of the four words intact.

Seal of the Illinois
Territory (sketch)

First Great Seal of the
State of Illinois

Second Great Seal of the
State of Illinois

Present Great Seal of the
State of Illinois
1868–Present

OTHER FACTS ABOUT ILLINOIS

Total area: 56,345 square miles.

Land area: 55,645 square miles.

Water area: 700 square miles.

Average elevation: 600 feet.

Highest point: Charles Mound, 1,235 feet.

Lowest point: Mississippi River, 279 feet.

Highest temperature: 117 degrees Fahrenheit.

Lowest temperature: -35 degrees Fahrenheit.

Population in 1990: 11,430,602.

Population density in 1990: 205.61 persons per square mile.

Population 1980-1990: 0.0 percent change.

Black population in 1990: 1,694,273.

Hispanic population in 1990: 904,446.

Native American population in 1990: 21,836.

White population in 1990: 8,952,978.

Capital: Springfield.

Admitted to Union: December 3, 1818.

Order of Statehood: 21.

Electoral votes: 24.

GEOGRAPHICAL CONFIGURATION

Seen from the air, the land of Illinois reveals graphically the agricultural importance of the State. Carved by intensive cultivation into an intricated mosaic of squares and rectangles, the level prairie resembles nothing so much as a vast stretch of modernistic tiles. In the grainfields no land is wasted; pasture adjoins field, farm fits snugly against farm, and between them is nothing but the straight line of a fence or hedgerow of osage orange.

Water Systems.

Lying between the Great Lakes and the Mississippi, Illinois enjoys a drainage system extraordinarily complete and extensive. Water from 23 of the 48 states crosses its surface and flows along its boundaries, eastward through Lake Michigan to the Atlantic Ocean and southward in the Mississippi to the Gulf. Although its topography presents no striking contrasts of surface contour, the State is separated into seven gentle but distinct basins, bearing the names of Lake Michigan, the Illinois, the Rock, the Kaskaskia, the Big Muddy, the Wabash, and the Ohio rivers. Arteries and branches of these great rivers serve 87.2 percent of the 56,665 square miles of the State's surface. The largest, the Illinois, runs from northeast to southwest and drains an area 250 miles long and 100 miles wide, comprising 43 percent of the State.

Land Area.

The conception of Illinois as an unrelieved table-top admits pleasant and unexpected contradictions. A portion of the hilly Wisconsin driftless area projects into the northwest corner; there, at Charles Mound, is the highest spot in the State, 1,235 feet above sea level. An extension of the Ozark Range, with several hills extending a thousand feet in altitude, crosses southern Illinois. The Mississippi and its tributaries, especially the Illinois, have carved long ranges of bluffs, the more rugged portions of which have been enclosed in State parks.

Elsewhere is prairie, but its original extent and appearance have been greatly altered. The earliest settlers found almost half the State in forest, with the prairie running in great fingers between the creeks and other waterways, its surface lush with waist-high grasses and liberally bedecked with wild flowers. Here occurred the transition from the wooded lands of the East to the treeless plains of the West.

Since this was the pioneer's first encounter with the prairie, Illinois came to be known as the Prairie State, although westward lay lands more worthy of the title than the semi-wooded surface of Illinois.

The pioneers admired the grasslands, but clung to the wooded waterways. At the time of early settlement, the fertility of the prairie was not known, nor was it available until the invention of plows capable of breaking the tough sod. The waterway furnished timber for fuel and building, a convenient water supply, and protection for the settlers' jerry-built cabins from prairie fires and windstorms. Fires invariably swept the grasslands in the late summer, when the Indians burned off the prairie to drive out game. When the settlers at last began to venture cautiously out from the groves, they took the precaution to surround their homesteads with several plowed furrows as a fire check.

The fame of the great stretches of treeless grasslands spread eastward, even to England, and magazines carried articles of description, speculating upon their origin (which is still unexplained) and the possibilities of their cultivation. Dickens, while visiting St. Louis in 1842, especially requested that he be shown the "paroarer," as he noted it was pronounced locally. A rumbling, ancient coach took him out to Looking Glass Prairie, near Belleville, and he returned to write:

"... there lay, stretched out before my view, a vast expanse of level ground; unbroken, save by one thin line of trees, which scarcely amounted to a scratch upon the great bank ... a tranquil sea or lake without water, if such a simile be admissible ... I felt little of that sense of freedom and exhilaration which a Scottish heath inspires, or even our English downs awakens. It was lonely and wild, but oppressive in its barren monotony."

Early Agriculture and Lumbering.

Lumbering activities and the pioneer's early preference for the woodland reduced the forests from their original extent, 42 percent, to little more than 5 percent. What is now commonly thought of as prairie is often the increment gained from the clearing of woodlands. Given over almost wholly to farms, the prairies were constantly in flux as the landscape altered with the agricultural season. April transformed the Illinois country into a vast patchwork quilt of fresh color. Spring planting brought forth teams and tractors that combed and dressed the land with geometric nicety. By summer the contours of the prairie were soft and round with ripening crops. July ushered in three months of intense industry. Crops were gathered, threshing machines built mounds of chaff, trucks and trains loaded with grain began to move toward the cities. When autumn came, the prairies, gashed by plows and stripped of their harvest, had a worn, desolate aspect that was heightened by the somber browns and yellows of the season. The prairies were dull throughout winter save for intermittent snowfalls, and then, in late March, the land would stir, splotches of green appeared, and farmers turned again to the soil.

Topography of the State.

The level aspect of Illinois topography has its explanation in the State's glacial history. As late as 25,000 years ago--a tick of the clock in geological time--there was still to be found in Illinois the last of the great ice sheets that had crept down from the North and with a leveling action comparable to that of a road-scraper, effaced hills and valleys carved by centuries of erosion. Ninety percent of the State's surface was covered by ice; the only unglaciated areas are Jo Daviess County in the extreme northwest, Calhoun County in the west-central section, and the seven southernmost counties. In these areas, the rugged terrain, sharply dissected by valleys, indicates the probable appearance of the whole of Illinois before the ice age. Elsewhere, save for sporadic outcrops, the uneven relief lies beneath a mantle of drift averaging 75 feet in depth.

The four ice-sheets that invaded the United States are definitely known to have reached Illinois. The next to last of these covered so great a portion of the State that it has been named Illinoisan by geologists. Occurring approximately 150,000 years ago, it pushed south to the northern edge of the Ozark Range, and there, halted by increased melting and the barricade of hills, piled up rock debris 20 feet deep on the hillsides. This was the greatest southern penetration of any of the North American glaciers.

The Winconsin Glacier, which moved into Illinois 50,000 years ago and receded 25,000 years later, covered only the northeast quarter of the State, but because of its geological lateness, its effects are more obvious to the layman. The great central portion of the State which was covered by the old Illinoisan sheet, but not overlaid by the Winsconsin, is much more nearly even in relief and mature in drainage. The terminal moraines--ridges of drift piled up where the glacial front stopped--are low and inconspicuous. Those of the last glacier, however, are among the largest known to geologists. Sharply defined and extensive in length, they comprise the chief topographical relief of the northeast portion of the State. The major ones are named for cities that have been built upon them; the Shelbyville, Bloomington, Marseilles, and Valparaiso moraines are four of the most important.

Marked with the characteristics of recent glaciation, the land bordering Lake Michigan near the Wisconsin State line is poorly drained, with many lakes and marshes formed by the melting Wisconsin glacier. Thus was created the lake region of Illinois, a major recreational area for the metropolis of Chicago. At the time of recession, the waters of the glacier were impounded between the Valparaiso moraine and the receding edge of ice, forming Lake Chicago, ancestor of Lake Michigan. The site of Chicago lay deep beneath the surface of this ancient lake, and deposition from its waters accounts for the table-top flatness of the city today. In successive stages the water receded north and east.

Agricultural Distinctions.

Glaciation and climate largely explain the agricultural distinction of the Illinois country. The average growing season varies from 160 days in the north to 211 days at Cairo in the south. The drift laid down by the ice had been gathered from so great a variety of bedrock that an ample percentage of essential minerals was assured. Lying at the southernmost reach of the ice-sheets, Illinois was not strewn with the boulders and heavy debris that pock-mark the land further north. Much of the State is veneered with a layer of loess, the finer particles of drift that were sorted out by the wind and spread across the land. Enriched by prairie grasses during thousands of years, it possesses an even texture which, with the regular terrain, fits Illinois admirably for mechanical cultivation.

Mineral Deposits.

Buried beneath the glacial drift, the rock strata of Illinois effect little influence upon the topography, but their minerals yield to the State an income, placing it high on the list of areas of the country with mineral output. All of the substructure that has been explored by geologists is sedimentary in nature, with the exception of a deep-lying mass of red granite encountered at 3,700 feet near Amboy, in the northern part of the State. At an unknown depth, the entire State is underlain with igneous rock, mother-rock of all formations, but vast processes of sedimentation have buried it beyond reach.

Of the five geological eras, the third, the Paleozoic, was by far the most important, both geologically and economically. Beginning some 600 million years ago, it was characterized by repeated submergences and uplifts. What is now Illinois was then covered by a series of shallow seas. In great cycles, the seas advanced, covered the land for millions of years, and then retreated to expose the surface again to weathering and erosion. The strata laid down during each submergence differ sharply from each other, the degree depending upon the depth of the sea and the nature of the land at its shoreline.

Sandstone and Dolomite. The oldest period of the Paleozoic Era was the Cambrian, during which thick layers of sandstone and dolomite were deposited over the entire State. This, like the igneous rock, does not outcrop in Illinois, but slants upward from the south to come to the surface in Wisconsin. Rainfall in the latter area, seeping through surface soil to the sandstone layers, follows these to northern Illinois, where it served as a reservoir for the wells of many municipalities.

Limestone. The second period of the Paleozoic Era was the Ordovician, which saw a series of submergences of long duration. Its first deposits, the Prairie du Chien group, included a limestone which was the basis of Utica's natural cement industry, important in earlier times, but later abandoned. Another of the early Ordovician deposits is a layer of St. Peter sandstone, which outcrops in Ottawa and nearby in a remarkably pure form that achieved national industrial importance as a source of silica sand, used in glass-making and a hundred other processes. St. Peter sandstone also forms the picturesque bluffs that comprise Starved Rock State Park. Platteville limestone, likewise an Ordovician deposit, is used in the manufacture of Portland cement. Late in the period, a layer of Galena dolomite was laid down. It bears the lead which gave Galena its name and its early mining boom. Related to this formation is the Kimmswick limestone, source of petroleum in the southwestern field at Dupo.

Oil. The third period, the Silurian, laid down several strata of dolomite and limestone. The latter is quarried extensively near Chicago and Joliet for road material, aggregate, and soil replenishment. The following period, the Devonian, is likewise chiefly important for its limestone. Among the Mississippian deposits are the sediments that store the southeastern oil pool, long a steadily producing field; this became the scene of a spectacular boom of revived activity during the early decades of the 20th century.

Coal Deposits. Near the end of the Paleozoic Era occurred the Pensylvanian period, when Illinois' great coal measures were deposited. The coal strata, but a small portion of the Pennsylvanian deposits, far outstrip all other geological periods in the wealth they have yielded. The land at this time was low and marshy, a few feet above sea level. A favorable climate encouraged the growth of giant trees and ferns that subsequent eons compressed into the coal veins that underlie two- thirds of the State. After a half-century of extensive mining operations, it was estimated that no more than one percent of Illinois' coal reserve had been tapped.

Following the close of the Pennsylvanian period, the greater portion of Illinois remained above sea level. Great land movements that raised the Appalachians in the east also folded the land of of Southern Illinois into the present Ozark range. The work of the seas was done, and now rain and wind attacked the surface to erode and crease it with great valleys and ridges. But then, following a climatic change, snow began to fall in the northern region, year after year, deeper in the winter than the brief summer sun could melt.

So began the glacial period, the *deus ex machina* in the making of Illinois. Even as the curtain descended upon the State's geological drama, the sheets appeared, effaced the ruggedness and retreated. Indian legends made awed mention of the Ice God that once came down from the North.

PRE-HISTORY AND ARCHEOLOGY

When Father Marquette and Louis Jolliet first set eyes on Illinois lands in 1673, they also met and tried to Christianize some members of the Confederated tribes of Cahokia, Tamaroa, Michigamea, Kaskaskia, and Peoria Indians. These tribes, called collectively the Illinois Indians, as well as tribes of the dreaded Iroquois alliance, were to begin a history of downfall and defeat from this point on. However, the descendants of these people have left an unwritten record of a long history of a successfully complex culture before the white man first arrived.

Prehistoric Indians: The Mound Builders.

The most conspicuous reminder of Prehistoric Indians in Illinois is the presence of thousands of large mounds of earth, usually located near rivers, in which skeletons, pottery, stone implements, and ruins of buildings are buried. Around these mounds have grown numerous stories about their origin. Some early settlers thought the people who built the mounds were a lost tribe of Israel. Others thought they might be related to the Mayas and Aztecs. Today, however, archaeologists simply think the mysterious mound builders were Indians who raised the earth for all sorts of reasons.

The precursors of these Indians came to North America as early as 25,000 years ago from Asia. They probably crossed the landbridge that connected Alaska and Russia at that time. As these tribes of people migrated south, some decided to remain in Illinois, where they underwent several cycles, including a period of mound-building, before Marquette and Jolliet arrived. As the culture evolved from migrating and hunting to agriculture (10,000-8,000 BC), these people were the first to cultivate squash, potatoes, corn, and other crops upon which much of the world depends for food today. They also devised tools and weapons from flint and other native rocks.

Many remnants of this early culture have been unearthed from the mounds throughout the State. But these mounds were not all of one period, nor were they all built for the same purpose. Some, like the effigy mounds in the northwestern part of Illinois, were of a ceremonial nature; many were built primarily for burial purposes; others were sites for buildings. Those of this last type seem to show influences which came from the Lower Mississippi, and possibly the more advanced cultures of Mexico and South America.

With the great tribal unrest among the Indians during the sixteenth and seventeenth centuries, largely due to the invasions of the Iroquois from the East, a great shifting of tribes occurred, so that by the time the first explorers came to Illinois, there were few mound-building Indians left in the region.

The Cycles of Indian History.

Of the cycles in Illinois Indian life, the Woodland culture is the oldest and most primitive, as discovered by excavating the mounds built during the Burial Mound Era (1000 BC-700 AD). A more advanced phase of development is the Hopewell culture, lasting from 200 BC to 400 AD. The Woodland tribes introduced the first domesticated plants. Hopewells were centered in southern Illinois at first, but soon spread to include a wide region of the State. They too cultivated plants but lived mostly on wild game and weeds. The mounds they built were fashioned in geometric and animal shapes. They also produced small art forms of stone, clay, and thin sheets of copper and mica. The dead were often buried under log tombs in the Hopewell mounds.

The latest era of development of these people is called the Temple Mound Period (700-1700 AD) and was dominated by a culture which not only cultivated plants on a larger scale, but settled into larger villages. These Mississippian tribes built larger earth mounds in which are found large stone statues of humans, pieces of art, and engravings in stone. One example of this type of mound is at Cahokia, which was at one time 100 feet high, 1,080 feet long, and 710 feet wide at the base. The Cahokia Mound is the largest earthwork in the world; eighty-five smaller mounds surround this main structure. The immensity of the project has been compared to the great pyramids of Egypt and Central America, which archaeologists believe indicated either slavery or fanatical religious beliefs.

Ancestors of the Iroquoians and other tribes who met the white man, the Mississippians also developed hot-fired pottery work, woven cloth, and permanent rectangular-shaped dwellings. The burial grounds were located near the mounds, and the dead were buried with pottery, charms and amulets, signifiers of a belief in the afterlife. Whereas Woodland and Hopewell Indians buried their dead in flexed positions, the Mississippians were interred lying prone.

Locations of Burial Grounds of Different Cultures.

More than 10,000 mounds are scattered up and down the State. The largest mounds are at Cahokia near East St. Louis, the Dickson mounds near Havana, and the Modoc Rock Shelter near Prairie du Rocher. Because Illinois was situated at the confluence of the great highways of primitive travel--the Mississippi, Missouri, Ohio, and Illinois rivers--various mound- building cultures shuttled back and forth across the State. Rock and minerals native to other regions are found here, and in the mounds of other states are found the kind of flint mined only in the ancient quarry in Union County, Illinois.

More primitive late-Woodland culture effigy mounds have been found in the northwestern part of Illinois. They possibly represent totems or clan symbols; usually no burials are found in them. Near Galena is a mound shaped like a serpent, which strikingly resembles the famed Hopewell Serpent Mound of Ohio. At the junction of Smallpox Creek with the Mississippi is the effigy of a bird with outspread wings. Also belonging to the Woodlands are 17 mounds on the bluffs overlooking East Dubuque and the Mississippi River, the largest of which is 70 feet in diameter and 12 feet high.

Thousands of small mounds, usually called bluff mounds, line the Illinois River. In culture, they are of two types, the Woodland and the Mississippi, separated by long lapses of time but buried in the same area. Other notable mounds in the State are the Montezuma Mounds near Pearl and the Beardstown Mounds in Cass County.

21

The Everyday Life of Early Tribes.

These risings in the earth tell us much about the everyday life of the early tribes. They all lived in substantial log- framed houses with walls of bark or poles, with roofs of bark or thatch. The Iroquois and their kindred tribes in Illinois wore warm leather clothing and fur in the winter. In each household, extended families of three or four generations lived closely together, and clan relationships were usually determined through the female line. Although clans were represented by a council of men with a clan chief, women often decided who would lead the group. The clan chiefs also sat on the tribal council, and tribes usually had two chiefs; one to take care of internal affairs and another to lead the tribe in war. This tribal organization was strong and well established by the time of the earliest French explorers.

Confederacies of the Illinois and Iroquois.

Of the historic Indians, the Illinois alliance was first in importance and one of the oldest. It was of Algonquian language, and consisted of the six tribes listed earlier. Once the Illinois Confederacy occupied most of the Illinois country, the early Jesuits found there had been vast movements of all the tribes of the region due to wars with the Iroquois. Closely related to them, if not at once time actually a part of the Confederacy, were the Miami, who lived for awhile in the region south of Chicago.

The Indians in the Illinois alliance called themselves the Illiniwek ("superior men") and indeed were physically well-built. They were generally friendly to the white explorers and helpful in their voyages. In war, they were reported to be excellent archers; they also used a war club and a kind of lance with dexterity; but their proud title of "superior men" was not earned in war, because they were often defeated by the Iroquois and northern lake tribes.

The Iroquois were to be feared because their confederacy was the strongest of all tribes north of Mexico at the time Champlain met them in the early 1600s. Their alliance of northern Illinois Iroquois and other Great Lakes area tribes were made in order to put up a united front against foreign tribes and later on, the white man.

Of the other confederacy, the Kaskaskia village near present-day Lake Peoria could be considered a "capital" village for all the Illinois tribes. LaSalle reported in 1680 that annual assemblies of all tribes were attended by 6,000 to 8,000 people.

The lodges of this town topped the banks of the Illinois for more than a mile. Corn, beans, and pumpkins matted the adjacent meadows, and maize, planted in the spring, was given special attention by the women. When the maize crop was gathered, it was usually stored in pits, often under the houses. Pumpkins were sliced into discs and dried. When the work of harvesting was over, the tribes began to file westward for the serious task of obtaining enough meat to last through the winter and early spring. The men stalked and killed the game; the women dried the meat and carried it back to the village. The Indians' diet was further supplemented by wild fowl, nuts, roots, berries, and fish, which they speared in the lakes and streams.

The usual totems of the Illinois tribes were the crane, beaver, white hind, and tortoise, although the Kaskaskia sometimes used the feather of an arrow, or two arrows fitted into a cross. Each village had several leaders, each of whom controlled from 30 to 50 young men. A reed mat with the feathers of various birds wrapped in it was carried on the warpath by the leader. The *De Gannes Memoir*, the most accurate description of the Illinois, probably written by Sieur Deliette, nephew of Henri de Tonti, notes that though women and children captives were spared as slaves, the male captives were tortured by fire, their bodies cut open, and their hearts eaten raw. Mothers then hastened to dip the feet of their male children in the blood of the thoracic cavity.

The Illinois, according to one account, did not immediately bury their dead; bodies were wrapped in skins, and attached by the foot and head to a tree. After the flesh had rotted away, the bones were gathered up and buried in rude sepulchres. The *De Gannes Memoir*, however, declares that the Illinois buried their dead in shallow trenches lined with planks. Both kinds of graves have been found in Illinois. Grave gifts for the deceased, to accompany him on his journey to the "land beyond the milky way", consisted of an earthen pot, his bow and arrows, a handful of corn and tobacco, and often a calumet pipe.

The *De Gannes Memoir* further states that men frequently had several wives. As all persons in the village addressed one another in terms of kinship, the sisters, aunts, and nieces of a man's wife were *nirimoua*, and they in turn called him by the same name. If a brave were a successful hunter, he could marry all the women thus related to him. When a man died, his wife was prohibited from marrying for a year; the penalty for breaking this tribal law was death, after which the offender's scalp was raised over the lodge of her husband's family. Many shamans, or medicine men, lived among the tribes, and attempted to cure illnesses by chants and ceremonies which they professed to have learned through visions. Once a year, they held a colorful dance at which they gave a preview of their nostrums and powers. In their leisure time, the warriors played a form of lacrosse, or gambled at a game of matching odd and even with sticks.

According to the *De Gannes Memoir* and the reports of Father Hennepin, the Illinois built their cabins like long arbors, and covered them with a double mat of reeds, which the women gathered from the rivers and wove into rectangles sometimes 60 feet long. Each house had four or five fires and accommodated eight to ten families. Some of the villages were enclosed within palisades; others were set in the open with a good view of the surrounding country.

A Century of Indian Wars.

About 1680, the Iroquois descended upon the Illinois tribes, wiped out the principal villages, and pursued some of the conquered bands down the Illinois River to the Mississippi. There they attacked the Tamoroa, and took 700 of their women and children prisoners. In 1682, LaSalle built Fort St. Louis at Starved Rock and gathered about it 3,000 warriors of the various Algonquian tribes in a confederation against the Iroquois; 1,200 of these were Illinois. Twenty years later, we find the Illinois dispersed again. Peoria, Cahokia, and Kaskaskia were centers for the tribes of those names. The Tamoroa were associated now with the Kaskaskia, and the Michigamea lived near Fort de Chartres on the Mississippi.

In 1729, Illinois warriors helped the French subdue the Natchez, and later fought in the Chickasaw War. Though they became involved in the Conspiracy of Pontiac at the conclusion of the French and Indian War in 1763, they had by then taken over many vices of the white man and had lost much of their vigor. When Pontiac was killed by a Peoria Indian near Cahokia in 1769, his tribes-- the Chippewa, Ottawa, and Potawatomi--descended from the north and east upon the Illinois and almost annihiliated them. A widespread but unauthenticated legend relates that a band of fugitives took refuge on Starved Rock, where they were besieged by the Potawatomi. Their provisions failed; the cords of bucket they dropped to the river for water were cut by the enemy; finally, decimated by thirst and hunger, they were attacked and killed.

In 1778, the Kaskaskia numbered 310 and lived in a small village three miles north of Kaskaskia. The Peoria and Michigamea lived a few miles farther up the river and together numbered 170. By this time, most had become demoralized through the use of liquor. In 1800, only 150 Illinois survived. In 1833, they sold their holdings in Illinois and moved west of the Mississippi. By 1855, the consolidated Peoria, Kaskaskia, Wea, and Piankashaw, living on an Indian reservation in Oklahoma, numbered 149, with much admixture of white blood.

In the seventeenth century, enemies other than the Iroquois came to make war on the Illinois and settle on their land. The Sauk and Fox moved down from Wisconsin to the northwestern part of the State and claimed all the territory between the Mississippi and the Rock rivers. Originally they had lived along the St. Lawrence; subsequently, harassed by the Iroquois, they moved to Wisconsin. Father Allouez set up a mission among them in Green Bay in 1669. After defeating the Mascoutens near the mouth of the Iowa River, they formed an alliance with the Potawatomi and forced the Illinois to move southward. Their defeat during the Black Hawk War in 1832, when they resisted the encroachments of the white men, caused their ultimate removal from the state.

By the time the French explorers came, the Winnebago sometimes drifted down from Wisconsin into northern Illinois, the Kickapoo had moved into the area at the foot of the lake and survived, and the Mascouten, friendly to the Illinois, lived in the great grassy plains east of the Mississippi. Along the Wabash dwelt the Piankashaw, and around the southern and western shores of Lake Michigan stretched the hunting grounds of the Potawatomi, a particularly warlike tribe who, in the Conspiracy of Pontiac, annihiliated the garrison at St. Joseph, and in 1812 were responsible for the Fort Dearborn massacre. Associated with the Potawatomi were the Chippewa and Ottawa, among the most energetic and powerful tribes of the Northwest; they lived on both sides of the Wabash. At one time the Shawnee dwelled in the southeastern part of the State.

The Spirit of the Indians.

Mythology of the Potawatomi shows rare beauty and imagination. According to Schoolcraft, they believed in two spirits, Kitchemonedo, the good spirit, and Matchemonedo, the evil spirit. Kitchemonedo made the world and all things in it. He peopled it with beings who looked like men, but were perverse, ungrateful, and wicked, and never raised their eyes from the ground to thank him for anything. At last the Great Spirit plunged the world into a huge lake and drowned them. He then withdrew the world from the water and made a single man, very handsome, but also sad and lonesome. Then, to allay his loneliness, Kitchemonedo took pity on the man and sent him a sister. One night the young man had a dream. When he awoke, he said to his sister, "Five young men will come to your lodge door tonight to visit you. You must not talk to the first four. But with the fifth, you may speak and laugh." She acted accordingly. The first to call was Usama (tobacco); being repulsed, he fell down and died. The second was Waupako (pumpkin); the third, Eshkossimin (melon); the fourth, Kokees (bean); all met the same fate. But when Tamin (maize) presented himself, she received him kindly. They were immediately married, and from this union the Indians sprang. Tamin buried the four unsuccessful suitors, and from their graves grew tobacco, pumpkins, melons, and beans.

As white civilization advanced westward, the Indians found their forests despoiled and their rivers polluted. Corrupted first with disease and liquor, they were used as pawns in colonial politics, and they were herded into reservations in the West, where their extinction was assured. In 1832, the year the Sauk and Fox were driven from Illinois after the Black Hawk War, the Winnebago ceded to the

United States all of their territory lying southeast of the Wisconsin and Fox rivers. In 1833, at a grand council of chiefs in Chicago, the Potawatomi, Ottawa, and Chippewa also ceded their holdings, and prepared to move across the Mississippi to Indian reservations, together with the Illinois.

HISTORY

The territory that now comprises the State of Illinois had, for ten thousand years, been home for a great variety of aboriginal tribes. Archaeologists have uncovered numerous important sites. At a very early period, for example, the so- called "Archaic hunters" set up camps along the prairie streams. The Modoc Rock Shelter, a lodge overlooking the Mississippi in Randolph County, was one important site.

Two of the most sophisticated Indian societies that flourished in the state were the Hopewellians (500BC-500AD), who practiced a limited agriculture, and the Middle Mississippians (c. 900 AD), who built giant earthwork mounds. The mounds involved a construction effort comparable to the building of the pyramids, and indicate a complex society with well-developed permanent towns and successful agriculture. The Mississippian society, like earlier Indian cultures, collapsed and disappeared for reasons (perhaps famine, or revolution, or genocide) that are not yet understood.

In the mid-sevententeenth century, the Illinois Indian group dominated the northern part of the State and southern Wisconsin. Numbering about 6,500, they were agriculturalists and hunted buffalo. Warfare with the Sioux, the Fox, and other tribes, abbetted by liquor supplied by the French, reduced their numbers to perhaps 2,000. Enemy tribes began a war of extermination in the 1760s, reducing the Illinois to a few hundred hapless survivors who sought asylum at Kaskaskia. The victors, the Potawatami, Sac, and Fox tribes, then occupied the former Illinois lands until whites forced them into Iowa in the early nineteenth century.

French explorers from Canada first reached Illinois in the late seventeenth century. In 1673, Louis Jolliet and Jacques Marquette traversed Wisconsin, floated down the Mississippi past what is now Cairo, then crossed over to Lake Michigan via the Illinois and Des Plaines rivers. The portage between those rivers and the lake, marking the closest connection between the Great Lakes and the Mississippi River basin, possessed an obvious geographical advantage. It was later to become the site of Chicago.

The French established small villages and forts in Kaskaskia and other points near St. Louis. Black slaves were brought in from the Caribbean to work as field hands and house servants. The French villages served as fur trading posts for commerce with the Indians. However, the Illinois settlements were far from the main centers of French activity, and at their peak probably included no more than 1,500 or 2,000 white inhabitants and 500 or so blacks.

The British assumed control of French America in 1765, but made it a policy to exclude Anglo-American settlers from the area. The rapid growth of the British-American colonies on the East Coast, however, led to demands for an opening of western lands. London reiterated its exclusionist policy in the Quebec Act of 1774, which became one of the grievances leading to Revolution. Virginia militia, led by land speculator George Rogers Clark, ousted the small British detachments at Vincennes and Kaskaskia in 1778 and 1779. Illinois, however, was too distant to attract American settlers, and the military alliances between the Indians and the British (extending as late as 1815), made the frontier too dangerous to occupy. During the late 1770s and 1780s, anarchy and violence disrupted the white-black French settlements in Ilinois, causing most of the inhabitants to escape to lands west of the Mississippi (which became American with the Louisiana Purchase of 1803).

Virginia ceded its claims to the national government in 1784, and in 1787 the Northwest Ordinance established the first effective American administration. A series of appointed governors and judges had legal authority in Illinois until its statehood in 1818. White settlers were very few before 1800, as nearly continuous warfare raged with the Indians. In 1809, the Illinois Territory was created, including all of present Wisconsin and small areas of Minnesota and Michigan.

Territorial status brought an influx of politicians, chiefly Virginia gentlemen (Virginians controlled by the White House), concerned with the trappings of prestige and the chance to grab huge quantities of empty land before the onrush of settlers arrived. The politicians doubled as military commanders, fighting a series of pitched battles with the Indians. The War of 1812, fought in large part in the Great Lakes basin, resulted in the final expulsion of British power. The Indians, facing the near certainty of extinction

at the hands of the better armed and .IX Indian Tribes--
Land cessions,

numerically dominant American frontiersmen, sold their
claims to the Federal government and retreated to Iowa.

By 1815, the rich lands of Illinois were practically uninhabited, but Kentucky to the south was rapidly filling up
with land-hungry frontiersmen; the era of massive settlement had dawned. There was soon plenty of work for surveyors and land agents, not to mention lawyers and judges
who had to straighten out the vague and overlapping land
claims.

Federal policy was to give the land away to war veterans (who usually sold their warrants to speculators), or to
sell modest 160 acre tracts on very easy credit at $1.25 or
$2 per acre. Even so, most of the settlers were squatters
who had little or no legal claim, but would soon move on,
perhaps selling their "quit claim deeds" to newcomers.
Eventually one settler would obtain a legal federal deed,
though the terms varied as Washington changed its land
policy several times in the first half of the nineteenth century. In contrast to Kentucky, however, it was relatively
easy to obtain clear title to land in Illinois.

The Structure of Government

Pressure for statehood came from politicians who
thought they would have a wider field of action and reward
if they were not held back by presidential appointees. The
Enabling Act, passed by Congress in 1818, finalized the
boundaries and gave the future State a miniscule three percent share of land revenues and outright ownership of eight
percent of the land. A convention wrote a new constitution,
largely copied from other states, including a provision to
allow slavery (still practiced in the remaining French villages) to die away. A rigged count provided "evidence" for
the minimum 40,000 population needed. Congress quickly
approved statehood, which came into effect in December,
1818.

Politics before the 1830s involved the highly personal-
ized squabbling of a few dozen headstrong Virginians eager
to seize power. Issues were nonexistent, save in 1824 when
an unsuccessful attempt was made to legalize slavery. (The

Northwest Ordinance had prohibited slavery "forever," but its provisions were defunct now that Illinois had become a sovereign state.) Legalized slavery carried the potential of building rich plantations, such as were emerging in neighboring Kentucky and Missouri.

The opposition, although led by men who considered slavery morally evil, succeeded by appealing to the racism of the poor white southerners who comprised the bulk of the population. Let slaves in and the rich slaveowners will seize all the good land, they warned, and the blacks will steal and rape.

In the first decades of statehood, neither the State nor the local goverments troubled the people very much. Taxes were low, and went mostly for officeholders' salaries (which, in turn, were greatly supplemented by inside land deals). Services also were few. Law enforcement, for example, was largely in private hands. If a neighbor caused trouble, or was even insulting, a private lawsuit was the remedy. Juries were stacked, judges prejudiced; not for decades would the concept of universal law, fairly applied by disinterested public servants, take hold among the people. If outsiders made trouble, the sheriff was of little help. A good rifle or a few good friends (otherwise known as a vigilante or "regulator" party) was the best protection. Gangs of outlaws roamed Illinois at will as late as the 1850s, and even later in more isolated parts of the State. Private wars also broke out. The Mormons, with their own private army, were finally forced out of the State in 1846 by massive vigilante bands (one of which murdered their leader, Joseph Smith).

Education was proclaimed a major State objective in many speeches and acts, but nothing much was done until the 1850s. If a father wanted his children educated, he and some neighbors might work out a deal with an itinerant Yankee, exchanging bed and board for the three R's. Stephen Douglas stayed alive this way for a while in the 1830s. Abraham Lincoln desperately sought an education; he was able to piece together about 18 months of schooling.

Other government services were minimal. Local officials had responsibility for roads. They allowed citizens to spend a few days, in lieu of road taxes, sprucing up the mud ruts that served as transportation arteries. Public health was unheard of. Welfare was handled by apprenticing orphans to families who could use a sturdy hand, and by allotting miniscule allowances to a few widows. Kinfolk and friendly neighbors provided what little succor was available for the helpless.

The most powerful officials were the judges, appointed by the General Assembly for life terms. A new constitution in 1848 made all judgeships elective, thus sharply enlarging the scope of democracy. With the formation of highly disciplined political parties in the 1830s, nomination to office was determined less by personal prestige than by service to the party. Wealthy and talented young men began to avoid governmental service, preferring to make their fortunes in land, business, banking and industry. While the democratization of politics did little to uplift the moral climate of Illinois politics, it did divert the creative energies of the people into economic pursuits, where the benefit to the total population proved dramatic.

Pioneer Life: 1818-1854

In the first decades of statehood, Illinois gained population rapidly: Tens of thousands of migrants poured into the southern third of the State--a region so promising that people called it "Egypt". With a population of 55,000 in 1820, 160,000 in 1830, 480,000 in 1840 and 850,000 in 1850, Illinois was the fastest growing area in the United States, or probably anywhere in the world.

Before 1840, most of the newcomers were southerners, arriving from Kentucky, Tennessee, or the Carolinas, either directly or, more likely, after two or three sojourns along the way. The migrants were young couples in their teens or twenties, as few people older than 35 or 40 cared for the risk and adventure of pioneering in a new land.

The southern pioneers, though willing to move about physically, remained closely tied psychologically to the traditional world-view of their ancestors. They were extremely poor--most had to pull their few belongings on a sled because they lacked horses. They sought wealth, and often gambled all they had in this endeavor, but showed little interest in hard work. Southern Illinois attracted these pioneers because its many streams made travel easy, its rolling hills teemed with deer and small game, and its fairly warm climate made well-built housing unnecessary.

Pioneers often lived in caves or dug-outs until they got around to raising a small log cabin (several days' work). By clearing five or ten acres, they could plant enough corn, sweet potatoes, pumpkins, tobacco, flax, and castor beans to provide for nearly all their daily needs. Barns and fences were not needed, as the pigs ran wild; a hog-call would attract one when fresh meat was wanted. Thirty to sixty days work per year sufficed for most of the pioneer men. The rest of the time they drank enormous quantities of corn whiskey, hunted, fished, tended the dogs, gambled or, occasionally, attended militia musters, court days, and political rallies.

If pioneer life was easy for men and horses, it was hard for oxen and women. Oxen were used for heavy plow work, and most of the work was done by the women, who grew much of the food, prepared all meals, hand sewed all the clothes, washed them occasionally, and tended to the children. With land so abundant and food so easy to obtain, the pioneer men could express their masculinity with very large families. Eight births, with two babies dying in infancy, was average on the early frontier. The women, who spent so much of their lives pregnant or nursing, aged rapidly. But they did not die any faster than the men, who frequently were hurt in hunting or farm accidents.

Life expectancy was higher than in the Old World, more because of the abundance of food than the healthiness of the land. Swamps and mosquitos were everywhere, and a mild form of malaria was epidemic. Scientific medicine was virtually unknown before the 1830s, and even then the traditionalists scorned it in favor of self-diagnosis and home remedies. Powerful emetics and laxatives, combined with charms and magical potions, either cured the disease or termined the case.

The frontier valued only masculine virtues. Physical strength, bravery, stamina, cunning, fighting, and shooting ability--not to mention drinking capacity--were appreciated more than hard work, book learning, or compassion for others. If danger threatened, men would fight or run--but they did not develop any long-term plans to circumvent future troubles. The men lived in the present, with their values and ideas fixed by the past.

Illinois was ideal because it was a safe refuge from the crowded conditions back east, and gave a man a chance to control his own life without interference from government, let alone the aristocracy, established church, heavy taxes, standing armies, and highly stratified society that burdened the peasants in Europe.

But Illinois was potentially too rich to stay forever the domain of lazy, individualistic frontiersmen. The prairie land in North America soon attracted a very different sort of settler, the farmers who planned to work hard and become rich. From the mid-1830s to the Civil War, scores of thousands of New England Yankees, Ohioans, and Pennsylvanians entered the State. They avoided Egypt and instead settled the prairies. Here farm making called for much hard work, plus some initial capital to get started. Special teams were hired to break the tough virgin soil. Fences had to be built to control the animals, and barns to shelter them. Warm housing was essential during the cold prairie winters. Tools and implements had to be bought and maintained. There was work enough for everyone: man, woman, and child, every day of the year. The rewards might be slow coming, but eventually the prairie farmers would become rich.

Before the full potential of prairie agriculture could be realized, Illinois needed to create a market-oriented economy, with suitable transportation and processing facilities.

In the 1820s, politicians realized that the subsistence-and- barter economy of the traditional pioneers would not make anyone rich. They promoted banks that would put paper money into circulation, permit more commerce and the growth of towns, and convert the potential wealth of the land into real dollars via mortgages and loans. The traditional southern pioneers were highly suspicious of paper money and extravagant speculation. Rallied by their hero, President Andrew Jackson, the traditionalists were organized into a new political party, later (and still) known as the Democrats. They sought, with considerable success until the Civil War, to keep banks out of Illinois. (However, out-of-state paper money did circulate.)

Businessmen and ambitious farmers, eager for wealth, realized that a modern transportation system was necessary to move crops and animals to market. No one could make money by driving herds overland, or rafting corn down the rivers. The State government borrowed millions of dollars

35

in the 1830s to create a transportation system, with rail-roads, turnpikes, and canals to connect every settled part of the State to outside markets.

Unfortunately, the politicians botched the scheme: canals were started everywhere and finished nowhere. The State was deeply in debt, and the traditionalistic Democrats were more firmly convinced than ever that economic modernization was a dangerous chimera.

The modernizers could not be stopped. Their party, the Whigs, preached the gospel of rapid economic growth through technology, banking , commerce, and industry. Abe Lincoln, though born to an extremely traditionalist back-woods family, adopted the new faith, becoming a spokesman for railroads, banks, and large- scale industry.

The modernizers, chiefly but not entirely of Yankee origin, also sought to improve society as a whole. They formed Congregational, Presbyterian, and Methodist churches, insurance companies and colleges, debating circles and stock-breeding farms, banks and temperance groups, small factories and abolitionist societies, corporation and newspapers. Thanks to the modernizers, by 1850 Illinois possessed all the institutions of a modern society. The people were still poor because the basic transportation problem had not yet been solved, but the structures were in place and ready for a takeoff into sustained and rapid economic growth.

Triumph of Economic Modernization, 1854-1900

The Whig party, for all its talk of creating a modern society, never managed to achieve dominance in politics. The Democrats were so successful that, after their sweep in 1852, ambitious Whig politicians like Lincoln (the party's leader) abandoned politics for business pursuits. But not for long. Senator Stephen Douglas, spokesman not only for Illinois Democrats, but the foremost national leader of his party, had apparently resolved the troublesome slavery issue with his Compromise of 1850.

In 1854, however, Douglas reopened the issue by proposing territorial status for Kansas and Nebraska under terms that would allow settlers to decide for themselves whether or not they wanted slavery. To Douglas this epitomized grass roots democracy in action. He envisioned a pluralistic society in which local communities could determine their own destiny, free from outside interference. His philosophy appealed to the traditionalistic folk, but it outraged the modernizers. Slavery was bad, and to allow it to spread threatened both moral self-respect and the practical interests of hard working farmers and artisans.

As the Whigs vanished, a new Republican party emerged across the North, and Abraham Lincoln soon became its outstanding western spokesman. Drawing off modernizing Democrats like Lyman Trumbull, the new party was a fair match for the old. The Republicans swept the State in their first attempt (1854), and sent Trumbull to the Senate. The new legislature vigorously promoted education, setting up the State's first real public school system.

Douglas succeeded in forcing his Kansas-Nebraska Act through Congress, but the upshot was a bloody civil war in Kansas; proof, the Republicans claimed, that the southern slave owners would use ruthless violence to suppress the honorable demands of free men. The Supreme Court's Dred Scott Decision in 1857, a victory for the slaveowners, further inflamed Republican passion. The Democrats shot back by accusing the Republicans of being Puritan fanatics who would forcibly "reform" traditionalists (by prohibition and nativism) whether the reformees liked it or not. To the agrarian traditionalists in Egypt, the Democrats added new strength by winning the support of urban traditionalists, especially Irish and German Catholic immigrants. With Douglas

proclaiming democracy the greatest good, and Lincoln standing for freedom, the two men met in the 1858 election for senator. Lincoln, as the hero of the more modern Illinoisians--the businessmen, prosperous farmers, professionals, railroad workers, clerks, and Protestants generally---won more votes. Douglas, however, was reelected by the legislature which, based on the 1850 census, was overrepresented in Egypt and underrepresented in the fast growing cities.

Both men gained national stature, becoming presidential nominees of their parties in 1860. The South, paranoid about the anti-slavery movement, and about northerners generally, chose to run its own candidates. Lincoln, by carrying nearly every northern state, even though he had zero support in the South, won the electoral vote. That was too much for the deep South. Seven states seceded, forming their own nation and seeking peaceful separation.

Lincoln was too much the American nationalist to agree to a breakup of the Union. He underestimated the determination of the Confederates, and called for troops when Fort Sumter was fired upon. Four border states then went over to the enemy, and the Civil War was on. Douglas was dead, and the rank-and-file traditionalist Democrats hated and feared the blacks. They were not willing to fight for the abolition of slavery. The Republicans still controlled the federal government and the governorship (they lost the legislature in 1862), and used strong tactics to suppress disunion at home.

No battles took place in Illinois. The state provided manpower and food for the army in great quantity. A quarter million young men (a majority of those eligible) served in the army. Battles were many, but Illinois regiments usually were on the winning side, so their casualties were light. One in 25 died in battle or from wounds. Twice that many died from diarrhea, typhoid, malaria, or dysentry, as medical progress and camp hygiene struggled to cope with masses of humanity in makeshift conditions. The men who marched home had become fervent supporters of Lincoln and staunch Republicans. For 70 years the Democrats would be on the defensive in Illinois.

The second half of the nineteenth century marked the modernization of every sector of Illinois economy. Railroads were the key factor. In 1850, only 111 miles of track had been built. Railroad men knew how to build and operate a system; the problem was to raise the $25,000 per mile needed for construction. The State's financial system was far too primitive to provide even a small fraction of the funding.

The solution was outside money. For decades, most of the stock in Illinois railroads would be held in Europe for funding the Illinois Central, which would traverse the State from Galena to Cairo and Chicago. (The government more than recouped its investment through sales of alternate squares of land to settlers.) Eastern roads needed no federal aid; they raced to extend their lines into Chicago, and then to Rock Island.

St. Louis promoters, fearful of losing trade to upstart Chicago, built lines eastward to Cincinnati. By 1860, 25,000 miles of track knitted the State with the nation; by 1890 100,000 miles of track brought the market economy to every city and large town in Illinois. Money poured into construction projects, and the yards, roundhouses, and depots employed tens of thousands of men. The largest direct benefit was the opening of a national, indeed, a world market for grain and livestock. City-made goods began to replace homemade goods in towns and on farms. Coal mines, providing fuel for trains and factories, expanded rapidly over a wide area of the State.

Manufacturing, which operated on a small scale for local markets before the war, also grew rapidly. By 1890, Illinois had become the third largest industrial State in the nation, with a quarter of its labor force engaged in meat packing, flour milling, steel making, and production of agricultural implements, furniture, liquor, stoves, men's clothes, and a thousand other items. Most of the factories were located in Chicago, but Peoria, Rockford, Joliet, Moline, Quincy, Elgin, and East St. Louis also became important industrial centers.

Service, commercial, and industrial functions of the State's towns and cities led to doubling of the downstate population, from 1,600,000 in 1860 to 3,200,000 in 1910. The growth of Chicago was even more phenomenal. From a little village in 1830, it reached 100,000 population in 1860, doubling again and again-- to 1,700,000 in 1900, and finally filling its boundaries with 3,400,000 people in 1930. Just behind Berlin and ahead of Paris, Chicago became the fourth city in size in the world.

Although Yankees had founded Chicago and controlled its economy until late in the twentieth century, they were soon greatly outnumbered by wave after wave of European immigrants. The Germans were the most numerous group (and still are, in terms of ethnic origins for the metropolitan area). Irish, British, and Scandinavian immigrants, arriving as young couples or teenagers, came in large numbers between 1840 and 1890.

Between 1890 and 1914, a number of new groups from Eastern and Southern Europe came to the city: Poles, Italians, Serbians, Jews, Lithuanians, Ukrainians, and many smaller groups.   Construction of a great metropolis in an era before power machinery demanded strong young men; fast growing factories, stockyards, and railroad yards needed unskilled labor in enormous numbers. Shops and offices were more particular in their hiring, demanding better educated young men (and, soon, women) to type, file, fill out forms, and sell the city's products to millions of consumers. Young women found work as servants, laundresses, waitresses, candy makers, seamstresses, and teachers.

Agriculture modernized as fast as any sector of the economy. The corn belt emerged, as farmers began to grow corn for feeding hogs and cattle, which the railroads shipped to Chicago and East St. Louis. The State's 36 million acres were sufficient for 250,000 farms, averaging 120-130 acres. By the mid-1870s, all the farm lands were occupied. The wetlands in the east central section of Illinois were drained, proving to be superb farm acreage.

Access to markets guaranteed that the hard work of building up a farm would pay off. Land prices began to shoot up, from $8 an acre in 1850 to $30 in 1870, $54 in 1900, and $108 in 1910. The average farm in 1910 was worth $16,000. The negative side of the coin was that young couples had a hard time acquiring ownership of a farm except by inheritance.

An increasingly large proportion of farmers became tenants, paying rent to an absentee owner. They made a reasonably good living, but did not share in the strong appreciation of land values. Since farmers were unwilling to subdivide their holdings into smaller plots, most of the children of farmers eventually had to move to nearby towns. The parents valued the rural lifestyle and were unhappy to see their children leave; often the youngsters were not equipped with enough schooling to allow them to make an optimal adjustment to urban living.

The southern third of the State had poor soil and was not suitable for corn-belt style agriculture. Out-migration was heavy, though the opening of coal mines provided a temporary lift to the region in the early twentieth century. When the mines cut back in the 1920s, the region plunged into a depression that, to a certain extent, still persists.

During the Civil War, the business community strongly supported the Republican party, and in turn received highly lucrative contracts to supply the army. Republicans in

Springfield, and especially in Washington, strongly promoted rapid economic modernization. New, national banking laws made it very profitable to be patriotic by the purchase of war bonds during the war. The State finally achieved a modern banking system that turned potential wealth into real cash, and channeled it into the most profitable enterprises. After 1865, businessmen were strong enough to prosper without aid from Springfield, though they continued to rely upon favorable federal tax law tariffs and monetary policies.

After the abortive attempt of Democrats to outlaw banks and restrict railroads in 1862, the triumph of the principle of rapid economic modernization was never in doubt. In the 1870s, small town merchants and farm groups succeeded in enacting "Granger Laws," the first attempt to regulate railroad freight rates. The compromise eventually reached established the principle that State agencies should regulate transportion rates (railroads, trucks, buses, etc.), as well as prices charged by utilities (electricity, telephones, gas). Laissez-faire, the predominant way to treat business, was thus moderated by State controls over vital industries, particularly those with monopolistic aspects.

Although the Civil War marked the victory of modernizers in the economic sphere, it did not end their conflicts with traditionalists. Democrats continued to complain about bankers and industrialists, appealing to the poorer farmers and unskilled laborers who benefited least from the new system. The main conflict shifted to cultural and social issues. In 1874, reformers returned to the goal of prohibiting the manufacture and sale of hard liquor. The Women's Christian Temperance Union, led by Evanston's energetic Francis Willard, played a leading role in agitating the issue. They scored some local victories (Evanston was dry until the 1970s), but intense opposition from the Germans, and from the Democratic party, postponed their triumph until 1920.

The modernizers sought to build schools and to compel not only their own children, but also the children of traditionalists to attend. In that way, all the youth would be inculcated into modern, middle class values, work habits, and ways of thinking, bringing the millennium of a perfectly modern society so much closer.

The farmers, not wanting their children to be enticed by urban ambitions, were willing to support small, neighborhood one- room schools, staffed by poorly-educated local teachers, but resisted the idea of high schools. The Catholics and German Lutherans, alarmed at the evangelical Protestant tone of the public schools, set up their own rival parochial system.

A bill which would require all children from age nine to fourteen to attend school three months a year died in 1874. Democrats charged that it would create a new crime: "the crime of liberty in education." By the 1880s, rural children attended school only 84 days a year. Conditions were much better in the towns. In Chicago, there was no way to keep track of the tens of thousands of immigrant children who experienced the English language schools and middle class teachers as an alien experience.

In 1889, the Republican General Assembly passed the Edwards Act, which banned child labor, made school attendance compulsory up to age 12, required basic instruction to be in the English language only, and authorized truant officers to compel parents to send their children to school. Catholics and German Lutherans were outraged at this intrusion of State power into the sphere of home and church. They swung to the Democratic party, and in 1892 elected John Peter Altgeld the first Democratic governor in 40 years.

Altgeld articulated the grievances of the traditionalists against the burden of social, cultural, and economic dislocations caused by the State's rapid modernization. His particular concern was the condition of the poor workingman, and he encouraged labor unions to organize the workers to do battle with the wicked industrialists. After he pardoned anarchists convicted of inciting violence at the Haymarket Riot of 1886, Altgeld drew the wrath of the State's middle classes.

A severe depression, with especially adverse effects on manufacturing, mining, and corn-belt agriculture, began early in Altgeld's term. At its nadir, Illinois Steel Company employed 225 men rather than its former 3,600; Pullman Palace Car, 1,700 out of 4,300; Deering Farm Implements, 600 out of 3,000; and McCormick Reaper, 440 out of 2,000. Since Democrat Grover Cleveland was president during the depression (1893-96), Altgeld's party drew most of the blame for the economic disaster.

In the spring of 1894, with the economy still in bad shape, the United Mine Workers called a strike in coal fields across the Midwest. Thirty-eight thousand Illinois miners were affected, but many were so hard pressed financially that they attempted to go back to work. This led to violence with the strikers. The goal of the strike was to raise prices, but the move failed.

The same spring, the Pullman workers in Chicago struck for lower rents in their company-owned houses. George Pullman, despite his paternalistic reputation, refused to negotiate. Thereupon Eugene Debs, leader of a new union of railway workers, entered the scene and called for a boycott of Pullman cars by the railroads. The roads refused, and Debs' men tried to shut down all the lines in the western two-thirds of the country. President Cleveland intervened, using federal court injunctions and army troops to end the boycott, which was marked by violence in Chicago and other rail centers.

Governor Altgeld protested bitterly at federal interference in State affairs, and launched a crusade to seize control of the Democratic party from Cleveland's supporters. The Republicans campaigned that fall on the premise that the disunited Democrats were hopelessly incompetent to govern a modern economy. The GOP won its most smashing victory in history in 1894, tightening its hold on the middle classes and winning majorities among the ethnic groups that traditionally favored Democrats.

Altgeld and his allies seized control of the Democratic party. With Altgeld running for reelection as governor (he would have been the presidential nominee save for his German birth), and young firebrand William Jennings Bryan for president, the anti-modern forces fielded their strongest possible ticket in 1896.

Bryan, born and raised in Illinois, realized that the Midwest, particularly Illinois, was key to the election. His vigorous campaign (317 speeches in October alone) galvanized Americans who feared that economic modernization produced hardship for the consumer and heavy debt for the farmer. Worst of all, America's democratic heritage was threatened by the excessive political power of the fast growing banks and corporations.

The Republicans, led by gubernatorial candidate John Tanner and presidential candidate William McKinley, fought back hard. Prosperity was the issue, they argued. The miners, factory hands, railroad employees, bankers, farmers, clerks, and professionals had a common interest in universal prosperity in a growth- oriented economy. Sabotage of the system in the name of purification was madness, they proclaimed.

The Altgeld-Bryan appeal to punish big business for wickedness failed in the industrial East and in the corn belt. Only in the colonial economies of the cotton South, the wheat- growing Plains, and the silver-mining West were they successful. Illinois, with a modern agriculture and diversified industry, voted for growth and prosperity. Not until the depression of the 1930s would the Democrats win a majority of the Illinois vote. The State had become solidly Republican, and was permanently committed to the policy of sustained economic growth.

Era of Prosperity, 1900-1929

McKinley's election brought a surge of business confidence, and inaugurated a reign of prosperity that continued unbroken for a third of a century. Every part of the State flourished. Chicago resumed its phenomenal growth. Industrial, mining, and railroad centers downstate grew quickly. The small towns and hamlets that serviced the needs of Illinois' prosperous farmers grew less rapidly, though they also shared in the ever-expanding wealth.

Yet plenty of poor people lived in the State. Most of them were new immigrants who had arrived penniless but ambitious for a better start in life. Many could not adjust to the furious pace of American industry, and returned to their peasant villages. Those who remained worked hard to achieve ownership of their own homes and a better life for their children. To assist them in assimilation into American life, reformers established a series of settlement houses in Chicago.

Jane Addams, daughter of a rural State senator, appealed to wealthy Chicagoans for funds to maintain the largest settlement, Hull House. Addams and her co-workers, mostly well-educated Yankee women, taught English to the illiterate Italians of the near west side, showed the ex-peasant women how to shop, cook, clean, sew, and maintain a home, helped with neighborhood problems like garbage disposal, and taught organizational skills. Hull House still exists on in its original site; it is now a museum, but it is also a decentralized social work organization that continues to help newcomers adjust to the city.

Chicago from 1890 to about 1910 suddenly and most unexpectedly became a major world cultural and intellectual center. Credit must go to the patrons--the self-made millionaires who decided to use their wealth and skill at creating large enterprises to modernize the organization of high culture. They set up and generously endowed universities, libraries, and museums, usually bearing their own names. Thus, between 1885 and 1930, a number of new cultural institutions were created: the Newberry and Crerar libraries, the Field Museum, the Art Institute, Shedd Aquarium, the Museum of Science and Industry, the Auditorium Theatre, the Lewis and Armour institutes (now merged as the Illinois Institute of Technology), and the Chicago Symphony Orchestra.

Largest and most important of the new institutions was the University of Chicago. The patrons knew how to select outstanding leaders and back them unswervingly with money. William Raney Harper was an outstanding cultural entrepreneur; in 1892, at age 36, he opened the new University of Chicago. He sought the best professors in the country (and a few from Europe), and enticed them with extraordinarily high salaries, a promise of the best laboratories and library collections, and the dream of building the greatest university in the world. Harper almost succeeded; his university was indeed one of the three or four strongest in the world. But after his death in 1906, it began slowly to slip below Harvard, Columbia, and Berkeley, and even the newly reinvigorated University of Illinois.

Chicago was not modest. In 1893, the World's Columbian Exposition brought in not only millions of tourists but thousands of the world's scholars and authorities to marvel at the dazzling architecture of the Fair and stand astonished that this raw city on the prairie had accomplished so much so quickly.

It was one thing to buy culture, but quite another to create it. The Chicago Symphony Orchestra, built by Theodore Thomas, played the greatest European music, but rarely performed anything composed in Chicago. Likewise, the Art Institute snatched up the best paintings from Paris, but had little exhibited from the Midwest. Chicago did have a literary renaissance, as novelists, poets, and writers like Carl Sandburg, Theodore Dreiser, and Harriet Monroe flourished there in the 1900s and 1910s. However, most of the talented young writers eventually drifted off to New York or even, like Oak Park's Ernest Hemingway, to Paris.

Architecture was an art form that stayed firmly rooted in Chicago. Many businessmen who patronized the arts wanted copies of European buildings for their museums, churches, colleges, and libraries. For their own homes, offices, stores, and warehouses, they sought out a remarkably original group of architects, of whom Louis Sullivan and Frank Lloyd Wright had the greatest impact.

The skyscraper, born in Chicago, was made possible by steel skeleton frames, electric elevators, and engineering ingenuity. Unlike other artists who drifted elsewhere, architects continued to return to the city. Ludwig Mies van der Rohe, trained in the German Bauhaus school, came to I.I.T. in 1938. He and his disciples, in firms like Skidmore Owens and Merrill, transformed the city's skyline after 1950 with great glass and steel towers that drew their stunning effect from a strictly functional composition.

Illinois needed reform as well as beauty in the early twentieth century, and the rapidly growing middle class appreciated the need to modernize the structure of government. Flagrant corruption was the rule in city politics, while inept administration produced a degree of waste intolerable to the efficiency-oriented businessmen. The chief obstacle to reform was the strongly entrenched political party system. Reformers introduced nonpartisan municipal government to most of the suburbs and downstate cities, but were never able to overcome the power of the corrupt Democratic and Republican machines in Chicago. Governor Frank Lowden (the son-in-law of George Pullman) drew national recognition for his efficient reorganization of parts of the State government in 1917.

The years of World War I reopened the scars of ethnic conflict. People were divided sharply on the wisdom of intervening in a terrible European War, with Jane Addams the outstanding advocate of pacifism. Anglophiles, led by utility magnate Samuel Insull (born in London), insisted that cultural ties and the duty to stop the reactionary Kaiser in the name of progress called for alliance with Britain. In this war, the State not only provided food and manpower, but also money, munitions, and supplies of all sorts for the Allied effort.

The Socialists denounced the war as a fraud on behalf of capitalism. They were rounded up, jailed, and their newspapers closed. The State's large German population had divided loyalties. Some enthusiastically endorsed the war; the majority feared that they would be persecuted as representatives of "Hun" culture. The fears proved correct. German-Americans were warned that they would be closely watched for signs of disloyalty, such as not buying enough war bonds. German language newspapers were tightly censored by the Post Office, German instruction was dropped from the public schools, street names were changed, and anyone with a kind word to say about the people of Germany was in serious trouble. The Americans of German descent were, in fact, completely loyal to their new country. Reluctantly they abandoned their native tongue in church services, cancelled their subscriptions to their newspapers, and wondered how vicious the persecutions would become.

Since victory came only 18 months after the United States declared war, the harassment of the German-Americans was not as bad as it might otherwise have become. The reformers did use the opportunity to identify beer with the hated German culture, thus rushing through prohibition. The political reaction of the Germans included votes for Socialist candidates in the 1917 Chicago elections, and for the Republican candidates in 1920. By 1920 the anti-German hysteria had vanished, and by 1928 or so the Germans' resentment had faded away. German-Americans in Illinois abandoned all traces of their distinctive heritage (except the Lutheran faith), and became so thoroughly assimilated as a protection against future threat that they lost all sense of their historic roots.

Bootleggers made Chicago famous in the 1920s, and pulled Cicero and Joliet into national headlines. Prohibition divided Illinois sharply into the modernizers, who endorsed the noble experiment, and the traditionalists, who felt their personal liberty had been outraged.

To supply the illegal demand, bootleggers built a complex business operation, with manufacturing facilities, a transportation network and a distribution system, together with financing, an active security and legal affairs division, and political connections. Publicity was handled by the general media. A multi-million dollar industry rapidly appeared, with its entrepreneurs as famous as Henry Ford. The problem was that it was all highly illegal.

Massive payoffs to corrupt police captains, judges, and aldermen kept the heat down. Competition was discouraged by machine guns, and uncooperative politicians worried about finding their automobiles wired to dynamite. Chicago and its ethnic suburbs were the center of the industry, but speakeasies and roadhouses, which also provided gambling and prostitutes, flourished in or on the outskirts of Peoria, East. St. Louis, Moline, and Springfield.

Although Republicans held most public offices, the governor and the mayor of Chicago for most of the 1920s were closely allied with machines that worked closely with the bootleggers. Al Capone even claimed credit for the election of Mayor "Big Bill" Thompson in 1927. The moralists were aghast at how badly their favorite reform had turned out. Only the vigilance of federal Treasury officials kept the bootleggers wary. Finally, the end of prohibition in 1933, together with prison sentences for many surviving crime figures, reduced the level of shocking violence and immorality to more tolerable levels.

Urban Illinois enjoyed unprecedented prosperity in the 1920s. Skyscrapers in the Loop and luxury high rise apartments along the lakefront symbolized the success of Chicago's elite in channelling the commerce of the entire region into their metropolis. Downstate cities fared well in less spectacular fashion, certifying their civic responsibility by new city halls, hospitals, paved streets, water plants, and high schools. The automobile finally broke the isolation of rural Illinois. Although corn, hog, and land prices did not match the heights of the 1910s, the farmers made out quite well. By 1927, 90 percent of downstate families owned an automobile, and the Sunday jaunt into the country, over newly built concrete highways, became a regular part of life. General stores in little hamlets shut down as farmers drove 10 or 20 miles to larger towns and cities to do their shopping. The smart thing for the rural shop-keeper was to open up a business in town: blacksmiths and livery stables adjusted quickly to the new era's demand for auto mechanics and service stations. Farmers who bought cars, trucks, and tractors discovered they could produce more with less work, and the old faithful horse was put out to pasture (more likely, sold to a glue or dog food factory).

Depression, War and the Suburban Era, 1929-1980

Average people across the State shook their fists at the "big guys": the speculators, entrepreneurs, brokers, and bankers on LaSalle Street. The curses were misdirected. The Great Depression was not caused by the stock market crash of 1929. (The cause of the depression is still not clear. Even historians and economists are not sure, but most are inclined to blame federal monetary policy for tightening up the supply of money and credit.) Other myths abounded. Hundreds of banks closed, especially small town or neigh-borhood operations, but eventually the depositors received about 90 cents on the dollar. Thousands lost their life savings because they had to spend the money to survive.

Unemployment was very high, but at any one time in the 1930s, at least 75 to 85 percent of people had jobs. Government employees, and white collar workers generally, were least likely to lose their jobs, although pay scales were lower and it took longer to get a promotion. The worst unemployment hit heavy industry such as steel, coal, and railroads. At the nadir only 52 percent of the normal factory work force was employed, often on a short week.

The State's large agricultural implement industry suffered, as farmers no longer invested in new John Deere tractors or International Harvester combines. The railroads shipped less coal, steel, meat, grain, and merchandise, forc-ing them to lay off half of their employees. Several lines went bankrupt. The Illinois Central barely stayed solvent, as its stock owners lost 95 percent of their equity between 1930 and 1932. Worst hit were the coal camps of southern Illinois, where the Red Cross had to set up emergency soup lines to keep whole towns from starving. Farmers suffered too; their average net income fell from $2,000 in 1928 and 1929 to a negative $500 in 1931 and 1932. Land prices also plunged, so that the average farm, which had been worth $27,000 in 1927, was worth only $18,000 in 1935. Farm income recovered somewhat in the mid-1930s, but only by slashing expenses could the farmers hang on. Local government and private charity tried to alleviate the distress, but soon ran out of money. The State government began imposing a sales tax of two percent to provide emergency help. The Hoover Administration finally provided loans for relief in late 1932.

The failure of the modern economy, together with the failure of prohibition, drove Illinois into the Democratic camp by huge majorities. Chicago judge Henry Horner became the first Democratic governor since Altgeld. Franklin Roosevelt blamed the speculators for the depression, and put on trial Samuel Insull, the man who built Commonwealth Edison, People's Gas, and many other utilities across the Midwest. Insull won acquittal by proving that his efforts to expand the electric power industry in the 1920s had no criminal motivation.

Nevertheless, the popular distrust of big business lingered on and contributed to the smashing margins Roosevelt and Horner secured in their reelection bids in 1936. Large scale relief, funded jointly by federal and State appropriations, was the hallmark of the New Deal. At any one time, about one family in six was on relief. Probably half the families in Illinois received some form of federal, State, or local relief at one time or another in the 1930s.

The largest program was the WPA, employing an average of 200,000 Illinois men between 1935 and 1940. The WPA and other work relief programs succeeded in endowing the State with many facilities: Lake Shore Drive, Midway Airport, and the subway in Chicago; parks, recreation buildings, roads, and sewage systems across the state.

Chicago Democrats used the relief programs to build an invincible political machine. Previously, the two parties had competed on equal terms in the city. Under the leadership of Mayors Anton Cermak and Edward Kelly, the machine attracted scores of thousands of previously apathetic men and women in the ethnic neighborhoods to join the party that provided relief. Chicago's black voters, previously Republican, switched over to the Democratic fold.

The Chicago Republican party became moribund in local affairs, never to recover. Chicago Democrats formed a close alliance with labor unions, which grew rapidly under the benevolent protection of federal agencies. Soon Chicago had the reputation as one of the strongest union towns in the country, with steel, garment, auto, meat, and electrical workers powerful in the factories, and the teamsters and building trades secure in their domains.

The middle class in Illinois, after giving considerable support to Democratic candidates in 1932, 1934, and 1936, began to sour on the New Deal. The return to prosperity was nowhere in sight, relief programs kept expanding, nasty strikes threatened the maintenance of law and order, the Democratic governor feuded bitterly with the Chicago machine, and Roosevelt's plan to pack the Supreme Court seemed to threaten one of the most sacred (and most conservative) national institutions.

Even worse, the big spending programs would have to be paid for, and that meant more taxes for the middle class. Indeed, State taxes quadrupled during the decade, and federal taxes went up sharply as well. Reaction was inevitable. In 1938, the Republicans scored well, and in 1940 they recaptured the governorship. Illinois was no longer safely Republican, nor would it be easy for either party to carry the State. Illinois became a major national battleground, with its electoral choice winning the presidency every time (except in 1976, when Ford narrowly beat Carter in Illinois).

Prosperity finally returned during World War II. Patriotic demand to whip the Axis produced an overexpanded economy, with men and women working longer hours than they wished. Illinois factories, shops, stores, and trains worked overtime to produce the munitions of war. Agriculture, though not as dominant in the economy as before, likewise expanded to feed the armies around the globe. Civilian volunteers in 561 draft boards across the state enlisted a million young men, three-fourths of whom served abroad.

In the highly mechanized and technological American style of war, casualties were relatively few. Only two percent of the soldiers were killed in battle, and four percent wounded. Heroes' welcomes greeted the returning veterans, as well as generous State and national bonuses. By 1980, federal and State government had paid out $6 million to Illinois veterans, with even more yet to come.

The veterans, and those who sweated and prayed on the home front, wanted most of all a return to peace and tranquil prosperity. Clean new suburbs with ample bedrooms, spacious lawns, fine schools, safe streets, and convenient central cities led to smaller towns either becoming static or losing in population. Much of this growth centered in Chicago's Cook and DuPage County suburbs, and in new housing developments on the outskirts of other large cities. By the mid-1960s, one third of the State's population lived in Chicago, another third lived in Chicago suburbs, and the last third lived in small towns and cities downstate.

Only four percent of the work force was still in agriculture; indeed, half the people who lived in farm houses commuted to jobs in stores, offices, or factories. With automobile ownership practically universal (and gasoline still cheap), the State expanded and improved its highway network, opened tollroads, and used federal gasoline tax money to build an impressive network of interstate highways criss-crossing the State.

The particular local flavor that once characterized individual towns or city neighborhoods yielded to a homogeneous way of life. The same supermarkets, service stations, drug stores, department stores, and fast food outlets provided everyone in Illinois the same standardized goods and smiles. Nostalgia for the old times eventually emerged in the 1970s, with historic preservation projects and reminiscent festivals reminding people of a way of life that was forever gone.

The last outpost of localism in rural Illinois was the neighborhood school district. Illinois had 12,000 separate districts in 1940, more than any other state. But they were inefficient, and provided an inadequate education for youth who would have to cope with a technological society. Consolidation proceeded rapidly in the 1940s and 1950s, until only 600 districts remained, each busing its students to a centralized plant where professionally trained teachers provided a homogeneous curriculum. Consolidation opened the way to high schools for rural youth.

To provide a college education for everyone who wanted it, the State upgraded its teachers' colleges into State universities, created a branch of the University of Illinois in downtown Chicago, and set up dozens of community colleges within easy commuting distance in Illinois.

Enrollment in higher education moved from 107,000 in 1940 to 164,000 in 1956, then began to soar, reaching 500,000 by 1980. The technological State needed well-trained men and women; money, hard work, imagination, and ambition provided the solution.

Political observers in the early 1950s speculated that suburbanization, extended schooling, and broadened wealth would soon make the GOP the majority party in the State and nation. Eisenhower's two landslides over Illinois Governor Adlai Stevenson in 1952 and 1956 seemed to confirm the trend. Actually, however, the proportion of Democrats held steady, while the Republican ranks diminished every year. The youth were becoming independent, and their parents stayed with the old party even as they moved to the suburbs. The GOP stayed alive in statewide elections by promoting brilliant young stars like Charles Percy and James Thompson. In the General Assembly, however, the shrinkage of the GOP voter base led to steady increments in Democratic gains, until the legislature in the 1970s finally fell to Democratic control.

Everywhere in America the old line political machines in the big cities were crumbling. The Chicago machine seemed to be losing its hold in the late 1940s and early 1950s, until Richard J. Daley took control as mayor and party boss. Daley used all the old techniques of patronage, ethnic recognition, and alliances with labor unions. But he also added a new ingredient: close cooperation with the business community to keep jobs and power inside his city. During his reign (1955-1976), Chicago won the accolade of "the city that worked."

After Daly's death, the machine stumbled along, amidst intense political infighting to secure control, and the reputation sagged. Discovery in late 1979 that the city's public school system was on the verge of bankruptcy proved that no metropolis was immune to the prospect of decay and disorder.

Illinois, like every urban state, was the scene of intense racial hostility and violence in the 1960s. Although legal segregation had been outlawed for a century, intense fear and dislike of the blacks had crowded them into slums in Chicago, East. St. Louis, Peoria, and every other city. National civil rights legislation, strongly promoted by Democratic Governor Otto Kerner and Republican Senator

Everett Dirkson, only highlighted the need for reform. Racial tension over jobs, housing, patronage, crime, and school integration simmered throughout the 1960s and 1970s, boiling over into short, sharp black riots in Chicago and a dozen other cities between 1966 and 1968.

Heavy spending on welfare ($2 billion a year by 1978), eased the overt tensions. The unsolved problem of integrating Chicago's public schools (only 20 percent white in 1980) guaranteed years of future difficulties in race relations. Meanwhile, however, young, well-educated black families finally reached income parity with their white counterparts. Black spokesmen like the Reverend Jesse Jackson promised that the combination of black self-awareness, hard work, and strong demands for racial justice would eventually overcome the inferior status Illinois blacks had always endured.

As if problems of race, poverty, and urban decay were not challenging enough for any state, the people of Illinois--and in many other parts of the nation generally--began to lose confidence in American values from the mid-1960s onward. Young people started to question the deep modern values to which their parents had been dedicated. The failure of the Vietnam War exacerbated domestic difficulties. Ambition for more and more no longer seemed so sensible, as youth demanded more autonomy. They turned increasingly to drugs, heavy rock music, sex, and protest politics.

Feminists began to challenge the old rule that careers, indeed, public roles generally, were reserved for men. Although Illinois refused to ratify the Equal Rights Amendment, the debate over it, over abortion, pornography, nudity, divorce, homosexuality, and cohabitation proved that sexual roles and codes of morality were undergoing drastic change.

The general malaise showed up most strikingly in widespread distrust of political leaders. As Watergate played out on the television, a series of powerful Illinois politicians, including ex-Governor Kerner, were sentenced to prison. Candidates for office ran against the system, warning that the incumbents were hopeless. The most spectacular example was the election of unknown Jane Byrne as mayor of Chicago against the united opposition of a supposedly invincible machine.

As more and more citizens lost faith in the system, they stopped voting, plunging election turnouts to the lowest levels since Illinois became a state. Clearly, the malaise was national in scope, and no state could hope to recover solely with its own resources. As the 1980s ended, the people of Illinois, like Americans generally, were fast becoming pessimistic about the future of their society, and there were no signs of hope anyone could offer, save those who realized that people had overcome adversity many times in their history.

(For more recent historical events see the Chronology.)

CHRONOLOGY

20,000 BC —Probable arrival of early man to the North American continent. These early hunters from Asia later developed into the primitive Paleo-Indian culture, the ancestors of Ilinois Indians.
-Ice sheet begins melting over Great Lakes.

8,000 BC — Descendants of the Paleo-Indians, the Archaic Indians, are the first men to arrive in Illinois.

2,500 BC — -Early Middle Woodland culture begins. Although these Indians mainly hunt, they also forage for nuts and roots and begin making pottery.

500 BC — Indians of the Middle Woodland culture, or the Hopewell culture, establish large settlements in the State. These first Illinois farmers are extremely artistic as the the Woodland culture reaches its zenith.

AD 200 — The Late Woodland period begins. The large settlements dissolve and the Indians leave farming. The artistry of the culture disappears.

AD 900 — Mound builders come to Illinois. Cahokia becomes the religious center for the sun worshippers during the Mississippian Period.

1540 — Hernando de Soto leads an expedition to the Mississippi River area. Smallpox and measles brought by the explorers wipe out families, villages and entire tribes.

1634 — Jean Nicolet reaches Green Bay, becoming the first white man to enter the midwest.

1671 — France takes possession of the "West" in a ceremony at Sault Sainte Marie.

1673 —   Father Jacques Marquette and Louis Jolliet explore the region.

1675 —   Marquette makes a second trip to Illinois area, founding the Mission of Immaculate Conception in the Indian village of Kaskaskia, near present-day Utica. On returning from the trip, he dies on the east shore of Lake Michigan.

1680 —   Robert Cavalier, Sieur de La Salle, builds Fort Crevecoeur along the Illinois River, near present-day city of Peoria.

1682 —   Cavalier builds Fort St. Louis after Fort Crevecouer is destroyed by mutineers.

1687 —   Cavalier is murdered by his own men.

1691 —   Henri de Tonti, Cavalier's lieutenant, moves Fort St. Louis to Pimitoui (now present-day Peoria) along the Illinois River. French settlers collect around the fort, making this the first white settlement in the State; the Mission of Immaculate Conception is moved to the settlement.

1699 —   Priests of the Seminary of Foreign Missions at Quebec establish the Mission of the Holy Family and the town of Cahokia.

1703 —   Jesuits move the Mission of Immaculate Conception to the town of Kaskaskia.

1712 —   French soldiers and their Indian allies begin a series of battles against the Fox.

1719 —   Fort Charles is built near Prairie du Rocher.

1731 —   Illinois becomes a royal province governed directly by the King of France.

1754 —   French-Indian War begins.

1763 —   French-Indian War ends.
           -Treaty of Paris is signed.
           -Illinois country is ceded to Great Britain.
           -Pontiac's Rebellion (May 7-Nov. 28).
           -Jesuits are expelled from Illinois by French government.

1765 —   A British detachment called "Black Watch captures Fort de Chartres and all the villages in Illinois from the French.

1769 —   Pontiac is killed at Cahokia by Indians.

1772 —   Fort de Chartres is destroyed by British.

1774 —   British Parliament passes the Quebec Act, enlarging Quebec's boundaries to include Illinois.
           -French civil law is reestablished.

1775 —   American Revolution begins.

1778 —   George Robert Clark captures Cahokia, Kaskaskia and other Illinois settlements for the Commonwealth of Virginia; the territory is declared a county of Virginia.

1779 —   Civil government is established. John Todd is named county lieutenant by Virginia's governor.

1783 —   War of Independence ends. The United States boundary is extended to the Mississippi River.
           -The first school in Illinois is established at New Design, in present-day Monroe County.

1784 —   Virginia cedes Illinois to the United States government.

1785 —   Congress adopts a plan for the orderly settlement of the Northwest Territory; townships are to be six miles square, divided into 36 sections, with each 16th section reserved for the support of common schools; minimum purchase of land is 640 acres, at no less than $1 per acre.

1787 — Northwest Territory, including Illinois, is officially recognized by Congressional Ordinance. Besides providing for government of the territory, the Ordinance prohibits slavery.
-General Arthur St. Clair is named governor.

1795 — Treaty of Greenville is signed; Indians cede vast areas of land to the U.S. government.

1796 — The first Baptist Church in state is established at New Design.

1800 — Congress creates Indiana Territory, which includes what is now Illinois, Indiana, Michigan, and Wisconsin (May 7).

1801 — William Henry Harrison assumes duties of first governor of Indiana Territory at the capital of Vincennes.

1803 — Fort Dearborn is erected on the south side of the Chicago River by Federal troops; the city of Chicago is later built on this site.
-Fort Wayne and Vincennes treaties are signed; Indians cede large tracts of land to whites.

1804 — Sauk and Fox tribes relinquish all their lands east of the Mississippi.
-Area's first U.S. Lands Office opens in Kaskaskia.

1809 — Feb.9. Illinois Territory is detached from Indiana Territory.
-Ninian Edwards is first governor.
-Kaskaskia is named capital.

1810 — Vandalia becomes new State capital.

1812 — Aug. 15. Indians attack Fort Dearborn; the fort is destroyed; evacuating soldiers and civilians are massacred.

1814 — -New Fort Dearborn is built.

1818— Illinois Enabling Act is passed by Congress, extending state territory northward.
-First state Constitutional Convention is held; the Constitution is adopted in August, and Kaskaskia named as capital.
-December 3. U.S. President James Monroe signs act to make Illinois 21st state of the Union; Shadrach Bond is elected first governor.

1820— Census reveals population is 55,211.
-State capital relocated to Vandalia.

1821— State Bank of Illinois is chartered by General Assembly.

1824— Convention to amend State constitution to allow slavery is voted down by populace.

1825— Erie Canal opens.

1827— 224,322 acres are given to State by Congress to help construct a major waterway from Lake Michigan to the Chicago River to the Des Plaines River and into the Mississippi; canal later becomes major factor in the early development of Chicago.
-A seminary is organized at Rock Springs; it is known today as Shurtleff College.

1830— Lincoln family moves from Indiana to Illinois.
-Population of State is 157,445.

1832— Black Hawk War brings complete defeat of Sauk and Fox.
-Chicago receives its first legal geographical locations; population of the town is 100.

1833— Last remaining Indian lands are ceded to government.

1834— Abraham Lincoln is elected to State Legislature.

-Feb. 11. Chicago is incorporated as a town.

1836 — Illinois and Michigan canal construction begins; sale of land along site of canal creates land boom.

1837 — Internal Improvement Act is passed by General Assembly, appropriating $10,000,000 for a network of canals, railroads, and roads throughout the state.
-John Deere revolutionizes prairie farming when he invents the first successful self-scouring steel plow.
-Chicago is incorporated as a city, with a population of 4,170.
-New York native William B. Ogden is elected Chicago's first mayor.
-Elijah P. Lovejay, editor of the anti-slavery *Alton Observer* newspaper, is murdered by a pro-slavery mob.

1839 — State capital is moved north to Springfield.
-Mormons, fleeing Missouri, found town of Nauvoo.

1840 — First steam railroad in Illinois, the *Northern Cross*, is completed, connecting Naples with Jacksonville.
-Liberty Party is organized.
-Irish immigrants begin settling in Chicago; these immigrants later play a major role in the city's politics.
-State population is 476,183.

1842 — Oldest German singing society in the United States, the Sacred Music Society, is organized in Chicago.

1844 — Mormon leaders Joseph and Hyrum Smith are murdered in Carthage, resulting in open warfare in Hancock County.

1845 — Free School law is enacted.

1846 — Brigham Young leads an exodus of Mormons from Illinois to Utah.
-Abraham Lincoln is elected to Congress.

Chronology

1847 —   Cyrus McCormick, inventor of the reaper, and his two brothers came to Chicago and open a farm machinery business. By 1850, the business has spread world-wide and Cyrus has become a millionaire.
              -*Chicago Tribune* begins publishing.

1848 —   Second state constitution is adopted.
              -Illinois and Michigan canal is completed, after 12 years of construction.
              -Chicago and Galena Union Railroad opens for business, establishing Chicago as an important railroad city.

1850 —   Population is 851,470.

1851 —   Illinois Central Railroad, the first land grant railroad in the United States, is chartered.
              -Allan Pinkerton is hired as Chicago's first detective.
              -Northwestern University, originally a Methodist college, is founded in present-day Evanston.

1853 —   Illinois State Agricultural Society is chartered.
              -First state fair is held.
              -Illinois Wesleyan University (Bloomington) opens.

1854 —   Republican Party is founded in state.

1855 —   First free public school system is approved by State legislature.

1856 —   Opposition to Kansas-Nebraska Act helps elect William H. Bissell as first Republican Governor.

              -Illinois Central Railroad is completed.
              -First cargo of wheat to leave Chicago through canals and head across the Atlantic establishes the city as an important international seaport.

1857 —   Original Fort Dearborn is torn down.
              -Illinois State University opens.

1858 —   Lincoln and Stephen Arnold Douglas hold series of debates throughout the State on the issue of free soil versus popular sovereignty; although Lincoln wins debates, Douglas is reelected to U.S. Senate by receiving large Democratic vote in Chicago.

1859 —　First University of Chicago opens; it is forced to close seven years later due to lack of funds.

1860 —　Republican National Convention in Chicago nominates Abraham Lincoln for President; Lincoln is subsequently elected President.
-Population is 1,711,951.

1861 —　Illinois begins supplying soldiers for Civil War effort; over the next few years, the State supplies 256,297 soldiers for the Union Army, 14,596 more than its quota.
-War creates business boom throughout the state.

1864 —　Democratic convention is held in Chicago.
-Lincoln is reelected President.
-"Chicago Conspiracy" to free confederate soldiers is uncovered.

1865 —　President Lincoln is killed; his body is laid to rest in Oak Ridge Cemetery in Springfield.
-Civil War ends. Over 34,000 men from State have lost their lives in the war.

1867 —　University of Illinois (Urbana) is founded.
-Phillip Armour opens meat-packing plant in Chicago.

1874 —　*Chicago Daily News* is established by Melville E. Stone.

1876 —　U. S. Supreme Court upholds right of the State to regulate business "clothed with a public interest" in the case of Munn v. Illinois.
-Lake Forest University opens.

1878 —　State Board of Health is organized.

Chronology

1880 —   Chicago surpasses St. Louis as the greatest interior city in America.
-Population is 3,077,871.

1882 —   Chicago Art Institute opens.
-Chicago Stock Exchange is established.

1884 —   Both Republican and Democratic National Conventions are held in Chicago.
-Chicago Conservatory of Music is established.
-Social unrest rises over labor conditions throughout the State; trade unions are formed; Knights of Labor demand eight hour workday.
-Construction begins on first modern skyscraper, the Home Insurance building, designed by William L. Jenny.

1886 —   Social unrest continues to grow; more than 1,000 labor- related strikes have taken place in the State.
-Sears, Roebuck and Company is established in Chicago.
-Chicago Symphony Orchestra is organized.
-May 4. The Haymarket Massacre takes place in Chicago; seven police are killed, and 70 persons injured. Four months later, seven foreign-born officials are sentenced to death for their participation in the riots; another is sentenced to life in prison.

1888 —   New State Capitol building is constructed.
-Chicago White Sox tour the world.

1889 —   State Historical Library is founded.
Jane Addams founds Hull House in Chicago, a prototype of other social settlement houses for immigrants in the U.S.

1890 —   Population is 4,821,550.

1891 —   Women are allowed to vote in school board elections.

1892 —   John P. Altgeld is elected governor; he is the first Democratic governor since the Civil War.

1893 — The World Columbian Exposition is held in Chicago; on the last day of the fair, Chicago Mayor Carter H. Harrison is assassinated (Oct. 26).
-Chicago Natural History Museum is founded.
-Illinois Factory Act is passed, providing the State with its first child labor laws.
-Governor Altgeld pardons three remaining convicts in the Haymarket Riot case (four had been executed, another had committed suicide) effectively ending his political career. The entire episode receives national attention and raises concern of whether the accused were actually guilty; this influences Illinois politics for many years.
-Armour College is opened.

1894 — Labor unrest in state climaxes; workers call strike against Pullman Car Company; American Railway Union joins strikers in show of support. Despite protests by Gov. Altgeld, President Cleveland sends in federal troops to end strike.

1895 — Sears, Roebuck and Co. revolutionizes farm purchasing by introduction of mail order department.

1896 — At Democratic National Convention in Chicago, former Illinois resident William Jennings Bryan is nominated for first of three unsuccessful bids for presidency.

1898 — DePaul University opens in Chicago.
-Illinois sends 12,000 men to fight in Spanish-American War.

1900 — William Raldolph Hearst begins publishing *Chicago Evening America* in Chicago.
-Population of State is 4,821,550; Chicago population is 1,698,575.

1901 —   Hearst begins publishing the *Examiner* in Chicago.

-Abraham Lincoln's body is moved to monument in Springfield.

1902 —   State adopts direct, popular election of U.S. Senators.

1903 —   596 persons are killed when Iroquois Theatre in Chicago   catches fire.
-State establishes eight-hour workday and 40-hour work week for children.

1904 —   At the Republican National Convention in Chicago, Theodore Roosevelt is nominated for presidency.

1905 —   The Rotarians, first luncheon club in the nation, begins in Chicago.
-A black newspaper, the *Chicago Defender*, is founded.

1906 —   State Highway Commission is organized.

1907 —   Legislature passes a law permitting local option for alcohol consumption.
-Hennepin Canal opens.

1908 —   Republican National Convention in Chicago nominates Taft for President.
-Frank Lloyd Wright creats Robie House in a Chicago suburb.

1909 —   Workday for women is limited to 10 hours.

1910 —   Primary Act is passed.
-Chicago Opera Company gives its first performance.
-Population is 5,638,591.

1911 —   Robert R. McCormick is appointed president of the *Chicago Tribune*.
-First workman's compensation law is passed.

1912 —   Republicans nominate Taft in national convention in Chicago; in revolt, Roosevelt supporters

launch progressive movement at Chicago's Orchestra Hall.
-Legal prostitution is abolished in Chicago.

1913 —   Women's suffrage is extended to all of State's nonconstitutional offices.

1915 —   812 persons are drowned when the steamer *Eastland* capsizes in the Chicago River.

1917 —   Over two years, Illinois contributes 351,153 men to fight in the United States Armed Forces in World War I.
-Major reforms take place within State's governmental structure; most noticable is reorganization of the Labor Department.

1918 —   Voters approve a 60 million bond issue for construction of a state-wide system of hard roads.
-World War I ends.

1919 —   June 10. Illinois ratifies 19th amendment, allowing women the same voting rights as men.
-Despite strong protests in Chicago and other areas of the State, National Prohibition Enforcement Act goes into effect. @COLUMN = -Race riots rage in Chicago for four days; forty-eight people die, another 520 are injured. The rioting, similar to riots two years earlier in East St. Louis, is caused by fear that Southern Blacks will be employed in Northern factories, denying jobs to white workers.

1920 —   Republican National Convention in Chicago nominates Warren G. Harding for presidency; Harding is chosen nominee by Republican Party bosses at a private meeting, in a smoke-filled room at the Blackstone Hotel.

1922 —   Voters overwhelmingly defeat a new state constitution.
-Coal strike in Herrin causes 22 deaths.
-Major anti-prohibition rallies are held in Chi-

cago; City Council sends letters to all major U. S. cities seeking their support to end prohibition; the Council also votes to oppose expenditures of city funds to enforce the prohibition law.

1923 — Legislature approves $100,000,000 Road Bond issue.
-Governor signs anti-Ku Klux Klan bill.

1924 — Richard Loeb and Nathan Leopold murder 14-year-old Robert Franks; defended by Clarence Darrow, the two escape death penalty and are sentenced to life in prison.
-Despite prohibition laws, Chicago has 15 breweries and 20,000 retail outlets for beer and alcoholic beverage sales.
-Underworld figure Al Capone moves his headquarters from Chicago to the outlying suburb of Cicero.
-Wrigley Building is constructed in Chicago.

1926 — Soldier Field is constructed in Chicago.
-Roman Catholic Church holds its Eucharistic Congress in Illinois.
-Open warfare begins between Al Capone's gang and the rival Dion O'Banion's gang throughout Chicago and suburbs.
-Chicago Municipal Airport is opened.

1927 — Capone returns to Chicago.

1928 — Children are required to finish elementary grades before being allowed to work; school year is increased from six to eight months.
-Seven of Al Capone's enemies are gunned to death in St. Valentine's Day Massacre.
-Stock Market Crash causes economic hardships throughout State.   Merchandise Mart opens in Chicago.

1930 — First planetarium in United States is built in Grant Park, Chicago.
-Population is 7,630,654.

1931 — Al Capone is found guilty of tax evasion.

1932 —   Franklin Delano Roosevelt is nominated for president at Democratic National Convention in Chicago; he is subsequently elected.
-National survey of cities reveals Chicago among hardest hit in country during depression.

1933 —   General Assembly enacts Retailer's Occupational Tax (sales tax) to raise money for the needy.
-Chicago Mayor Anton Cermak dies of gunshot wounds received in attempted assassination of president-elect Roosevelt in Miami.
-Chicago World's Fair, The Century of Progress, is held.

1936 —   Old age security law, occupational disease law, compensation law, and permanent registration law are enacted by General Assembly.

1936 —   Legislature passes law requiring examination for venereal disease before a couple can be married.

-Workday for women is limited to eight hours.
-Ohio River floods in southern Illinois, leaving thousands homeless.

1937 —   Oil is found in central to southern parts of State, creating major boom.

1940 —   Communists are mobbed while circulating petitions to get party on ballot; the party is later barred from ballot.
-Governor Horner dies in office; Lt. Governor Stelle is governor.
-Dwight Green is elected Governor.
-Population is 7,897,241.

1941 —   General Assembly passes bill barring Communist Party from ballot.
-*Daily Illinois* student editorial opposing U.S. entry into World War II brings condemnation from Illinois Senator C. Wayland Brooks.
-Over the next five years, Illinois supplies over 900,000 residents for Armed Forces to fight in World War II; State also supplies an estimated $27,000,000,000 worth of war goods.

1942 — First controlled nuclear chain reaction is conducted by Enrico Fermi and group of American scientists at a top-secret laboratory beneath stands of Stagg Field at the University of Chicago.

1943 — U.S. Court of Appeals upholds State's right to levy an oil tax.
-Two Illinoisans, General MacArthur and Col. R. R. McCormick, enter primaries as Republican Presidential candidates.
-Alumnus vote to erect art gallery at University of Illinois.
-Attempted revolt occurs at Illinois State Penitentiary.

1944 — School children buy Keyes copy of Lincoln's Gettysburg Address for the State.
-A Senate committee investigation into State's absentee ballots finds no irregularities.
-Governor Green is reelected.

1945 — General Assembly commends Hitler for dying.
-World War II ends.

1946 — Electorate approves war veteran aid proposal.
-Use of voting booths is adopted.

1947 — Proposed U.S. Constitutional Amendment limiting Presidential tenure is ratified.

1948 — Legal battle erupts when Progressive Party is denied access to State ballot.
-Governor Green is defeated by Adlai E. Stevenson.

1949 — Over 50 Illinois publishers, editors, and newsmen are revealed to have been on State payroll during governor Green's administration in order to favorably publicize the "Green Machine".

1950 — *Chicago Daily News* and *St. Louis Post- Dispatch* are awarded Pulitzer Prizes for exposing newspaper personnel on governor's payroll.
-Population is 8,712,176.

1952 —   Stevenson is defeated by Dwight D. Eisenhower
in bid for presidency.
-Stratton defeats Dixon for Governor.
-University of Illinois President Stoddard resigns
after trustees reject vote of confidence; L.
Morey is named president.   -Il-
linois toll-road commission established.

1955 —   U.S. Senate gives State exclusive rights to Land
of Lincoln emblem.
-Richard Daley is elected mayor of Chicago, establishing 25 years of dominance of the
Democratic machine in the city.
-University of Illinois announces plans to probe
any staff member who evokes Constitutional
rights to avoid testifying on Communist ties.
-Robert R. McCormick of the *Chicago Tribune*
dies; the death of this colorful and influential
newspaper publisher marks the passing of a
great period of personal journalism in State.

1956 —   State Auditor General Hodge pleads guilty in
Federal and State courts of embezzlement of
over $1 million in State money; political corrup-
tion ravages the State.
-Besides Hodge, several other state officials and
private citizens are convicted over the next few
years.
-Despite bad press for the Republican party
during this election year, the party loses no
footage in State races.

1957 —   Political corruption cases enter second year.
-Executive L. Marcus, an associate of Hodge,
Southmoor Bank and Trust Company, is killed.
-*Chicago Daiiy News* receives Pulitzer Prize for
Hodge expose.
-House approves freedom of information bill,
requiring most govcrnmental bodies to hold open
meetings.
-University of Illinois receives $300,000 from
H.C. Kramet for construction of art museum.
-Chicago seeks to divert additional water from
Lake Michigan, but is fought by six other Great
Lakes states and Canada.

1959 —   Despite Canadian protests, U.S. House of Representatives votes to let Chicago divert 1,000 more cubic feet of water per second from Lake Michigan for sewage system.
-Daley is reelected in Chicago.

1960 —   Kerner defeats Stratton for governorship.
-Census shows Chicago has overtaken New York as America's leading industrial city.

1961 —   Democratic minority in house elects P. Powell as Speaker in rump session after Republicans walk out.
-Constitutional crisis erupts.

1962 —   Students occupy University of Chicago President Beadle's office, protesting segregation in university housing.

1963 —   Daley is reelected mayor of Chicago by more than 137,000 votes to his closest opponent.

1964 —   Entire Democratic slate of 118 candidates is elected to State House of Representatives.

1965 —   New University of Illinois campus opens in Chicago.
-After two years of court battles, Rock Island stockholders approve merger with Union Pacific Railroad.

1966 —   1,000 Puerto Ricans riot, protesting alleged police brutality.
-Interior of State capitol is remodeled.

1967 —   Supreme Court upholds Chicago's increased diversion of water for Lake Michigan.
-Chicago mayor Richard Daley is reelected by record 516,208 votes.

1968 —
Rioting erupts outside Democratic National Convention in Chicago.

-Trial of radical "Chicago Seven" begins; after several years of court battles, charges against the seven are dropped.
-G. Brooks is named Illinois Poet Laureate.
-Stamp is issued commemorating 150 years of statehood.
-Governor Kemer resigns to accept federal judgeship; Lt. Gov. Shapiro succeeds to governor; later that year, Richard Oglivie is elected governor.
-Pitzler family donates $12 million to University of Chicago for construction of Medical School.

1969 —
Bill establishing new State flag is signed.
-Former State capitol is restored to appear as it did in Lincoln's time.

1970 —
New state constitution is adopted.

1971 —
Federal Judge Kerner is indicted by Federal Grand Jury on charges of conspiracy, bribery, perjury and mail fraud from his alleged purchase of Illinois racetrack at a huge discount while he was governor; other major political figures in state also indicted in related charges.
-Daley is reelected to fifth term as Chicago mayor.
-City observes 100th anniversary of the Great Chicago Fire that killed over 300 people.

1974 —
U.S. Senator Adlai Stevenson III leads Democratic party to its biggest political win in State in years.
-Federal district court in Washington orders Treasury Department to cut off funds to Chicago for having used money in ways to discriminate against women, blacks, and other minorities; quarterly payments of $19,195,633 to city halted.

1975 —
U.S. Appeals Court denies motion to release the $76 million frozen by the Treasury department

because of the alleged biases.
-Chicago Mayor Daley is easily reelected to his sixth four-year term.
-Illinois restores the death penalty.

1976 —   Chicago borrows $55 million from banks to fill city needs   left void by judicial freeze.
-Daley dies December 20 of heart attack at age of 74.

1977 —   Michael Bilandic named Chicago mayor for re-maining two years of Daley's term.

1978 —   *Chicago Daily News* folds.

1979 —   Blizzard virtually paralyzes city of Chicago; billions in damage done.
-Jane M. Byrne upsets Mayor Bilandic and the Democratic machine in Chicago mayorial race; she is elected mayor by a 5-1 margin.
-U.S. Supreme Court rules Illinois election code violates the equal protection clause of the 14th amendment.
-Federal Judge Nicholas S. Bua rules that Chicago's patronage system is unconstitutional.

1980 —   Midwest struck by dozens of tornadoes; two touch down in Illinois.

1981 —   Fire sweeps through Royal Beach Hotel on Chicago's North Side; residents are trapped in rooms by smoke and spreading flames; 19 die, 14 others injured in blaze.

1982 —   Air National Guard jet tanker explodes over northern Illinois, killing all 27 people aboard.
-Nov. 2. Thompson wins gubernatorial election over Adlai E. Stevenson by little more than 5,000 votes; it is the closest Statewide race in modern Illinois history.
-Dec. 2-9. Severe storms, heavy floods hit Mississippi Valley; 22 persons dead, $600 million damage in Illinois, Missouri and Arkansas.
-Dec. 10. U.S. Attorney Dan K. Webb of Chicago announces grand jury investigation of possible fraud in Nov. 2. election; inquiry investigates charges of votes cast for persons not at polls, absentee-ballot irregularities.

1983 — U.S. Agriculture Dept. declares drought disaster for Illinois and other areas of nation.

-Harold Washington wins mayoral race in Chicago, becoming first black mayor to be elected in the city.

1985 — Illinois Attorney General Neil Hartigan drops out of State gubernatorial race.

1986 — Widespread ticket-splitting affects election in Illinois; different parties elected in State race for senator and governor.

1987 — Mayor of Chicago Harold Washington dies while in office.

-Governor Thompson outlines agenda for reforms in education, welfare, environmental, judicial offices, and political campaigns in a State of the State address, saying he does not want to preside over "last generation of Illinoisans to dream or live the American dream."

1989 — Richard M. Daly wins mayoral election in Chicago; he will hold the same post his father had for 21 years in city.

1990 — Federal grand jury indicts five Chicago political figures on corruption charges, including fixed trials; charged are Alderman Fred Roti, Alderman Pasquale (Pat) Marcy, Judge David J. Shields, Attorney Pasquale (Pat) De Leo, and Senator John A. D'Arco Jr.

1991 — Illinois misses redistricting deadline written into State constitution; control of process is shifted to federal courts.

1992 — Underground flood devastates Chicago; reports estimate damages to exceed $1 billion; President Bush declares city a disaster, allowing city and businesses to become eligible for federal disaster relief.

1993 — United Mine Workers union ends coal strike in Illinois and four other states; health care costs among issues to be negotiated in reopened contract talks.

1993 — June. Chicago Bulls win third NBA championship over Phoenix Suns.

-Chicago Bulls superstar guard, Michael Jordan, announces his resignation from basketball.

DIRECTORY OF STATE SERVICES

ADJUTANT GENERAL, OFFICE OF
1301 N. MacArthur Blvd.
Springfield, IL 62702-2399

ADMINISTRATION, DEPARTMENT OF
401 S. Spring St.
Springfield, IL 62706

AERONAUTICS, OFFICE OF
One Langhorne Bond Dr.
Springfield, IL 62707-8415

AGING, DEPARTMENT OF
421 E. Capitol Ave.
Springfield, IL 62701

AGRICULTURE, DPEARTMENT OF
State Fairgrounds
Springfield, IL 62706

AIR POLLUTION CONTROL, DIVISION OF
2200 Churchill Rd.
P.O. Box 19276
Springfield, IL 62794-9276

ALCOHOLISM, DEPARTMENT OF
100 W. Randolph St.
Chicago, IL 60601

ARCHIVES AND RECORDS, DEPARTMENT OF
Office of the Secretary of State
Archives Bldg.
Springfield, IL 62756

ARTS AND HUMANITIES, DEPARTMENT OF
State of Illinois Center, Room 10-500
100 W. Randolph St.
Chicago, IL 60601

ATHLETICS BOARD
State of Illinois Center, 9th fl.
100 W. Randolph St.
Chicago, IL 60601

ATTORNEY GENERAL, OFFICE OF
500 S. 2nd St.
Springfield, IL 62706

AUDIT, DEPARTMENT OF
Marriott Commerce Bldg., Room 151
509 S. 6th St.
Springfield, IL 62701-1878

BANKING
Reisch Bldg., Room 100
117 S. 5th St.
Springfield, IL 62701-1291

BUDGET, DEPARTMENT OF
State Capitol, Room 108
Springfield, IL 62706

CHILD WELFARE SERVICES
406 E. Monroe St.
Springfield, IL 62701

CIVIL DEFENSE, DEPARTMENT OF
110 E. Adams St.
Springfield, IL 62706

CLERK OF THE HOUSE
State Capitol, Room 115
Springfield, IL 62706

COMMERCE, DEPARTMENT OF
620 E. Adams St.
Springfield, IL 62701

COMMUNITY AFFAIRS, DEPARTMENT OF
620 E. Adams St.
Springfield, IL 62701

COMPTROLLER, OFFICE OF
State Capitol, Room 201
Springfield, IL 62706

CONFLICT OF INTEREST BOARD
State of Illinois Center, Room 3-300
100 W. Randolph St.
Springfield, IL 60601

CONSUMER AFFAIRS, OFFICE OF
500 S. 2nd St.
Springfield, IL 60726

CORRECTIONS, DEPARTMENT OF
1301 Concordia Court
P.O. Box 19277
Springfield, IL 62794-9277

COURT ADMINISTRATION, OFFICE OF
Supreme Court Bldg.
Springfield, IL 62704

DATA PROCESSING
201 W. Adams St.
Springfield, IL 62706

DEVELOPMENTAL DISABILITIES DIVISION
William G. Stratton Office Bldg.
401 S. Spring St.
Springfield, IL 62706

DRUG ABUSE, DEPARTMENT OF
State of Illinois Center, Room 5-600
100 W. Randolph St.
Chicago, ILL 60601

ECONOMIC DEVELOPMENT, DEPARTMENT OF
620 E. Adams St.
Springfield, IL 62701

ECONOMIC OPPORTUNITY, DEPARTMENT OF
State of Illinois Center, Room 3-400
100 W. Randolph St.
Chicago, IL 60601

EDUCATION (HIGHER)
4 W. Old Capitol Square
Springfield, IL 62701

EDUCATION (PRIMARY, SECONDARY, AND
VOCATIONAL)
100 N. 1st St.
Springfield, IL 62777

ELECTIONS DIVISION
1020 S. Spring St.
P.O. Box 4187
Springfield, IL 62708

EMPLOYMENT SECURITY, DEPARTMENT OF
401 S. State St., Room 615 South
Chicago, IL   60605

ENERGY AND NATURAL RESOURCES, DEPARTMENT OF
325 W. Adams St., 3rd Floor
Springfield, IL   62704

ENVIRONMENTAL AFFAIRS
2200 Churchill Rd.
Springfield, IL   62706

FEDERAL-STATE RELATIONS
William G. Stratton Bldg., Room 801
401 S. Spring St.
Springfield, IL   62706

FINANCE, DEPARTMENT OF
William G. Stratton Bldg., Room 801
401 S. Spring St.
Springfield, IL   62706

FISH AND GAME DIVISION
600 N. Grand Ave. West
Springfield, IL   62706

FOOD AND DRUGS DIVISION
525 W. Jefferson St.
Springfield, IL 62761

FORESTRY DIVISION
600 N. Grand Ave. West
Springfield, IL 62706

GENERAL SERVICES, DEPARTMENT OF
William G. Stratton Bldg., Room 505
401 S. Spring St.
Springfield, IL 62706

GEOLOGY DIVISION
Natural Resources Bldg., Room 121
615 E. Peabody Drive
Champaign, IL 61820

HANDICAPPED, COUNCIL ON
623 E. Adams St.
Springfield, IL 62794-9429

HAZARDOUS MATERIALS, DIVISION OF
1808 Woodfield Dr.
Savoy, IL 61874

HEALTH, DEPARTMENT OF
535 W. Jefferson ST.
Springfield, IL 62761

HIGHWAY SAFETY, OFFICE OF
IDOT Administration Bldg., Room 319
2300 S. Dirksen Pkwy.
Springfield, IL 62764

HIGHWAYS DIVISION
IDOT Administration Bldg., Room 300
2300 S. Dirksen Pkwy.
Springfield, IL 62764

HISTORIC PRESERVATION AGENCY
Old State Capitol
Springfield, IL 62701

HOUSING, DEPARTMENT OF
620 E. Adams St. B-5
Springfield, IL 62701

HUMAN RIGHTS, DEPARTMENT OF
State of Illinois Center, Room 10-100
100 W. Randolph St.
Chicago, IL 60601

INSURANCE, BUREAU OF
Bicentennial Bldg.
320 W. Washington St.
Springfield, IL 62767

JUVENILE DELINQUENCY
1301 Concordia Ct.
P.O. Box 19277
Springfield, IL 62794-9277

LABOR, DEPARTMENT OF
310 S. Michigan Ave.
Chicago, IL 60604

LAW ENFORCEMENT PLANNING
120 S. Riverside Plaza
Chicago, IL 60606

LEGISLATIVE RESEARCH, DEPARTMENT OF
222 College St. 3rd Floor, Suite A
Springfield, IL 62704

LIBRARY SERVICES, OFFICE OF
Centennial Building, Room 275
Springfield, IL 62756

LICENSING (CORPORATE)
Centennial Bldg., Room 330
Springfield, IL 62756

LICENSING (OCCUPATIONAL AND
PROFESSIONAL)
320 W. Washington St.
Springfield, IL 62786

LIQUOR CONTROL COMMISSION
State of Illinois Center, Room 5-300
100 W. Randolph St.
Chicago, IL 60601

LOTTERY DIVISION
676 N. St. Clair, Suite 2040
Chicago, IL 60611

MASS TRANSIT DIVISION
310 S. Michigan Ave., Suite 1608
Chicago, IL 60604-4205

MENTAL HEALTH DIVISION
401 S. Spring St.
Springfield, IL 62706

MINING AND MINERALS, DEPARTMENT OF
William G. Stratton Bldg., Room 704
401 S. Spring St.
Springfield, IL 62706

MOTOR VEHICLES, DEPARTMENT OF
Centennial Bldg., Room 312
Springfield, IL 62756

NATURAL RESOURCES, DEPARTMENT OF
325 W. Adams St., 3rd Floor
Springfield, IL 62704

NUCLEAR ENERGY, DEPARTMENT OF
1035 Outer Park Dr., 5th Floor
Springfield, IL   62704

OIL AND GAS, DIVISION OF
William G. Stratton Bldg., Room 704
401 S. Spring St.
Springfield, IL   62706

OMBUDSMAN
201 W. Monroe St.
Springfield, IL   62706

PARKS AND RECREATION, DEPARTMENT OF
600 N. Grand Ave., West
Springfield, IL   62706

PERSONNEL, OFFICE OF
William G. Stratton Bldg., Room 715
401 S. Spring St.
Springfield, IL   62706

PLANNING DEPARTMENT
William Stratton Bldg., Room 107
401 S. Spring St.
Springfield, IL   62706

POLICE DEPARTMENT
103 Armory Bldg.
Springfield, IL   62706

PRINTING AND PUBLISHING DIVISION
425 S. 4th St.
Springfield, IL 62701

PROBATION AND PAROLE, STATE BOARD OF
319 E. Madison St., Suite A
Springfield, IL 62701

PUBLIC DEFENDER, OFFICE OF
300 E. Monroe St.
Springfield, IL 62701

PUBLIC UTILITIES, DEPARTMENT OF
State of Illinois Center, Suit 9-100
100 W. Randolph St.
Chicago, IL 60601

PUBLIC WORKS, DEPARTMENT OF
William G. Stratton Bldg., 3rd Floor
401 S. Spring St.
Springfield, IL 62706

PURCHASING DIVISION
William G. Stratton Bldg., Room 801
401 S. Spring St.
Springfield, IL 62706

RAILROADS DIVISION
IDOT Administration Bldg.
2300 S. Dirksen Pkwy., Room 307
Springfield, IL 62764

REAL ESTATE, COMMISSION ON
Bicentennial Bldg.
320 W. Washington St.
Springfield, IL 62786

REFUGEE RESETTLEMENT, OFFICE OF
201 S. Grand Ave., East, 2nd Floor
Springfield, IL 62763

RETIREMENT, DEPARTMENT OF
2815 W. Washington St.
P.O. Box 19255
Springfield, IL 62794-9255

SECRETARY OF STATE
State Capitol, Room 213
Springfield, IL 62756

SECRETARY OF THE SENATE
State Capitol, Room 401
Springfield, IL 62706

SECURITIES REGISTRATION DIVISION
188 W. Randolph St., Room 426
Chicago, IL 60601

SOCIAL SERVICES DIVISION
406 E. Monroe St.
Springfield, IL   62701

SOLID WASTE MANAGEMENT
2200 Churchill Rd.
Springfield, IL   62706

STATE-LOCAL RELATIONS
620 E. Adams St.
Springfield, IL   62701

SURPLUS PROPERTY DIVISION
3550 Great Northern Ave.
P.O. Box 1236
Springfield, IL   62707

TAXATION AND REVENUE
Willard Ice Revenue Center
101 W. Jefferson St.
Springfield, IL   62794-9014

TEXTBOOKS
Alzina Bldg.
100 N. 1st St.
Springfield, IL   62777

TOURISM, OFFICE OF
State of Illinois Center, Room 3-400
100 W. Randolph St.
Chicago, IL   60601

TRANSPORTATION, DEPARTMENT OF
IDOT Administration Bldg.
2300 S. Dirksen Pkwy.
Springfield, IL   62764

TREASURER
State Capitol, Room 219
Springfield, IL   62706

UNCLAIMED PROPERTY DIVISION
State of Illinois Center, Room 15-700
100 W. Randolph St.
Chicago, IL   60601

UNEMPLOYMENT
401 S. State St.
Chicago, IL   60605

VETERANS' AFFAIRS, DEPARTMENT OF
208 W. Cook St.
P.O. Box 19432
Springfield, IL   62794-9432

VITAL RECORDS AND STATISTICS BUREAU
605 W. Jefferson St.
Springfield, IL 62702-5097

WATER POLLUTION CONTROL
2200 Churchill Rd.
P.O. Box 19276
Springfield, IL 62794-9276

WATER RESOURCES
IDOT Administration Bldg.
2300 S. Dirksen Pkwy.
Springfield, IL 62764

WEIGHTS AND MEASURES DIVISION
State Fairgrounds
P.O. Box 19281
Springfield, IL 62794-9281

WELFARE, DEPARTMENT OF
Harris II Bldg.
100 S. Grand Ave., East
Springfield, IL 62704

WOMEN
State of Illinois Center, 16th Floor
100 W. Randolph St.
Chicago, IL 60601

WORKERS' COMPENSATION
State of Illinois Center, Room 8-272
100 W. Randolph St.
Chicago, IL 60601

GOVERNORS

EDWARDS, NINIAN (1775-1833), first territorial governor of Illinois (1809-1818) and third State governor (1826-30), was born in Montgomery County, Maryland. His parents were Benjamin and Margaret (Beal) Edwards. After attending private schools and graduating from Dickinson College in Pennsylvania, Edwards studied law and was admitted to the Kentucky bar in 1798, and to that of Tennnessee in 1799. Soon afterwards he was made Judge of the General Court in Kentucky, then Circuit Judge (1803), Judge of the Court of Appeals, and Chief Justice of Kentucky (1806).

In 1804, Edwards also served as the Democratic Presidential Elector. In 1809, President James Madison appointed him governor of the new Illinois Territory, a position he held until 1818, when Illinois became a State. During his administration, Edwards placed great emphasis on the State's military defense, and organized companies of volunteer rangers. He also built stockades in a line along the Missouri and Wabash rivers, which were highly valued during the War of 1812 in border wars with the Indians. In 1816, he was appointed one of three commissioners to deal with the Indian tribes.

When Illinois became a State in 1818, Edwards was elected one of the first two U. S. Senators from the State. After he resigned in 1824, he accepted an appointment as Minister to Mexico. However, he soon resigned this new office as well, when Secretary of the Treasury William H. Crawford pressed charges against him. He lost no popularity in Illinois, however, and in 1826, Edwards was elected third Governor of the State as the Republican-Democratic candidate.

Under his second administration, Edwards urged for the removal of Indians from the State, insisting that the State had the right to the land within its borders. He also urged growth in the State, and within two years, the population tripled.

Edwards married in 1802, and had five children. He died at Belleville, Illinois in 1833.

BOND, SHADRACH (1773-1832), first governor of the State, (1818- 1822), was born in Maryland. His parents were Nicholas and Rachel (Stevenson) Bond, plantation owners. Although members of his family had lived in Maryland for over a century, he moved to the Northwest Territory in 1794 and engaged in agricultural pursuits in present-day Monroe County, Illinois.

From 1805 to 1808, he served on the Legislative Council of the Indiana Territory and was appointed Justice of the Peace in St. Clair County in 1809. After participating in the militia, Bond helped in the organization of Illinois Territory in 1809. From 1812 to 1814, he represented Illinois in Congress, and soon afterwards, President Madison appointed him receiver of public monies for the Territory. He served in that capacity at the General Land Office in Kaskaskia until 1818, when he was elected without opposition as the first State governor.

Soon after inauguration, Bond was concerned with providing for the State's growth. He pushed for a canal to connect Lake Michigan with the Illinois River, emphasized State education, and advised that provisions be made for leasing salt springs.

In 1819, the State capitol moved from Kaskaskia to Vandalia, and a State bank was formed. The first State Constitution prohibited a governor from serving two terms, so Bond left office in 1822. He quickly took an appointment as Register of the Land Office in Kaskaskia, a position he held until his death in 1832. A county in the central part of the state was named in his honor.

COLES, EDWARD (1786-1868), second governor of Illinois (1822- 1826), was born in Virginia, the son of Col. John and Rebecca (Tucker) Coles. He left William and Mary College before earning a degree due to ill health. In 1808, he inherited a large plantation with a number of slaves, but hated the idea of slavery and decided to move to a free state.

He served as private secretary to President Madison from 1809 to 1815. While in this post, Cole corresponded with Thomas Jefferson, a friend of his family, and asked him to use his influence in advocating emancipation of the slaves. He received a favorable response from Jefferson, and continued throughout his career to advocate black people's freedom.

After returning from a diplomatic trip to Russia, Coles settled in Edwardsville, Illinois in 1818, where he served as Register of the Land Office. He attended the State convention in Kaskaskia to draft a State constitution, and persuaded the Congress to prevent recognition of slavery in the document. In Edwardsville, Coles freed all slaves in the area and presented each family with 160 acres of land. As the Democratic-Republican candidate, he was elected governor of the state in 1822.

During his administration, Coles was faced with the confusion and disorganization of a new State. He was concerned about the mania for establishing banks at that time, and the fluctuating condition of the circulating medium. He also pushed for the proposed canal between the Mississippi and the Great Lakes. He prevented Illinois from becoming a slave State in spite of opposition from many citizens as well as fellow politicians. He accomplished this by gaining support of other anti-slavery proponents and distributing pamphlets on the character and effects of slavery. He also bought Vandalia's only newspaper, the *Intelligencer* in order to push the anti-slavery issue.

Coles also successfully pushed for laws to repress kidnapping, and for a reorganization of the State's judiciary into both Circuit and Supreme courts.

After his term in office, Coles retired in Pennsylvania, where he married Sally Logan. A county in Illinois was named in his honor. He died in 1868.

REYNOLDS, JOHN (1788-1865), fourth governor of the State, (1830- 34), was born in Pennsylvania to Robert and Margaret (Moore) Reynolds, Irish immigrants. While he was still an infant, the family moved to Tennessee, but fear of the local Indians caused them to move again in 1800 to Kaskaskia, Illinois.

Reynolds entered the College of Tennessee at Knoxville in 1809, and the next year began to study law. As a scout during the War of 1812, he was nicknamed "Old Ranger." Two years later, he passed the bar and began a law practice in Cahokia, Illinois, dealing mostly in litigation over land titles.

His political career began with his 1818 election as Justice of the Illinois Supreme Court. Although he was unsuccessful in his attempts in 1823 for a U.S. Senate seat, Reynolds served in the State House of Representatives from 1826-30. He aided in the attempt in 1824 to revise the State constitution in favor of slavery. Six years later, he was elected governor by a small margin of those voting.

During his administration, the Black Hawk War (1831-2) represented the culmination of conflicts between settlers and Indians concerning hunting and farming rights. Reynolds, acting as ex-official commander in chief of the militia, asked for volunteers to help fight the Indians. The Governor's forces finally defeated the Indian tribes under Chief Black Hawk, forcing the Indians out of the State and across the Mississippi.

Reynolds resigned the governorship in 1834, after being elected to the U.S. House of Representatives. However, he was unsuccessful in his attempts for a State Senate seat (1848) and the State Superintendent of Schools post (1858). He was elected an anti-Douglas delegate to the 1860 Democratic National Convention, but when he discovered Abraham Lincoln's popularity, he publicly stated his support for Douglas, and advised Southerners to take up arms against the North.

Reynolds was known for his simple manners and genial disposition. His speech often leaned toward the vernacular and he introduced slang of his own. He died at Belleville, Illinois in 1865.

EWING, WILLIAM LEE D. (1795-1846), senator and fifth (acting) governor of the State (1834), was born near Nashville, Tennessee, the son of Rev. Finis Ewing and Peggy, daughter of a American Revolution War general. He moved in 1818 to the new town of Shawneetown, near Kaskaskia, and began to practice law.

After serving as Receiver of Public Monies in the land office at Vandalia, he took on the post of Brigadier General of the State militia, and was Colonel of the "Spy Battalion" during the Black Hawk War. In 1832, he was elected State

Senator, and two years later he was chosen Speaker. This position led him into the governor's post, as Governor Reynolds and Lt. Governor Casey had resigned to take seats in Congress.

After Joseph Duncan was inaugurated, Ewing was elected to the U.S. Senate, where he served from 1835-37. In 1840, he represented Fayette County in the Legislature and was once again chosen Speaker of the House. In 1843, he was appointed the Legislature's Auditor of Public Accounts, where he worked until his death.

DUNCAN, JOSEPH (1794-1844), sixth governor of the State (1834- 1838) , was born in Kentucky, the son of Maj. Joseph and Ann (McLaughlin) Duncan. In 1812, he was commissioned as an ensign in the Seventeenth Infantry with Col. Croghan. The infantry occupied Fort Stephenson, now Fremont, Ohio, with a force of less than 150 men, but was able to fend off an English army of 500. Duncan won a gold medal for his efforts in the defense there.

After peace was declared, he retired from the army and moved to Illinois to farm near Kaskaskia. From 1821-1823, he served as Justice of the Peace for Jackson County; he was also commissioned Major General in the Illinois militia in 1823.

Duncan's political career began when he was elected a State Senator. In 1826, he was elected Illinois' sole representative to Congress, where he served three terms, until 1833. His major effort in Congress was to convince the government to subsidize a canal to be built between the Illinois River and Lake Michigan. He also endorsed a State public school system.

When Duncan became governor of the State in 1834, he repeated his efforts for the schools, but had little public support. However, two private institutions of higher learning opened in the State during his term. Although a southerner, he opposed slavery for Illinois and looked upon it as "a great moral and political evil."

Duncan ran for governor of the State again in 1842, but was unsuccessful in winning the office. He died at Jacksonville, Illinois in 1844.

CARLIN, THOMAS (1789-1852), seventh governor of the State (1838- 1842), was born in Kentucky, son of Thomas Carlin. Chiefly self- educated, he motivated himself to study after he matured. He volunteered under General Howard during the War of 1812, and commanded a battalion during the Black Hawk War soon after moving to the Illinois Territory.

He married Rebecca Hewitt and fathered 13 children. The family moved around the State, pioneering some areas. He served two terms on the State Senate and the House of Representatives. President Jackson appointed him Receiver of Public Monies at Quincy, Illinois in 1834, and Carlin worked in that position until he was elected governor in 1838. Under his administration, he pushed for better transportation within the State; the Sangamon and Morgan Railroad opened to traffic, and a four billion dollar loan was negotiated to help in the construction of an intrastate canal.

While Carlin was governor, the Mormons emigrated to Illinois and were granted a charter for the city of Nauvoo. However, the State's finances were not as booming; the State Bank at Shawneetown decreased its circulation by fifty percent, rendering the only money in the State worthless and devastating many families.

After his governorship, Carlin retired to his farm in Carrollton. He died in 1852.

FORD, THOMAS (1800-1850), eighth governor of the State (1842- 1846), was born in Pennsylvania, the son of Robert and Elizabeth Logue (Forquer) Ford. When his father died, his mother took the family westward and settled near St. Louis at a town called New Design. Ford studied at home, and then at Transylvania University in Kentucky.

After studying law and passing the bar, he began a law practice at Waterloo, Illinois. Moving to Edwardsville, he was appointed State's Attorney of the Fifth Judicial District from 1829 to 1835. During the Black Hawk War, he enlisted in the "Spy Battalion" and later was elected Judge of the Ninth Circuit Court in 1839.

He served for a year beginning in 1841 as a State Supreme Court Judge, but resigned to campaign for the governorship. During his term, he successfully reduced the State's indebtedness by closing the State banks and instituting tolls along the Michigan-Illinois Canal. Violent conflicts between the Mormons in Nauvoo and their neighbors caused Ford to call out the militia to maintain order in the western part of the state.

Congressman John Wentworth said of Ford that he, more than any other in the State, attempted to remove regional divisions within the State, and other State leaders attributed much of the Illinois' success to Ford's liquidation of the public debt.

After his governorship, Ford resumed his law practice in Peoria and wrote the *History of Illinois, From its Commencement as a State in 1818 to 1847*, considered one of the best authorities on that period.

FRENCH, AUGUSTUS (1808-1864), ninth governor of the State (1846- 1853), was born in New Hampshire. His father died while he was a child, and his mother died when he was 19; he became responsible for the care of his four younger brothers and sisters. He attended public school irregularly, but entered Dartmouth College and later studied law.

After admittance to the New Hampshire bar in 1823, he decided to move to Albion, in Edwards County, Illinois, to practice the next year. In 1825, he moved to Paris, Illinois for a more profitable position. In 1837, he was elected to the State legislature, where he served for two years before receiving an appointment as Receiver of Public Monies at Palestine.

His political career continued in 1844 when he was voted elector in the presidential race, favoring Polk. Two years later, he was elected governor of the State after his popular platform advocating a war with Mexico. As governor, French continued the work of his predecessors to keep the State budget solvent.

The last of the Mormons left Illinois during his term, since their city charter at Nauvoo was revoked by the Legislature. In addition, the Michigan-Illinois Canal was completed; a new State constitution was approved, and a township organization was adopted. Under the new constitution, French was eligible for reelection. He won a second term in 1848. During this term, his main accomplishment was liquidation of the State's debt.

In 1853, French took a professorship in law at McKendree College, and nine years later was elected to the State constitutional convention. He died at Lebanon, Illinois in 1864.

MATTESON, JOEL ALDRICH (1808-1873), tenth governor of the State (1853-57), was born in New York, the son of Elnathan and Eunice (Aldrich) Matteson, wh were farmers in Jefferson County, N. Y. Joel taught school in his native state, but in 1834 began work as a foreman on the first railroad in South Carolina. Before that, he had moved to Kendall County, Illinois to continue farming, but sold his land and moved to Joliet in 1836 during the speculation rush that year.

His business interests in the city led him to secure a contract for the Illinois and Michigan Canal in 1848, and in 1842 he was elected governor. While he was in office, a great boom in railroad building took hold in the State. The Illinois Central, the Chicago and Rock Island, Burlington and Quincy, the Alton and St. Louis, and the Chicago and Galena Union were all built during this time.

Matteson was also a proponent of growth in education within the State; in 1854 , he appointed Ninian Edwards a special officer of public instruction, which helped in that expansion. His governorship didn't interfere with his business career, however, since Matteson held the presidency of the Chicago and Alton Railroad for several years, and a controlling interest in several banks.

He died in Chicago in 1873, after many years of private life.

BISSELL, WILLIAM HENRY (1811-1860), eleventh governor of the State (1857-60), was born in New York to Luther and Hannah Bissell. After attending local schools and later teaching, he gathered enough money to enter Cooperstown Academy. Later, he graduated from Jefferson Medical College (1835) and from the law school at Transylvania University (1841).

For a few years, he practiced medicine in New York, but in 1837, he moved to Waterloo, Illinois where he taught school. Three years later, he was elected to the State Legislature, where he was encouraged to remain in public life. His graduation from law school helped him politically, and after practicing in Belleville for awhile, he was appointed Prosecuting Attorney for the Second Illinois Judicial District. When the Mexican War broke out, he organized a group of volunteer soldiers and was elected colonel.

He was elected three times to the House of Representatives, serving in Washington from 1849-1855 as an independent Democrat. However, he conflicted with the Southern Democrats in Congress because of his anti-slavery position, having spoken out against the Missouri Compromise. His speech also made claims of the superiority of Northern soldiers over Southern, which so inflamed Jefferson Davis that the latter challenged him to a duel. Bissell accepted, but Col. Davis' friends cooled his temper before a duel could take place.

Soon afterwards, Bissell became a Republican and was elected Governor under that new party. He found substantial opposition in the Legislature, however, and not many of his bills passed. While he was governor, the "Illinois and Michigan canal scrip fraud" was uncovered, and a northern penitentiary and institutions for the mentally ill were appropriated.

Bissell never finished his term. He died at Springfield, Illinois (the State's new capitol). He was married and had two daughters.

WOOD, JOHN (1798-1880), twelfth (acting) governor of the State (1860- 61), was born in New York. His parents were Daniel and Catherine (Crouse) Wood. He arrived in Shawneetown, Illinois in 1819 after leaving home with the intention of settling in Tennessee or northern Alabama.

He decided to stay at a farm in Pike County, Illinois, however, and lived there for two years before building the first cabin at what is now Quincy. He and Willard Keyes established claims there, and Wood became a leader in a settlement called "The Bluffs." He helped defeat those who pushed for a State constitution recognizing slavery in

1824, and his anti- slavery beliefs prevented him from moving to Missouri.

Wood was a private in the Black Hawk War. In 1825, he petitioned the State Legislature to create Adams County, and was successful in retaining Quincy as the county seat. Throughout his lifetime, Woods continued to direct the city situated on the Mississippi as its trustee and mayor.

Wood was elected to the State Senate in 1850. In 1856, he was elected Lieutenant Governor of the State. This position led him to the gubernatorial chair when William Bissell died in 1860. A year later his successor, Richard Yates, appointed him one of the five delegates to the Peace Convention in Washington. But when war broke out, he was appointed quarter-master of the State, and then colonel of the 137th Illinois Volunteers in 1864. Later that year, he retired and returned to his business in Quincy. He died in 1880 and was buried at Quincy.

YATES, RICHARD (1818-1873), thirteenth governor of the State (1861-1865), was born in Kentucky, the son of Henry and Millicent Yates. He moved to Sangamon County, Illinois in 1831. He was educated at Miami University in Ohio, Georgetown College in Kentucky, and was a graduate of the first class of Illinois College in 1835.

After graduation, Yates moved back to Kentucky to study law at Transylvania University. In 1837, he returned to Jacksonville to begin a law practice. In 1842, he began a career in public life as a member of the State legislature, holding his seat until 1845, and again in 1848-1849.

Yates also served as a Whig in the U.S. House of Representatives for four years, beginning in 1851. Although unsuccessful in his attempts for reelection in 1854, he became a delegate to the Republican State Convention that year, and was also a delegate to the Republican National Convention in 1860. During that time, he also practiced law and controlled the interests of a new railroad company, the Tonica and Petersburg, later renamed the Chicago and Alton.

In 1860, Yates won the State gubernatorial race on the Republican ticket. In his inauguration speech, he stood against any concession or compromise with the South, thereby establishing his loyalty to newly-elected President Abraham Lincoln and the Union. He declared that "the whole material of the government, moral, political, and physical, if need be, must be employed to preserve, protect, and defend the constitution of the United States."

When Lincoln called for troops, Yates sent more than double the State's quota for volunteers. Yates also appointed West Point-educated Ulysses S. Grant as Mustering Officer for Illinois, which gave him the reputation of being the State's "war governor."

The State Legislature, usually in opposition with the governor, passed a resolution to compromise with the seceded states, but Yates prorogued the Legislature until a Republican majority came into power a year later. He actively supported emancipation of black slaves, recommending to Lincoln that "loyal blacks" be enlisted in the Union cause. After his governorship, he was elected to the U.S. Senate, where he continued to fight against "Southern sympathizers," as well as for reconstruction efforts.

In 1871, Yates retired from public life, except for a position as U.S. Commissioner to inspect land subsidy railroads. He continued his law practice until his death in 1873 in St. Louis, Missouri.

OGLESBY, RICHARD JAMES (1824-1899), was the fourteenth (1865- 1869), sixteenth (1873), and twentieth (1885-1889) governor of the State. He was born in Kentucky to Isabel Walton and Jacob Oglesby. Orphaned at the age of eight, Oglesby was sent to Decatur, Illinois to live with an uncle. After attending local schools and, later, the law school of Silas W. Robbins in Springfield, he began a law practice in Sullivan, Illinois.

When the Mexican War broke out, Oglesby was commissioned a first lieutenant in Company C of the Fourth Illinois Infantry. In this capacity, he took part in battles at Vera Cruz and Cerro Gordo. The next year, he returned to Illinois to practice law at Decatur, and later graduated from the school of law in Louisville, Kentucky. For a time, Oglesby traveled around California mining for gold, but soon returned to practice law and enter political life.

He was an unsuccessful candidate in the race for U.S. House of Representatives in 1858, but was elected to the State Senate in 1860. After only one session, however, he responded to the call to arms and became colonel to a volunteer infantry. After a show of courage at Fort Henry, Oglesby was made a brigadier general. In a subsequent battle, however, he was so severely wounded that he was forced to return home.

After an eight month recuperation, in 1864 he addressed the State legislature. His speech denounced certain Democratic members of the Senate and House for "treason" because of their efforts to nullify Governor Yates' war measures. Many were impressed by Oglesby's speech, and a few months later he resigned his appointment as Major-General of the State's volunteers to accept an election as State governor.

His first term in office set the tone for the State's growth. During that time, a State board of equalization was formed; two amendments to the constitution were ratified; a penitentiary was built; and other institutions and asylums were constructed. He returned to private practice in 1869, but was reelected under the Republican party ticket several years later.

Oglesby's second term only lasted a few months, however, since he was elected to the U.S. Senate. His third term, which began more than 10 years later, was characterized by changes in the State's election processes. For example, the Citizen's Election Bill was passed, limiting the number of persons able to vote in a district to 450.

Oglesby was often referred to fondly as "Uncle Dick." After his unprecedented time in office, he retired to private life in Elkhart, Illinois, where he died in 1899.

PALMER, JOHN MCAULEY (1817-1900), fifteenth governor of the State, (1869-73), was born at Eagle Creek, Kentucky, the son of Ann Hansford Tutt and Louis D. Palmer. His family moved to Illinois in 1831 because of strong anti-slavery principles. They settled near Alton and three years later, John entered Shurtleff College at Upper Alton. He taught school while studying law and was admitted to the bar in 1839.

After starting a practice at Carlinville, Palmer was appointed Probate Judge of Macoupin County in 1845. In 1847, he helped reframe the State constitution. Under the new constitution, he was elected County Judge in 1848, and gained enough support to be elected to the State Senate in 1852. Two years later he resigned, however, because of political differences among his colleagues.

For a few years, he became involved in Republican party activities, presiding over the first party convention in the State in 1856, and serving as a delegate to the national convention in 1859. He was also an elector to the ticket in 1860. After serving as a delegate to the Peace Convention in Washington in 1861, Palmer was commissioned a colonel in the Fourteenth Regiment of the State volunteer army. He was honorably mustered out after five years of service, which included his command of the first brigade of the First Division Army of the Mississippi and other major roles for which he was well-honored.

Palmer returned to his Carlinville law practice, but soon became engaged in State politics again in Springfield. He was elected on the Republican ticket for governor in 1869. In 1871, he was successful in giving relief for victims of the Chicago fire.

During his governorship, Palmer also switched party loyalties, becoming a Democratic in order to support Horace Greeley for President. After 1873, Palmer once again returned to his law practice, this time in Springfield. He served as a delegate to the Democratic National Convention in 1884, and was elected as the liberal, pro-labor candidate for the U. S. Senate in 1891. He did not run for reelection in 1897, and in 1896, he was unsuccessful in a candidacy for President.

After returning once again to his law practice, Palmer died at his Springfield home in 1900. His family published his memoirs, *Personal Recollections of John M. Palmer-- The Story of an Earnest Life,* in 1891.

BEVERIDGE, JOHN LOURIE (1824-1910), seventeenth governor of the State (1873-1877), was born in New York, the son of Ann Hoy and George Beveridge, who were farmers. The family moved to the rich soils of Dekalb County, in Somonauk in 1842.

In 1845, Beveridge moved to Tennessee to study law and teach school. He was admitted to the bar there, but returned in 1851 to practice law in Dekalb County, and later in Evanston. In 1855, he entered into a law partnership with John F. Farnsworth, which he held until the Civil War broke out.

When Farnsworth was commissioned to organize a cavalry regiment, Beveridge enlisted in it. He was elected major in his regiment, and later was promoted to Colonel of the Seventeenth State cavalry. After an appointment as Brigadier General, he resigned in 1866.

Beveridge's political career began when he returned home and was elected Sheriff of Cook County in 1866. In 1871, he was elected to the U. S. House of Representatives, a seat he held until 1873. He ran successfully for Lieutenant Governor of Illinois in Oglesby's gubernatorial campaign. When Oglesby resigned to take his U.S. Senate seat, Beveridge filled out the remainder of his term as governor.

While Beveridge was the State's leader, several charitable and reformatory institutions were funded, the State militia was increased, and the State government occupied offices at Springfield's new capitol for the first time. He also authorized payment of the State debt.

After a four-year position as sub-treasurer at Chicago, Beveridge moved to Hollywood, California in 1895. He was married and had two childen. He died in Hollywood, California in 1910.

CULLOM, SHELBY MOORE (1829-1914), eighteenth governor of Illinois (1877-1883) was born in Kentucky to Richard Northcraft Cullom and Elizabeth Coffey. His family moved to Tazewell County, Illinois to farm, and during that time, his father represented his district in the Illinois Legislature.

Cullom began to study law in the office of Stuart and Edwards in Springfield in 1853, and two years later was admitted to the bar. He was elected City Attorney of Springfield in 1855, and was a presidential elector the next year. In 1856, he was elected to the State Legislature, where he served through 1862. After serving as the House Speaker,

Cullom was appointed by Abraham Lincoln to settle claims against the U.S. government for property purchased by volunteers in the army.

In 1864, Cullom was elected to represent the State in Congress, and was reelected to that seat until 1871, when he returned to the State Legislature. While in Congress, he chaired a committee on territories, pushed for severe penalties against the practice of polygamy in Utah, and his "stringent measures for suppression" were passed by the House. He also gained an appropriation of $320,000 for the new federal building at Springfield.

Upon his return to State government, Cullom engaged in banking, and after four years as a State legislator, he was nominated and subsequently elected governor by the Republican party.

Cullom was the first governor to hold his position for six years, having been reelected in 1880. During his lengthy term, he established the Board of Fish Commissioners, and $80,000 was allocated by the Legislature to pay for military suppression of riots in 1877.

In 1883, he stepped down from the governorship and into the position of U. S. Senator from Illinois. He chaired a senate committee on interstate commerce which investigated and recommended federal regulations on railroad corporations. A bill bearing his name established an interstate commerce commission, and it became law in 1887. He was reelected to the Senate through 1913, during which time he chaired the new interstate commerce commission, and was involved in "committees dealing with the governments of Cuba and Hawaii." He served as a Regeant of the Smithsonian Institution from 1885-1913, and as commissioner of the Lincoln Memorial from 1913-14. He died in Washington, D. C. in 1914.

HAMILTON, JOHN MARSHALL (1847-1905), nineteenth governor of the State (1883-85), was born in Ohio, the son of Nancy McMorris and Samuel Hamilton. In 1854, the family moved to Illinois to farm in Wenona, a part of Marshall County.

Hamilton enlisted in the 141st regiment when the Civil War broke out, and he served in Kentucky and Tennessee in guerrilla warfare until the regiment was discharged. He taught school for a time when he returned to Illinois, and after two years at Wesleyan University, he graduated with honors in 1868. He continued his career in education as a tutor at an academy in Marshall County.

In 1869, Hamilton began the study of law. While pursuing his law studies, he was also a professor of languages at Wesleyan University until his admittance to the bar in 1870. At that time, he formed a law partnership with Captain J.H. Powell which lasted 12 years. He was elected to the State Senate in 1876 and to the Lieutenant Governorship in 1880.

When Governor Cullom resigned in 1883, Hamilton took over his duties as leader of the State. During his administration, he authorized a Compulsory Education Act for children between the ages of eight and 14, and supported an appropriation to complete the State House. He also signed legislation making foreign insurance companies and railroad companies subject to State regulation.

When he left office, Hamilton resumed his law practice in Chicago until his death in that city in 1905.

FIFER, JOSEPH WILSON (1840-1938), twenty-first governor of the State (1889-1893), was born at Staunton, Virginia to Mary Wilson and John Fifer. When Fifer was 17 years old, his family moved to McLean County, Illinois, where he helped his father build a log cabin and establish a farm. He studied during the winter at local schools.

In 1861, when the Civil War broke out, he enlisted as a private. Although he was severely wounded in 1863, he served three months after his term of duty was over. Returning to his home in 1864, he continued his education at Wesleyan University in Bloomington. After graduation in 1868, he studied law at an office in Bloomington and was admitted to the bar in 1869.

After his law practice was established, in 1871 he was elected the city's Corporation Counsel. He served as State Attorney from 1872 to 1880 before being elected to the State Senate. He resigned the legislature in 1884, however, to resume his law practice. As an advocate, he was known for speaking without obvious preparation or notes, although he was generally successful in his arguments.

In 1888, he defeated the Democratic candidate and former governor, John M. Palmer. During his administration, he supported measures to codify the State public school laws and an anexation act for State consolidation of cities. He lost reelection in the 1893 campaign to Democrat John Altgeld.

Soon afterwards, Fifer resumed his practice at Bloomington, where he died in 1938. He was often called "Private Joe" by his friends and admirers.

ALTGELD, JOHN PETER (1847-1902), twenty-second governor of the State (1893-97), was born in Germany to John Peter and Mary Altgeld. When his family immigrated to the U.S., they originally settled in Ohio, where Altgeld attended school. In 1863, he enlisted in the 164th Infantry and served until the end of the Civil War.

Although he had little formal education, Altgeld taught school after his war duty, and in 1869, he traveled west to Missouri, where he continued teaching and began studying law. After admission to the bar, he was elected city attorney of Savannah and state attorney of Missouri in 1874.

Several years later, Altgeld moved to Chicago to expand his law practice. His involvement as a Democrat led to an election to the Cook County Superior Court in 1886, where he sat until 1891. He campaigned for governor against incumbent candidate Joseph Fifer in 1892, when the political mood of the State was changing.

Altgeld was a promoter of social and political reforms in the State. He favored labor unions and other "radical" ideas of his time. During his campaign, he strove to keep the gubernatorial campaign free of the old Republican issues of the Civil War and reconstruction, placing more emphasis on questions directly concerning a growing State, such as legislative reforms and public school issues. It was the first time in 40 years that a Democrat was elected to the governorship, and Altgeld also represented the first foreign-born man to hold that office.

Altgeld's term in office was not always as successful as his campaign. His high ideals led to discontent among voters and the non-Democratic legislature. When he lost his bid for reelection in the next campaign, Democrats in the State's administration also went out of office, and the Democratic party had little influence in State politics for the next four terms.

However, under Altgeld, new business methods were introduced in government agencies. Reformatory institutions were built, and women were appointed for the first time to important boards and other positions. Also, for the first time in 20 years, the Illinois and Michigan Canal was in a position to turn money back into the State treasury. Altgeld supported taxation on corporations and passed legislation for fair and unbiased grand juries in the State.

After leaving office, he was a delegate to the Democratic National Convention (1896) and appeared as a platform speaker from time to time. He ran unsuccessfully for mayor of Chicago in 1899, and continued to practice law in that city until his death in 1902. He wrote of his experiences with the State's legal system in *Our Penal Machinery and its Victims* (1884).

TANNER, JOHN RILEY (1844-1901), twenty-third governor of Illinois, (1897-1901), was born in Booneville, Indiana to Eliza Downs and John Tanner. He lived on the family farm until 1861, when he enlisted in the army with all other male members of his family. Until 1865, he fought with the 98th Illinois infantry, and afterwards returned north to purchase his own farm in Clay County, Illinois.

Five years later, he was elected sheriff of the county, and from 1872 to 1876 served as clerk of the Circuit Court. In 1880, he was nominated for State senator of his district and won. He continued his political career with an appointment as U. S. Marshall in 1883, and an election as State Treasurer in 1886.

Under Governor Fifer's administration, Tanner worked as Railroad Commissioner, but he resigned in 1891 to fill an appointment as U.S. Treasurer in Chicago. He was a gubernatorial candidate on the Republican ticket in 1896. His efforts to reorganize the party two years earlier, while he was still a State central committee chairman, helped him become the campaign's victor.

Although Tanner's accomplishments in party organization brought forth Republican representation in the legislature and in the governor's seat, his term in office was tumultuous from the beginning. Coal strikes in Virden, Pana, and Carterville broke into violence after he refused to send troops to protect strikebreakers. After some lost their lives, Tanner sent guards, but gave them strict orders not to allow strikebreakers into the mines.

He became unpopular with voters when he approved the Allen Bill, allowing city councils to grant 50-year franchises to street railway companies. Financial problems also caused the governor embarassment. When he took office, there were deficits in almost every State agency, and no money was left in the treasury to pay the bills. He reached an agreement with some companies to buy products at wholesale prices and on credit. By the end of his term, the State debt had been paid. The governor was also involved in the war with Spain, sending 10,000 troops within two days of his call for volunteers.

Despite his successes, Tanner lost favor with the majority of the State and decided not to run for reelection. After his term ended, he was an unsuccessful candidate for the U. S. Senate. He died at Springfield in 1901.

YATES, RICHARD (1860-1936), twenty-fourth governor of the State, (1901-05), was born at Jacksonville, Illinois, the son of Catherine Geers and former governor Richard Yates. The junior Yates was the first native-born Illinoisan to become governor.

In 1880, he received a Bachelor of Arts degree from Illinois College and three years later, he earned a master's degree from that institution. Following the example of his father, Yates won honors for his oratory skills in college, and afterwards studied the law. He graduated from the law school at the University of Michigan in 1884, and was admitted to the bar that year.

From 1885 to 1890, Yates served as City Attorney of Jacksonville. After losing as the Republican candidate for U. S. Congress in 1892, he was elected Judge of Morgan County. He resigned that post five years later when President McKinley appointed him U.S. Collector of Internal Re venue for the Central District of the State, based at Springfield.

His political connections soon gained him the nomination for governor, and he defeated the Democratic candidate by a close margin of 60,000. His nomination came on the 40th anniversary of his father's nomination for the same office. While in office, Yates strove for more thrifty administration of public funds. He vetoed a bill for improvements on the executive mansion, as well as legislation to allow racetracks in the State. Yates also protected blacks with State troops when race riots broke out in Saline County.

Yates lost the renomination for governor at the Republican convention in 1894, however, and the next year he left office. He was also unsuccessful in gaining the nomination in 1908 and 1912. From 1914 to 1917, he was a member of the State Public Utilities Commission, and was elected to the U. S. House of Representatives in 1918, where he served until 1933. After losing a reelection in 1932, he retired from politics. He died at Jacksonville and was buried at his birthplace in 1926.

DENEEN, CHARLES S. (1863-1940), twenty-fifth governor of the State (1905-13), was born in Edwardsville, Illinois, the son of Mary F. Ashley and Samuel Deneen. After attending public schools, Deneen graduated from McKendree College in Lebanon, where his father was professor of Latin and ancient history (1882).

He received his law degree from Union College in 1888 and was admitted to the bar that same year. He practiced law in Chicago from 1890 to 1904, and also became active in public affairs. In 1892, he was elected to the State Legislature, and in 1895-1896, was attorney for the Chicago Sanitary District. For the next eight years, he was State's Attorney for Cook County; the cases he prosecuted gained him national attention.

In 1904, Deneen won the gubernatorial election as a Republican candidate, and in 1908 he was reelected, defeating Democrat Adlai E. Stevenson. While in office, Deneen led the Legislature's passage of the first statewide primary law, as well as the Presidential Preference Primary Law in 1912, the first in the nation. The State Geological Survey and Highway Commission were formed under his administration, and large increases in the education budget were approved. Reforms in labor were also instituted during Deneen's two terms, including workmen's compensation provisions and a child labor law.

When Deneen tried for a third term in 1912, he lost to popular Progressive movement candidate, Edward Dunne. After leaving office, he returned to Chicago to practice law until 1925, when he was appointed to the U.S. Senate to fill the unexpired term of Medill McCormick. He left that seat in 1931 after helping promote expansion of waterways in the upper Mississippi River Valley.

He once again returned to Chicago to practice law after 1931, and was active in many service groups and clubs until his death in 1940.

DUNNE, EDWARD F. (1853-1937), twenty-sixth governor of the State (1913-1917), was born in Connecticut the son Delia Lawler and P.W. Dunne, a member of the Illinois General Assembly.

In 1877, Dunne earned a law degree from Union College, and for the next few years practiced his profession in Chicago. He ran successfully for Cook County Circuit Court judge in 1892, where he served until 1905. For the next two years, he was mayor of the city of Chicago, then returned to his law practice in 1907.

In the upsurge of the Progressive movement, Dunne defeated incumbent Republican governor Charles Deneen by more than 100,000 votes in the 1912 election. Under his administration, Deneen supported better roads in the State, holding a series of conferences with the Illinois Highway Improvement Association. He also pushed through the legislature a bipartisan committee to regulate public utilities, and a law allowing local governments to purchase electric and gas plants.

Dunne held great faith in the public sector, as evidenced by a speech made in 1916: "We are learning as a people to conduct our public affairs as economically, as honestly, as scientifically, as we do our private affairs."

Dunne lost in the 1916 gubernatorial race to Republican candidate, Frank Lowden. From 1930-37, he served as Cook County Board of Election Commissioners' attorney, and in 1933, he published a history of Illinois, *The Heart of the Nation*. He died in 1937 and was buried in Chicago.

LOWDEN, FRANK 0. (1861-1943), twenty-seventh governor of the State, (1917-21), was born in Sunrise, Minnesota, the son of Nancy Elizabeth Breg and Lorenzo Lowden. His father was the town blacksmith, farmer and Justice of the Peace.

In 1885, he graduated from the University of Iowa. Two years later, after receiving a degree from Union College of Law, he passed the bar. Until 1906, he practiced law in Chicago, and in 1899 was given a professorship at Northwestern University School of Law.

During the Spanish American War, Lowden was a lieutenant colonel in the first Infantry of the Illinois National Guard. In 1900 and again in 1904, he was a delegate to the Republican National Committee. Although he was an unsuccessful candidate for governor in 1904 against Charles Deneen, he was elected to represent the State in Congress in 1906, and in 1916, he defeated incumbent Democrat Edward Dunne for the governorship.

While he was in office, World War I began its rage, and Lowden urged support for the president. In 1917, he pushed through the Legislature a State Council of Defense to organize all the State's resources for victory in the war. Lowden also was concerned with cuts in government bureaucracy, as evidenced by his administrative reorganization, which combined 128 overlapping agencies into nine departments, saving the State over one million dollars a year. State taxes were reduced by seven million dollars by 1921, and a large State surplus remained when he left office.

Lowden also continued his predecessor's support of increased and improved roadways in the State. Although he was intent on trimming government expenditures, Lowden produced a plan by which the new highways would be financed through car license fees, and the State acquired 3,000 miles of cement roads by 1920. However, the governor slowed down construction soon afterwards, since the price of cement was raised markedly.

Lowden also supported women's suffrage while in office, urging the Legislature's ratification of the constitutional amendment, and was instrumental in the passage of anti-religious and anti-race discrimination legislations.

In 1921, after Lowden left office, he returned to his farm and estate, which he kept as a legally-protected bird sanctuary. He also owned cotton plantations in Arkansas, and became known as one of Chicago's elite because of his ties with his father-in- law, George Pullman, and his view of civic reformism. In 1920, he received 300 votes for the presidential nomination at the Republican National Convention, but he declined the vice presidential nomination in 1924.

Lowden remained in private life until his death in 1943. He was married to Florence Pullman, daughter of railroad man George Pullman, in 1896.

SMALL, LENNINGTON (1862-1936), twenty-eighth governor of the State (1921-29), was born in Kankakee, Illinois, the son of Calista Currier and Abram Small; his father was a doctor. After attending local schools and, later, the Northern Indiana Normal School, he was a member of the State Senate beginning in 1905.

In 1904, he was a member of the State Treasury, a position he held until 1908. In 1912, he was assistant treasurer in charge of the U. S. Subtreasury in Chicago, and in 1917, he won in the race for State Treasurer. He registered as a Republican, and in 1920, was elected governor under that party.

When he took office, he worked for improvements in the State's highway system. In his inaugural address, Small recognized the growing need for more roadways. He said: "The greatest economic good that can be accomplished for the country districts of our State is to push this road system to completion." During his eight years in gubernatorial office, the State's highways grew to be the longest in the United States as he replenished the funds available for building.

Small's efforts for road building were aided by the economic boom of the early twenties, and as the number of automobile purchases increased, so did the demand for roads. Small used this to his advantage politically, by nominating local candidates for election, promising to build roads in the area if his proteges were elected, and then living up to that promise. Despite criticism of his "machine" methods of party politics, Small was reelected in 1924. By the time he left office, State roadways spanned 7,000 miles in concrete.

Small came under attack for charges of corruption early in his term in 1921, when he was tried on charges of conspiracy and embezzlement from his years as State Treasurer. He was not found guilty, but was forced to pay $650,000 to settle a civil suit in that case.

In 1932, Small ran for governor once again, and although he won the Republican nomination, he lost to Democratic candidate Homer. He tried again in 1936, but was not nominated to his party for governor. Small continued to live on his farm in Kankakee during this time, and published the town's *Daily Republican* newspaper. He died at his farm in 1936.

EMMERSON, LOUIS LINCOLN (1863-1941), twenty-ninth governor of the State (1929-33), was born in Albion, Illinois, the son of Fannie Saurdet and Jesse Emerson, who were local farmers. He attended area schools, and in 1883 moved to Mount Vernon, Illinois to take a partnership in a general store. In 1901, he took one of the first few cashier jobs at The Third National Bank of that city, and eventually he became president of the bank.

Emmerson ran unsuccessfully for State Treasurer in 1912, but in 1916 was elected Secretary of State, serving until 1929. While in office, he collected an unprecedented amount of automobile fees, which helped construct a new State roads system. In 1928, he was successful in his bid for governor as a Republican, defeating Democrat Floyd Thompson by more than 400,000 votes.

By signing into law a gasoline tax, Emmerson was able to administer the completion of 5,300 miles of roads which had been planned for the State. He also lobbied for federal aid in order to complete the Lakes-to-Gulf Waterway. Despite these signs of growth, Emmerson was faced with cutbacks because of the oncoming Depression. In 1931-32, special sessions of the Legislature were called to institute relief measures for cities and the unemployed people of the State. Emmerson created the first Unemployment Commission; he also signed new laws to ease the taxpayers' burden by extending penalty deadlines for payment as well as providing for emergency bonds.

Thinking the chances for a Republican victory in the middle of the Depression were slim, Emmerson quit politics after his term and resumed his private life. After leaving office, he was given honorary law degrees from both Illinois College and Milliken University. He was buried at Mount Vemon, Illinois in 1941.

HORNER, HENRY, (1879-1940), thirtieth governor of the State, (1933-40), was born in Chicago to Dilah Horner and Solomon A. Levy. His parents separated when he was four years old, and his mother took her maiden name and gave it to her young son. After attending public schools and a manual training school in the city, Horner went to the University of Chicago and then studied law at Chicago-Kent College.

Horner was admitted to the State bar in 1898 and began to practice law in Chicago. In 1914, he was elected Judge of the Probate Court of Cook County, where he served until 1933. As judge of the largest court of its kind in the world, he heard as many as 46,000 cases in a year. Consequently, Horner instituted several timesaving procedures for the court and strove to help the underprivileged through more direct court hearings. His "Horner Plan" to give free legal aid to war veterans as well as his work to obtain better facilities for the insane helped him gain the renown necessary to win the Democratic nomination for Governor in 1932, defeating the Chicago "machine" candidate in a bitter contest.

He won the State election over former Republican governor Len Small by some 600,000 votes. Taking office at a time when almost everyone in the State was destitute from the Depression, Homer was faced with problems of relief and maintaining the State budget. He abolished the State real estate tax through the legislature and instituted a two percent sales tax to cover the revenue losses. Farmers received help from Horner's administration, which consolidated farm debts through the State.

119

Horner also signed the State's repeal of Prohibition and presided at the formal ratification of the Twenty-First Amendment to the U.S. Constitution. At the same time, he had to contend with Chicago "machine" supporters, led by Mayor Edward Kelly, and attempted to restrict their power by requiring voters to match signatures on file by election officials.

Horner was reelected in 1936 despite Chicago opposition. Two years later, he was incapacitated by illness and Lieutenant Governor Stelle took over his duties. The governor died in October 1940, and Stelle finished the term. He was buried at Winnetka, Illinois, after donating his extensive collection of Abraham Lincoln memorabilia to the state Historical Society.

STELLE, JOHN H. (1891-1962), thirty-first (acting) governor of the State, 1940-41), was born in McLeansboro, Illinois, the son of Laura Blades and Thompson Beveny Stelle. His father, a county judge, sent him to Western Military Academy in Alton after an elementary education, and from 1914-15 he studied law at Washington University in St. Louis.

Stelle practiced law in his hometown until 1917, when he enlisted in the State's National Guard. As an officer in the U.S. Army, he was sent to France in the 115th Machine Gun Battalion and, in 1919, was discharged as a captain after being wounded in battle. After recuperating and spending several years involved in business interests, Stelle served as Assistant State Auditor from 1933 to 1934, and as State Treasurer from 1934 until 1936. That year, he was elected Lieutenant Governor under Governor Horner.

When Horner became ill in 1938, Stelle took over his duties, At Horner's death, Stelle officially took over the governorship until the end of his term, in January of the following year. While in office, Stelle fired Horner's appointees and appointed his friends to the State administration.

He did not receive the Democratic nomination for the next term in 1940, and returned to his business interests. In 1941, he became president and owner of Arketex Ceramic Corporation; he was also president of the Evansville Coal Company and McLeansboro Shale Products Company.

Stelle died in McLeansboro, his hometown, in 1962.

GREEN, DWIGHT H. (1897-1958), thirty-second governor of the State (1941-49), was born in Ligonier, Indiana to Minnie Gerber and Harry Green. He studied at Wabash College from 1915 until the World War I broke out, and enlisted in the U.S. Army Air Service for two years (1917-19), serving as second lieutenant.

He studied at Stanford University for a year and, in 1920, received a PhD. from the University of Chicago. Two years later, he graduated with a law degree from that university. While studying there, he wrote news stories for the Chicago *American* and worked as a law clerk.

After passing the bar, Green practiced law in Chicago until 1926. At that time, he was appointed Special Attorney for the Bureau of Internal Revenue in Washington, which helped him the next year in an appointment as special assistant on income tax matters and the State's Northern District Attorney. Working out of Chicago, Green prosecuted a number of infamous gangsters of that era, including Al Capone for income tax evasion. The Capone case gained national recognition for him in 1931, which helped him gain the appointment as U. S. District Attorney for the Northern District in 1932. He held that post for three years.

Green lost the 1939 Chicago mayoral race, but in 1940, he won the nomination for governor and took the seat as the Republican candidate. He was reelected in 1944. A new law requiring all public schools to teach U. S. history was passed while Green held office, and many provisions for veterans were instituted.

Green also appointed an interacial commission to deal with problems between blacks and whites in the cities, focusing on housing and unemployment, and sat on several postwar commissions, including the Midwest Postwar Planning Conference of State Governments in 1943.

After his gubernatorial term, Green was active in the Republican party's State affairs, and was a delegate to the National Convention in 1952 and 1956. He also served as a trustee of Wabash College and was a member of the board of directors of the Research Foundation, as well as other charitable organizations. He died at Chicago in February 1958.

STEVENSON, ADLAI E. (1900-1965), thirty-third governor of the State (1949-1953) was born in Los Angeles, California to Helen Louise Davis and Lewis Green Stevenson. His grandfather was vice president to Grover Cleveland.

When he was 18 years old, Stevenson left home to join the U.S. Naval Reserve as an apprentice seaman. He studied at Princeton University, graduating in 1922. From that time until 1926, he completed his study of law at Northwestern University in Evanston while working as assistant managing editor of the Bloomington *Daily Pantagraph*. He also became a resident of Illinois.

In 1927, Stevenson set up a law practice with the firm of Cutting, Moore and Sidley, which led him to the position of special counsel for the Agricultural Adjustment Administration in 1933. His legal knowledge also helped him gain an appointment as Assistant Counsel for the Federal Alcohol Control Administration in 1934. During World War II, he was Special Assistant to the Secretary of the Navy, at which time he was appointed head of the Italian Section of the Foreign Economic Mission. He also served as senior advisor in the San Francisco conference of 1945, where the United Nations was formed; the next year he was a member of the United States delegation to that body.

His renown in both international and State services led him to be elected governor of Illinois in 1948, defeating the Republican incumbent by about 600,000 votes. His platform was for liberal reform in the State. His success triggered a reform movement within the Democratic party, which at that time had grown almost indistinguishable from Republicans in its orientation and platforms.

While in office, Stevenson sponsored mining law revisions, and effectively broke up syndicated gambling, prostitution, and loan shark rings in Rock Island, Peoria, Joliet, Decatur, Springfield and East. St. Louis by putting State police on the merit system. Corrupt links between the underworld and politicians in these cities diminished markedly. He also increased the State gasoline tax to finance the State's highway system. However, in spite of his successes, Stevenson has been called by some an ineffective governor. He found it difficult to deal with local and legislative officials, and showed a preference for international affairs.

In 1952, he did not run for gubernatorial reelection and was instead nominated for the Democratic Presidential race. He was defeated by Eisenhower both that year and in 1956. He continued his law practice and was, from 1955 through 1960, in partnership with Rifkind and Wirtz. From 1961 until his death, he served as U.S. Ambassador to the United Nations. He was buried at Bloomington, Illinois in 1965.

STRATTON, WILLIAM G. (1914-), thirty-fourth governor of the State (1953-1961), was born in Ingleside, Illinois, the son of Zula Van Wormer and William Stratton. His mother taught school, and his father was prominent in the State's Republican party, having been the Director of Conservation and, later, the Secretary of State of Illinois.

Stratton attended local schools before attending the University of Arizona, from which he graduated in 1934. He majored in political science, and was a member of that state's National Guard while in college, but decided to return to Ingleside after graduation.

While working as a salesman, he was a delegate to several Republican State conventions during the next five years and, in 1940, was nominated by his party for the U.S. House of Representatives, where he served for one term. As the youngest member of the House, Stratton voted against arming merchant ships, extending military service to 18 months, and the ship seizure bill, but favored registering teenagers for military service.

He returned to Illinois in 1942 and served four years as State Treasurer. In 1945, he joined the U.S. Navy with the rank of lieutenant. On the way home from his duty abroad, Stratton learned from a radio broadcast that he was once again nominated to represent the State in Congress. He served in Washington until 1950, with a record of overriding at least six significant Presidential vetos. After this term, took the position of Illinois State Treasurer.

Two years later, Stratton was elected the Republican candidate for governor of the State. In 1953, he appointed the first woman ever to a governor's cabinet post, approved a bond issue to finance expressways, and began an open door policy toward his constituents. He held a weekly open house in Springfield so that people could speak with him directly about State affairs. During his second term in office, Stratton approved an increase in State sales tax to raise money for schools, and pushed for reform in State hospitals for more beds.

Although he disapproved of presidents holding office for more than two terms, Stratton ran again for a third term as governor in 1960, but lost to Otto Kerner, a Democrat. After his term ended, he returned to his Black Angus cattle farm. He tried again for Governor in 1968, but finished third in the primary race.

KERNER, OTTO, JR. (1908-1976), thirty-fifth governor of the State, (1961-68) was born in Chicago, Illinois, the son of Rose B. Chmelik and Otto Kerner. His father was a lawyer and served as judge of the Cook County Circuit Court and the U.S. State Court of Appeals.

Kerner received his degree from Brown University, and after a year's study at Cambridge University, England, began studying law at Northwestern University in Evanston. He was admitted to the State bar in 1934 and joined a law firm, where he dealt with corporate legal questions. During World War II, he joined the U.S. Army and rose to the rank of Major General within 10 years (1936-46).

Kerner began his political career in 1947, when he was appointed U. S. District Attorney for the Northern District of Illinois. Meanwhile, he was also a member of Chicago Bar Association committees on constitutional amendment, criminal law, and war activities. From 1950-53, he was a member of the Chicago Crime Prevention Council, which may have led to his candidacy for Cook County Judge, where he served from 1954 until taking office as governor of the State in 1961.

His campaign against the Republican incumbent Stratton was characterized by mud slinging. Kerner criticized Stratton's third term plan and cited scandals in the State administration. Stratton in turn claimed Kerner would be a pawn in Chicago Mayor Daley's majority.

In the first months of his gubernatorial term, Kerner approved raises in the State sales and corporate taxes to pay for his unprecedented three billion dollar budget. He also supported passage of a fair employment practices law, a consumer credit law, and a new criminal code. Although he faced opposition by party lines in both houses of the State Legislature, most of his bills were passed. In 1964, Kerner was reelected to a second term, but he resigned in 1968 to become a judge in the U.S. Court of Appeals in Chicago.

His judicial term proved less successful than his governorship, however, as he was indicted and convicted of bribery, conspiracy, income tax evasion, mail fraud, and perjury charges while on the bench. He went to jail after resigning in 1974 from his judgeship.

Kerner died in his home town in 1976. He was buried at Arlington National Cemetery.

SHAPIRO,SAMUEL H. (1907-1987), thirty-sixth governor of the State (1968-1969), was born in Kankakee, Illinois, the son of Tillie Bloom and Joseph Shapiro. After attending St. Victor College, he received his law degree from the University of Illinois in 1929.

Shapiro practiced law in Kankakee for three years before being appointed City Attorney for his home town in 1933. In 1936, he was appointed State's Attorney for the county.

Shapiro ran successfully for Lieutenant Governor in 1960, and was reelected in 1964. When Governor Otto Kerner resigned, Shapiro took over his duties. But despite his efforts to stand on his own feet politically, he was unable to win the Republican nomination for governor in 1968. However, the race was a tight 2,307,295 to 2,279,501.

While Shapiro was in gubernatorial office, the controversial Democratic National convention was held in Chicago. After his short term as governor, Shapiro returned to his law practice. He died in March 1987.

OGILVIE, RICHARD B. (1927-1988), thirty-seventh governor of the State, (1969-73), was born in Kansas City, Missouri to Edna May Buell and Kenneth S. Ogilvie. He studied at Yale University after attending schools in his home town, and in 1942 enlisted in the U.S. Army, where he served for three years. He suffered face and jaw wounds in action as a tank commander in France.

After his discharge, Ogilvie returned to Yale and graduated in 1947, afterward attending law school at Chicago-Kent College. Upon passing the bar, he began practicing law in Chicago, from 1950 to 1958. He also held a job as Assistant U S. Attorney in 1954-1955, and his political involvement became deeper when he became Special Assistant to the U.S. Attorney General between 1951 and 1961.

Ogilvie was a leader in the movement against Chicago mobsters, heading a special Midwest office on organized crime. The reputation he gained in this position led to his election as the Republican candidate for Cook County Sheriff in 1962, and in 1966 he was elected president of the county's Board of Commissioners. Two years later, he was voted into the governor's seat, defeating Democratic incumbent Shapiro over 120,000 votes.

While in office, Ogilvie kept up the modernist reform movement that had swept the state in the mid-60s. He hired young "whiz kids" to streamline and improve the quality of executive agencies and bring the State budget under control. A new income tax law doubled the State's income during his term, allowing more funding for local schools and police departments. Direct revenue sharing for local governments was also begun in these years. Ogilvie helped begin a massive road-building plan for the State, as well as the fast-growing higher education complex.

However, Ogilvie lost in the next gubernatorial election, and accepted an appointment as chairman of the Young Republicans of Cook County. He died in March 1988.

WALKER, DANIEL (1922-), thirty-eighth governor of the State, (1973-77), was born in Washington, D.C., the son of Virginia Lynch and Lewis W. Walker. His father was a chief radioman for the U.S. Navy, and his son was raised at the San Diego, California base.

Walker served as a seaman in the Navy from 1939 to 1942, and after graduating from the Naval Academy in 1945, he entered Northwestern Law School in 1947, where he was editor of the university's *Law Review*. He ranked second in his 1950 graduating class.

For a year afterward, Walker worked as a law clerk to Supreme Court Justice Fred M. Vinson. In 1951, he assisted Illinois Governor Adlai Stevenson. After practicing law with two successful law firms, he took a position as vice president and general counsel for Montgomery Ward Company in 1966. Two years later, he was vice president and general counsel for MARCOR, Incorporated.

He tried and failed in his first bid for public office, losing the Democratic nomination for State Attorney General in 1960. However, Governor Kerner appointed him to the Illinois Public Aid Commission to oversee the State's welfare programs. In other commissions, he fought for more open occupancy of middle income housing in the traditionally white suburbs of Chicago, and published two pamphlets disclosing local business interests of mobsters. These activities gave him the reputation of a liberal; in 1968, he was chosen by the National Commission on the Causes and Prevention of Violence to lead an investigation on the bloody confrontations between Chicago police and antiwar demonstrators at that year's Democratic National Convention.

Three months after the unrest, a comprehensive account of the incidents of August 1968 was made public; it came to be known as the "Walker Report." The report found fault on both sides of the conflict, but criticized some Chicago policemen in particular for "unrestrained and indiscriminate violence ... inflicted on persons who had broken no law." This amounted to "what can only be called a police riot," the report summarized, and Walker blamed municipal government orders, particularly from Mayor Daley, for police disorderliness in the week-long black riots earlier in the year.

Although his accomplishment caused much local criticism for Walker, he also received supportive national recognition. After serving as campaign manager in Adlai Stevenson's successful bid for the U.S. Senate in 1970, Walker announced his intentions to run for governor in 1972 as a reform Democrat.

His alienation from the large Chicago Democratic "machine" did not defeat Walker. Instead, he won the primary and defeated incumbent Governor Ogilvie in a close race. While in office, he trimmed the State payroll by 10 percent, and sought for austerity in his office by dismissing personal security guards and substituting his own Dodge for three official limousines. He also implemented energy-saving measures for State buildings, and approved a Regional Mass Transit Authority.

Even though he instituted a zero-based budget, a $156 million "shortfall" led Walker to call for a six percent budget cut for fiscal year 1976. Despite his fiscal conservatism and support of affirmative action employment in State government, many poiltical observers found contradictions between Walker's professed idealogies and the scandalous histories of some of his administrators. In his attempt for second term, he was defeated at the Democratic primary by a Chicago "machine" candidate, Michael J. Howlitt.

THOMPSON, ("BIG JIM") JAMES ROBERT (1936-), thirty-ninth governor of the State (1977-), was born in Chicago, Illinois, the son of Agnes Josephine Swanson and Dr. James Thompson; his father was a pathologist. He grew up on the west side of Chicago, in Garfield Park, where he became interested in politics at an early age. By the time he was 11, he decided his ambition was to be President of the United States, one which he still holds today.

Thompson attended the University of Illinois from 1953 to 1955, and Washington University from 1955 to 1956. In 1959, he graduated from Northwestern University School of Law and was admitted to the bar that year. For the next few years, he served as an assistant on the prosecutorial staff of the Cook County State Attorney (1956-64).

After becoming an associate professor of law at Northwestern University for four years, from 1969-1970 he was Assistant Attorney General of the State. He also lectured at the University of California, Davis and at Michigan State University. His specialty is criminal law, and in 1967 he was a member of the president's task force on crime.

Thompson used his expertise in the Attorney General's office to become chief of the Criminal Division and chief of the Department of Law Enforcement and Public Protection. In 1970, he became first assistant to the United States Attorney for the Northern District of the State, and the next year was appointed U.S. Attorney for the district, where he served until 1976. During his years as U.S. Attorney, he rose from relative obscurity to what *Washington Post*'s David Broder described as "the busiest, the boldest, best-publicized office holder in the Midwest."

Thompson's efforts produced convictions and sentences for 90 percent of over 300 indictments he handled, some of which included corrupt public employees. His prosecution of a Chicago police officer for brutality against a young black ended in the first civil rights conviction against a policeman in the city's history. Other convictions included city aldermen and a former Cook County clerk. But Thompson's most significant success was in the case of former governor Otto Kerner for 17 counts of tax evasion, bribery, fraud, perjury, and conspiracy in connection with a racetrack scandal.

These successes led Thompson to vaulting fame, and in 1976, he was elected Governor of the State on the Republican ticket by almost a two to one vote. Soon after he took office, he worked with Chicago officials to establish a mass transit and highways program, and pushed through a stringent anti-crime law as well as a plan for a balanced State budget in spite of the Democratic- controlled State legislature.

Although he originally planned to serve a two-year term in order to prevent Illinois gubernatorial elections from coinciding with presidential elections, he was reelected to a four-year term in November 1978. He was subsequently reelected until the 1990 election, when Republican James Edgar won the gubernatorial office.

EDGAR, JAMES (1946-   ), thirty-ninth governor of Illinois (1991-   ), was born in Charleston, Illinois on July 22, 1946. After receiving his early education in Charleston's public schools, he earned his degree at Eastern Illinois University.

Edgar began his political career in 1968 as a key aide in the State House of Representatives and Senate. In 1976, he was elected to the State House, and was reelected again in 1978. In 1981, he was appointed to fill a vacancy as Secretary of State; was elected to the office in his own right in 1982, and was reelected again in 1986.

While he was Secretary of State, Edgar led a drunk driving crackdown program that earned him national recognition. He also pioneered an adult literacy program that became a model for the nation; marshalling support from public and private sectors, he established a volunteer tutoring program to assist some of the two million Illinois adults who are functionally illiterate.

Edgar sought funding increases for library construction, improvements in library services for the disabled, and technological advances in public libraries via computers, to make libraries "computer-age doorways to a world of information" needed in education, research, and business.

Edgar ran for governor of Illinois in the 1990 election; he was inaugurated on January 14, 1991. During his administration, he has worked to streamline and downsize State government; the day after he became the State's leader, he cut his staff budget by $1 million. However, his top priority continues to be education, and he has sought to protect funding for education and essential human services while also holding the line on taxes.

He is chairman-elect of the Education Commission of the States, and president of the board of the Council of State Governments; he also chairs one of three committees of the National Governors' Association.

Edgar is married to the former Brenda Smith; the couple has two children.

CHICAGO

In the Beginning

The natural landscape of the Chicago region as viewed by Jolliet and Marquette, and by the Indians before them, was the result of millions of years of geologic action--for although the chronicle of man in Chicago is brief, the story of the land on which metropolitan Chicago spreads began eons ago.

Many millions of years ago the first living creatures appeared in the ancient tropical sea that covered the mid-continent. Through the millenia of geologic eras, the limy skeletons and shells of countless sea creatures settled over the ocean bottom where, eventually, they formed the rock known as limestone. In time the ocean receded, but the limestone remained to form the bedrock upon which rest Chicago's skyscrapers. The limestone, retrieved from numerous quarries in the area, provided a basic building material.

In the mild and fertile swampy areas bordering the receding shallow inland seas, giant fern trees took hold, forming thick jungles of vegetation. As the plants and trees died, layer upon layer of dead vegetation, often buried by sediment, decomposed into the harder fuel, coal, which was eventually mined in the southwestern fringe of the Chicago region just beyond Joliet, at Coal City and Braidwood.

Effects of the Glaciers

Many thousands of years ago, changes in climate brought on the glacial period. At least four successive sheets crept down from Canada and covered much of the northern part of the United States, including most of Illinois. These glaciers, advancing and retreating, greatly altered the landscape.

The moving ice masses ground down elevations, polished rough surfaces, and gouged and deepened such areas as the basin of Lake Michigan. The glaciers left behind a covering of glacial drift--a jumble of clay, sand, gravel, and boulders over the limestone bedrock. In some places this drift reached a depth of more than 150 feet, with an average depth of between 60 and 70 feet. Later some of the drift was commercially quarried.

In the Chicago region, the last glacier receded about 13,500 years ago, having sculptured what is essentially the basic land. Most significant, especially in regard to the drainage pattern, is the outer crescent-shaped ridge around the southern end of Lake Michigan, stretching from southeastern Wisconsin into southwestern Michigan. It is known as the Valparaiso Moraine or Upland and borders the southern and western part of the Lake Plain. Its inner edge is followed approximately by the Tri-State Tollway. It averages about 15 miles wide and in general stands a dozen or so miles from Lake Michigan. The elevation of the moraine ranges from less than 100 to over 500 feet above the level of Lake Michigan.

The northern part of this moraine is rugged and irregular, exhibiting a surface characterized by rounded hills and intermediate undrained depressions. In Lake County, Illinois and crossing into Wisconsin, many of these depressions are now occupied by about 100 small lakes and ponds. This inland lake region has become an important recreational and residential area, with sizeable settlements developing around some of the larger lakes such as Fox Lake, Pistakee Lake, Round Lake, Long Lake, Grays Lake, and Lake Zurich.

On the lake side of the northern part of the Valparaiso Moraine is the much smaller Lake Border Upland. It is an elongated bell of nearly north-south ridges, with a width of five to 15 miles. The main segment extends northward from about Des Plaines and Winnetka, with a narrow extension south into the Lake Plain as far as Oak Park. Some ridges rise to about 200 feet above the lake level and are interspersed by gentle sags which are occupied by several small streams and an occasional marsh such as the Skokie Lagoons. Lakeward of the Valparaiso Upland and the Lake Border Upland spreads the flat Lake Plain on which Chicago is situated.

The Lake Plain

As the last glacier retreated, water drainage to the north was blocked by the ice. Consequently, the glacier meltwater filled the depression between the receding ice front and the Valparaiso Moraine. This created a lake, marginal to the ice, that at its highest elevation rose to a level of about 60 feet above the present surface of Lake Michigan. This enlarged Lake Michigan, geologically known as Lake Chicago, as well as a portion beyond it. The boundary line of the lake reached from approximately what is now Winnetka through the present communities of Maywood, La Grange, and Homewood, crossing the State line at Dyer and then continuing eastward beyond Chesterton, Indiana.

The accumulated water eventually receded in stages, finding its way westward into the Illinois-Mississippi River drainage system by enlarging two outlets through the Valparaiso Moraine drainage divide. These outlets were later to become important transportation corridors. One outlet was through the Sag Valley south and southwest of the city; it now holds the Calumet Sag Channel. The other outlet, to the southwest, is sometimes known as the Chicago Portage; it contained first the Illinois-Michigan Canal, and later the Chicago Sanitary and Ship Canal as well as other important transportation arteries, including railways and highways.

The lake bottom of Lake Michigan left the Chicago area remarkably flat--a lake plain--except for a few small islands that had existed in the lake such as Mount Forest Island, Blue Island, and Stony Island, and some spits, sand bars and crescent- shaped beach ridges that emerged as the water receded in three distinct stages. Beach ridges stand about 60 feet, 40 feet, and 20 feet higher than the present level of Lake Michigan-- approximately 580 feet above sea level. Today, driving away from the lake on an east-west street, such as Devon Avenue or 111th Street, will take one over each of the three beach ridges of Lake Chicago within a distance of 10 to 15 miles.

Because they were often the best-drained ground in an otherwise marshy area, some of the sandy spits, bars, and beaches of the area later became Indian trails, and some are now parts of modern roads such as Green Bay Road, Ridge Avenue, North Clark Street, Vincennes Avenue, and U. S. routes 6, 20, 30, and Interstate 94. The good drainage also

133

made these areas attractive for the location of cemeteries and golf courses. Both Graceland and Rosehill spits bear the name of large cemeteries on them.

Three small lakes in the vicinity of the Chicago-Hammond State line boundary are merely isolated remnants of the glacial Lake Chicago. Beach ridges separate them from present Lake Michigan. A series of such beach ridges has hampered drainage in the entire Calumet district. Each of the three lakes has, in recent decades, declined in size because of marginal filling and drainage alterations. Lake George, on the Indiana side, has virtually disappeared; Wolf Lake has been preserved as a recreational area; and Lake Calumet is being developed as the major port of Chicago.

After the Glaciers

The topography of the area that developed through these geologic epochs resulted from the superimposition on the limestone bedrock of an uneven layer of glacial drift and, later, of the deposits of Lake Chicago. Since the Ice Age, a number of limited changes have occurred in the topography of the area. Through weathering wind and water deposition, and vegetative growth, the present soils have been formed on the surface of the deposits of the glacial period. The soil is generally of rich, fine quality, agriculturally very productive except where there are major drainage problems or where extensive sand deposits have accumulated, such as along the shore at the head of Lake Michigan, especially in northwestern Indiana. A magnificent concentration of dunes has developed there due to the continued action of the lake current and winds sweeping sand southward.

Another noteworthy change since the glacial era has been the development of the very scenic bluffs and ravines along the lake between Winnetka and Waukegan, due to the erosion of the shore line. Some of the bluffs are almost 100 feet high, and many of the more than 20 major, deep, V-shaped ravines extend a mile or so inland. The effect of lakeshore erosion in this area is dramatically illustrated by the following report:

In 1845 and for about 10 years following there was a village located in the southeast comer of what is now the Fort Sheridan grounds. This village was known as St. Johns. The chief industry was brick making, the yards employing as many as 80 men ... North of the clay pit remnants of a foundation and of an orchard are at the very margin of the lake cliff. Reports differ as to the amount of land that has been cut away at this point, but all agree that it was more than 100 feet. Some old settlers insist that 300 to 400 feet have been removed, and that the cliff and even overhanging are reported by some to have been in the yard to the west of the westernmost house in the village. If this is true, the entire side of the village of St. Johns is east of the present shore line.*

The Chicago River

Across the rather featureless Lake Plain that contains the city of Chicago, the most distinguishing topographic feature is the Chicago River. Though short and sluggish, (the important South Branch is only about half-a-dozen miles in length), the river has been a major factor in the establishment and growth of the city. It was the early connecting route between the East and the commercial wealth of the Middle Prairie. Early Chicago centered around the river and, in the century of its greatest use, the river handled huge cargoes of grain, lumber, and manufactured goods.

The main channel of the river with its two branches forms a Y, with the junction near the Merchandise Mart. This river configuration has, by tradition, divided Chicago into three broad sections: North, South, and West Sides.

The North Branch of the Chicago River originates in Lake County, Illinois, as three small streams flowing southward in the sags of the moraines of the Lake Border Upland. The three streams join in the north part of Cook County and flow southeastwardly toward the junction with the main channel.

The South Branch was usually navigable only as far as west as Leavitt Avenue (2200 West). Often however, during spring high water, it was possible to push canoes across the marshy divide all the way to the Des Plaines River (near 49th Street and Harlem Avenue) by using sea-

135

sonal Mud Lake, which bridged most of the six-mile portage between the two rivers.

The Chicago River of today has been greatly modified since it was navigated by the Indians and early explorers. It has been straightened and widened in parts. The sand bar which blocked the river's mouth and caused it to bend southward and flow into the lake opposite the foot of Madison Street has been removed. An artificial island, Goose Island, has been created and a sharp bend has been by-passed by the construction of the mile-long North Branch Canal. Most importantly, the portage has been eliminated and the South Branch of the river has been connected with the Illinois-Mississippi River waterway system, first by the Illinois and Michigan Canal, and later by the Chicago Sanitary and Ship Canal. And the flow of the Chicago River has been reversed to flow now into these connecting waterways.

The Calumet River

At the southeastern end of the city is Chicago's other important river: the Calumet. Unlike the Chicago River, the Calumet River played an insignificant role in the early history of Chicago, but today it is one of the most industrialized rivers in the world, "the Ruhr of America," and it carries considerable tonnage.

The early settlers found the Calumet to be a strange, erratic, meandering stream that had formed an elongated loop parallel to the lake. The river flowed westward from its source in Indiana and then looped back only two or three miles to the north, flowing in the opposite direction to empty into Lake Michigan near Miller, Indiana. Frequently, the mouth of the river was nearly closed by sand drift.

Later man altered this river to suit his purposes. Its mouth, located at Miller, was blocked, and a channel was dug from the Calumet River near Hegewisch to an outlet into Lake Michigan at about 90th Street in South Chicago. The river was again altered in 1922 when the Calumet Sag Channel was dug. The Calumet River was reversed to flow into the Calumet Sag Channel near Riverdale, and thus drain the Lake Plain of southern Chicago and northwestern Indiana westward into the Chicago Salutary and Ship Canal, and eventually into the Illinois-Mississippi system.

The Drainage Pattern

The reverse of the Chicago and Calumet rivers altered the unusual drainage pattern of the Chicago region. Glacial action, in creating moraines parallel to Lake Michigan, also resulted in the creation of a divide parallel to the lake and relatively close to it. The divide, which separates water flowing on one side into the St. Lawrence River system, and on the other side into the Gulf of Mexico, is less than four miles from the lake in the Waukegan, Illinois area, and at its furthest point, south of Hammond, Indiana, only about 20 miles.

A few short rivers, such as the Chicago and Calumet on the eastern side of the divide, broke through sand bars to reach Lake Michigan. But the major rivers, such as the Fox, Des Plaines, and Kankakee, never penetrated through the moraines; instead, they flow into the Mississippi Basin. In places, the divide is less than 100 feet above Lake Michigan; at its lowest point, the Chicago outlet at Summit, Illinois, it is a barely discernable 15 feet.

Because the land is flat, the rivers are generally sluggish, and drainage of the area is poor. Furthermore, layers of impermeable clay left by the glaciers hampered the drainage of surface water, created a high water table, and helped to make early Chicago, for at least part of the year, a virtual sea of mud. To get adequate gradient for storm and sanitary sewers, the Metropolitan Sanitary District of Greater Chicago had to provide more than a dozen pumping stations to enhance the flow to the extensive drainage canal system.

Vegetation

The Chicago region is a transition zone between the vegetative patterns of the great eastern forests of North America and the prairies further to the west. The transition zone once contained both forests and prairies. The solid stands of forest diminished westward in Illinois largely because of declining rainfall. The zone's average annual rainfall of about 34 inches is substantially less than the 40 to 50 inches further east that nurtured a beech-maple forest. However, there is enough rain to support drier oak-hickory stands and extensive tall-grass prairie. The percentage of forestland generally increased to the east and to the north, and was prevalent and more varied in wet bottomlands, as along the rivers.

The natural vegetation of the Chicago area is indicative of its position as a meeting ground for plants of a number of regions. The plants fall chiefly into three categories: "hangovers" of species of the north that had persisted locally since the glacial era; returned plant migrants from the southeastern states that had been driven out during glacial times; and a few species that migrated from the semi-arid southwest.

Within a generation or two of the start of intensive settlement of the area, most of the forest and prairie grass had disappeared except in a few isolated patches, and on the moraines and along the rivers where drainage was often poor. Many of the remaining wooded areas, especially along the rivers, later became part of the extensive 63,000-acre system of Cook County Forest Preserves.

The cosmopolitan character of the vegetation in the area was especially evident under the unusual and largely untouched conditions of the Indiana sand dune.

Early Settlement

A century after Marquette and Jolliet had passed through the area in 1673, Chicago still did not have any permanent settlers. During the period of French rule, which lasted until the cession of the land to the British in 1763, there had been sporadic but limited activity in the area. Other French explorers, notably Robert Cavelier, Sieur de La Salle, and his companion Henri de Tonti, had passed through the area around the 1680s. Later, because of its excellent geographical location and portage, a number of French voyageurs, trappers, and fur traders also traversed the area. Indians, mainly Potawatomi, who were the most powerful tribe around the south end of Lake Michigan, hunted, traded furs, and occasionally camped in the area they called "Checagou," evidently referring to the garlic, wild onion smell which permeated the air.

The territory was under British rule for 20 years, until the Treaty of Paris of 1783 which ended the American Revolution and made the area part of the new United States.

The British, nonetheless, lingered on illegally until the Jay Treaty of 1794 pledged British evacuation.

Indian resentment at being driven from their lands continued to make permanent settlement of the area hazardous. A turning point for the Chicago area came with the defeat of the Indians at Fallen Timbers, Ohio, by the army of "Mad Anthony" Wayne. The ensuing Treaty of Greenville of 1795 forced the Indians to concede "one piece of land, six miles square at the mouth of the Chicago River." The treaty cleared the title to Chicago and opened to settlement a 36-square mile area encompassed by the lake, Cicero Avenue, Fullerton Avenue, and 31st Street. In 1803 Fort Dearborn was constructed at an elevated point at the bend of the river, near its mouth, to secure the area and protect the important waterway linkage, which became of even greater importance with the Louisiana Purchase the same year.

In the late 1770s, even before the building of the fort, Jean Baptiste Point du Sable, whose father was French and whose mother was a Negro slave, had built a cabin on the north bank of   the river in the vicinity of the present Tribune Tower. This was probably Chicago's first permanent dwelling From here, for about two decades, du Sable carried on trade with the Indians. Later, the house was occupied by another trader, John Kinzie, a famous early settler of Chicago.

Despite the fort, settlement in this part of Illinois remained very sparse, unlike southern Illinois, which was rapidly becoming occupied by settlers. A major reason was the continued hostility of the Indians, who were angered by the takeover of their lands. This was brutally manifested in the War of 1812 when a group of soldiers and settlers, who had been ordered to evacuate Fort Dearborn in order to contract the western military perimeter against the British, were ambushed by the Indians along the shores of the lake at about what is now 18th and Calumet Avenue. Fifty-three men, women, and children were killed. The Indians burned Fort Dearborn to the ground, and once more Chicago lapsed into a prairie wilderness.

In 1816, Fort Dearborn was reestablished following peace between Great Britain and the United States. News of the outpost's reestablishment attracted a few settlers, tradesmen, and agents to the vicinity of the fort. But large-scale settlement did not start until the conclusion of the

Black Hawk War in 1832. The treaty with the Indians provided for their relocation payments in cash and goods.

The Indians gathered in Chicago for their final payments in 1835. Gathering there were also a motley group of wayfarers-- horse dealers and horse stealers, peddlers, grog sellers, and "rogues of every description, white, black, brown and red-- half-breeds, quarter-breeds, and men of no breed at all." By ruse, whiskey, and thievery, they managed to take from the Indians a good part of their money and goods. About 800 Indians joined in a last, defiant dance of farewell before crossing the bridge over the South Branch of the Chicago River and heading westward until Chicago saw them no more.

Town and City

No longer held off by fear of the Indians, the trickle of newcomers to the little military and trading outpost grew into a stream. The westward movement of people and trade was aided by the opening of the Erie Canal in 1825, and the subsequent establishment of regular, cheap, and convenient steamboat service from the east via the Great Lakes. Migration was also helped by improvements in land transportation to the Chicago area as competing Atlantic ports fostered the building of canals and roads westward to tap the growing midwestern hinderland.

The rapid push westward to this area was also due to a variety of difficulties experienced in other areas--especially in the eastern United States and in western Europe. Men were drawn to Chicago by plenty of cheap land, jobs, and a speculative fervor stimulated by plans for a canal that would connect Lake Michigan with the Mississippi River.

Settlers came in increasing numbers, some to fan out into adjacent lands and some to remain in Chicago. In 1833, Chicago, with a population of around 350, was incorporated as a town. The town was only 3/8 of a square mile in size, and was centered around the main channel of the Chicago River. Its boundaries were the present Kinzie Street on the north, Madison Street on the south, State Street on the east, and Des Plaines Street on the west. Also in the same year, Congress appropriated $25,000 for major improvements of the harbor. In 1834, a channel was opened through the sand bar at the mouth of the river and, to protect the entrance to the harbor, 500 foot piers were constructed on either side.

In the year of its incorporation, Chicago was described by a Scottish traveler, Patrick Shirreff, as follows:

Chicago consists of about 150 wood houses, placed irregularly on both sides of the river, over which there is a bridge. This is already a place of considerable trade, supplying salt, tea, coffee, sugar, and clothing to a large tract of country to the north and west; and when connected with the navigable point of the river Illinois, by a canal or railway, cannot fail of raising to importance. Almost evevy person I met regarded Chicago as the germ of an immense city, and speculators have already bought up, at high prices, all the building-ground in the neighborhood.

Chicago's growth was reflected in a number of ways. In 1883, black bear were being killed on the fringes of what is today's Loop. Only four lake steamers had entered the harbor that year; by 1836, this had increased to 450. A parcel of land at South Water and Clark Streets costing $100 in 1832 was sold for $15,000 in 1835. And by 1837, when Chicago was incorporated as a city, the population exceeded 450 people. The city, as first incorporated in 1837, encompassed some 10 square miles. Its boundaries were North Avenue on the north, 22nd Street on the south, the lake on the east, and Wood Street on the west. Ten years later, as the population grew, the boundary was extended westward to Western Avenue.

The burgeoning Chicago of 1848 was portrayed by the author John Lewis Peyton:

...The city is situated on both sides of the Chicago River, a sluggish, slimy stream, too lazy to clean itself, and on both sides of its north and south branches, upon a level piece of ground, half dry and half wet, resembling a salt marsh, and contained a population of 20,00M. There was no pavement, no macadamized streets, no drainage, and the 3,000 houses in which the people lived, were almost entirely small timber buildings, painted white and this white much defaced by mud....

...Chicago was already becoming a place of considerable importance for manufacturers. Steam mills were busy in every part of the city preparing lumber for buildings which were contracted to be erected by the thousand the next season. Large establishments were engaged in manufacturing agricultural implements of every description for the farmers who flocked to the country every spring. A single establishment, that of McCormick, employed several hundred hands, and during each season completed from 1,500 to 2,000 grain-reapers and grass mowers. Blacksmith, wagon and coachmaker's shops were busy preparing for a spring demand, which with all their energy, they could not supply. Brickmakers had discovered on the lake shore near the city and a short distance in the interior, excellent beds of clay, and were manufacturing, even at this time, millions of brick by a patent process, which the frost did not hinder, or delay. Hundreds of workmen were also engaged in quarrying stone and marble on the banks of the projected canal; and the Illinois Central Railway employed large bodies of men in driving piles, and constructing a track and depot on the beach. Real estate agents were mapping out the surrounding territory for 10 and 15 miles in the interior, giving fancy names to the future avenues, streets, squares, and parks. A brisk traffic existed in the sale of corner lots, and men with nothing but their wits, had been known to succeed in a single season in making a fortune- sometimes, certainly, it was only on paper ...*

By 1850, Chicago's population had grown to about 30,000 and its future role as a great transportation and industrial center was already clearly evident. The Illinois and Michigan Canal, 97 miles long, had been opened in 1848 connecting the Great Lakes with the Mississippi Valley. Shortly thereafter, there began a period of vigorous railroad building which brought railroad tracks focusing on Chicago from almost every direction.

Chicago's geographical location and its excellent transportation connections with the rich agricultural hinderland helped to create strong bonds of interdependence between the farmers of the Midwest and Chicago. The farmers funneled their produce to Chicago; the city provided stockyards, food processing commodities eastward. And back from Chicago to the farmers went clothing, processed food, household items, lumber, and farm equipment. Many of the farm machines and implements were manufactured by the McCormick Reaper factory which had been established in 1847 on the north branch of the river at the site of the former du Sable cabin. Cyrus McCormick of Virginia was one of the first of a long line of commercial and industrial entrepreneurs who, with their employees, were to contribute toward making Chicago "Hog Butcher for the World, Tool Maker, Stacker of Wheat, Player with Railroads and the Nation's Freight Handler."

Political and economic dominance, on the whole, was held initially by men who were predominantly from the eastern United States. With remarkable combinations of thrift, shrewdness, and drive, they acknowledged no barriers to successful expansion of a wide range of enterprises. In climbing to the top, often with little regard for others, perhaps they did what had to be done to raise a city out of a swamp.

Among these early leaders was William B. Ogden, who came from New York and, in 1837, became the city's first mayor. One of the first of many Chicagoans to promote the building of railroads, he later was the first president of the Union Pacific. Potter Palmer appeared on the scene in 1852. He made a fortune in dry goods and cotton speculation, and added to his wealth by developing State Street. Marshall Field came from Massachusetts; by 1867 he became a part-owner in the firm that was later to bear his name. Two farm youths from the east, Philip D. Armour and Gustavus Swift, helped Chicago become the meat packer of the nation. A new era in railroad travel was begun when George Pullman invented the sleeping car. Later his shops for building passenger and freight cars spread over 3,500 acres near Lake Calumet. Julius Rosenwald, a native of Springfield, Illinois, learned the clothing business, went to work for Sears, Roebuck and Company, and eventually became President and Board Chairman as well as one of the nation's greatest philanthropists. Sears' major competitor had been founded shortly after the Chicago Fire of 1871 by A. Montgomery Ward, who had lost everything in the conflagration except $65 and the clothes he wore. He later earned the nickname "watchdog of the lake-front" for his long but successful struggle to save the Grant Park area from being commercialized--contrary to an 1836 legal provision which designated the areas as "public ground, forever to remain vacant of building."

The Street Pattern

Fundamental to Chicago's internal development was its street pattern. The Federal Ordinance of 1785, with its land survey provisions, imparted to early Chicago a basic pattern of land subdivision and roads. Even today it is still a strong determinant in the pattern of streets, traffic flow, commercial development, and the arrangement of lots and parcels.

The survey divided the land into square-mile sections using a rectangular grid system. The section lines, a mile apart, and running either north-south or east-west, became the city's main traffic thoroughfares, and later the major routes of public transportation. The section-line streets also became endless ribbons of commercial development that in time became too extensive and inefficient. Intersections of section lines, such as 63rd and Halsted, and Madison and Pulaski, often became major shopping areas.

In Chicago, there are typically 16 blocks to the mile in one direction and eight blocks in the other. The street numbering system of Chicago, with a few exceptions, is based on a theoretical 800 numbers to the mile. Thus there are the section line streets of 31st, 39th, 47th, 55th, etc., and in the other direction Halsted (800 W.), etc. Frequently half mile steets, halfway between the section lines, became important thoroughfares and shopping streets, such as California Avenue (2800 W.) and 51st Street.

In time, as a result of tradition, zoning laws, and actual development, this rigid rectangular grid system became virtually fixed as the basic pattern of Chicago. This had an advantage in that the right angle pattern eliminated travel dangers associated with streets meeting at acute angles (with the major exceptions of Chicago's few diagonal streets, many of which began as Indian trails). Also, the subdividing of lots and assigning of street addresses were simplified. On the other hand, the rectangular pattern led to a monotonous uniformity, made virtually all streets througb streets, and fostered unneeded commercial ribbons. Furthermore, the grid system discouraged some pleasing patterns such as distance-saving diagonals, curvilinear streets, cul de sacs, streets following terrain, drainage, or scenic conditions, and planned housing and shopping developments-- features that have been adopted in many of the newer suburbs of the metropolitan area.

Mudhole of the Prairies

The main problem of the streets of early Chicago was the mud. In 1848 Chicago:

... could boast of no sewers, nor were there any sidewalks except a few planks here and there, nor paved streets. The streets were merely graded to the middle, like country roads, and in bad weather, were impassable. A mud hole deeper than usual would be marked by signboards with the significant notice thereon, 'No bottom here, the shortest road to China'... Wabash Avenue between Adams and Jackson Streets, was regarded as out of town, where wolves were occasionally seen prowling about.*

Chicago's problem was that it was flat and low, being only about two feet above the river level. Moreover, the sewage that did drain off into the river flowed into the lake, which also supplied the drinking water. The resulting epidemics of cholera, typhoid, and other diseases were not finally curtailed until the flow of the Chicago River was literally reversed in 1900. In the meantime, Chicago tried to lift itself from this quagmire by actually raising the elevation of the city. Street levels were raised by piling fill several feet deep; sometimes the fill was obtained from the dredgings of the waterways.

George M. Pullman in 1854 demonstrated successfully, with the help of 500 men and 2,500 jackscrews, how even one of the largest of Chicago's buildings, the Tremont Hotel, could be lifted eight feet "without disturbing a guest or cracking a cup." The idea caught on in this spirited community of ardent boosters, and within two decades, several thousand acres had been raised three to five feet above its former level. For a time, however, Chicago exhibited a somewhat confusing pattern of disjointed sidewalks, some up and some down, depending on whether the owner had raised his property or not. And even today, especially in the inner city, one can find yards and homes below the raised street level, some with stairs leading down to the first floor.

The Fire

Despite these problems, Chicago continued to grow and prosper. It was buoyed by the opening of the Illinois and Michigan Canal, the coming of the railroads, the development of substantial industry fueled somewhat by the Civil

War, the further settling of its rich hinderland, and the accelerating influx of settlers.

The disastrous Chicago Fire of 1871, however, cast a temporary pale on the future growth of Chicago. Chicago in 1871 was a city of wood--wooden houses, wooden roofs, even wooden sidewalks. After an unusually long period of drought, the city became tinder dry. The stage was set for the fire that broke out on October 8 in Mrs. O'Leary's barn at 558 De Koven Street (at the site of the present Chicago Fire Academy). Fanned by a southwest wind, the fire spread rapidly. When it finally subsided two days later, it had thoroughly gutted about four square miles of the city. It took more than 250 lives, destroyed some 1,700 buildings, and left almost 100,000 people, about a third of the population, homeless. Property loss reached nearly $200,000,000.

The fire virtually consumed the entire area from Roosevelt Road on the south to Fullerton Avenue on the north, and westward nearly to Halsted Street, including the entire downtown area. Only a handfull of buildings were spared; of these the Chicago Avenue Water Tower is the only remaining landmark.

The positive faith in Chicago was underscored the day after the fire, when Joseph Medill's Chicago Tribune, printing from an improvised plant in the unburned area, editorialized:

CHEER UP!

In the midst of a calamity without parallel in the world's history, looking upon the ashes of 30 years' accumulations, the people of this once beautiful city have resolved that CHICAGO SHALL RISE AGAIN!

And Deacon Bross, one of Chicago's greatest boosters and aformer Lt. Governor declared:

I tell you, within five years Chicago's business houses will be rebuilt, and by the year 1900 the new Chicago will boast a population of a million souls. You ask me why? Because I know the Northwest and the vast resources of the broad acres. I know that the location of Chicago makes her the center of this wealthy region and the market for all its products. What Chicago has been in the past, she must become in the future--and a hundredfold more! She has only to wait a few short years for the sure development of her manifest destiny!

Rebuilding and Further Expansion

The determined Chicagoans, who had already created a city on marsh land, immediately turned to the task of rebuilding it. By 1875, little visible evidence of the catastrophe remained. The peoples' indomitable spirit and vitality, visions of a profitable future, and generous amounts of outside aid totaling over $5,000,000, including about $1,000,000 from abroad, all contributed to building a new Chicago that was to emerge bigger and better than ever.

The fire accelerated the out movement of residential homes from the central business district. The new buildings that rose in the downtown area were larger and higher, conforming to the new city ordinance outlawing wooden buildings in the downtown region. And outside this area, thousands of homes were going up, many of brownstone and brick. The rebuilding activities attracted to Chicago thousands of laborers and numerous achitects. In the 1880s many of them helped in the construction of the first skyscrapers using the innovative steel skeleton, elevators, and somewhat later, the floating foundation. The "progenitor" of the true skyscraper was probably William Le Baron Jenney's Home Insurance Building, built in 1885 with an iron and steel framework. It was on the northeast corner of La Salle and Adams Streets, where today the La Salle Bank Building stands.

Despite the fire, depressions, and sporadic violent labor strife, such as the Haymarket Riot, Chicago continued to grow rapidly. Besides its commercial and transportation importance as a major handler of grain, cattle, and lumber, the city was becoming increasingly a major center of diversified manufacturing.

After increasing its size from 43 square miles to 168 square miles by the annexation in 1889 of four sizeable but relatively sparsely populated communities--the towns of Jefferson and Lake, the City of Lake View, and the Village of Hyde Park--the 1890 census showed that Chicago already had 1,009,850 people. In the preceding decade the output of many of its major industries had more than doubled.

From Fire to Fair

In 1893, just 22 years after the fire had leveled the heart of the city, Chicago again attracted attention of the world with its dazzling, classically styled World's Columbian Exposition. With its usual audacity, the city built the Fair on an apparently impossible sandy site along the lake front, eight miles south of the river. The Fair sparked a feverish real estate boom on the south side, especially in the Hyde Park-Woodlawn area around the Exposition grounds. As a legacy to the city, it left Jackson Park, the Midway, and the Museum of Science and Industry (the Fine Arts building of the Fair).

The many contrasting facets of Chicago in the last decade of the century were portrayed by George W. Steevens, an English journalist, who wrote this sprightly account of the city in 1896:

... Chicago! Chicago, queen and guttersnipe of cities, cynosure and cesspool of the world! Not if I had a hundred tongues, every one shouting a different language in a different key, could I do justice to her splendid chaos. The most beautiful and the most squalid, girdled with a twofold zone of parks and slums; where the keen air from lake and prairie is ever in the nostrils, and the stench of foul smoke is never out of the throat; the great port a thousand miles from the sea; the great mart which gathers up with one hand the corn and the cattle of the West and deals out with the other the merchandise of the East; widely and generously planned with streets of 20 miles, where it is not safe to walk at night; where women ride straddlewise, and millionaires dine at mid-day on tbe Sabbath; the chosen seat of public spirit and municipal boodle, of cut-throut commerce and munificent patronage of art; the most Americann of American cities, and yet the most mongrel; the second American city of the globe ... the first and only veritable Babel of the age; all of which 25 years ago next Friday was a heap of smoking ashes. Where in all the world can words be found for this miracle of paradox and incongruity?

The growth of Chicago continued unabated during the first three decades of this century despite periodic depressions, the turmoil of World War I with its curtailment of European immigration, and the notorious ganster era of the prohibition years which created an image of lawlessness, an image hard to overcome despite the city's many accomplishments. The population almost doubled during this period, from 1,698,575 in 1900 to 3,376,808 in 1930. Virtually the entire city area, except for some small patches mainly on its fringes, had been occupied. In addition, especially since World War I, population was increasingly overflowing into the suburbs.

To celebrate a century of remarkable growth, Chicago staged the Century of Progress Exposition of 1933-1934. The very colorful and modernistic structures of the World's Fair were located on artificially created land along the lake shore from Roosevelt Road to 39th Street. Despite being held in the depths of the Great Depression, the Fair attracted over 39 million people and was an unqualified financial success.

Source of Early Settlers

Chicago's unprecedented growth from a marshy wilderness to a city of well over 3 million people in less than a century and a half was largely a result of an almost constant stream of settlers into the area--although their major points of origin changed with the passing decades. At first settlers came largely from the eastern United States, then from northwestern Europe, later from eastern and southern Europe, and more recently from our South and the Caribbean areas. In all, Chicago is an amalgam of over 40 identifiable ethnic and racial strains.

They came because opportunities in Chicago were much brighter than in their native areas, where they often had encountered economic, political, and religious difficulties. They came because Chicago had the network of waterways, roads, and rails that made it highly accessible. And they contributed with brawn and brains to the development of the great Midwest Metropolis.

The first permanent settlers in the city and surrounding farmland came mainly from the east--New England, the Middle Atlantic States, and nearby Ohio and Indiana. Many were sons of pioneers emulating their parents. Unlike the early settlement of southern Illinois, very few of Chicago's early settlers came from the south.

In the early decades of Chicago's growth, some of the settlers of eastern origin became the city's political and economic leaders. Many lived in the fashionable areas along Michigan and Wabash Avenues in what is now the downtown area.

European Immigrants

Foreign immigration into Chicago first began on a large scale in the 1840s. The first large group was the Irish, fleeing from the famine caused by the failure of the potato crop and from the burden of absentee landlords. They were followed by large numbers of Germans, especially after the suppression of the democratic revolutions of the 1840s. William Cullen Bryant, in letters in 1846 to his newspaper, The *New York Evening Post,* noted about Chicago that:

... Any one who had seen this place, as I had done five years ago, when it contained less than 5,00O people, would find some difficulty in recognizing it now when its population is more than 15,000. It has its long rows of warehouses and shops, its bustling streets; its huge steamers, and crowds of lakecraft, lying at the wharves; its villas embowered with trees; and its suburbs, consisting of the cottages of German and Irish laborers, stretching northward along the lake, and westward into the prairies, and widening every day. The slovenly and raw appearance of a new settlement begins in many parts to disappear. The Germans have already a garden in a little grove for their holidays, as in their towns in the old country, and the Roman Catholics have just finished a college for the education of those who are to proselyte the West.

Scandinavians also began to come in large numbers, together with smaller numbers of English, Welsh, and Scots. By 1860, over half of Chicago's population of 112,172 were foreign born, Movement of immigrants to Chicago had been spurred by the opening of the first rail connection between New York and Chicago in 1853 as well as by organized solicitation of settlers and by the glowing reports of Chicago's opportunities sent home by Chicago's foreign settlers. By 1890, about 78 percent of Chicago's one million people were either foreign born or the children of immigrants. Tbe Germans, Scandinavians, and the Irish, in order, were the three largest foreign-born groups in 1890. In 1900 Chicago had more Poles, Swedes, Bohemians, Dutch, Danes, Norwegians, Croatians, Slovakians, Lithuanians, and Greeks than any other American city.

The flow of Europeans to Chicago continued unabated until the outbreak of World War I in 1914, but the geographic sources of immigration already had started to shift markedly about 1880. For about the next half century, until foreign immigration quotas went into effect in 1927, the majority of the migrants came from eastern and southern Europe--with the Poles, Italians, Eastern European Jews, Bohemians, Lithuanians, Russians, Greeks, Serbians, and Hungarians among the largest groups, although there were migrants from almost every area in Europe. At the peak of immigration, Chicago was the largest Lithuanian city, second- largest Bohemian city, and third-largest Irish, Swedish, Polish, and Jewish city in the world.

When immigration was sharply curtailed in 1927, the foreign- born whites comprised about 27 percent of Chicago's total population. Because of deaths and some migration back to the old country, this figure was about 20 percent in 1940, 15 percent in 1950, and 11 percent in 1970.

By 1970, the median age of the foreign born was 62 years-- foreshadowing a further decline of the group which at one time had constituted a majority of the people of Chicago. Their decrease also marked the decline of one of Chicago's most colorful eras--a period when much of Chicago was a microcosm of Europe and the city was enriched by many cultures. The city was filled with the sounds of dozens of languages, exotic dress, and a myriad of ethnic shops, schools, churches, synagogues, cafes, coffeehouses, and newspapers. The immigrants cherished the security of their own institutions in their own neighborhoods, as they endeavored to work their way upwards economically and socially, despite occasional hostility encountered from "native Americans," many of whom were themselves the children or grandchildren of immigrants.

The Ethnic Checkerboard

The new immigrant groups usually sought housing in the congested low-rent areas around the Loop, especially on the near west side in areas abandoned by earlier immigrant groups who had moved upward economically and outward geographically.

The desire to be close to their own people and to create in their new land the institutions they had cherished in their homelands was instrumental in the formation of numerous ethnic neighborhoods. A traverse of Halsted Street a half century ago from the north side going southward would take one successively through Swedish, German, Polish, Italian, Greek, Jewish, Bohemian, Lithuanian, and Irish neighborhoods, Centrally located on Halsted Street was Jane Addams' Hull House, catering to the immigrants who were often needy, poorly educated, and bewildered by the unfamiliar urban setting.

Jane Addams described the conditions of the immigrant groups:

Between Halsted Street and the river live about 10,000 Italians. To the south on Twelfth Street are many Germans, and side streets are given over almost entirely to Polish and Russian Jews. Still farther south, these Jewish colonies merge into a huge Bohemian colony. To the northwest are many Canadian French and to the north are Irish and first-generation Americans. The streets are inexpressibly dirty, the number of schools inadequate, sanitary legislation unenforced, the street lighting bad, the paving miserable and altogether lacking in the alleys and smaller streets, and the stables foul beyond description. The older and richer inhabitants seem anxious to move away as rapidly as they can afford it. They make room for newly arrived immigrants who are densely ignorant of civic duties. Meanwhile, the wretched conditions persist until at least two generations of children have been born and reared in them.*

In time, with some acculturation and economic success, the immigrant groups and especially their offspring moved outward from their crowded islands near downtown, often migrating in an axial pattern. Thus many of the Germans moved outward along Lincoln Avenue, and the Poles along Milwaukee Avenue. The Bohemians moved westward out of the congested Pilsen colony in the Halsted-Ashland area south of 16th Street into South Lawndale, and later into Cicero and Berwyn. Each migration outward was usually accompanied by a further loosening of the old world ties as each new generation became more assimilated, geographically dispersed, and active as leaders in the civic and economic affairs of the city.

Recent Migration

The 1970 U.S. Census figures for Chicago indicated a population of 3,336,957 down substantially from the peak of 3,700,000 estimated in 1955. This decline resulted largely from the sizeable exodus of white families to the suburbs, and a lower population density in the city caused by considerable redevelopment, including housing and expressway construction. Population data also indicated a substantial change in the population composition of Chicago. In 1970 native whites of native parentage comprised about 1,400,000 people, or only a little over 40 percent of the population; native whites of foreign or mixed parentage comprised under 20 percent of the population; foreign born were less than 10 percent; while, in contrast, blacks numbered about 1,000,000 or nearly a third of the population. The population of Latin American origin rose to about 200,000; the Japanese, Chinese, and Filipino groups each number around 10,000; the American Indian population in the city was about 7,000.

This changing composition of population resulted from the fact that the most recent wave of migration to Chicago was not from Europe, but was mainly from our southern states, and to a lesser extent, from Mexico, Puerto Rico, and more recently, Cuba. It was spurred by the continuing demand for labor, especially during World War I, and later during World War II and its subsequent boom years. Blacks have lived in Chicago since its earliest days; Chicago was a terminal point of the underground railway, and by the time of the Civil War there were several hundred blacks in the city. However, they remained but a relatively small percentage of the city's population until the World War I period. In 1919 blacks constituted only two percent of the total population; by 1919 this figure had reached four percent; seven percent in 1930; in 1970, the black population was 32 percent, and 1990 population figures for blacks were almost 40 percent.

153

When the number of blacks was small, they were widely scattered in the city. As they grew in number, they became increasingly concentrated in the older, deteriorated neighborhoods of the inner city that had been abandoned by earlier immigrant groups, especially on the south side. The major axis of black settlement was between State Street and South Parkway (Dr. Martin Luther King, Jr. Drive), with smaller black settlements on the near west side and near north side. As the black population increased during World War I, the black neighborhoods became grossly overcrowded, with all the resulting social ills. Attempts at residential expansion were often stymied by hostility and sometimes violence. Prejudice and restrictive real estate practices attempted to confine the ghetto within certain fixed boundaries. The result was poor housing, overcrowding, higher rents, school segregation, loss of employment opportunities because of difficult accessibility to available jobs, and racial tension.

The large black migration to Chicago during and after World War II built up a strong housing demand. The artificial ghetto boundaries began to give way--Cottage Grove Avenue, Stony Island Avenue, Ashland Avenue, etc. On a map, the black residential areas resembled an inverted L, with the main segment pushing south toward the city limits and another segment pushing west toward the city limits. The expansion of the black ghetto was on a block by block basis, but was almost always confined to the periphery of the established black ghetto.

As with immigrant groups who preceded them, the blacks had taken over the worst jobs and worst residential areas. But, unlike the earlier immigrant groups, the second and third generation blacks could not readily escape from the ghetto--even if they could afford to, and an increasing number could. Even with wealth and education, their world usually remained the ghetto. Expansion was into the adjacent neighborhoods that had formerly housed whites who had fled to the city's periphery or into the suburbs.

As in the case of the white settlement patterns, the black residential areas in the city also reflect an economic stratification. The quality of neighborhoods, homes, educational level, job status, etc., generally improves as one proceeds outward from the inner city.

Although most of the suburbs began to enact open-housing laws, the percentage of blacks in the suburbs increased only slightly. Many of the suburbs still house few blacks, and some have merely token integration. Sizeable black populations in predominantly white suburbs are found in only a few communities.

OTHER FACTS ABOUT CHICAGO:

Population in 1990: 2,783,726.

Black population in 1990: 39.07 percent.

Hispanic population in 1990: 19,61 percent.

Persons with college education: 13.8 percent.

Per capita income: $10,275.

January mean temperature: 21.4 degrees F.

July mean temperature: 73 degrees F.

Annual precipitation: 33.3 inches.

PEORIA

Population: 135,000; Area Code: 309; Elevation: 608

The third largest city in Illinois, Peoria is situated on a bluff overlooking the north bank of the Illinois River, at the point where it widens to form the Peoria Lake. At the midpoint between Chicago and St. Louis, Missouri, Peoria has grown into a large industrial and trade center, mostly because of its convenience to extensive river routes. It is also an important railroad center, with tracks coming into the city from points all over the eastern half of the country.

Much of Peoria's trade comes from the rich agricultural land surrounding the city limits. Corn is a major product in the region, which, along with the pure river water, has helped make the city into an important liquor manufacturing center. Agricultural implements, grain feed, meat and dairy products, and glucose and alcohol are also produced in the city. Manufacturers of corn products in Peoria are able to obtain the largest amount of starch from every ear of corn because the underground water supply used in the process maintains a temperature of 53 degrees Fahrenheit year round.

Steel and mechanical products have long been a trademark of Peoria; tractors, furnaces, road machinery, washing machines, and diesel engines are all made in the city's factories. Lake Peoria was the site of the first operable gasoline motorboat, and Charles E. Duryea built the first successful gasoline engine in the U. S. at Peoria.

Not the least of the city's firsts is the claim of some Peorians that it is the oldest settlement in Illinois. Although Cahokia is acknowledged as the longest continually-occupied city in the State, Peoria was first settled in 1691 by explorer Henri de Tonti and his crew at Fort Pimiteoui ("fat lake"). The fort was not continuously occupied in the following years, but it was in fact the first settlement in Illinois that is still occupied today.

The first white men to see and record the Peoria region were Louis Joliet and Pere Marquette in 1673, when they descended the Illinois River towards the Mississippi. After Tonti's fort was built in 1691, the area was populated from time to time by the French until late 1812. The village carried several names during that time, including au Pe and Fort le Pe until about 1790, when it was first referred to as Peorias (the "s" was not pronounced), named after the Indians of the same name who populated the region when the first French explorers arrived.

These Indians were friendly, the food was abundant, and the river provided excellent transportation, and so Peorias thrived as a trading post. There were a few squabbles with the English over the settlement; during the American Revolution, it was visited by American military expeditions which destroyed an Indian village there, but afterwards the French resettled it as a trading village.

After the War of 1812, Americans erected Fort Clark in order to protect them against hostile Indians. In 1819, the first American village began to grow around the fort and, in 1825, Peoria County was first incorporated. For about six years, the Peoria settlement was the seat of business for about one-fourth of the State. The town itself was not incorporated until 1835, but at that time, there were already 500 inhabitants, much more than the stripling settlement at Chicago. The city was chartered 10 years later, with a population of about 2,000.

In 1854, Abraham Lincoln was in town to hear Stephen Douglas speak for his campaign for the senatorship. After an afternoon of Douglas' lecturing, Lincoln stood up at his seat and asked the audience to return in the evening to hear his rebuttal. That night, Lincoln delivered a longer version of his public statement against slavery, delivered 12 days earlier at Springfield. This was not, however, one of the famed Lincoln-Douglas debates occurring four years later.

The city continued to grow in the 1800s, as pork and beef packing became big industries. Between 1850 and 1870, plows, threshing machines, and fanning mills were major products, which caused a large industrialization in the city as well as a quadrupling of population. But the largest-growing industry became distilling, and by 1860 the city had seven factories that later became part of a "Whiskey Trust" that centralized the business interests in that field and increased the average output of liquor several hundredfold.

With the early 1900s came the era of Prohibition, however, and for awhile the great industry of liquor ended. However, the distilleries bounced back in the 1930s with unexpected strength, and soon the city once more was first in production. Today, the world's largest distillery, Hiram Walker and Sons, Ltd., is located on the banks of the Illinois River in south Peoria. Pabst Brewing Company is also headquartered here. These and other distilleries in the city still draw much of the region's corn crop.

Cultural places in Peoria include a civic theater with a player's group, a city library system, and the Bradley Polytechnic Institute, a college of the arts and sciences. There are three general hospitals in the city, and a county courthouse that was built in 1876 in the Italian Renaissance style (a new courthouse has replaced the old one for daily business, however). Another point of interest is the site of Fort Clark, located at Liberty and Water Streets, marked with a bronze plaque.

OTHER FACTS ABOUT PEORIA:

Population in 1990: 113,504.

Black population in 1990: 20.87 percent.

Hispanic population in 1990: 1.6 percent.

Persons with college education: 19.4 percent.

Per capita income: $12,481.

January mean temperature: 21.5 degrees F.

July mean temperature: 75 degrees F.

Annual precipitation: 34.9 inches.

ROCKFORD

Population: 147,370; Area Code: 815;
Elevation: 715-742

Located 18 miles south of the Wisconsin line and 65 miles west of Chicago, Rockford is the second largest city in Illinois. It was named for the shallow rock-bottomed ford across the Rock River, which was used by travelers on the Chicago-Galena line before any settlement existed here. The area is heavily wooded, causing many residents to call it "The Forest City," and small creeks meander through the main areas of town as well as the residential districts. Surrounding Rockford are endless acres of farmland, in which dairying and the raising of grain and livestock have helped make the city an important trading center.

However, the city has a long history of manufacturing and industry, and this is how the small town has maintained steady growth since the early 1800s. The manufacture of agricultural implements and furniture are the most important activities in the city, but machine tools, air conditioning, and heating equipment, auto parts, textiles, hardware, pianos, and sewing machines are also made here.

In fact, Rockford's first settlement grew around the industry of sawmilling. In 1834, Germaricus Kent and Thatcher Blake of Galena dammed a tributary of the Rock River, using the city's best resources at that time: cheap water power to transport logs. The timber was cut for new homes for the rush of emigrating New Englanders. In 1839, there was a substantial enough population that Rockford was incorporated as a town, and became the seat of Winnebago County. Much of the reason for naming Rockford the county seat was because of the supposed navigability of the Rock River. However, only two steamers ever made it through the shallows and rapids from the Mississippi. The economic importance of the town to the agricultural communities around it weighed out its need as a river port, and within a few years, industrialization brought even more money into Rockford.

In the 1850s, the Chicago and Galena Railroad reached through the town; the Rockford Water Company began

159

operations; a permanent dam was built on the river; and John H. Manny, inventor of a combination reaper and mower, arrived in Rockford. All of these brought people and business into the small prairie town.

Manny came to Rockford in 1853, and began turning out 150 of his machines in the first year here. That year, Rockford was incorporated as a city. After a few improvements, Manny's new plant was able to increase production, and by 1854, over 1,000 reapers were being made. He was sued the next year by another reaper inventor, Cyrus H. McCormick of Chicago, for stealing patented ideas. Manny won the case however, and continued making his machines, which increased agricultural production in the Midwest, especially in Illinois, many hundred-fold.

Other manufacturers moved to Rockford during this period, including makers of plows, pumps, cultivators, and threshing machines. In the 1870s, hosiery became an important business here, and new machines were invented to make them, including the first fully automatic one in Rockford.

Swedish immigrants and their descendants made up a substantial portion of Rockford's population. Many of this nationality moved to the area in the early days of the city and began making furniture in the tradition of the Swedish masters.

The city today continues the art of furniture making, and other arts are preserved by several organizations sponsoring events such as concert series. A 70-piece symphony orchestra entertains residents frequently, and an art gallery, several theaters, and events at Rockford College provide other kinds of cultural exposure.

Rockford College, situated on the banks of the Rock River, was founded in 1847 as a women's seminary. It is one of the oldest original all-female institutions in the country. Today it is co-educational, and concentrates mainly on the liberal arts.

Many public and parochial schools, and a several-branched public library system are also located here. Two large parks in the city limits, Sinnissippi and Black Hawk, allow space for all kinds of recreation.

OTHER FACTS ABOUT ROCKFORD:

Population in 1990: 139,426.

Black population in 1990: 14.97 percent.

Hispanic population in 1990: 4.19 percent.

Persons with college education: 14.9 percent.

Per capita income: $11,634.

January mean temperature: 18.3 degrees F.

July mean temperature: 73 degrees F.

Annual precipitation: 36.8 inches.

SPRINGFIELD

Population: 105,227; Area Code: 217; Elevation: 598

The capital of Illinois, Springfield is located at the rough center of the State, near a widened area of the Sangamon River. Farms and coal veins surround the city, which accounts for its many factories that supply bread and other wheat products as well as the prevalence of mining-related businesses.

Industrial and capital areas of the city are divided into two distinct sections, delineated by Ninth Street. The western end is the seat of wealthy homes and government buildings; the eastern end is the factory and low-income housing section of Springfield.

More than anything, however, Springfield is known as a monument to a national hero. More than a century ago, Lincoln left the city for Washington, never to return alive, telling a farewell group of friends, "No one not in my situation can appreciate my feelings of sadness at this parting. To this place and the kindness of this people I owe everything. Here I have lived a quarter of a century, and have passed from a young to an old man ..." The city remembers him at every turn, from the numerous Bronze plaques marking the site of his activities, to the large monument at his tomb in Oak Ridge Cemetery.

Springfield did not exist in 1818 when Illinois became a State, however. It was first settled in 1820 by Elisha Kelly and his family, who found the area rich in plant as well as animal life. Soon other adventurous people settled in this valley of plenty along the Sangamon. When the county by that name was established in 1821, Kelly's Colony had the most facilities to house government officials. The name "Springfield" came that same year, so called because of nearby Spring Creek as well as Kelly's fields. The farmer was then commissioned by the State to build the first cut-log courthouse for $42.50.

In the following years, a new and larger courthouse was built, and a steamboat floated up the river from St.

Louis. The town newspaper, the *Sangamon Journal*, declared in 1832, 169Springfield can no longer be considered an inland town ... we cordially invite emigrating citizens from other states to come hither and partake of the good things ..."

As more and more "emigrating citizens" moved northward to Springfield and into regions of the Great Lakes, many citizens wanted to change the capital from Vandalia to Springfield. In 1837, they got their wish, after Abraham Lincoln and eight other legislators insisted on it. Lincoln himself moved to the prairie town that year. By 1840, Springfield was incorporated as a city and, by 1860, over 9,000 people lived within its limits. In 1868, the cornerstone of the present-day Capitol was laid; however, the final building was not completed until 1857 because of quarrels within the Legislature over funding.

In the early twentieth century, a centennial building was constructed in the city to commemorate 100 years of Illinois statehood. It was built on the site of Lincoln's home; a museum located within the building contains many historical items from his life. Along with the the museum area, the old structure houses many State offices, as does an addition built in 1930.

In 1868, Myron Howard West drew up a plan for civic improvement in Springfield, which included the creation of a widened area of the Sangamon River to be named Lake Springfield. Gambling, prostitution and other crime syndicate rings were rampant in the east end of town from the 1920s until the late 1940s, when Governor Adlai Stevenson hired law enforcement officials specifically to suppress these activities.

The Archives Building was built in 1937; there, State and court records are preserved in filtered air, and old newspapers are filed on microfilm. Other locations of importance are the Library and Art Gallery, housed within the Centennial Building. The site of the Globe Tavern, where Lincoln lived in 1842, is marked on Adams Street, as well as the site of his brother-in- law's (C.M. Smith) store, where Lincoln's fateful Inaugural Address was held.

A 100 foot obelisk in the Oak Ridge Cemetery marks the tomb of Abraham Lincoln, his wife, and three of their children. Eleven years after Lincoln's death, a fantastic attempt was made here to steal his body. Ben Boyd, engraver for "Big Jim" Kenealy's gang of counterfeiters, had been caught and sentenced to Joliet for 1O years. Unable to replace Boyd, an excellent craftsman, the gang decided to "kidnap" Lincoln's body, bury it in the Indiana Dunes, and then secretly inform Boyd of the burial place. With this knowledge, Boyd was to force the governor to "ransom" the body by granting him a pardon.

The Secret Service learned of the plot and decided to catch the graverobbers actually desecrating the tomb. Just as the ghouls were about to open the casket, one of the officers shot off his gun accidentally. Confusion caused the servicemen to shoot at each other and the gangsters escaped, although they were captured later and prosecuted.

Activities in Springfield today are less wild, but every year in late August, farmers as well as other citizens attend the Illinois State Fair on 376 acres of grounds at the northern city limits.

OTHER FACTS ABOUT SPRINGFIELD:

Population in 1990: 105,227.

Black population in 1990: 13.01 percent.

Hispanic population in 1990: 0.83 percent.

Persons with college education: 20.8 percent.

Per capita income: $12,192.

January mean temperature: 24.6 degrees F.

July mean temperature: 76.5 degrees F.

Annual precipitation: 33.8 inches.

DICTIONARY
OF PLACES

This is a gazetteer of geographical places in the state.

It contains listings of all of the *incorporated* and many other populated places (1990 census figures); prominent physical features and cultural locations. Many points of interest are included as well as the names of nationally recognized Historical Sites. Details on the Historical Places can be found in the section of the book titled Historical Places. They are arranged in that section by County, so it will be necessary to note the name of the County when cross-referencing.

It is anticipated that additional populated places and other geographical entities not included in this edition will appear in subsequent editions, along with updating, correcting and expanding entries presented here.

● **ABINGDON,** City, Knox County; Pop. 3,597; Area Code 309; Zip Code 61410; W. Central Illinois; 10 miles S of Galesburg; Located in an agricultural region and is a noted trade and shipping point for livestock, corn, wheat, fruit, and poultry. Manufactures clothing, pottery, and plumbing supplies. Of note is the 83-foot totem pole in town. The gigantic pole features two wing spans and has the cardinal, Illinois' state bird, on top. Incorporated 1857.

● **ADAMS COUNTY,** W. Illinois; Area 866 square miles; Pop. 66,090; Seat Quincy; Established January 13, 1825. Named for President John Quincy Adams, the western boundary is formed by the Mississippi River.

● **ADDISON,** Village, Du Page County; Pop. 32,058; Area Code 708; Zip Code 60101; NE Illinois; W of Chicago; Named for the 18th century essayist, Joseph Addison. The village has been a center for the German Lutheran faith since 1840, and has the Kinderheim, a training school for children of Lutheran parentage. Of note are the many century-old buildings, a number of which are still in use. The post office dates from 1852.

● **ALBANY,** Village, Whiteside County; Pop. 835; Area Code 815; Zip Code 61230; NW Illinois; On the Mississippi River just S of Clinton, Iowa; Formerly a river port, Albany was practically destroyed in 1860 by a tornado. Today, it remains mainly a sportsman's retreat. The sloughs near the village attract many ducks and geese every fall, and as a result of this, many hunters and sportsmen arrive every year. Numerous camp developments have been built to stimulate business.

● HISTORICAL PLACES: (See Hist. Pl. Sect. for Details.)

Albany Mounds Site.

● **ALBERS,** Village, Clinton County; Pop. 700; Area Code 618; Zip Code 62215; SW Ilinois; 21 miles E. of East Saint Louis.

● **ALBION,** City, Edwards County seat; Pop. 2,116; Area Code 618; Zip Code 62806; SE Illinois; 16 miles W of Mount Carmel in an agricultural region; Founded in 1818 by Morris Birkbeck and George Flower, English settlers who came to establish a colony. Incorporated in 1869; many old houses have been restored. Greek and Georgian architectural styles are reflected in the public library, built in 1842. The library houses the collection of the first public library in Illinois. Economy based on the manufacturing of clothing, flour, and bricks.

● **ALEDO,** City; Mercer County seat; Pop. 3,681; Area Code 815; Zip Code 61234; NW Illinois; 23 miles SSW of Rock Island; Incorporated 1885.

Aledo is a trade and shipping center for coal, corn, oats, livestock, poultry, and dairy products. It has a large and modern business district, and in town is the Roosevelt Military Academy.

● **ALEXANDER COUNTY,** SW tip of Illinois; Pop. 10,626; Area 226 square miles; Pop. 12,015; Seat Cairo; Established March 4, 1819. Named for William M. Alexander, early Illinois settler.

Bounded to the west by the Mississippi River, and to the SE by the Ohio River. Area was originally the site of large Indian settlements, as evidenced by mounds left by prehistoric tribes. The Old Courthouse is at Thebes, the county's first seat.

● **ALEXIS,** Village, Mercer-Warren County line; Pop. 908; Area Code 309; Zip Code 61412; NW Illinois; 11 miles NW of Galesburg; Located in an agricultural and bituminous coal region.

● **ALGONQUIN,** Village, McHenry County; Pop. 11,663; Area Code 708; Zip Code 60102; NE Illinois; 42 mi. NW of Chicago; Located on the Fox River, which once crossed with an Indian path. The first residents were the Potawatomi Indians who eventually ceded the land after the Black Hawk War in 1832. The first white settler, in 1834, was Samuel Gillilan, who resided there with his wife Margaret and their children. The original name of the village was Cornish's Ferry, named after Dr. Andrew B. Cornish, the area's first postmaster, and it was also called Osceola for a time. The name Algonquin was settled on in 1844, suggested by Samuel Edwards. Thriving on the tourist trade, the village is located in a picturesque dairy and lake region, and the area's industry includes corn and gravel mining.

● **ALHAMBRA,** Village, Madison County; Pop. 709; Area Code 618; Zip Code 62001; SW Illinois; 28 miles NE of East Saint Louis in a mainly agricultural area.

● **ALLENDALE,** Village, Wabash County; Pop. 476; Area Code 618; Zip Code 62410; SE Illinois; 8 miles NNE of Mount Carmel; Located near the Wabash River in a mainly agricultural region.

● **ALLERTON,** Village, Champaign-Vermilion County lines; Pop. 274; Area Code 217; Zip Code 61810; E Illinois; 22 miles SW of Danville; Founded in 1887 and incorporated in 1902.

●**ALMA,** Village, Marion County; Pop. 388; Area Code 618; Zip Code 62807; S central Illinois; 18 miles NE of Centralia; Founded in 1855, and incorporated that same year.

● **ALORTON,** Village, St. Clair County; Pop. 2,960; Area Code 618; Zip Code 62207; SW Illinois; SE of East Saint Louis; Formerly known as Alcoa, the village was incorporated in 1944.

●**ALPHA,** Village, Henry County; Pop. 753; Area Code 309; Zip Code 61413; NW Illinois; 16 miles N. of Galesburg in an agricultural and bituminous coal mining area; Alpha was founded in 1871 and incorporated as a village in 1894.

●**ALSIP,** Suburban village, Cook County; Pop. 18,210; Area Code 708; Zip Code 60658; NE Illinois, just S of Chicago; The first known settlers, in the 1830's, were Joseph and Hannah Lane. The area was incorporated in 1927 when the only industry was a brick plant owned by the Alsip family, who resided in Chicago. The village lies on the Calumet Sag Channel. In its early years, it was largely an agricultural area, but that has diminished substantially, and now there's mostly industry, including: steel, oil, bottling, paper, medical equipment, pumps, and chemical preparations, among several others.

● **ALTAMONT,** City, Effingham County; Pop. 2,296; Area Code 217; Zip Code 62411; SE central Illinois; 12 miles WSW of Effingham; Incorporated as a village in 1872, and as a city in 1901. Named for a highland area a mile to the west. Located at the junction of the Pennsylvania and Baltimore and Ohio railroads. Altamont is a shipping point for wheat and manufactures clothing and egg cases.

● **ALTON,** City, Madison County; Pop. 32,905; Area Code 618; Zip Code 62002; SW Illinois; On the bluffs overlooking the Mississippi River, and 17 miles N of St. Louis; Through a merger of three hamlets, Alton was incorporated as a city in 1837. Because of its location near the Mississippi River and Missouri River confluence, the city prospered during the steamboat days.

A monument to Elijah Parish Lovejoy (1802-1837), an abolitionist editor, is in town. The editor was killed by a mob while trying to protect his press. On William Street, a parking lot covers what was once the Civil War prison of Andersonville, the first Illinois state prison. Due to poor sanitary conditions, a smallpox epidemic broke out in 1863, and an unknown number of prisoners died. They were buried on an uninhabited island in the river. The last of the Lincoln-Douglas debates was held in Alton in 1858.

Today, heavy industry dominates Alton's economy. Products include steel, scrap iron, farm tools, ammunition, chemicals, and food products. Shurtleff College (1827) is in town. Recreational facilities can be found at Alton Lake and in the slough region along the Mississippi River.

POINTS OF INTEREST:

● Alton Lock and Dam. Riverfront Park offers a good view of operation.

● Alton Museum of History and Art. 121 E Broadway.

● Confederate Soldiers' Cemetery. Rozier St., W of State Street.

● Pere Marquette State Park. Approx. 20 miles W on IL 100.

● Piasa Bird Painting Reproduction. On the bluffs NW of town, best seen from the river and McAdams Hwy.

● HISTORICAL PLACES: (See Hist. Pl. Sect. for Details.)

Alton Military Prison Site; Guertler House; Haskell Playhouse.

● **ALTONA,** Village, Knox County; Pop. 559; Area Code 309; Zip Code 61414; NW central Illinois; 16 miles NE of Galesburg; Founded 1868 and incorporated in 1857.

● **AMBOY,** City, Lee County; Pop. 2,377; Area Code 815; Zip Code 61310; On the Green River, which is bridged here; 11 miles SSE of Dixon; Incorporated in 1857. Amboy was the birthplace of the prestigious mercantile firm of Carson, Pirie, Scott, & Company which was opened here in 1858. By the end of the Civil War, the headquarters had been moved to Chicago. A drinking fountain, commemorating the first store, was given to Amboy by the company in 1934. The first newspaper in Lee County, was published in the city in 1854 by Charles Dickens' brother, Augustus Noel Dickens. The town has railroad shops, and manufactures dairy products and gasoline filters.

● **ANDALUSIA,** Village, Rock Island County; Pop. 1,052; Area Code 309; Zip Code 61232; NW Illinois; On the Mississippi River; In the 1830s Clark's Ferry from Andalusiato Buffalo, Iowa was the most famous river crossing above St. Louis. Plans for a paper town, and thriving steamboat wharves fell through, and today the only industry in the village is the manufacture of pearl buttons from clam shells gathered in flatboats from the shallow sloughs and lagoons of the Mississippi.

● **ANNA,** City, Union County; Pop. 4,805; Area Code 618; Zip Code 62906; SW Illinois; 28 miles SW of Marion.

Anna, which was incorporated in 1865, is located in the scenic Illinois Ozarks, and in its earlier days was engaged in a traditional form of folk art, stoneware making. The products were usually crude, and the craft was eventually abandoned for the more lucrative business of fruit farming. The city is a leading shipping center for fruit, wheat, and corn, and manufactures wood products. Granite and marble works are nearby. It is also the seat of the Anna State Hospital.

● **ANNAWAN,** Village, Henry County; Pop. 802; Area Code 309; Zip Code 61234; NW Illinois; 33 miles ESE of Moline; Located in a bituminous coal area, the village is a center for coal mining. Surrounding the village are active and inactive

Encyclopedia of Illinois

strip mines. Reclamation of this land has begun to restore the natural ecology. Annawan residents also deal in livestock farming and selling.

● **ANTIOCH,** Lake resort village, Lake County; Pop.6,105; Area Code 708; Zip Code 60002; NE Illinois; On the Wisconsin border 15 miles WNW of Waukegan; Antioch was settled in 1836 and was incorporated in 1857. The village is the principal community in the Chain-0'-Lakes country and has a thriving tourist business. It is also an important agricultural center for dairy products, flour, and feed.

POINTS OF INTEREST:

● Chain O'Lakes Area.

● Chain O'Lakes State Park. 6 miles W on IL 173; 39947 N State Park Road, Spring Grove.

● Hiram Butrick Sawmill. Gage Brothers Park on Sequoit Creek.

● Wilmot Mt. Ski Area. 3 miles N on IL 83, then W on WI County C; 1 mile S of Wilmot, WI near Illinois state line.

● **APPLE RIVER,** Village, Jo Daviess County; Pop. 414; Area Code 815; Zip Code 61001; NW Illinois; 23 miles NW of Freeport in a resort and agricultural area (corn, dairying, livestock). Apple River citizens make cheese and dairy products.

● **ARCOLA,** City, Douglas County; Pop. 2,678; Area Code 217; Zip Code 61910; E. Central Illinois; 37 miles ESE of Decatur; Originally called Okaw, it was later named after a town in Italy. Arcola was platted in 1855 and incorporated in June of 1873. Noted for its "corn brooms" made out of broom corn, which has a finer leaf than grain corn and a brushy tassel. The city has a local broom factory and a poultry hatchery, and there is also some agriculture produced such as corn, beans, and wheat. Nearby is an Amish colony as well as Rockhome Gardens, which have artistic rock and flower gardens.

POINTS OF INTEREST:

● Rocome Gardens. 5 miles W on IL 133.

● **ARENZVILLE,** Village, Cass County; Pop. 432; Area Code 217; Zip Code 62611; W central Illinois; 12 miles NNW of Jacksonville in an agricultural region. Founded in 1840; Named for Francis Arenz and incorporated in 1893.

● **ARGENTA,** Village, Macon County; Pop. 940; Area Code 217; Zip Code 62501; Central Illinois; 21 miles NE of Decatur. Center for corn, wheat, and soybeans. Known originally as Friends Creek, the area was founded in 1874 and was incorporated as a village in 1891.

● **ARLINGTON HEIGHTS,** Residential village, Cook County; Pop. 75,460; Area Code 312; Zip Code 600%; NE Illinois; NW suburb of Chicago. Settled in the 1830s and incorporated in 1887. Home of the Arlington Park Race Track (1929) which is the largest of the race tracks in the Chicago area. Manufactures mostly furniture and beverages. Nearby is the Deer Grove and Camp Reinberg Forest Preserve which has two small lakes and some camping sites.

POINTS OF INTEREST:

> ● Historical Society Museum. 500 N Vail Avenue.
> ● Long Grove Village. 1 mile N, jct. IL 53, 83 in Long Grove.

● **AROMA PARK,** Village, Kankakee County; Area Code 815; Zip Code 60910; NE Illinois. At the confluence of the Kankakee and Iroquois rivers and SE of Kankakee in a mainly agricultural area.

● **ARTHUR,** Village, Douglas-Moultrie County lines; Pop. 2,112; Area Code 217; Zip Code 61911; E Central Illinois; 16 miles NNW of Mattoon in a farming region. Originally an Amish colony, the village was platted in 1873 and incorporated in 1877. The village has two broom factories, and also manufactures road machinery, burial vaults, and office equipment. The Amish colony is still in existence and the members make their own rules and regulations exclusive of the village council.

● **ASHKUM,** Village, Iroquois County; Pop. 650; E Illinois; 16 miles SSW of Kankakee in an agricultural area. Ashkum produces fertilizer and farm chemicals.

● **ASHLAND,** Village, Cass County; Pop. 1,257; Area Code 217; Zip Code 62612; SE corner of W central Illinois; 20 miles WNW of Springfield. Platted in 1857 and incorporated in 1869. Center for grain, dairy products and livestock.

Ashland is the birthplace of Henry Clay, statesman and Whig political leader, who died in 1852.

● **ASHLEY,** City, Washington County; Pop. 583; Area Code 618; Zip Code 62808; SW Illinois; 13 miles S of Centralia. Named for John Ashley, one of the early settlers. Located in an agricultural and bituminous coal area. The city is noted for corn, wheat, fruit, and dairy products.

● **ASHMORE**, Village, Coles County; Pop. 800; Area Code 217; Zip 61912; 18 miles E of Mattoon in an agricultural area. Ashmore is a farm trade center for feeds, fertilizer, and seeds.

● **ASHTON**, Village, Lee County; Pop. 1,042; Area Code 815; Zip Code 61006; 13 miles E of Dixon. Many of the inhabitants are of German descent. Ashton manufactures cheese and cement vaults.

● **ASSUMPTION**, City, Christian County; Pop. 1,244; Area Code 217; Zip Code 62510; Central Illinois; Economy based on manufacturing, coal mining, and some farming.

● **ASTORIA**, Town, Fulton County; Pop. 1,205; Area Code 309; Zip Code 61501; W Central Illinois; 28 miles SSW of Canton. Astoria was platted as Washington in 1836, and in the following year Vienna was platted to the west. The villages were combined and incorporated in 1839 and named for John Jacob Astor. In its early days it was a manufacturing center, but remains today only as a retired farmers' town, its principal activity being the buying and selling of farm products.

● **ATHENS**, City, Menard County; Pop. 1,404; Area Code 217: Zip Code 62613; Central Illinois; 10 miles N of Springfield. Founded in 1831 and incorporated in 1859. In 1837 in a little building on Main Street, Abraham Lincoln and eight members of the Sangamon County legislative delegation were honored with a banquet for the influence they had in transferring the state capital from Vandalia to Springfield. Coal mines are nearby, and the city is a manufacturer of radiator guards.

● **ATKINSON**, Village, Henry County; Pop. 950; Area Code 309; Zip Code 61235; NW Illinois, 27 miles ESE of Moline; Founded in 1856 and incorporated in 1867. Located in a bituminous coal region, the landscape surrounding Atkinson is scarred by numerous mounds and pits of strip mines. A vigorous program of land reclamation has been initiated in order to restore the ecology.

● **ATLANTA**, City, Logan County; Pop. 1,807; Area Code 217; Zip Code 61723; Central Illinois; 18 miles SW of Bloomington. Founded in 1853 as Xenia, the name was changed by the state legislature on February 14, 1855, after Richard T. Gill, who had visited Atlanta, Georgia and loved its beauty, suggested it for this area. The city was incorporated in 1869.

Located in the heart of the Illinois corn belt, Atlanta is a shipping point for corn, especially to Memphis, where it is made into furfural and used in synthetics, abrasives, and lubricants. Other industries include a fertilizer company, two seed companies, a trucking line, and the manufacture of farm equipment.

●**ATWOOD,** Village, Douglas-Piatt County line; Pop. 1,253; Area Code 217; Zip Code 61913; E central Illinois; 26 miles E of Decatur. Established in 1874 and incorporated in 1884. The village basically is located where Douglas, Piatt, and Moultrie counties meet. Shopping center for the surrounding farm area and shipping point for soybeans, corn, and wheat.

●**AUBURN,** City, Sangamon County; Pop. 3,724; Area Code 217; Zip Code 62441, 62615; Central Illinois; 15 miles SSW of Springfield. Incorporated in 1865. Known as the "redbud city of Illinois," with hundreds of the trees planted throughout the community. The only industries include a wood shop and a hosiery plant. The Auburn Printing Company puts out weekly newspapers for the city as well as for Chatham, Divernon, and Pawnee.

●**AUGUSTA,** Village, Hancock County; Area Code 217; Zip Code 62311; W Illinois; 30 miles NE of Quincy in an agricultural and bituminous coal mining region. Founded in 1834 and incorporated in 1859, after which it flourished as a farm trade center.

●**AURORA,** Industrial city, Kane County; Pop. 99,581; Area Code 708; Zip Code 605%; Elev. 638; NE Illinois; 37 miles W of Chicago. On both sides of the Fox River, which is bridged here.

First settlers arrived in the area in 1834. At that time there was a large Potawatomi village on the river, and 500 Indians lived in peace with the white men and traded with them, particularly foodstuffs. Soon, other settlers trickled in. Two brothers, Joseph and Samuel McCarty dammed the river and built a sawmill. Joseph, in fact, was the first settler and had originally gone to Chicago after building his cabin near the river. After seeing Chicago and describing it as "more promising for the raising of bullfrogs than

173

humans," he decided the Fox River area was more palatable. The sawmill was completed in 1835, and within a year, the community had 30 families and a post office. Aurora was platted in 1836. For 15 years the village grew up as two separate units along the river, tied to it for the only suitable source of power for the first industries. 1848 brought the forerunner of the Burlington Railroad and a period of expansion followed in which the railroad business dominated the economy. The large railroad shops were also established at this time. The name Aurora, for the Roman goddess of dawn, was adopted by the two communities, and the town was incorporated in 1857.

In 1881, Aurora became the first town in Illinois to light its streets with electricity. Although the illumination left much to be desired, it was a start, and the citizens were fascinated by the yellow glow on top of the high steel towers. Many have thought that the name Aurora was chosen because it means light and so referred to the electrical lighting, but this is not the case since it was chosen well before the electric light came to the community. The town was to have been called Waubonsie after a local Indian chief, but another town was already so named. Aurora was the second choice and it was appropriate since Waubonsie also means "morning light."

By 1890, Aurora's population swelled to 20,000 and had become an industrial city in its own right. It is engulfed in the growing metropolitan area of Chicago, and the location of tollways has brought it within easy reach of O'Hare International Airport. Urban renewal projects have largely renovated the central business district. An $800,000 police-court building and several parks are noteworthy examples. Water power no longer plays an important role in manufacturing in Aurora, but several of the 250 factories have sought riverfront sites. The railroads still boost the economy, and the city is served by the Burlington Northern, Chicago Northwestern, the Elgin, Joliet, and Eastern railroads, and also a new belt line.

Manufacturing plants of international reputation, such as Caterpillar, Barber-Greene, and Thor Power Tool, are located here. Noteworthy products are aluminum goods, construction equipment, elevators, furniture, office supplies, auto accessories, clothing, hardware, parachutes, and belt conveyors.

The city is the seat of Aurora College (1912) which is affiliated with the Advent Christian Church. Located on 22 acres with seven main buildings, it is a coeducational institution with an emphasis on the liberal arts. Waubonsee Junior College was founded in 1967.

The Aurora Historical Museum has period furnishings in a 17- room house built in 1857. Local historical relics are displayed, including a collection of mastodon bones which were excavated in the area. Also of note are the Aurora Public Library, Jennings Seminary, and Memorial Bridge (1921) which spans the Fox River at the end of Stolp's Island.

Nearby is Pioneer Park, a restoration of an Illinois farm village (1880-1910). Several turn-of-the-century shops and stores, as well as a museum and a blacksmith shop are on the grounds.

POINTS OF INTEREST:

- Aurora Historical Museum. Oak Avenue at Cedar Street.
- Fermilab Particle Accelerator. 2 miles N on IL 31, 2 1/2 miles E on Butterfield Rd. (IL 56), then N on Kirk Road at Pine Street.

● **AVA,** City, Jackson County; Pop. 674; Area Code 618; Zip Code 62907; SW Illinois; WNW of Herrin; Founded in 1857, the village was originally known as Headquarters. Incorporated in 1901 and developed as a farming town.

● **AVISTON,** Village, Clinton County; Pop. 924; Area Code 618; Zip Code 62216; S. Illinois; 26 miles W of Centralia in farming and mining area. Aviston also manufactures wooden farm buildings, kitchen cabinets, and sink tops.

● **AVON,** Village, Fulton County; Pop. 1,013; Area Code 309; Zip Code 61415; W central Illinois; 20 miles S of Galesburg. Early names were Woodsville and Woodstock. On April 4, 1852, the Postmaster General of the United States designated the area as Avon, and the village was later incorporated on March 8, 1867. Some of the early manufactures included tile, brick, and cabinet-making, as well as shoe and harness-making. The area's first mill was built near Avon in 1851.

In 1857, the Avon Town Band was formed, and later had the distinction of playing at the Lincoln-Douglass debate in Galesburg. The first electrical lighting manufac tured for the town was in 1892 by the Avon Milling & Manufacturing Co., and the first telephone lines appeared in 1899.

One of the first contemporary factories, built in the 1950's, made television antennas that were shipped all over the world. The area is now largely agricultural, and produces such products as corn, beans, wheat, oats, hogs, cattle, sheep and dairy products.

● **BANNOCKBURN**, Village, Lake County; Pop. 1,388; Area Code 708; Zip Code 60015; Extreme NE Illinois; 25 miles NNW of Chicago in an agricultural area noted for feed grains and livestock. Named for Bannockburn, Scotland and was incorporated in 1929.

● **BARRINGTON**, Village, Cook-Lake County line; Pop. 9,504; Area Code 708; Zip Code 600%; NE Illinois; 32 miles NW of Chicago and founded in 1845.

Early pioneers in Barrington included Quakers; Some came from Great Barrington, Massachusetts and gave the Illinois counterpart its name; Main Street in Barrington is the dividing line of Cook and Lake counties; The economy is based on the manufacture of clothing, furniture, tableware, and coffee and tea packing; The Jewel Food Stores Plant is perhaps the most conspicuous of the industrial complexes; The landscape around Barrington is quite heavily wooded and gives way to pastures and wood lots.

POINTS OF INTEREST:
- ● Barrington Area Historical Museum. W Main Street.
- ● Wauconda Orchards. 2 miles NE of Wauconda.

● **BARRINGTON HILLS**, Village, encompasses 30 sq. miles of Cook, Lake, McHenry, and Kane counties; Pop. 4,202; Area Code 708; Zip Code 600%; NE Illinois. The community is comprised mainly of white collar workers who commute elsewhere. Near Barrington; incorporated in 1959.

● **BARRY**, City, Pike County; Pop. 1,391; Area Code 217; Zip Code 62312; W. Illinois; 24 miles SE of Quincy. Founded in 1836 by veterans of the War of 1812 and incorporated as a city in 1859; named for Barre, Vermont. Shipping point for apples, and trading center for corn, wheat, and hay. Marble and granite works are nearby.

● **BARTELSO,** Village, Clinton County; Pop. 412; Area Code 618; Zip Code 62218; S Illinois; 18 miles W of Centralia; Founded in 1885; incorporated, 1898.

● **BARTLETT,** Village, Cook-Du Page County lines; Pop. 19,373; Area Code 708; Zip Code 60103; NE Illinois; 31 miles W of the Chicago Loop. Located in a hilly area, the village is mainly based on light industry with the largest of three plants producing flexible metal tubing. Founded in 1873 by Luther Bartlett, the first postmaster, who also bought the site in 1844. Incorporated in 1891.

● **BARTONVILLE,** Village, Peoria Coulrty; Pop. 5,643; Area Code 309; Zip Code 61607; NW Central Illinois; 7 miles SW of Peoria. Founded in 1881, the suburb grew rapidly and was incorporated in 1903. Bartonville is served by four railroads and has come into its own as an industrial community. The Keystone Steel and Wire Company alone employs 3,600 people. Other industries include coal mining and fence-making. At the edge of town is the Peoria State Hospital.

● **BATAVIA,** Industrial city, Kane County; Pop. 17,076; Area Code 708; Zip Code 605%; NE Illinois; 35 miles W of Chicago. On the Fox River, which is bridged here. Batavia was founded in 1834 and made an excellent site for sawmills and gristmills who depended on the waterpower of the river. Abundant natural resources contributed to the early prosperity of Batavia and its industrial career began early in 1837 with the construction of a flour mill. "Rock City," as it was known 1842, conducted a profitable limestone quarrying business which has carried over to the present day. Batavia produces refrigerator truck bodies, windmills, cosmetics, coats, kitchen cabinets, and metal products. The central business district is on an island, as is the civic center and other municipal buildings.

Fox Hill Home (1853) on Union Avenue was a mental disorder sanatorium, and one of its distinguished patients was Mary Todd Lincoln, widow of the President. Bellevue Sanitarium is also in the city.

● **BATCHTOWN,** Village, Calhoun County; Pop. 225; Area Code 618; Zip Code 62006; W Illinois; 27 miles WNW of Alton in an apple growing area. Founded in 1879 and incorporatcd in 1897, it was formerly known as Batcheldersville. Batchtown produces crushed stone from local quarries.

● **BATH,** Village, Mason County; Pop. 388; Area Code 217; Zip Code 62617; Central Illinois; On the Illinois River and 36 miles NW of Springfield. Founded in 1834, and in 1837 it was mapped by Abraham Lincoln when he was a surveyor. Incorporated in 1857, Bath was revisited by Lincoln many times when it was the county seat (1843-1851). Its prosperity peaked in the steamboat days when it was an important river port. Today it remains only a "playground for Chicago millionaires," with its exclusive private hunting club and a golf course.

● **BEARDSTOWN,** City, Cass County; Pop. 5,270; Area Code 217; Zip Code 62618; W Central Illinois; On the Illinois River, and 45 miles WNW of Springfield. Beardstown was settled in 1819 as a ferry crossing and was originally called Beard's Ferry. It was here that Lincoln was commissioned as a captain in the Black Hawk War and where he successfully defended his client, Duff Armstrong, in the "Almanac Murder Trial" of 1854. Every July, the citizens of Beardstown stage a mock trial in the old courtroom which is preserved in its original condition.

Beardstown is located on the Illinois Water Trail and on the western offshoot of the Lincoln Heritage Trail (q.v.). It is a trade and shipping center (flour, gloves, cigars) and conducts an extensive clam fishing business. The Beardstown Indian Mounds and the Sanganois Conservation Area (q.v.) are nearby.

● **BEAVERVILLE,** Village, Iroquois County; Pop. 278; Area Code 815; Zip Code 60912; E Illinois; 15 miles SE of Kankakee. Formerly known as St. Mary's, it was established in 1857 and incorporated in 1872.

● **BECKEMEYER,** Village, Clinton County; Pop. 1,070; Area Code 618; Zip Code 62219; S Illinois; 16 miles WNW of Centralia. Established in 1905, the village was named for the Beckemeyer family, which owned a large portion of coal-producing land.

Incorporated in the same year, the village went into the coal mining business, but the mine closed in 1930. Today, the only industries in town are a die-casting firm and a silo plant. It's future lies in recreational facilities, based on its proximity to Carlyle Lake.

● **BEDFORD PARK,** Village, Cook County; Pop. 566; Area Code 708; Zip Code 60499, 60501, 60638; NE Illinois; W of

Chicago. Incorporatd as a village in 1940. Manufacturing center for shipping containers, electronics equipment, iron work, chemicals, vacuum cleaners, foods, steel tubing, paper products, and automobile parts.

● **BEECHER,** Village, Will County; Pop. 2,032; Area Code 708; Zip Code 60401; NE Illinois; 35 miles S of Chicago. Named for Henry Ward Beecher (1813-1887), noted leader of the anti-slavery movement. Platted in 1870 and incorporated in 1883. Beecher is based on an agricultural economy, but also produces welding equipment, wooden cabinets, pillows, and foil products.

● **BEECHER CITY,** Village, Effingham County; Area Code 217; Zip Code 62414; SE Central Illinois; 14 miles WNW of Effingham. Founded in 1872 and incorporated 1895.

● **BELGIUM,** Village, Vermilion County; Pop. 511; Area Code 217; E Illinois; 3 mi. S of Danville; Belgium's past economy was based on coal mining, but the coal seams were eventually exhausted. Miners in town now commute to distant strip mines.

● **BELLEVILLE,** City, St. Clair County; Pop. 42,785; Area Code 618; Zip Code 622%; SW Illinois; just SE of East Saint Louis. In 1814, Belleville became a county seat, even before the state of Illinois was created. St. Clair County was established in 1790 by Gen. Arthur St. Clair, the first governor of the Northwest Territory.

Belleville, situated on the high bluffs of the eastern rim of the American Bottom, has earned the name "beautiful city"; The city was incorporated in 1819, and within nine years, coal was discovered beneath the city which brought an influx of German mineworkers. Many 19th century houses are preserved, such as the courthouse (1857), and numerous one-story brick cottages built when Belleville constructed its many brick manufacturing plants.

Illinois' first free circulating library was established here, as was the nation's secord oldest philharmonic society. Of special interest is the national Shrine of Our Lady of the Snows, which is visited by millions of people of all faiths every year. Built in 1958 by Oblate Fathers, the shrine has a 20,000-seat amphitheater and outdoor altar, as well as a replica of the grotto at Lourdes in France, the Stations of the Cross, and a reflection pool with four Angelus bells.

Major industries include coal-mining, boiler making, bricks, chemicals, and metal products. Nearby is Scott Air Force Base.

POINTS OF INTEREST:

● National Shrine of Our Lady of the Snows. 2 miles NW on IL 15.

● **BELLEVUE,** Village, Peoria County; Pop. 1,491; Area Code 309; N central Illinois; just W of Peoria. Bellevue was a subdivision of Peoria up until 1941, when it was incorporated as a village. Main products are television and radio towers.

● **BELLFLOWER,** (alt. BELLE FLOWER), Village, McLean County; Pop. 405; Area Code 309; Zip Code 61724; E Illinois; 20 miles W of Rantoul.

● **BELLWOOD,** Industrial village, Cook County, Pop. 19,811; Area Code 708; Zip Code 60104; NE Illinois; 13 miles W of Chicago; Founded around 1842, and incorporated on May 21, 1900, the first enterprise in town was a blacksmith shop (1870). Today, Bellwood has expanded its horizons to include such well- known industries as the Chicago Screw Company, Armour Grocery Products, Northern Illinois Gas, and Taylor Forge and Pipe Works. The area's most famous citizen was astronaut Eugene Cernan who spent his boyhood here.

● **BELVIDERE,** City; Boone County seat; N Illinois; Area Code 815; Zip Code 61008 on the Kishwaukee River, which is bridged here; Founded in 1836, the city is chiefly a manufacturing community, specializing in dairy and grain products, sewing machines, machine parts, clothing, and hardware. In 1965, due to its central location near transport routes, a new Chrysler plant was built which employs up to 5,000 workers. Also in town is the Boone County Historical Museum, and the grave of Big Thunder, a locally popular 19th century Potawatomi chieftain.

● **BEMENT,** Village, Piatt County; Pop. 1,668; Area Code 217; Zip Code 61813; Central Illinois; 19 miles ENE of Decatur in a primarily agricultural area. Founded in 1855, it was named for an official of the Great Western Railroad. Located at the midpoint between Decatur and Champaign-Urbana, the village is a shipping point for farm products, especially soybeans. It was in Bement that Abraham Lincoln met Stephen A. Douglas in 1858 to discuss plans for a series of debates. (See entry on Bryant Cottage State Memorial.)

● **BENLD,** City, Macoupin County; Pop. 1,604; Area Code 618; Zip Code 62009; SW Illinois; 25 ENE of Alton; Established and incorporated as a village in 1900, it was named for Ben L. Dorsey, an early settler. It was incorporated as a city in 1930 when the population exceeded 3,000.

● **BENSENVILLE,** Village, Du Page County; Pop. 17,767; Area Code 708; Zip Code 601%; NE Illinois; WNW of Chicago; Named for Bensen, Germany and incorporated in 1894. Originally a dairy town, an industrial park has taken over which is served by the Chicago, Milwaukee, Saint Paul, and Pacific railroads. It is a center for primary metal industries.

●**BENSON,** Village, Woodford County; Pop. 410; Area Code 309; Zip Code 61516; Central Illinois; 26 miles ENE of Peoria; Established 1873 and incorporated in 1878.

● **BENTON,** City, Franklin County; Pop. 7,216; Area Code 618; Zip Code 62812; S Illinois; 25 miles S of Mount Vernon. Founded in 1840, the city was named for Thomas Hart Benton, U. S. senator from Missouri. The city is involved in part of the Rend Lake State Park project (q. v.). Located only a few miles from the artificial lake, the added water supply will help boost the addition of new industries. Manufacturing center for flour, electrical machinery, and metal products. New coal resources have been mapped, and shafts have been sunk into the low sulphur coal seams which have favorable deposits for the production of metallurgical coke.

POINTS OF INTEREST:

　　● Rend Lake. 5 miles N via I-57.

●**BERKELEY,** Village, Cook County; Pop. 5,137; Area Code 708; Zip Code 60163; NE Illinois; W suburb of Chicago. Incorporated in 1924, it was named for Berkeley, California. The village has an industrial park.

● **BERWYN,** residential city, Cook County; Pop. 45,426; Area Code 708; Zip Code 60402; NE Illinois; 10 miles W of Chicago. Named for a town in Pennsylvania, Berwyn was, unlike most Illinois cities, pre-planned by two realtors. It was chartered in 1908, and has been able to keep industry out for the most part. There is some manufacturing (machine tools, leather products, electrical equipment), but most of the population commutes to Chicago and Cicero. Berwyn has many recreational facilities--there are swimming pools, wading pools, six parks, and a field house. Racetracks, golf courses, and forest preserves are nearby.

Disaster struck Berwyn on July 24, 1915 when the "Eastland", an excursion boat, rolled over in the Chicago River; The majority of the 812 persons drowned were from Berwyn.

● **BETHALTO,** Village, Madison County; Pop. 9,200; SW Illinois; 8 miles E of Alton in a bituminous coal and agricultural area. Bethalto began as an industrial community in its own right (1854), but in recent years it has taken on a residential-suburban character with most workers commuting to nearby Alton and Saint Louis. It is a livestock and dairy farming center. In 1954 Bethalto celebrated its centennial.

● **BETHANY,** Village, Moultrie County; Pop. 1,369; Area Code 217; Zip Code 61914; Central Illinois; 16 miles SE of Decatur. The original settlement was known by the unlikely name of Marrowbone, conjured up by two trappers who ate the leftovers of the previous night's venison steak at this exact spot. The missionaries from the Bethany Cumberland Presbyterians of Tennessee changed it to its present designation in 1831. The economy centers on the Bethany Grain Company, but there is a newspaper, the *Beamy Echo,* as well as a lumber yard and a bank. Seventy-five percent of the population is employed in Decatur.

● **BIGGSVILLE,** Village, Henderson County; Pop. 349; Area Code 309; Zip Code 61418; W Illinois; 13 miles ENE of Burlington, Iowa. Formerly known as Grove Farm (1856), it was incorporated as a village in 1879.

● **BISHOP HILL,** Village, Henry County; Pop. 131; Area Code 309; Zip Code 61419; NW Illinois; 20 miles NE of Galesburg. Bishop Hill is a restored Swedish village and Illinois' first commune (1846). It was named for Biskopskulla, Sweden, the birthplace of Erik Jansson, the religious communal leader and founder of the village. The settlement prospered here for a time until internal dissent and the murder of Jansson in 1850 disrupted the organization. By 1862 all the property was divided equally among the inhabitants. The colonists were then converted to the Methodist and Seventh-Day Adventist faiths, and many moved to nearby Galva.

Today, Bishop Hill is merely a relic of the past, and many of the buildings are of historic and ethnic interest. 10 out of 18 main buildings built by the Janssonists are still standing, though some are in great disrepair. Colony Church (1848) and the "Steeple Building" (1854) are largely unchanged. In the blacksmith shop, Swedish folk crafts, such as weaving and candle- dipping, are demonstrated every summer to the many visitors, largely first, second, and third generation descendants of immigrants, who come to Bishop Hill. Along the Edwards River are the Oxpojke, Wildlife and Bird Study nature trails.

Bishop Hill has been declared an Illinois state memorial.

POINTS OF INTEREST:

● Village Tours.

● HISTORICAL PLACES: (See Hist. Pl. Sect. for Details.)

Bishop Hill Historic District.

●**BLANDINSVILLE,** Village, McDonough County; Pop. 762; Area Code 309; Zip Code 61420; W Illinois; 12 miles WNW of Macomb in an agricultural area noted for livestock and dairy products. Argyle Lake State Park (q.v.), with its 95-acre lake, is located in the vicinity.

●**BLOOMINGTON,** City; McLean County seat; Pop. 48,483; Area Code 309; Zip Code 617%; Central Illinois; 35 miles ESE of Peoria.

Bloomington was settled in 1822 at a crossroads of several Indian trails, and for many years it was known as Keg Grove, supposedly because of a keg of liquor found there by a local Indian tribe. Forests abounded in the region, and the name of Keg Grove was eventually changed to Blooming Grove because of the profusion of wildflowers that bloomed in the forest glades.

Many of the early inhabitants were British and much of the Victorian architecture still in existence today is a reflection of their staid and formal lifestyle.

In 1830, James Allin, a local resident, deeded a parcel of land to the state of Illinois. Allin had the foresight to know that Fayette County (q.v.), in which the village was then located, would soon be sub-divided. He offered the parcel, just north of the village, as a site for a future courthouse, and indeed, in December of 1830 the legislature at Vandalia created the county of McLean and accepted Allin's offer of land. Bloomington was subsequently platted in 1831, Allin became one of the founding fathers, and the city acquired a new courthouse as well as title of new county seat.

Bloomington is built on the Bloomington Moraine, one of the four huge, serpentine glacial ridges laid down during the last ice age. The moraine is one of the largest known to geologists and comprises the chief topographical feature upon which the city is built. The area around Bloomington is pleasantly hilly, and agriculturally, the morainic soils are among the most productive in Illinois. The city's economy early on was based on dairying, farming (corn, livestock fodder, seed crops), and the manufacture of agricultural machinery and farm products. It expanded its horizons, however, in 1850, with the founding of Illinois Wesleyan University. With the advent of students, faculty, and general university staff, came new prosperity, and in 1854, railroad tracks were laid through Bloomington which consequently opened up new communications with the rest of the state. Bloomington was no longer a quiet farming community, and railroad repair shops boosted the city's economy and population.

The repair shops continued to dominate the economy well into the 1940s, but today they have been overshadowed by prospering specialty manufacturing such as air-conditioning systems, ironworks, farm machinery, and rubber products. Coal mining, concrete products, vacuum cleaners, snack foods, corrugated packing materials, printing, radio broadcast equipment, and automobiles are some of the other industries in the area. Important manufacturers include the Firestone Tire Rubber Company, The Funk Brothers Seed Company, Illinois Agricultural Association, and the Beich Candy Company. Agriculture continues to be very important, with record yields in corn, wheat, and soybeans.

Politically, Bloomington has remained in the forefront since 1856 with the founding of the state's Republican Party. Abraham Lincoln spoke at the Anti-Nebraska Convention there, and the speech made him a power in the new party. Aligned with Lincoln was the Bloomington *Pantagraph,* a daily newspaper which has been published continuously since 1846. Of interest today is the Old Majors Hall erected on the site where Lincoln made his speech.

Bloomington is the burial place of both Adlai Stevenson I, and Adlai Stevenson II. The elder Stevenson was a former U.S. assistant postmaster general, and the vice president under President Grover Cleveland. His son was the former governor of Illinois, twice a presidential candidate, and an ambassador to the United Nations.

Other points of interest include Miller Park and Zoo and the Funk Gem and Mineral Museum also on the Illinois State University campus. An annual event since 1923, is the American Passion Play held at the Scottish Rite Temple. A cast of 200 performs the Biblical play which is usually seen by more than half a million people from around the country.

Recreational facilities are available at nearby Lake Bloomington, a 500-acre reservoir impounded by a dam at Money Creek.

POINTS OF INTEREST:

- David Davis Mansion (1870). 1000 E Monroe.
- Illinois State University (1857). 1 mile S of jct. US 51, I-55 in Normal.
- Illinois Wesleyan University (1850). 210 E University St. North side residential area on US 51, Business 55, IL 9.
- Miller Park Zoo. On Morris Avenue, 1/2 mile N of I-55 Business.

- HISTORICAL PLACES: (See Hist. Pl. Sect. for Details.)

  Clover Lawn (David Davis Mansion); McLean County Courthouse and Square; Stevenson House.

- **BLUE ISLAND,** City, Cook County; Pop. 21,203; Area Code 708; Zip Code 60406; NE Illinois; Located on the Calumet Sag Canal just S of Chicago.

Blue Island was first settled in 1835 by German and Italian pioneers and was named for the ridge upon which it grew. The ridge is a glacial remnant on the otherwise flat Chicago Lake Plain. At times a blue haze could be seen enveloping the densely wooded ridge which rose like an island from the surrounding marshlands. Blue Island became incorporated in 1872 and based its economy on farming and dairying.

Today it is an important industrial suburb of Chicago whose manufactures include wire steel and iron products, brick, lumber, petroleum products, and tile. A major industry is canning, and the city is the site of the Libby, McNeil, Libby Packing Plant. Agriculture, although not the mainstay, is still important and the area around Blue Island is noted for truck crops.

Encyclopedia of Illinois

● **BLUE MOUND,** Village, Macon County; Pop. 1,161; Area Code 217; Zip Code 62513; Central Illinois; 12 miles SW of Decatur. The area around Blue Mound is noted for agriculture and is a producer of soybeans, corn, wheat, and oats.

● **BLUFORD,** Village, Jefferson County; Pop. 747; Area Code 618; Zip Code 62814; S. Illinois; 8 miles E of Mount Vernon in an agricultural area. Bluford also manufactures vinyl products.

● **BOND COUNTY,** S Central Illinois; Area 388 square miles; Pop. 14,991. Seat Greenville since 1821, Perryville in 1817-1821. Established January 4, 1817. Named for Shadrach Bond, first governor of state. County is cut through by Shoal River. Dairy and poultry producing region.

● **BOONE COUNTY,** N Illinois; Area 293 square miles; Pop. 30,806; Seat Belvidere. Established March 4, 1837. Named for Daniel Boone, pioneer. Borders on Wisconsin state line. Dairying region.

● **BOURBONNAIS,** Town, Kankakee County; Pop. 13,934; Area Code 815; Zip Code 60914; NE Illinois, 3 miles NNW of Kankakee.

Bourbonnais was the earliest settlement on the Kankakee River, established as a trading post there in 1832. The town is named for Francois Bourbonnais, one of the French fur traders who established the post and went on to become historian of the area.

Bourbonnais' economy is based on agriculture (corn, truck crops, feed grains) and limestone quarrying. Many of the town's building are constructed from the quarried stone and are architecturally reminiscent of a centuries-old French village. The town is the site of Olivet Nazarene College and of a Roman Catholic convent which dates back to 1852.

Close to town is Rock Creek State Park, a scenic 2,675-acre woodland containing a canyon and several rapids. It is also known as Kankakee River State Park (q.v.). Beyond the park boundaries are several small caves which have been formed from solution of the underlying limestone by the waters of the Kankakee River and its tributaries. The caves, though small, are a favorite with local spelunkers who are able to explore them with primitive carbide lamps.

186

● **BOWEN,** Village, Hancock County; Pop. 462; Area Code 217; Zip Code 62316; W Illinois; 27 miles NE of Quincy in an agricultural area noted for livestock and feed grains. Bituminous coal mining is also important to the village's economy.

● **BRACEVILLE,** Village, Grundy County; Pop. 587; Area Code 815; Zip Code 60407; NE Illinois; 23 miles SSW of Joliet in an agricultural and strip coal mining area. Apparently Braceville had a hard time surviving in the 1890s due to a lack of sophisticated mining technology. Remnant slag piles still exist from those days and lay in mute testimony to an era when miners were barely able to survive in a coal-mining occupation. Today, strip mining has revived the economy to some extent, although agriculture is most heavily relied on by most of the county's population.

● **BRADFORD,** Town, Stark County; Pop. 678; Area Code 309; Zip Code 61421; NW Central Illinois; 14 miles ESE of Kewanee. The town's economy is based on agriculture, coal mining, and the manufacture of horse collars.

● **BRADLEY,** Village, Kankakee County; Pop. 10,792; Area Code 815; Zip Code 60915, 62907; Elev. 648; NE Illinois; N of Kankakee and near the Kankakee River.

Bradley was founded in 1892 as North Kankakee but the name was changed later in honor of David Bradley who started an agricultural implement factory there. That industry is still a major one today as is the manufacture of furniture and wood products.

● **BRAIDWOOD,** City, Will County; Pop. 3,584; Area Code 815; Zip Code 60408; Elev. 585; NE Illinois; 19 miles SSW of Joliet.

Braidwood was settled in 1865 when coal was accidentally struck by a local resident who was drilling a well. The coal seam was about three feet thick and covered a large area, enough so that mining syndicates were attracted there from all parts of the country. Braidwood thrived on its newfound economic base and by 1873 the population had grown so large that Braidwood became incorporated as a city. During the boom days, miners of all nationalities lived in and around the area and the city became a site for numerous labor meetings and organizations. The area around Braidwood is covered with long, serpentine mounds of "badlands" produced by repeated strip mining. Lagoons formed between the huge mounds of shale, and some of the land is being reclaimed for parkland. The lagoons have been stocked with fish and a new resource, tourism, has come to Braidwood.

Braidwood is famous worldwide for its fabulous fossil assemblages which are found in the concretions (iron oxide nodules) scattered throughout the shale beds. They have become known as the Mazon Creek fauna, for the stream running through the area, and constitute a rich collection of prehistoric plants and animals. Over 500 species of plants are represented and at least 200 species of insects and other animals. When split open, the concretion reveal perfect halves of the fossils. Accommodations in Braidwood have sprung up in order to house the thousands of eager rockhounds, scientists, and tourists who pass through the area each year in hopes of finding these fossils.

Strip mining is still carried out, but the economy is also based or agriculture and in the manufacture of clothes, macaroni, and beverages.

● **BREESE,** City, Clinton County; Pop. 3,567; Area Code 618; Zip Code 62230; Elev. 458; SW Illinois; 34 miles E of East Saint Louis.

Breese was settled around 1860 and was named after Judge Sidney Breese, an Illinois jurist who once lived there. Incorporated in 1905, when it flourished as a coal mining center, Breese's economy is presently based on agriculture (corn, wheat, fruit), bituminous coal mining, livestock raising, and dairying.

Just outside of town is the Cholera Cross, a monument to those people who perished in the cholera epidemic that struck the city in 1849.

● **BRIDGEPORT,** City, Lawrence County; Pop. 2,118; Area Code 618; Zip Code 62417; Elev. 449; SE Illinois; 4 miles W of Lawrenceville. The city was the center of an early oil boom and today it is still a center for petroleum products and natural gas. A typical prairie town with many retired farmers and an economy heavily reliant on agriculture. A major oil company has a pumping station here and other industries include oil refining and the manufacture of electronics equipment. Incorporated as a city in 1865.

Dictionary of Places

● **BRIDGEVIEW,** Village, Cook County; Pop. 14,402; Area Code 312; Zip Code 60455; NE Illinois; SW suburb of Chicago. Bridgeview, which became incorporated in 1947, is mainly residential with small businesses and a population which is largely commuter-oriented. It is basically a community which relies upon the job market in Chicago. There is some manufacturing which includes paper and allied products.

● **BRIGHTON,** Village, Jersey-Macoupin County line; SW Illinois, 10 miles N of Alton.

Located in the Mississippi Valley, Brighton is a bituminous coal mining and agricultural center. Major crops include corn, soybeans, apples, and wheat.

Outdoor recreation is plentiful in the sloughs and inlets of the Mississippi River which flows past nearby Alton.

● **BRIMFIELD,** Village, Peoria County; Pop. 797; Area Code 309; Zip Code 61517; Central Illinois; 17 miles WSW of Peoria in an area noted for feed grains and livestock. Recreation is plentiful in the area which has several noted conservation districts.

● **BROADLANDS,** Village, Champaign County; Pop. 340; Area Code 217; Zip Code 61816; E Illinois; 19 miles SE of Champaign in an agricultural area noted for feed grains and livestock.

● **BROADVIEW,** residential suburb, Cook County; Pop. 9,110; Area Code 708; Zip Code 60153; Elev. 625; NE Illinois; 10 mi. W of Chicago.

The area, which was originally a settlement of Chippewa, Ottawa, and Potawatomi Indians, was officially founded on June 25, 1835, by Frederick Bronson, who bought a plot known as "80 acres." It was later incorporated as a village on January 22, 1914. The name was chosen by Elizabeth Mueller Cote, daughter of Jacob Mueller, the first village president.

In later years, the village had an automobile race track, Speedway Park (1915-18), and an airport, Checkerboard Field (1920-27). Just east of town is the Loyola University Medical Center. Printing and publishing businesses are located here, and the area's main manufactures are fabricated metal products.

189

● **BROCTON,** Village, Edgar County; Pop. 322; Area Code 217; Zip Code 61917; E Illinois; 14 miles WNW of Paris.

The village, located in an agricultural area, is a grain shipping center.

● **BROOKFIELD,** Residential village, Cook County; Pop. 18,876; Area Code 312; Zip Code 60513; Elev. 620; NE Illinois; W of Chicago.

Brookfield was founded in 1893 following extensive land purchases by members of the Ogden, Armour, McCormick, and Rockefeller families. Then known as Grossdale, the name was changed to its present form in 1905.

Brookfield is perhaps best known for the Chicago Zoological Park (Brookfield Zoo) which opened in 1934. It is one of the nation's most outstanding zoological parks where fine animal, bird, and reptile collections are housed in enclosures resembling the native habitat. Against a backdrop of artificial rocks and thickets of shrubbery, the animals appear to roam free. Moats effectively replace bars and cages, and the Seven Seas Panorama is a unique seaquarium in which fish and porpoises can be viewed either from ground floor portholes or from a surrounding deck.

POINTS OF INTEREST:

● Brookfield Zoo (Chicago Zoological Park). 31st St. & 1st Ave.

● **BROOKPORT,** City, Massac County; Pop. 1,070; Area Code 618; Zip Code 62910; Elev. 335; S Illinois; On the Ohio River and just opposite Paducah, Kentucky.

Brookport was incorporated in 1888 and has since flourished as a trade center and shipping point for wheat, corn, and hay. Diverse manufacturing includes buttons, railroad ties, and agricultural products.

Brookport has been plagued by floods and in 1937, six to fourteen feet of water inundated the town, causing severe damage to buildings.

● HISTORICAL PLACES: (See Hist. Pl. Sect. for Details.)

Kincaid Site.

● **BROWN COUNTY,** W Illinois; Area 306 square miles; Pop. 5,836; Seat Mount Sterling; Farming region bordered to W by Illinois River.

Dictionary of Places

● **BROWNING,** Village, Schuyler County; Pop. 193; Area Code 217; Zip Code 62624; W central Illinois. On the Illinois River and 27 miles SE of Macomb in a region noted for agriculture and bituminous coal mining.

●**BROWNSTOWN,** Village, Fayette County; Pop. 668; Area Code 618; Zip Code 62418; S Central Illinois; 8 miles E of Vandalia in an oil producing area. Brownstown's economy is based on agriculture.

● **BRYANT,** Village, Fulton County; Pop. 273; Area Code 309; Zip Code 61519; W Central Illinois, 7 miles SSW of Canton in an area noted for agriculture and bituminous coal mining. In the surrounding area are huge strip mine dumps left by many years of digging and removal of vast deposits of coal.

● **BRYANT COTTAGE STATE MEMORIAL,** restored cottage in Bement, Illinois, in which the first meeting between Abraham Lincoln and Stephen A. Douglas was held in 1858 to discuss plans for a series of joint debates. Located on Wilson Street, tours are given daily by the Bement Guide Service.

●**BUCKLEY,** Village, Iroquois County; Pop. 557; Area Code 815; Zip Code 60918; E Illinois, 37 miles SSW of Kankakee in an agricultural area noted for corn.

●**BUCKNER,** Village, Franklin County; Pop. 478; Area Code 618; Zip Code 62819; S Illinois, 12 miles N of Herrin in an area noted for agriculture and coal mining.

●**BUDA,** Village, Bureau County; Pop. 648; Area Code 309; Zip Code 61314; N Illinois; 13 miles ENE of Kewanee. Founded in 1823, and originally called French Grove, the townspeople later considered other names such as Watusa and Concord; however, the postal authorities made the decision to name the area Buda. A large portion of the land during that time was owned by John Stevens.

Agriculturally, the area produces corn, beans, and hogs. Manufactures include chimneys, smoke ducts, farm and feed equipment, and undergarments.

● **BUFFALO,** Village, Sangamon County; Pop. 503; Area Code 217; Zip Code 62515; Central Illinois, 12 miles ENE of Springfield in an agricultural and coal producing area.

● **BUFFALO GROVE,** residential suburb; Lake and Cook County line; Pop. 36,427; Area Code 312; Zip Code 60089; NE Illinois. 15 miles NW of Chicago in an agricultural area noted for feed-grains.

●**BUNKER HILL,** City, Macoupin County; Pop. 1,700; Area Code 217; Zip Code 62014; SW central Illinois, 15 miles NE of Alton.

The area was platted in 1836, and later incorporated in 1873. It is a shipping center for grain, and agriculturally produces corn, wheat, and beans. It is also a manufacturing site for burial vaults and monuments.

● **BUREAU COUNTY,** N Illinois; Area 866 square miles; Pop. 35,688; Seat Princeton; Farming and fruit growing region. The Fox River flows through the SE corner of county. The Amish settled here in the 1830s.

● **BUREAU JUNCTION,** (alt. BUREAU), Village, Bureau County; Pop. 350; Area code 815; Zip Code 61315; N Illinois, on Bureau Creek; 14 miles W of LaSalle.

Farming and coal mining community; south of town are the Putnam and Marshall county conservation areas which offer excellent recreational facilities (fishing, camping, boating marinas).

● **BURLINGTON,** Village, Kane County; Pop. 400; Area Code 312; Zip Code 60109; NE Illinois; 13 miles W of Elgin in a dairying, livestock, and farming area.

●**BURNHAM,** Village, Cook County; Pop. 3,916; Area Code 312; Zip Code 60633; NE Illinois; At the Indiana line just N of Calumet City. It is an industrial suburb of Chicago, with an oil-refining plant and petroleum products factories.

● **BURR RIDGE,** Residential suburb, DuPage County; Pop. 7,669; Area Code 312; Zip Code 605%NE Illinois; W of Chicago in an agricultural area.

● **BUSH,** Village, Williamson County; Pop. 351; Area Code 618; S Illinois; 6 miles WNW of Herrin in an agricultural and coal mining area. Bush is the site of the Southern Illinois Children's Service Center.

● **BUSHNELL,** City, McDonough County; Pop. 3,288; Area Code 309; Zip Code 61422; W Illinois; 28 miles S of Galesburg.

Bushnell, incorporated in 1865, is an important rail and industrial center in an agricultural and coal mining area. In town are distilleries, nurseries, and stockyards, and diversified goods include garden tools and equipment, candy, beverages, and agricultural products. Bushnell is also a shipping point for livestock, poultry, corn, and wheat.

● **BYRON,** City, Ogle County; Pop. 2,284; Area Code 815; Zip Code 61010; Elev. 729; NW Illinois; On the Rock River and 12 miles SW of Rockford.

Named after poet Lord Byron. It was founded in 1835 by New Englanders, and was a stopover point for the Underground Railroad, the Civil War freedom train for runaway slaves who made their way to safe havens in the North and Canada. Many of the townspeople offered their houses and farms as temporary quarters for the fugitives.

Byron flourished early as an agricultural center and dairying and farming are still the mainstay of the city's economy; there is a cheese factory in town.

Of interest is the Soldiers' Monument (1866), a memorial to Civil War soldiers of Illinois.

● **CAHOKIA,** Village, St. Clair County; Pop. 17,550; Area Code 618; Zip Code 62206; Elev. 407; SW Illinois; On the Mississippi River just E of East St. Louis.

Cahokia is one of Illinois' earliest settlements and the state's oldest permanent village. Originally an Indian village site which became a French missionary post in 1699. The village derived its name, in fact, from the Indian village, which at that time housed about 2,000 Tamaroa and Cahokia Indians.

The Fathers Jolliet de Montigny, Antione Davion, and Jean Francois Buisson de St. Cosme from the Seminary of Quebec, Canada, ran the mission, and under their leadership was built the first church in Illinois. A trading post was later established which flourished on a vigorous river trade between Cahokia and the settlements along the Mississippi all the way to New Orleans.

Cahokia became a center of French influence in the Upper Mississippi Valley, but it was to exchange hands several times before falling into American jurisdiction on July 4, 1778. Even then, the village remained almost totally French in character.

For many years, Cahokia was the seat of St. Clair County, but for political and geographical reasons, it lost that title to Belleville in 1814. The economic rise of St. Louis and East St. Louis as well as the frequent floods which inundated Cahokia contributed to its hasty decline.

Cahokia was incorporated in 1927, but its former importance is reflected only in its historic relics and monuments. It never regained its original status.

Tourism has brought some measure of prosperity to the village which contains many relics from the eighteenth century. Of note are the Cahokia Court House State Memorial (1737), a log structure believed to be the oldest building in Illinois, the Church of the Holy Family which has been used continuously since 1799 even though it has been under French, British, and American rule, and the Jarrot Mansion (1798-1806), the oldest brick building in the state. Cahokia is also the seat of Parks College of Aeronautical Technology (1927) (not affiliated with St. Louis University).

The most notable feature associated with the village is Cahokia Mounds State Park (q.v.) northeast of there. The park contains a complex of 85 prehistoric Indian mounds including the largest earthwork in the United States.

POINTS OF INTEREST:

- Cahokia Mounds State Historic Site. 5 miles E of East St. Louis on Collinsville Road.
- Historic Holy Family Mission Log Church. 120 E St. at jct. IL 3, 157.

- HISTORICAL PLACES: (See Hist. Pl. Sect. for Details.)

    Church of the Holy Family; Jarrot, Nicholas, House; Old Cahokia Courthouse (Francois Saucier House).

- **CAHOKIA MOUNDS STATE PARK,** St. Clair County, SW Illinois, NE of Cahokia and 4 miles NE of East St. Louis.

The scenic 649-acre park is the site of over 300 prehistoric Indian mounds believed to have been built between 1200 and 1500 AD. They had been noted as early as the 1700s but were not fully explored until 1921. Professor W. K. Moorehead of the University of Illinois completed excavations there and concluded that the builders were of a culture more advanced than other early American Indians. Along with human remains, he found large quantities of flints, beads, pottery shards, and other artifacts. Moorehead concluded that the mounds were the hub of a village which spread for seven to eight miles along Cahokia and Canteen creeks.

Most of the 300 mounds have been destroyed through consequent cultivation of now existing farmlands, but 85 of them remain, and eighteen of the best preserved mounds are contained within the immediate park. Monk's Mound, not only the largest in the park, is the largest earthwork in the nation. The mound has a 7-acre base and is 104 feet high, 100 feet wide, and 1,000 feet long, and its shape is that of a truncated pyramid with four terraces. Computations show that construction by primitive methods would entail two years labor by 2,000 men. A museum at the base of Monk's Mound contains many of the artifacts found in the area.

Farther to the south is a broad, shallow pit, occasionally filled with rainwater (Lake Cahokia) believed to be the place where the Indians dug the earth used in constructing the mounds.

Cahokia Mounds State Park also contains excellent facilities for picnicking, hiking, and camping.

● **CAIRO,** City, Alexander County seat; Pop. 4,846; Area Code 618; Zip Code 62914; Elev. 315; SW Illinois; At the confluence of the Ohio and Mississippi rivers and 125 miles SE of Saint Louis, Missouri.

Cairo is located on a fertile delta which juts out to the confluence of the rivers. Pere Marquette and other explorers had noted the finger of land, and in 1702 a French colony was established there with a fort and a tannery. Disease eventually wiped out most of the population.

A subsequent settlement in 1818 was named Cairo by a St. Louis merchant who thought it resembled the city in Egypt. The name stuck, and even today, southern Illinois is popularly referred to as Little Egypt. Cairo was not successfully developed until 1837 when the Illinois State Legislature formed the Cairo City and Canal Company. A huge levee, which still encircles the city, was constructed, along with stores and houses. At first, through exhaustive advertising, stocks were eagerly purchased in the company, but the venture failed in 1840. Many of the new inhabitants lost their fortunes and the city went into a long decline.

After 13 years of suspended animation, Cairo got a second chance. Investors had several years earlier purchased 10,000 acres of land around the city in hopes of making it a terminus for a railroad. They were affiliated with the Illinois Central Railroad Company which consequently acquired an additional land grant from the federal government. The railroad was built, Cairo took root once again, flourished, and became incorporated as a city in 1857.

Every month that passed brought increasing business to the new city. Vigorous trade was carried on between Cairo and Chicago (the northern terminus) and all the settlements along the route. Cairo might have been destined to become the commercial capital of the Midwest had not the Civil War dammed up the developing trade route. During the Civil War, General Ulysses S. Grant had his headquarters in Cairo, and the laden gunboats that clogged the rivers forced trade goods to be increasingly diverted to Chicago. This pattern did not change after the war and Chicago became the regional trade center. Cairo once again was in danger of losing its prosperity, but the citizenry were not about to let that happen. They recognized its strategic location as both a railroad terminus and as a river port. Its location on the delta also gave Cairo an immediate access to fertile river-bottom lands. The soils were well suited to many crops and they became immediately cultivated and planted in cane, cotton, soybeans, and corn. The drier elevations were turned into pasture, and the heavily wooded timberlands became the target for lumber and sawmills. Local plants were built to process cottonseed oil, agriculture became an economic mainstay, lumber mills flourished, river barge traffic increased, and seven new railroads eventually were built into the city. The additional transportation lines brought in even more business and Cairo became an industrial, agricultural, and shipping center for farm and dairy products, wood products, drugs, beverages, and clothing. There are several sawmills, flour mills, foundries, and machine shops in Cairo that have survived since the 1800s.

Cairo came into the spotlight again in 1937. In that year, the Ohio River rose to 60 feet, and Cairo, because of its protective levee, became the only city in the Ohio and Mississippi River valleys that was not inundated by floodwaters. It was a close call, however, for the catastrophe had been anticipated. As the floodwaters rose, residents sandbagged the levee, and when the water reached to within four inches of the crest, the people knew they had made a wise choice in protecting their city.

Cairo, somewhat exotic for Illinois, has streets lined with magnolias and gingko trees and is surrounded by cane-brakes and cottonfields. The levee and the buildings along the rivers still bespeak of the steamboat era; Victorian in architectural style, the buildings are profusely decorated with comices, gargoyles, and wrought iron balconies. Many have fallen into disrepair, others have been preserved as historic relics. Of note is the Magnolia Manor (1869), built when Cairo had hopes of passing Chicago as a trade center. The mansion is filled with Victorian antiques and much of the original furniture. The Ohio Building (1858) was the headquarters of General Grant between 1861-1862.

Several bridges connect Cairo with Missouri and Kentucky. Many of them were built at the turn of the century but can still handle the heavy traffic characteristic of the present.

Of interest is Fort Defiance State Park (*q.v.*) at the southern edge of town. The park is the site of a Civil War fort. Farther north is the Horseshoe Lake State Conservation Area, wintering ground for large flocks of Canadian geese.

POINTS OF INTEREST:

- Fort Defiance State Park. 39 acres. On US 51 at S edge of town.
- Horseshoe Lake State Conservation Area. 7 miles NW on IL 3.
- Magnolia Manor (1869). 2700 Washington Avenue.

- HISTORICAL PLACES: (See Hist. Pl. Sect. for Details.)

Magnolia Manor; Old Customhouse.

- **CALHOUN COUNTY,** W. Illinois; Area 247 square miles; Pop. 5,322; Seat Hardin; A rolling, sparsely populated strip of land squeezed between the Mississippi and Illinois rivers; Established 1825. An "Act to Abolish Calhoun County" because it was so heavily wooded and full of a transient lumberjack population, was defeated by the State Assembly in 1837. Named for J. B. Calhoun, of the Illinois Central Railroad. Today's main industry is apple growing and shipping.

- **CALUMET CITY,** Industrial city, Cook County; Pop. 37,840; Area Code 312; Zip Code 60409; Elev. 585; NE Illinois; 20 miles S of Chicago on the Indiana border.

Calumet City proper was platted in 1833 but owed much of its growth to the real estate boom of the 1920s. The city developed as part of the residential-industrial complex of Gary-South Chicago-Hammond. It was called West Hammond until 1924 when it gained its present name, which is derived from the French meaning "peace-pipe of the Indians."

Manufactures include chemicals, pickles, packed meat, and glue. Calumet City is the site of several glue and chemical factories, meat packing plants, and steelworks.

● **CALUMET PARK,** Village, Cook County; Pop. 8,418 Area Code 312; Zip Code 60643; NE Illinois; S of Chicago. Originally known as Burr Oak, the name was changed to Calumet Park in 1925. The packing plant of the Libby, McNeil & Libby Company is located here.

● **CAMBRIA,** Village, Williamson County; Pop. 1,230; Area Code 618; Zip Code 62915; S Illinois; 5 miles W of Herrin in a noted agricultural and coal mining area.

● **CAMBRIDGE,** Village, Henry County seat; Pop. 2,124; Area Code 309; Zip Code 61238; NW Illinois, 21 miles SE of Moline.

Cambridge was incorporated in 1861 and has thrived as an agricultural and coal mining community. Another industry is furniture.

● **CANTON,** City, Fulton County; Pop. 13,922; Area Code 309; Zip Code 61520; Elev. 655; W central Illinois; 25 miles WSW of Peoria.

Canton was settled in 1825 by Isaac Swan, a native New Yorker who came to this spot and surveyed out a number of lots. These lots he offered free to anyone who wanted to make his home there. Swan built the first solid structure, a log cabin, which he offered as temporary quarters for would-be settlers. He later named his settlement Canton in the belief that it was located exactly on the opposite side of the world from Canton, China.

Canton thrived as a farming and coal mining community. A tornado, which struck in 1835, heavily damaged the town, but it survived and prospered despite this setback.

It was incorporated as a city in 1854 and has become the leading manufacturing center for Fulton County. Its many diversified products include coal, farm implements, lumber, clay goods, and overalls. Canton is a shipping point for agricultural products such as corn, wheat, livestock and poultry.

Much of the population of the city is employed in its coal mines which lie in the center of the world's largest strip mining area. Visitors to the city enjoy going out to the mines to watch the huge shovels carve the landscape into miniature valleys, canyons, and mountains.

Canton is the site of Spoon River College, opened in 1959.

Nearby recreational facilities can be found at Lake Canton and at the 2,370-acre Rice Lake Conservation Area (*q.v.*).

● HISTORICAL PLACES: (See Hist. Pl. Sect. for Details.)

Orendorff, Ulysses G., House.

● **CAPRON,** Village, Boone County; Pop. 682; Area Code 815; Zip Code 61012; NE Illinois, 19 miles ENE of Rockford in a noted agricultural region (feed grains, livestock). Industries include tile and brick.

● **CARBON CLIFF,** Town, Rock Island County; Pop. 1,492; Area Code 309; Zip Code 61239; Elev. 570; NW Illinois, just E of East Moline in an agricultural area.

● **CARBONDALE,** City, Jackson County; Pop. 27,033; Area Code 618; Zip Code 629%; Elev. 416; SW Illinois; 19 miles WSW of W Frankfort.

Carbondale was founded in 1852 after the arrival of the Illinois Central Railroad, and it was subsequently named for the huge coal fields upon which it is built. The coal fields provide income for much of the area population. The city, which depends both on agriculture and mining, attains a large share of its income from lumbering.

Carbondale is also the seat of Southern Illinois University, a coeducational institution which opened as a normal school in 1874.

Carbondale is situated on the edge of the Illinois Ozarks and is surrounded by the Shawnee National Forest. As a result, the area around the city is very scenic and offers a multitude of picturesque attractions and recreational facilities for tourists who arrive here by the thousands year-round. Just S of town is Giant City State Park (*q.v.*), one of Illinois' largest, with its unusual rock formations and wooded bluffs.

Crab Orchard National Wildlife Refuge (*q.v.*) has camping, fishing, swimming, hiking, and hunting available and is a well known wintering ground for Canadian geese.

Carbondale also has the honor of being the city where in 1868, General John A. Logan, commander-in-chief of the Grand Army of the Republic issued the order making May 30, Memorial Day, a holiday.

POINTS OF INTEREST:

- Bald Knob. 16 miles S on US 51 to Cobden, then 4 miles W to Alto Pass.
- Giant City State Park. 10 miles S on US 51, then E on unnumbered road.
- Shawnee National Forest. S, W and E of town, via I-57, I-24, US 51, IL 13/127, 148.
- Southern Illinois University at Carbondale (1869). S on Illinois Avenue, US 51.

#

● **CARLINVILLE**, City, Macoupin County seat; Pop. 5,416; Area Code 217; Zip Code 62626; Elev. 627; SW central Illinois; 37 miles SSW of Springfield.

Carlinville is especially noted for its courthouse (1870) which is one of the most expensive buildings for that time period ever built in the Midwest. Even today's architects come to study its design. The building is shaped in two rectangles of limestone that cross in the middle and are surmounted by a dome which rises 191 feet above the ground. Forty foot columns support the roof and portico, and the entire interior is finished in a Corinthian style.

Blackburn College, a coeducational school, is also located in the city.

Carlinville is an important agricultural and coal mining center for the county and is a shipping point for corn, wheat, and livestock. Production of natural gas is high and important manufactures include bricks, gloves, and nursery products. The city was incorporated in 1837.

● **CARLYLE**, Town; Clinton County seat; Pop. 3,474; Area Code 618; Zip Code 62231; Elev. 461; S Central Illinois; 35

miles E of St. Louis; Incorporated, 1836; On man- made Lake Carlyle; Named for Thomas Carlyle by English settlers.

Site of John Hill's fort, which in 1812 stood six blocks south of the present courthouse. The town experienced a large miner's boom in the 1880s, but became quiet after the turn of the century. While Lake Carlyle was under construction (1966-68), land speculation along the Kaskaskia River Valley increased, and lots nearby that went for $50-100 in 1961, cost $2,000 in 1966. Many new industries have opened nearby.

Of interest is the General Dean Suspension Bridge, a swinging foot bridge, dedicated to the famous Korean War general who grew up in Carlyle.

North of the city is the 15,680-acre Eldon Hazlett State Park (q.v.) which provides recreational facilities. Lake Carlyle is the main attraction.

POINTS OF INTEREST:

- Carlyle Lake 1 mile NE via IL 127N.
- Eldon Hazlet State Park. N off IL 127.

- HISTORICAL PLACES: (See Hist. Pl. Sect. for Details.)

    General Dean Suspension Bridge.

- **CARLYLE LAKE,** Reservoir; 26,000 acres; Clinton and Fayette Counties; S Central Illinois; Formed by a damming of the Kaskaskia River (1968); Largest artificial lake in state; 4 miles wide by 10 miles long; Large recreation area serves campers, fishermen, and boaters.

- **CARMI,** City, White County seat; Pop. 5,564; Area Code 618; Zip Code 62821; Elev. 399; SE Illinois; 32 miles NE of Harrisburg;

Located on the Little Wabash River, Carmi was settled in 1816 and immediately became the seat of the county. The Robinson- Stewart House (1815), now private, served as the town's first courthouse.

Carmi is located in a transition zone of rolling hills between the level prairies and the southern, rugged Illinois Ozarks. It is in the center of the huge Tri-State oil-producing area, and many of the leading oil companies have their offices located in the city. Most important to the economy, however, is agriculture, and Carmi is a leading shipping center for melons, corn, soybeans, wheat, fruit, and poultry.

Manufactures include men's underwear, waterflood equipment, pistons, millwork, and clothing.

The Lincoln Heritage Trail (*q.v.*) enters Illinois just NE of Carmi. The 460-mile historical trail is dedicated to preserving Abraham Lincoln's memory.

The Radcliff Inn is a museum containing local historical exhibits. Annual events include the White County Fair (August) and the Kiwanis Corn Day (October).

● HISTORICAL PLACES: (See Hist. Pl. Sect. for Details.)

Ratcliff Inn; Robinson-Stewart House.

● **CAROL STREAM,** residential suburb, DuPage County; Pop. 31,716; Area Code 312; Zip Code 60188; NE Illinois; 10 miles W of Chicago in an agricultural area noted for feed grains. Other industries include tubular rivets, clay products, boxes, and laboratory equipment.

● **CARPENTERSVILLE,** Village, Kane County; Pop. 22,049; Area Code 312; Zip Code 60110; Elev. 805; NE Illinois; On the Fox River and 38 miles WNW of Chicago.

Carpentersville was settled in 1834 by Angelo Carpenter of Massachusetts. He established a saw and gristmill, a woolen mill, and a grocery store there and subsequently platted the village in 1851. He became associated with the Illinois Iron and Bolt Company, the village's economic mainstay. Carpentersville is also an agricultural center for feed grains, livestock, and dairy products.

● HISTORICAL PLACES: (See Hist. Pl. Sect. for Details.)

Library Hall.

● **CARRIER MILLS,** Village, Saline County; Pop. 1,991; Area Code 618; Zip Code 62917; Elev. 392; SE Illinois; 6 miles SW of Harrisburg in the picturesque foothills of the Illinois Ozarks (*q.v*).

Carrier Mills was established in 1894 and developed as a noted bituminous coal mining community. The village is also an agricultural trade center (wheat, dairying, livestock) for the area.

● **CARROLL COUNTY,** NW Illinois; Area 456 square miles; Pop. 16,805; Seat Mount Carroll; Hilly Mississippi Valley region bordered to the west by the Mississippi River.

● **CARROLLTON**, City; Greene County seat; Pop. 2,866; Area Code 217; Zip Code 62016; Elev. 625; W Illinois; 30 miles NNW of Alton.

Carrollton was settled in 1818 and incorporated in 1861 and has since become a leading trade center (livestock, grain, poultry, tile and brickwork) for the area. The city is the home of the Lower Illinois Valley Archaeological Museum, containing Indian artifacts, and of the Greene County Historical Society. The latter has pioneer artifacts and was once visited, when it was an inn, by Abraham Lincoln.

● **CARTERVILLE**, City; Williamson County; Pop. 3,630; Area Code 618; Zip Code 62918; S Illinois; 5 miles SW of Herrin.

Carterville was incorporated in 1892 and developed as a leading strip coal mining center for the region. Agriculture is also important (corn, wheat, dairy products, and fruit), and there are several sawmills in the area. Nearby Crab Orchard Lake provides recreational facilities.

●**CARTHAGE**, City; Hancock County seat; Pop. 2,657; Area Code 217; Zip Code 62321; Elev. 676; W Illinois; 14 miles E of Keokuk, Iowa.

Carthage was laid out in 1833 and subsequently became an anti-Mormon stronghold. Joseph Smith, founder of the religion, and his brother, were captured, and jailed there for treason. Shortly thereafter, both he and his brother Hyrum were killed by an angry mob as they tried to escape from the jail. The old Carthage Jail was later acquired by the Mormon Church which now regards it as a shrine to Smith. After the Mormons left Illinois, Carthage resumed its normal pace and settled down to become a peaceful farming community which is now a trade center for livestock, soybeans, wheat, and poultry.

Carthage College (1870) was established there as the first Lutheran college in the Midwest.

● HISTORICAL PLACES: (See Hist. Pl. Sect. for Details.)

Carthage Jail.

●**CARY**, Village; McHenry County; Pop. 10,043; Area Code 815; Zip Code 60013; Elev. 811; NE Illinois; 12 miles N of Elgin.

Located near the Fox River, Cary is in the center of a noted dairying and resort area; Site of an annual ski-jumping meet.

● **CASEY**, City; Clark County; Pop. 3,026; Area Code 217; Zip Code 62420; Elev. 648; E Illinois; 24 miles ESE of Mattoon.

Casey was incorporated in 1896 and was a quiet farming community until the early 1900s when oil and natural gas was discovered underneath the area. There followed a tremendous oil boom and Casey flourished with it. Much of the population got rich, and grand old houses, still in existence, bespeak of this prosperous era.

Much of Casey's income at the present time is still generated from gas and oil production, but the supply has diminished considerably, and other businesses have developed to supplement the economy.

Casey is a trade center for agricultural products such as grain and livestock, and is a producer of limestone.

● **CASS COUNTY**, W Central Illinois; Area 371 square miles; Pop. 13,437; Seat Virginia. Bordered to the west by the Illinois River and to the north by the Sangamon River. This is one of the oldest settled regions in Illinois. Named for General Lewis Cass, Secretary of War under President Jackson and Secretary of State under President Buchanan.

● **CATLIN**, Village, Vermilion County; Pop. 2,173; Area Code 217; Zip Code 61817; E Illinois; 6 miles SW of Danville.

Catlin is located in a noted bituminous coal mining area and is an agricultural trade center for corn, wheat, soybeans, poultry, and livestock.

● **CAVE-IN-ROCK,** Village, Hardin County; Pop. 381; Area Code 618; Zip Code 62919; Elev. 340; SE Illinois; On the Ohio River and 26 miles SE of Harrisburg.

Cave-in-Rock is located in the scenic hill country of the Illinois Ozarks (*q.v.*) and is named for the nearby natural cavern located midway between the summit of the river bluff and the waterline.

The cave was long a landmark for Ohio River boatmen and can be seen from the ferry which crosses the river at Cave-in-Rock. The 64-acre state park by the same name encompasses the cave and has excellent camping, picnicking, and boating facilities. Cave- in-Rock, although basically a farming community, enjoys a brisk tourist trade from the visitors who annually come to the park. The village is especially noted for its restaurants which serve Ohio fiddler catfish, a local delicacy.

● **CEDARVILLE,** Village, Stephenson County; Pop. 751; Area Code 815; Zip Code 61013; Elev. 781; N Illinois, 5 miles N of Freeport.

Cedarville is a quiet farming community whose main claim to fame is being the birthplace of Jane Addams, founder of Chicago's famous social center, Hull House (1889). The birthplace is a Greek revival style, two-story brick building nestled among trees on a 450-acre estate. Two picturesque limestone caves are located on the property.

● **CENTRAL CITY,** Village, Marion County; Pop. 1,390; Area Code 618; Elev. 498; S Illinois; On the Crooked River; N Suburb of Centralia.

Central City depends on agriculture and coal mining, and in addition has several large nurseries. Central City was settled by German immigrants and was incorporated as a village in 1857.

● **CENTRALIA,** City, Marion-Clinton County line; Pop. 14,274; Area Code 618; Zip Code 62801; Elev, 495; S Illinois; 55 miles E of East St. Louis.

Centralia was founded in 1853 by members of the Illinois Central Railroad System, after which it is also named. Like Center City to the north, Centralia was settled by German immigrants who put a substantial amount of their own monies into developing the city. Their influence can still be seen today in the many German businesses, schools, and churches scattered throughout Centralia.

Incorporation to city status came in 1859, just four years after the railroad shops for the Illinois Central were established there. It was in these shops that the first locomotive to burn Illinois coal was successfully converted from a wood-burning engine. The coal, in fact, was extracted from local underground mines which still are large producers. The city boomed in the 1930s with the discovery of oil and natural gas in the area. Oil production surpassed coal mining, although the latter continues to be important.

Centralia is still very much the railroad town, and the railroad shops continue to be the main industry. But the economy is boosted by coal mining, oil and natural gas production, agriculture (fruit, corn, wheat, livestock, poultry, dairy products) and a considerable amount of light manufacturing. Centralia has several tool and die companies, publishing firms, a meat packing plant, and a cannery and is also a manufacturer of automobile parts, paperboard, clothing, and fiberglass products.

One of the nation's worst coal mining disasters occurred in Centralia on March 25, 1947. An explosion, caused by entrapped dust in Centralia Mine #5, killed 111 men. The company was cited for negligence and fined a mere $1,000.

Kaskaskia Junior College opened its doors in 1965 and remains the only institution of higher learning in the city.

Of note is Fairview Park, in town, which has a picnic ground, swimming pool, and the "Old Steam Locomotive 2500" which offers tours to visitors.

POINTS OF INTEREST:

- Centralia Carillon. North Elm and Noleman.
- Fairview Park. W on IL 161, at W Broadway & 4th St.
- Fishing, boating, camping. Raccoon Lake. 3 miles E on IL 161, then 1/2 mile N on Moon Glow Road.
- Lake Centralia. 8 miles NE on Green Street Road.

●**CENTRAL PARK,** Village, Vermilion County; Pop. 2,676; Area Code 217; E Illinois, 2 miles S of Danville in an agricultural and bituminous coal mining area.

●**CENTREVILLE,** City, St. Clair County; Pop. 7,489; Area Code 618; SW Illinois; 4 miles SE of St. Louis; Missouri in an agricultural and industrial area.

●**CERRO GORDO,** Village, Piatt County; Pop. 1,436; Area Code 217; Zip Code 61818; Central Illinois; 12 miles ENE of Decatur.

The village was incorporated in 1873 and is a shipping center for grain.

● **CHADWICK,** Village, Carroll County; Pop. 605; Area Code 557; Zip Code 61014; NW Illinois; 24 miles SW of Freeport.

Chadwick developed as a farming community and has a feed mill. There is some light manufacturing and products include picnic table frames and steel outdoor fireplaces.

●**CHAMPAIGN,** City, Champaign County; Pop. 63,502; Area Code 217; Zip Code 618%; Elev. 740; E Illinois; Adjoining its sister city Urbana.

Champaign was settled in 1854, and for a time it was known as West Urbana when the Illinois Railroad ran its tracks two miles west of the present city of Urbana. The town was re- incorporated as Champaign in 1860 and flourished as a trade center.

The city shares the University of Illinois (1868) with Urbana (*q.v.*), but the latter is usually regarded as the main site. Whereas Champaign is an industrial center, Urbana remains basically residential. Champaign, in addition, is a leading agricultural trade center for soybeans, corn, wheat, livestock, and poultry. Farm products are shipped from the city to all parts of the state. Over the years, Champaign has become increasingly industrial and manufactures a diversity of products including transmitters, refrigeration equipment, mattresses, furniture, foods, electronics equipment, radiators, and canvas products. An oil refinery is also located there.

Nearby recreational facilities can be found at Lake of the Woods Forest Preserve. The preserve has a small lake which offers boating, swimming, and fishing. The site also has a 100-foot observation tower, a carillon, and a covered bridge.

POINTS OF INTEREST:

● Champaign County Historical Museum. 709 W University Avenue. Located in the Victorian Wilber Mansion (1907).

● Lake of the Woods County Park. 10 miles W on I- 74, then 1/4 miles N on IL 47.

● University of Illinois (1867). Wright Street.

● **CHAMPAIGN COUNTY,** E Central Illinois; Area 1,000 square miles; Pop. 173,025; Seat Urbana; Established 1833. Tributaries of the Sangamon and Wabash Rivers flow through the region, as does the Kaskaskia River. It is the site of the

University of Illinois and Chanute Air Force Base, and is a prairie and agricultural area.

● **CHANDLERVILLE,** Village, Cass County; Pop. 689; Area Code 217; Zip Code 62627; Elev. 464; Central Illinois; 30 miles NW of Springfield near the Sangamon River.

Chandlerville was named after, and settled by, Dr. Charles Chandler who hired young Abraham Lincoln to survey his land. The village is a farming community in a region noted for feed grains and livestock.

● **CHANNAHON,** Village, Will County; Pop. 4,266; Area Code 815; Zip Code 60410 ; Elev. 530; NE Illinois; 14 miles SW of Joliet in an agricultural area noted for corn and livestock.

The name Channahon is derived from the Indian words meaning "meeting of the waters," since the village is located where the Du Page River joins the Des Plaines River. It grew quickly after its birth in 1832, due to the building of the Illinois and Michigan Canal. The canal carried corn to Chicago on canal boats drawn by mules along the towpath. The village once boasted six grain elevators and was a noted limestone quarrying center. With the decline of the canal came the decline of Channahon, now a quiet farming community. Many of the residents work and commute to either nearby Joliet or Chicago. Remains of the locks and canal are preserved in the Channahon Parkway, a scenic little park just on the western edge of the village. The towpath on either side of the canal is still visible, and the park is a favorite with local fishermen and picnickers.

Left from Channahon, on its northern border, are the Briscoe Mounds, two unexcavated Indian earthworks measuring respectively 90 and 45 feet in diameter.

● **CHAPIN,** Village, Morgan County; Pop. 632; Area Code 217; Zip Code 62628; W Central Illinois; 10 miles WNW of Jacksonville.

Chapin is a farming community (feed grains, livestock) and has light manufacturing. The village has a meat processing plant and two plants which rebuild diesel cylinder heads.

● **CHARLESTON,** City; Coles County seat; Pop. 20,398; Area Code 217; Zip Code 61920; Elev. 686; E central Illinois; 47 miles ESE of Decatur.

Charleston was settled in 1826 by Benjamin Parker. The area was platted in 1831, organized as a village in 1835, and incorporated in 1865. Originally called Coles Courthouse, it was changed in 1843 to Charleston in honor of Charles Morton, its first postmaster. Charleston has been the county seat since 1831, but remained a quiet farming community until 1858 when it became the focus for the fourth debate between presidential candidates Abraham Lincoln and Stephen A. Douglas. Twelve thousand persons came to hear the speeches and parades, and celebrations were the order of the day.

In the Charleston debate, Lincoln was accused by Douglas of advocating interracial marriages. Lincoln admirably defended his position on equality for blacks, the Mexican War, and several other issues. The site of this debate is located at the Coles County Fairgrounds on the western edge of town. For several years, Lincoln had practiced law in the area, and his father and stepmother lived in a cabin 8 miles south of town. They are both buried in Shiloh Cemetery, one of the stops on the historic Lincoln Heritage Trail (q.v.). The original sandstone grave marker has been destroyed, chipped away piece by piece by greedy souvenir hunters.

Charleston is located in a fertile agricultural area noted for livestock raising and dairying. The city, although mainly residential, is an important trade center for ceramic fittings, urethane insulation, "six pack" holders, concrete tile, iron castings, wood products, modular homes, burial vaults, truck-trailers, and vocational equipment. It is the seat of Eastern Illinois University (1899) founded originally as Eastern Illinois State Normal School. The university is well-known for its Center for Lincoln Studies.

The tourist trade is rather brisk in Charleston due to its historical importance as one of Lincoln's stopovers places. The city and area surrounding it are filled with landmarks and Lincoln memorabilia. Of particular interest is the Lincoln Log Cabin State Park (q.v.), site of the reconstructed log cabin built by Lincoln's father, Thomas, in 1837. The cabin is built upon the original foundation and contains the pioneer furnishings. The Moore Home State Memorial (q.v.) is the house where Lincoln ate his last meal with his stepmother and her daughter before leaving for his inauguration.

Recreational facilities can be found at nearby Fox Ridge State Park (*q.v.*) with its rugged scenery, and at Lake Charleston, site of the Lincoln Reservoir project.

POINTS OF INTEREST:

- Coles County Courthouse (1898). Charleston Square.
- Eastern Illinois University (1895).
- Fox Ridge State Park. 10 miles S on IL 130.
- Lincoln Log Cabin State Historic Site. 1 mile S of Moore Home.
- Moore Home State Historic Site. 9 miles S on unnumbered road.

● **CHATHAM,** Village, Sangamon County; Pop. 6,074; Area Code 217; Zip Code 62629; Central Illinois; 9 miles SSW of Springfield in an agricultural and bituminous coal mining area. Industries include refrigeration equipment, mufflers, and oil control systems.

● **CHATSWORTH,** Town, Livingston County; Pop. 1,186; Area Code 815; Zip Code 60921; Elev. 736; E central Illinois; 40 miles NE of Bloomington.

Platted in 1858, Chatsworth grew with the coming of the Toledo, Peoria & Western Railroad. It was incorporated in 1867 and is an agricultural trade center, has light manufacturing (truck caps, drain tiles, windows, rolling door hardware), and makes brick and tile from clay taken from local quarries.

● **CHEBANSE,** Village, Iroquois-Kankakee County line; Pop. 1,082; Area Code 815; Zip Code 60922; Elev. 667; E Illinois; 8 miles SSW of Kankakee.

The village, whose name is derived from the Indian words meaning "little duck," is a German farming community and shipping center for grain. The area around Chebanse is noted for corn and livestock. The village also manufactures concrete burial vaults.

● **CHENOA,** City, McLean County; Pop. 2,500; Area Code 815; Zip Code 61726; Elev. 722; Central Illinois; 23 miles NE of Bloomington.

Chenoa was platted in 1856 by Matthew T. Scott and developed around the junction of the Peoria & Oquawka and Chicago & Mississippi railroads. The city flourished despite two great fires which entirely destroyed all the false front buildings in the central business district. Agriculturally, Chenoa's products include corn, beans, wheat, oats, and seeds. Its manufactures are limestone quarrying, traffic signs, fertilizer, cabinetry, and drilling equipment.

● **CHERRY,** Village, Bureau County; Pop. 487; Area Code 815; Zip Code 61317; Elev. 682; N Illinois, 7 miles N of Spring Valley.

Cherry, a bituminous coal mining community, was the scene, in 1909, of a mine disaster which killed 270 men. It was caused by a mine fire, and the resultant smoke and gas overwhelmed the miners, with only 20 surviving. A stone marker bearing the inscription "Memorial to the Victims of the Cherry Mine Disaster" stands in the village cemetery.

● **CHERRY VALLEY,** Village, Winnebago County; Pop. 1,500; Area Code 815; Zip Code 61016; N Illinois; Originally called Grigg's Ford, and Butler, the village was incorporated in 1896. On the Kishwaukee River and 7 miles ESE of Rockford, the area was an agricultural one for years, and is now a residential and business community. There is still a small amount of agriculture, with such products as livestock, corn, and soybeans. Manufacturing includes the production of trusses, steel products, machine shop equipment, cabinetry, and industrial heat treating furnaces.

● **CHESTER,** City; Randolph County seat; Pop. 8,194; Area Code 618; Zip Code 62233; Elev. 381; SW Illinois; 50 miles SSE of East St. Louis.

Located on the Mississippi River near the mouth of the Kaskaskia River, Chester was founded in 1819 by an Ohio land company which hoped to establish a commercial center which rivaled the then dominant town of Kaskaskia. Chester developed as a river trade community, was incorporated in 1855, and became the county seat. There are several grain elevators and flour mills in the city, and it is a shipping center of the surrounding agricultural area for soybeans, livestock, food products, wheat, and corn. Chester has diversified manufacturing which includes the production of clothing, aluminum and brass castings, aluminum doors, porch enclosures, and leather goods, Nearby quarries and mines yield coal, stone, sand, and gravel.

Chester, picturesquely situated on the river, has several historic landmarks in its environs and is a favorite tourist center. Fort Kaskaskia, 10 miles N of the city, is the site of a French fort built in 1736 which played an important role in Illinois' history. At the foot of the hill where the fort stood, is the Pierre Menard Home (1802), a lavish mansion which was the former residence of the first lieutenant governor of the state (1818). The house has often been referred to as the "Mt. Vernon of the West."

Chester is also the site of the Menard Branch of the Illinois State Penitentiary (1877) and the Illinois Security Hospital (1889).

● HISTORICAL PLACES: (See Hist. Pl. Sect. for Details.)

Mary's River Covered.

● **CHICAGO:** See article — page 131.

POINTS OF INTEREST:

● Adler Planetarium. 1300 S Lake Shore Dr, on a peninsula in Lake Michigan.

● Auditorium Building (1889). 430 S Michigan Ave.

● Balzekas Museum of Lithuanian Culture. 6500 S Pulaski Rd.

● Batcolumn (1976). Outside the Social Security Administration Great Lakes Program Service Center, 600 W Madison.

● Bertoia Sculpture (1975). Standard Oil Plaza, 200 E Randolph.

● Calder Stabile. Federal Center Plaza, Adams & Dearborn Sts.

● Carson Pirie Scott & Co. State & Madison Sts.

● Chagall Mosaic. First National Plaza, Monroe & Dearborn Sts.

● Chicago Academy of Sciences (1857). 2001 N Clark St in Lincoln Park.

● Chicago Board of Trade (1929). 141 W Jackson Blvd at La Salle St.

● Chicago Fire Academy. 558 W DeKoven St.

● Chicago Historical Society. Clark St at North Ave.

● Chicago Mercantile Exchange (1983). 30 S Wacker Dr.

● Chicago Public Library Cultural Center. 78 E Washington St at Michigan Ave.

● Chicago Temple (First United Methodist Church of Chicago, 1831). 77 W Washington St.

● Chicago Tribune Tower (1925). 435 N Michigan Ave.

● Chinatown. Wentworth St & Cermak Rd.

● Civic Opera Building (1929). 20 N Wacker Dr.

● Civic Theatre. Civic Opera Building, 20 N Wacker Dr.

● DePaul University (1898). (13,000 students) Lincoln Park campus, Fullerton & Halsted St; Loop campus, 25 E

Dictionary of Places

Jackson Blvd.

● Du Sable Museum of African-American History. 740 E 56th Pl.

● Field Museum of Natural History. Roosevelt Rd at Lake Shore Dr.

● Fourth Presbyterian Church. Michigan Ave at Delaware Pl.

● Garfield Park and Conservatory. 300 N Central Park Blvd.

● Grant Park. Stretching from Randolph St to McFetridge Dr.

● Greek town. W of the Loop, Halsted St from Madison St S to Van Buren.

● Holy Name Cathedral (Roman Catholic). 735 N State St.

● Illinois Institute of Technology (1892). (6,000 students) 3300 S Federal St.

● International Museum of Surgical Sciences. 1524 N Lake Shore Dr.

● Jane Addams' Hull House. 800 S Halsted on campus of University of Illinois at Chicago.

● John G. Shedd Aquarium. 1200 S Lake Shore Dr. At Roosevelt Rd.

● John Hancock Center (1969). 875 N Michigan Ave.

● Lincoln Park. Largest in Chicago, stretches almost the entire length of the north end of the city along the lake.

● Loyola University (1870). (14,252 students) 6525 N Sheridan Rd.

● Marina City (1963). 300 N State St, N side of Chicago River.

● Marshall Field's. 111 N State St.

● McCormick Place-On-The-Lake. E 23d St & S Lake Shore Dr.

● Merchandise Mart (1930). Wells St at Chicago River.

● Michigan Avenue. From Chicago River to Oak St (1000 north).

● Miro Sculpture. Daley Plaza across from the Picasso.

● Monadnock Building. 53 W Jackson Blvd.

● Moody Church. 1630 N Clark St.

● Morton B. Weiss Museum of Judaica. 1100 E Hyde Park Blvd.

● Mundelein College (1929). (1,500 students) 6363 N Sheridan Rd.

● Museum of Contemporary Art. 237 E Ontario St.

● Museum of Holography. 1134 W Washington Blvd.

- Museum of Science and Industry. 57th St & Lake Shore Dr.
- Navy Pier. At E end of Grand Ave.
- New Town. From 2800 to 3400 N on Broadway.
- Northwestern University Chicago Campus (1920). (5,984 students) Lake Shore Dr & Chicago Ave.
- O'Hare International Exposition Center. 5555 N River Rd.
- Old Town. From 1400 to 1700 N on Wells St.
- Orchestra Hall. 220 S Michigan Ave.
- Oriental Institute Museum. 1155 E 58th St, on University of Chicago Campus.
- Our Lady of Sorrows Basilica (1890-1902). 3121 W Jackson Blvd.
- Peace Museum. 430 W Erie St.
- Picasso Sculpture. Richard J. Daley Plaza, Washington & Dearborn Sts.
- Polish Museum of America. 984 N Milwaukee Ave.
- Prairie Ave Historic District. Prairie Ave between 18th & Cullerton Sts.
- Richard J. Daley Center and Plaza. Randolph & Clark Sts.
- Robie House. 5757 S Woodlawn Ave.
- Rockefeller Memorial Chapel. 5850 S Woodlawn Ave, on University of Chicago campus.
- Roosevelt University (1945). (6,000 students) Entrance at 430 S Michigan Ave.
- Rush Street. From Chicago Ave N to Division St.
- Sears Tower (1924). 233 S Wacker Dr.
- Shubert. 22 W Monroe St.
- Soldier Field Stadium. Lake Shore Dr & E McFetridge Dr.
- Spertus Museum of Judaica. 618 S Michigan Ave.
- State Street Mall "That Great Street,", from Congress Pkwy to Wacker Dr.
- Sun-Times Building. 401 N Wabash Ave.
- Telephone Museum. 225 W. Randolph St.
- Terra Museum of American Art. 666 N Michigan Ave.
- The Art Institute of Chicago. (1879). Michigan Ave & Adams St. In Grant Park.
- The "Gold Coast." Lake Shore Dr from Chicago Ave to North Ave.
- The Newberry Library (1887). 60 W Walton St.
- The Rookery (1886). 209 S La Salle St.
- United States Post Office (1933). 433 W Van Buren St.
- University of Chicago (1892). (7,800 students) 5801 S

Ellis Ave.

• University of Illinois at Chicago (1965). (25,000 students) Near I-94 & I-290.

• Water Tower (1869). Chicago & Michigan Aves.

• Water Tower Place (1976). 835 N Michigan Ave. Atrium Mall.

• Wicker Park. Bounded by Augusta Blvd & Armitate, Western and Ashland Ave.

• Wrigley Building. 400 N Michigan Ave.

• HISTORICAL PLACES: (See Hist. Pl. Sect. for Details.)

Alta Vista Terrace Historic District; Auditorium Building, Roosevelt University; Carson, Pirie, Scott and Company; Charnley, James, House; Chicago Public Library, Central Building; Clarke, Henry B., House; Delaware Building (Bryant Block); Dewes, Francis J., House; First Self-Sustaining Nuclear Reaction, Site of; Getty Tomb; Glessner, John J., House; Halsted, Ann, House; Heller, Isadore H., House; Hitchcock, Charles, Hall; Hull House; Jackson Park Historic Landscape District and Midway Plaisance (Site of the World's Columbian Exposition of 1893); Jewelers' Building; Kekilath Anshe Ma'ariv Synagogue (Pilgrim Baptist Church); Lathrop, Bryan, House; Madlener, Albert F., House; Marquette Building; McClurg Building (Ayer Building); Monadnock Block; Old Stone Gate of Chicago Union Stockyards; Prairie Avenue District (Fort Dearborn Massacre Site); Pullman Historic District; Reliance Building; Robie, Frederick C., House; Rookery Building; Room 405, George Herbert Jones Laboratory, University of Chicago; Second Presbyterian Church; Shedd Park Fieldhouse; Taft, Lorado, Midway Studios; Tree Studio Building and Annexes; U.S.S. Silversides; Wells-Barnett, Ida B., House.

• **CHICAGO HEIGHTS,** Industrial city, Cook County; Pop. 33,072; Area Code 312; Zip Code 60411; Elev. 694; NE Illinois; 25 miles S of Chicago.

The city was settled at the junction of the historic Sauk and Old Vincennes trails in the 1830s and has been known respectively as Thorn Grove, Bloom, and Chicago Heights (1892). It developed independently of Chicago's influence and became the area's first steel-producing city. Factories were established there, encouraged by the Chicago Heights Land Association, and today the city is a diversified industrial and manufacturing community, whose products include automobile body stampings, chemicals, textiles, soap, furniture, asphalt, linseed, castings, heating and air-conditioning equipment, foods, paints and varnishes, lumber, office equipment, candles and railroad cars.

In town is the Svoboda Nickelodeon Museum, which houses one of the world's largest collections of music boxes. Prairie State College was established in Chicago Heights in 1958.

● **CHICAGO RIDGE,** Village, Cook County; Pop. 13,643; Area Code 312; Zip Code 60415; NE Illinois; SW of Chicago in an agricultural area. Manufacturing center for formica sink tops, structural steel, wood products, grave statuary, railroad cars, conveyors, and asphalt.

● **CHILLICOTHE,** City, Peoria County; Pop. 5,959; Area Code 309; Zip Code 61523; Elev. 490; Central Illinois; 15 miles NNE of Peoria.

Chillicothe developed along the N end of Lake Peoria and along the Illinois River. It became incorporated in 1861. The city has some light manufacturing (diesel engine products, concrete blocks, road construction equipment, yeast, and water wagons) and is located in a noted bituminous coal mining area. Local quarries yield an abundance of sand and gravel.

● **CHRISMAN,** City, Edgar County; Pop. 1,136; Area Code 217; Zip Code 61924; Elev. 645; E Illinois; 22 miles S of Danville,

Chrisman was platted in 1872 by Matthias Chrisman and flourished as an agricultural center. At the present time, farming is still the economic base, and the city is a shipping point for corn, soybeans, wheat, poultry, and livestock.

● **CHRISTIAN COUNTY,** Central Illinois; Area 709 square miles; Pop. 34,418; Seat Taylorville; Bordered to north by Sangamon River; Agricultural.

● **CHRISTOPHER,** City, Franklin County; Pop. 2,774; Area Code 618; Zip Code 62822; S Illinois; 11 miles N of Herrin.

Christopher, which was incorporated in 1910, developed as an important coal mining center for the area. It also has some manufacturing, including the production of cisterns, septic tanks, metal stampings, and tools.

● **CICERO,** Town, Cook County; Pop. 67,436; Area Code 312; Zip Code 60650; Elev. 610; NE Illinois; E of Chicago.

Cicero was founded in 1857 on a swampy lowland. It grew slowly until the Civil War when the rich bottomlands around the settlement were perceived to be agriculturally productive. The community developed steadily as settlers from the East poured into the area. Incorporation came in 1867 as agriculture and the closeness to Chicago spurred industrial growth. Fifty miles of swamplands were drained and put into crops and Cicero eventually became economically independent of its great neighbor.

One of Cicero's biggest industrial concerns is the Western Electric Company, established in 1902, and which employs 14,000 people. It is a manufacturer of telephone switching equipment.

Other major industries manufacture iron castings, pumps, engines, chemicals concrete products, foods, truck cabs, screw machine products, water treatment equipment, dental instruments, and refrigeration equipment.

The city gained notoriety in Prohibition days (until 1931), as being the headquarters of gangland leader Al Capone. He stayed in a hotel near the Western Electric Company, and from there, organized a chain of speak-easies, honky-tonks, and gambling casinos. At his height of power, Capone was attended by over 200 henchmen. He was finally indicted in Chicago in 1931. Cicero, its reputation hurt by Capone's presence, immediately made plans to eradicate any evidence of his activities. In the process, the local government, infiltrated by mobsters, was purged and Cicero was on its way to a fresh start.

POINTS OF INTEREST:

- Hawthorne Race Course. 3501 S Laramie Avenue.
- Sportsman's Park Race Track. 3301 S Laramie Avenue.

●CISCO, Piatt County; Pop. 282; Area Code 217; Zip Code 61838; Central Illinois; 16 miles NE of Decatur in an area noted for livestock and feed grains.

●CISNE, Village, Wayne County; Pop. 645; Area Code 618; Zip Code 62823; SE Illinois; 28 miles ENE of Mount Vernon in an agricultural, natural gas, and oil producing area.

●CISSNA PARK, Village, Iroquois County; Pop. 805; Area Code 815; Zip Code 60924; Elev. 684; E Illinois; 37 miles S of Kankakee.

Cissna Park is located in an area which has a large Amish population. Most of the village's inhabitants are

217

members of the Apostolic Church which was founded in Switzerland. The religion forbids ornamentation, the bearing of arms, and participation in government. The members keep to themselves, lead a spartan life dressed in simple dark clothing, and live in bare frame houses devoid of decoration. Their chief occupation is farming, and such is the economy of Cissna Park which has several grain mills and a meat-processing and slaughtering plant. The only manufacturer is the Cissna Park Tile Company which makes concrete drain tiles and feed bunkers.

● **CLARENDON HILLS,** Village, DuPage County; Pop. 6,994; Area Code 312; Zip Code 60514; NE Illinois; W of Chicago.

Incorporated in 1924, the town grew to become one of the 25 most affluent suburbs of Chicago, based on median family income. Although largely a residential commuter development, Clarendon Hills has a number of small manufacturers. Products include microfilm storage cases, wire goods, fiberglass, concrete mixing equipment, and plastic molds.

●**CLARK COUNTY,** E Illinois; Area 505; Pop, 15,921; Seat Marshall; bordered to west by Wabash River and Indiana State Line; Established 1835, with Clark Center as seat, but seat was changed in 1837.

●**CLAY CITY,** Village, Clay County; Pop. 929; Area Code 618; Zip Code 62824; Elev. 429; S Central Illinois; 14 miles W of Olney.

Settled in the early 1830s, Clay City developed with the building of the Ohio and Mississippi Railroad. It flourished as a trade and shipping center for the surrounding agricultural area whose soils yielded an abundance of fruit (apples, peaches, pears), feed grains, and wheat. In 1937, oil was found just SE of the village and the boom which followed joined the ranks of the others from several fields discovered all over southern Illinois. Ten leading oil companies and many independents eventually bought up 2,000,000 acres of oil producing land in the southern half of the state.

Oil and natural gas production is still important, as is agriculture and light manufacturing, including the production of water filters, pumps, garden tools, lumber and oil tanks.

● **CLAY COUNTY,** SE Central Illinois; Area 464 square miles; Pop. 14,460; Seat Louisville. Little Wabash River flows diagonally across land rich in fruit orchards. The area was once drilled for its oil fields.

● **CLAYTON,** Village, Adams County; Pop. 726; Area Code 217; Zip Code 62324; W Illinois; 25 miles ENE of Quincy in an agricultural area noted for livestock, poultry, corn, wheat, and soybeans.

● **CLIFTON,** Village, Iroquois County; Pop. 1,347; Area Code 815; Zip Code 60927; E Illinois; 12 miles SSW of Kankakee in an agricultural area noted for corn and livestock.

● **CLINTON,** City; DeWitt County Seat; Pop. 7,437; Area Code 217; Zip Code 61727; Elev. 746; Central Illinois; 19 miles N of Decatur.

Settled in 1836, Clinton flourished as an agricultural community (corn, wheat, oats, livestock) and later became a rail and manufacturing center for the county. Products include clothing, medicines, fertilizer, cooking utensils, copper tubing, and store fixtures.

Clinton is of interest historically as being one of the cities in which Abraham Lincoln practiced law. On the courthouse lawn is a life-size Lincoln statue. The Barnett Hotel on Grant Street was a favorite stopping place for the former President.

Nearby is Weldon Springs State Park (*q.v.*), a 370-acre facility with a lake, campground, and picnic area.

● **CLINTON COUNTY,** SW Central Illinois; Area 499 square miles; Pop. 33,944; Seat Carlysle. Site of Carlysle Reservoir, a widened point in the Kaskaskia River. It is a mining and agricultural region.

● **COAL CITY,** City, Grundy County; Pop. 3,907; Area Code 815; Zip Code 60416; Elev. 562; NE Illinois; 21 miles SSW of Joliet.

Coal City was founded in 1875 as a site for bituminous coal mining. The original mines were shaft mines, but they proved to be too expensive to operate. Strip mining was consequently introduced and the huge serpentine mounds of tailings dug up by giant shovels surround the city today. Coal mining is still important but Coal City has developed into an important manufacturing center for clothing, clay products, wallpaper, chemicals, concrete, and wire rope.

● **COALTON,** Village, Montgomery County; Pop. 359; Area Code 217; S central Illinois; 20 miles ENE of Litchfield in an agricultural and coal mining area.

● **COAL VALLEY,** Village, Rock Island County; Pop. 2,683; Area Code 309; Zip Code 61240; NW Illinois; 7 miles SE of Rock Island in an agricultural area. Coal Valley has light manufacturing including the production of septic tanks, lumber goods, and meat products.

● **COBDEN,** Village, Union County; Pop. 1,090; Area Code 618; Zip Code 62920; Elev. 594; S Illinois; 36 miles N of Cairo.

Cobden is an agricultural community which was incorporated in 1875. It became an important fruit shipping center on the Illinois Central Railroad. Located in the Illinois Ozarks (*q.v.*), the soils of the village and surrounding area are highly productive of fruit, truck crops, wheat, and corn. Cobden is also a manufacturing center for mobile homes.

The Cobden Museum has an interesting display of Indian artifacts and pioneer tools.

● **COLCHESTER,** City, McDonough County; Pop. 1,645; Area Code 309; Zip Code 62326; W Illinois; 6 miles WSW of Macomb.

Colchester, which was incorporated in 1867, flourished as a farming and coal mining community. There are several clay pits in the area, and the clay quarried from them is used to make brick and tile. The city is a shipping center for corn, wheat, hay, livestock, and poultry. There is also some light manufacturing including the production of electronics equipment, security systems, boats, agricultural implements, and concrete.

● **COLES COUNTY,** E Central Illinois; Area 506 square miles; Pop. 51,644; Seat Charleston; Little Wabash, Kaskaskia, and Embarras Rivers flow through agricultural region. This is the site where Thomas Lincoln, father of Abraham, lived after 1831. Lincoln practiced law in the old County Courthouse, built in 1832.

●**COLFAX,** Village, McLean County; Pop. 854; Area Code 309; Zip Code 67728; Central Illinois; 20 miles ENE of Bloomington.

Colfax, which is located on the Mackinaw River, is mainly a farming community and cheese is one of its major products. Tornado shelters are also built here and the village is one of the main producers of farm equipment and farm feeds for the surrounding area.

●**COLUMBIA,** City, Monroe County; Pop. 5,524; Area Code 618; Zip Code 62236; Elev. 490; SW Illinois; 12 miles S of East Saint Louis.

Columbia was founded in the 1840s by German immigrants who quarried the beautiful Keokuk limestone found in the area. Columbia was incorporated as a village in 1859 and as a city in 1933. It has since flourished as an agricultural (corn, wheat, livestock) and trade center for the area. Limestone is still quarried and is used in the making of metallurgical, glass, and flux stone.

● HISTORICAL PLACES: (See Hist. Pl. Sect. for Details.)

Lunsford-Pulcher Archeological Site.

● **COMPTON,** Village, Lee County; Pop. 343; Area Code 815; Zip Code 61318; N Illinois; 24 miles N of LaSalle in a rich agricultural area noted for corn and livestock. Main industrial plant produces grain augers, elevators, and bale movers.

● **COOK COUNTY,** NE Illinois; Area 954; Pop. 5,105,067; Seat Chicago, Established 1830; Major population center of the state. It is cut through by the Illinois and Des Plaines rivers, and its eastern border is formed by Lake Michigan as well as the Indiana state line. Its organization is based on a township and county system, with 10 commissioners from Chicago and five from outlying townships serving on the county board.

Area first discovered by whites in 1696 when Friar Pinet, a French missionary established the Mission of the Guardian Angel. In 1803, Captain John Whistler, an American, built a fort on site of Chicago, and a fur trading post was established. After Chicago was incorporated in 1833, the population began to explode, with a wave of 20,000 newcomers in the first year.

Much of the county revolves around the city. Most towns are residential suburbs. A large industrial area produces steel, chemicals, diesel engines, electrical and agricultural machinery, and plastics.

(See "Chicago" chapter.)

● **CORDOVA**, Village, Rock Island County.; Pop. 638; Area Code 309; Zip Code 61242; NW Illinois; 17 miles NE of Moline.

Cordova is mainly a farming community located on the Mississippi River. Rich bottomlands produce feed grains and seeds. The village is also a manufacturer of chemicals, butter, and wood products. Limestone is taken out of local quarries.

● **CORNELL**, Village, Livingston County; Pop. 556; Area Code 815; Zip Code 61319; Central Illinois; 9 miles NNW of Pontiac.

The area around Cornell has rich agricultural lands which yield feed grains and is also an important producer of bituminous coal. The village has one grain mill.

● **CORTLAND,** Town, DeKalb County; Pop. 963; Area Code 815; Zip Code 60112; N Illinois; 22 miles NW of Aurora in an agricultural region noted for corn and livestock. Manufactures include canvas products, steel forgings, machine tools, and lumber.

● **COTTAGE HILLS,** Village, Madison County; Pop. 1,261; Area Code 618; Zip Code 62018; SW Illinois; E of Alton.

Cottage Hills is part of the Alton-Wood River Metroplex, a conglomeration of progressive communities whose economies are based on agriculture and industry. The superb soils of the Mississippi Valley yield corn, soybeans, wheat, apples, and peaches, and livestock and poultry raising is a major pastime. Cottage Hills' two major industries include tool and die work and aluminum ingot remelting.

● **COULTERVILLE,** Village, Randolph County; Pop. 984; Area Code 618; Zip Code 62237; SW Illinois; 40 miles SE of East St. Louis in a rich agricultural area noted for corn, wheat, dairying, and livestock. The village has a lumber mill and produces wood products and raw lumber.

● **COUNTRY CLUB HILLS,** Village, Cook County; Pop. 15,431; Area Code 312; Zip Code 60478; NE Illinois; S of

Chicago; Mainly residential with a large share of the population working in Chicago. Main industry manufactures include industrial lift truck batteries and chargers.

● **COUNTRYSIDE**, Village, Cook County; Pop. 5,716; Area Code 312; Zip Code 60525; NE Illinois; W of Chicago.

A suburb of Chicago, the village has an independent economy based on manufacturing. Diversification is the key to its survival and products include hardboard, TV parts, packaging materials, conveyors, power hydraulic machines, pollution control equipment, and crushed stone.

● **COWDEN**, Village, Shelby County; Pop. 599; Area Code 217; Zip Code 62422; Central Illinois; 40 miles S of Decatur in an agricultural and bituminous coal mining region. A farming community whose only manufacturing consists of cattle feeders and livestock equipment.

● **CRAINVILLE**, Village, Williamson County; Pop. 1,019; Area Code 618; S Illinois; 5 miles SSW of Herrin in an agricultural and bituminous coal mining area.

● **CRAWFORD COUNTY**, E Illinois; Area 443 square miles; Pop. 19,464; Seat Robinson; Bordered to west by Wabash River and Indiana state line; Embarras River flows through Southwest area of County.

● **CREAL SPRINGS**, City, Williamson County; Pop. 791; Area Code 618; Zip Code 62922; S Illinois; 16 miles SE of Herrin in an agricultural region.

● **CRESCENT CITY**, (alt. CRESCENT), Village, Iroquois County; Pop. 541; Area Code 815; Zip Code 60928; E Illinois; 24 miles S of Kankakee in an agricultural area noted for feed grains and livestock. The Sea Sprite Boat Company, a national manufacturer of fiberglass boats and runabouts, is the main industry.

● **CREST HILL**, Village, Will County; Pop, 7,460; Area Code 815; Zip Code 60435; NE Illinois; W of Joliet; In an agricultural area noted for corn and livestock. It is a manufacturing and trade center for the local area, and a diversification of products marks its prosperity. Plastic foam chemicals, silk screens, boxes and containers, foods, and sheet metal fabrication items are its major trade goods.

● **CRESTON**, Village, Ogle County; Pop. 535; Area Code 815; Zip Code 60113; N Illinois; 24 miles SSW of Rockford in an agricultural area noted for feed grains.

● **CRESTWOOD,** Village, Cook County; Pop, 10,823; Area Code 312; Zip Code 60445; NE Illinois; SW of Chicago in an agricultural and industrial region. Manufacturing trade center for air dryers, wood cabinets, bowling equipment, chemicals, screw machine products, lawn and garden equipment, and air ventilators.

●**CRETE,** Village, Will County; Pop. 6,773; Area Code 815; Zip Code 60417; Elev. 720; NE Illinois; 30 miles S of Chicago in an agricultural area.

Platted in 1849, Crete began as a farm town along the Chicago Vincennes Road. Hog raising was a major activity in the 1820s and droves of hogs could sometimes be seen roaming the prairie between Crete and Danville, a distance of almost 100 miles. The hogs were herded to Chicago where they were sold and butchered.

Crete was incorporated in 1880, and the economy eventually became structured on manufacturing. Several industrial plants are located in the village and products include locks, machine shop items, wire, and custom steel articles.

● **CREVE COEUR,** Village, Tazewell County; Pop. 6,851; Area Code 309; Zip Code 61611; Central Illinois; 4 miles S of Peoria. Originally called Wesley City, in early years it was inhabited by Indians and French traders. The area was platted and surveyed in 1836, and was incorporated as Creve Coeur in 1921.

Located on the Illinois River, the village was named after the first French fort built in the West and in Illinois (1680- 1682), and which site is located nearby at Fort Creve Coeur State Park (*q.v.*).

In the 1930's, Creve Coeur became a boom town, and in 1936, was named as the fastest growing town in the country. This was due to the growth of industry in the area, and at that time, over 40% of the workers were employed by one company. One of the area's biggest manufactures currently, is the production of heavy equipment.

● **CROSSVILLE,** Village, White County; Pop. 805; Area Code 618; Zip Code 62827; SE Illinois; 24 miles SW of Mount Carmel in an agricultural area noted for livestock, feedgrains, and wheat.

● **CRYSTAL LAKE,** City, McHenry County; Pop. 24,512; Area Code 815; Zip Code 600%; NE Illinois; 13 miles N of Elgin.

Crystal Lake is named for the small lake around which it developed, and it is one of the main resort cities of NE Illinois. It was founded in the 1820s after the advent of the Erie Canal. Crystal Lake incorporated in 1914 and was originally only a resort spot. It expanded gradually and eventually became a manufacturing and trade center for McHenry County when the Chicago and Northwestern Railroad laid its tracks two miles NE of the city limits. Several small businesses as well as a number of larger manufacturers have their home offices in Crystal Lake, partially due to its desirable aspects, and partially due to its strategic location near major transport routes. Manufactures include plastic molds, steel dies, concrete products, hydraulic pumps, chemicals, tools, cabinets, sporting goods, screw machine products, industrial adhesives, boats, and agricultural equipment.

● **CUBA,** City, Fulton County; Pop. 1,440; Area Code 309; Zip Code 61427; W Central Illinois; 34 miles WSW of Peoria in an agricultural (corn, livestock), and bituminous coal mining area.

Cuba was incorporated in 1853 and flourished for a time as a bituminous coal mining center. Mining operations grew increasingly expensive, and the city's economy eventually swung over to agriculture. The city's only grain elevator supplies fertilizer, agricultural chemicals, and feeds to local farmers.

● **CULLOM,** Village, Livingston County; Pop. 568; Area Code 815; Zip Code 60929; E central Illinois; 18 miles E of Pontiac in an agricultural and bituminous coal mining area. Cullom is the home of Hahn Industries, one of the largest manufacturers of ornamental concrete figurines in the United States.

● **CUMBERLAND COUNTY,** SE Central Illinois; Area 347 square miles; Pop. 10,670; Seat Toledo; Named for old Cumberland Road, constructed in the early nineteenth century for freight and stagecoach travel to the West; The Embarras River cuts through the area.

● **CUTLER,** Village, Perry County; Pop. 523; Area Code 618; Zip Code 62238; SW Illinois; 40 miles SSW of Centralia in an agricultural and bituminous coal mining area.

● **DAHLGREN,** Village, Hamilton County; Pop. 512; Area Code 618; Zip Code 62828; SE Illinois; 15 miles ESE of Mount Vernon in an agricultural area noted for feedgrains.

● **DAKOTA,** Town, Stephenson County; Pop. 549; Area Code 815; Zip Code 61018; N Illinois; 8 miles NE of Freeport in an agricultural area.

● **DALLAS CITY,** City, Hancock-Henderson County lines; Pop. 1,037; Area Code 217; Zip Code 62330; W Illinois; 13 miles SE of Burlington, Iowa.

Dallas City was settled in 1836, platted in 1848, and incorporated in 1859. It was named for George Dallas, vice-president of the United States from 1845 to 1849. The city is picturesquely situated on the E bank of the Mississippi River and its location there has helped it develop as a commercial fishing center. Barges ply the waters, bringing and taking away trade goods. Manufacturing and agriculture are the mainstay of the economy and Dallas City is a trade center for soybeans, corn, poultry, dairy products, sectional homes, foundry sand conditioners, crushed stone, sand, and honey bee supplies.

The Dallas City rock quarry is famous for its ornamental blue chert and is a haven for rockhounds who explore it for chert, geodes, fish scales, and calcite crystals.

It is interesting to note that Dallas City, in the early 1900s, was one of the few Illinois cities used as experimental sites for early automobile manufacturers. The early makes were eventually discontinued and ranked among the many cars that were classed as failures in the automobile industry.

● **DALTON CITY,** Village, Moultrie County; Pop. 573; Area Code 217; Zip Code 61925; Central Illinois; 10 miles SE of Decatur in an agricultural area.

● **DALZELL,** Village, Bureau County; Pop. 587; Area Code 815; Zip Code 61320; N Illinois; 4 miles WNW of LaSallle in an agricultural and bituminous coal mining area.

● **DANFORTH,** Village, Iroquois County; Pop. 457; Area Code 815; Zip Code 60930; Elev. 658; E Illinois; 21 miles

SSW of Kankakee in an agricultural region. Named for A. H. Danforth who purchased land here in 1850, and induced 30 families from the Netherlands to emigrate here.

●**DANVERS**, Village, McLean County; Pop. 981; Area Code 309; Zip Code 61732; Central Illinois; 9 miles WNW of Bloomington in an agricultural area.

●**DANVILLE**, City, seat of Vermilion County; Pop. 36,660; Zip Code 618 ; E central Illinois; 36 mi. E of Champaign.

Danville was founded in 1765 on the site of a Piankashaw Indian village which was located next to the Vermilion River. The neighboring Kickapoo tribe next ceded a large parcel of land to the federal government. The land contained numerous salt springs whose concentrated brines lured speculators into the area. They in turn sunk wells and turned the salines, as they were called, into profit. Danville became known as Salt Works and consisted of a tavern and 12 cabins. After the brine supplies were depleted in the 1880s, the settlement remained stagnant. Eventually, a local surveyor donated 100 acres of land next to Salt Works, whereupon the state of Illinois would build the new Vermilion County Courthourse. Danville was incorporated on April 10, 1827, and named for the area's surveyor, Dan W. Beckwith; it was also designated as the county seat.

Vast deposits of coal were discovered in the early 1880s and Danville became the leading coal mining center in Illinois. The industry eventually dwindled to a few strip mines and left thousands of miners jobless. For a while it looked like Danville would become a ghost town, but its long experience in coal mining gave it the foundation for a manufacturing economy, and the city became a leader in the production of advanced coal mining machinery. Most 150 manufacturers have their offices in Danville which has become one of the state's leading trade centers. Diversified manufactures include agricultural products such as corn and beans, as well as lumber, glass, chemicals, electronics equipment, prefabricated buildings, burial monuments, playground equipment, meat packing, animal feeds, fireworks, clothing, paper boxes, transformers, and batteries.

A monument to coal mining days is Kickapoo State Park (*q.v.*), 1,500 acres of strip mine land which have been reclaimed for camping, picnicking, hiking, and water sports.

POINTS OF INTEREST:

- Forest Glen Preserve. 10 miles SE.
- Kickapoo State Park. 4 miles W on US 150, I-74.
- Vermillion County Museum. 116 N Gilbert Street.

● **DAVIS,** Village, Stephenson County; Pop, 541; Zip Code 61019; N Illinois; 14 miles NE of Freeport in an agricultural region noted for dairying. The village's only industrial venture is the manufacture of swiss cheese.

● **DAWSON,** Village, Sangamon County; Pop. 536; Zip Code 62520; Central Illinois; 10 miles ENE of Springfield in an agricultural and bituminous coal mining region.

● **DECATUR,** City, seat of Macon County; Pop. 83,885; Zip Code 625 ; Central Illinois; 37 miles E of Springfield.

Decatur is located at a bend in the Sangamon River, about 160 miles southwest of Chicago. In 1923, the river was dammed to form Lake Decatur, and the city rests on a mound of grassland which overlooks the water as well as the flatlands beyond.

Decatur is both a manufacturing and a college town. Since it is at the middle of the State, main highways run through the city. Railroad lines have made the northeast section of town a maze of tracks. This helped make Decatur the home of several major railroad repair shops.

With corn and soybeans readily available from nearby farms, factories in the city began processing these grains for nationwide consumption. Some residents still claim they live in the "Soybean Capital" of the world. Other products, from fly swatters to steel bridges, area also made in city factories.

Millikin University students play a large part in shaping the city's character, especially in the west end of town. Named after James Millikin, a Decatur pioneer, the University was founded in 1903. Today, several buidings on 35 acres house studies in engineering, liberal arts, and the fine arts.

The town was founded and named the seat of Macon County in 1829, although no one had settled on the site at that time. James Renshaw built the first log cabin there later that year. In 1830, Abraham Lincoln settled near the town with his family. He studied law at the home of the county's first peace officer, Major Warnick. At what is now known as Lincoln Square, the young man made political speeches, and on nearby farms he split logs and worked the plow. Richard J. Oglesby, former governor of the State, also lived in Decatur as a boy. He was a friend of Lincoln's, and also worked as a farmhand on nearby fields.

In 1854, Decatur's eoonomy flourished from the agricultural products of the area. As railroads began chugging through town that year, manufacturing also began to supply the needs of farms and smaller towns nearby. In the following years, industrialization brought more people and money, and the discovery of coal veins in the region gave Decatur a reputation as a major Illinois city. Here in 1860, Abraham Lincoln received his first party convention nomination for the presidency.

In the early 1900s, a university was founded, a large dam was built on the river, thousands of homes were built, and most of the present day business district was erected. The town's architecture mainly follows Frank Lloyd Wright's conception of the prairie: low to the ground with horizontal lines. However, some of the more ornate designs of the Victorians are also evident.

After the 1920s boom, however, Decatur felt the pinch of the Great Depression. Wages decreased, layoffs were common, and the first strikes occurred among the city's factory workers. By 1938, however, industry and farming income for the country had returned to former levels, and the discovery of oil in southern Illinois raised even more hope for the economy.

Some of the history of Decatur is preserved at the Lincoln Log Cabin Courthouse, which was the original Macon County seat, as well as at the site of the Wigwam Convention Hall. A plaque from the 1860 State Republican Convention which nominated Lincoln for President is located here. Other places of interest are the Decatur Civic Institute Building, which houses a large local art collection, and Lake Decatur, where water sports are practiced year round. An Ice Carnival is held there each winter.

POINTS OF INTEREST:

- Decatur Historic District. Bounded by Eldorado, Church Street, Haworth Avenue and the Sangamon River.
- Fairview Park. Jct. US 36, IL 48.

- Friends Creek Regional Park. 16 miles NE via I- 72, Argenta exit.
- Lake Decatur. SE edge of town, on the Sangamon River.
- Lincoln Trail Homestead State Park. 10 miles W on US 36, then S on County 27.
- Macon County Museum Complex. 5580 N Fork Road.
- Millikin University (1901). 1184 W Main St., on IL 48, 1 blk. S of US 36.
- Rock Springs Center for Environmental Discovery. S on IL 48, E 2 miles on Rock Spring Road.
- Scovill Gardens Park. E shore of Lake Decatur, S of US 36. Children's zoo.
- Weldon Springs State Park. 22 miles N on US 51, S off IL 10 near Clinton.

- HISTORICAL PLACES: (See Hist. Pl. Sect. for Details.)

    Millikin, James, House.

- **DEER CREEK,** Village, Tazewell-Woodford County lines; Pop. 630; Area Code 309; Zip Code 61733; Central Illinois; 15 miles ESE of Peoria in an agricultural and bituminous coal mining area.

- **DEERFIELD,** Village, Lake County; Pop. 17,327; Area Code 312; Zip Code 600 ; NE Illinois; NNW of Chicago.

One of the most affluent suburbs of Chicago, Deerfield was founded in 1836 on the site of a Potawatomi Indian village. It was incorporated in 1903 and though it is mainly a residential community, it has attracted some big industries. The main offices of Baxter Laboratories are there and Deerfield has profited as a trade center for packaging materials, bakery goods, construction machinery, swimming pools, and pharmaceuticals.

Recreational activities are available on Lake Michigan, 3 miles east, and on the Fox River and the surrounding small lakes.

- **DEER GROVE,** Village, Whiteside County; Pop. 44; Area Code 815; Zip Code 61243; NW Illinois; 13 miles S of Sterling in an agricultural area noted for livestock. Site of the Deer Grove Forest Preserve.

- **DE KALB,** City, De Kalb County; Pop. 34,925; Area Code 815; Zip Code 60115; Elev. 886; N Illinois; 24 miles WSW of Elgin; On the South Branch of the Kishwaukee River which is bridged here.

De Kalb was named for Baron Johann De Kalb of the American Revolutionary Army, but for a long time was known as "Barb City" after Joseph E. Glidden, who invented twisted barbed wire there. The new type of fencing was a revolution for agriculture and was a key element in the development of the cattle industry. Another inventor, Jacob Haish, patented his own barbed wire process about the same time Glidden did, and a long, drawn-out patent suit resulted. Eventually, both men were credited, and De Kalb has several memorials to each, among them the Glidden Hospital and the Hiash Memorial Library.

De Kalb is a manufacturing city with 18 factories which produce a diversified number of products. Some of these are television equipment, agricultural products, pianos, road paving equipment, drugs, toys, appliance motors, mica pellets, and delivery trucks.

Northern Illinois University was founded in De Kalb in 1895. It is one of Illinois' most prestigious universities with 20,000 students, 63 buildings, and a wooded campus which sprawls over 450 acres by the Kishwaukee River. Kishwaukee College (1968) is a few miles west.

POINTS OF INTEREST:

- Ellwood House Museum. 509 N 1st Street.
- Northern Illinois University (1895). West Lincoln Hwy (IL 38).
- HISTORICAL PLACES: (See Hist. Pl. Sect. for Details.)

   Glidden, Joseph F., House.

● **DE KALB COUNTY,** N Illinois; Area 636 square miles; Pop. 77,932; Seat Sycamore; Named for Baron Johann De Kalb, of the Revolutionary War; Cut through by the Kishwaukee River. There is rich farmland in the area, noted for corn raising.

● **DE LAND,** (alt. DELAND), Village, Piatt County; Pop. 458; Area Code 217; Zip Code 61839; Central Illinois; 24 miles NE of Decatur in an agricultural region noted for livestock; De Land has a meat processing plant and is a distributor for de-ionized bottled water.

● **DELAVAN,** City, Tazewell County; Pop. 2,000; Area Code 309; Zip Code 61734; Central Illinois; 23 miles S of Peoria.

Delavan was founded in 1836 by Jonas R. Gale, and Edward Cornelius Delavan of Rhode Island, the latter of whom auctioned off parcels of wild prairie land in that section of Illinois. Abraham Lincoln was a visitor to the area in 1841. Growth was slow, and at the time of incorporation in 1872, Delavan had only 500 inhabitants. Even though it never reached the status of a city, Delavan managed to profit from its rich agricultural land and from its strategic location on the Illinois Central and Gulf, Mobile, and Ohio railroad routes.

Agriculturally, its products include feed grains, corn, wheat, soybeans, hay, and cattle. Industries include scales and tool and die products.

● **DEPUE**, (alt. DE PUE) Town, Bureau County; Pop. 1,729; Area Code 815; Zip Code 61322; Elev. 473; N Illinois; 11 miles W of La Salle.

Depue was founded in the early 1800s on a glacial moraine by the Illinois River. It flourished for a time as a riverboat trade center and became incorporated as a town in 1861. When the steamboat era ended, Depue turned its interests elsewhere. A zinc smelter was built which saved the town from financial ruin. Unfortunately, because of the lack of pollution control laws, emissions from the smelter destroyed all the surrounding vegetation. Stricter controls of chemical pollutant levels have corrected the problem, and most of the land has been reforested.

Depue is the site of the National Champion Outboard Races, held on Lake Depue, a land-locked arm of the Illinois River.

● **DE SOTO**, Village, Jackson County; Pop. 1,500; Area Code 61 8; Zip Code 62929; Elev. 386; SW Illinois; 11 miles W of Herrin in an agricultural and bituminous coal mining region. De Soto was destroyed and 38 of its inhabitants were killed by a tornado that struck in 1925. Much of the village was never rebuilt and it has since suffered from a long economic decline. Farming is the main occupation.

● **DES PLAINES**, City, Cook County; Pop. 53,223; Area Code 312; Zip Code 600 ; Elev. 643; NE Illinois; NW of Chicago.

Des Plaines was founded in the 1830s as Rand in honor of its first settler, Socrates Rand. It is located on the Des Plaines River, after which it was renamed in 1869. It flourished early as a lumber center whose main mill produced timbers for a plank road between Jefferson Park and Chicago and for ties for the railroad built in 1853.

Its nearness to Chicago, and its strategic location to major transport routes, spurred Des Plaines' rapid growth. Notably, as many commuters travel from Chicago to work in Des Plaines as from Des Plaines to Chicago. Over 200 companies have their offices in the city. Diversified manufactures produce a wide range of products including electrical equipment, cement blocks, abrasives, screw machine products, burial vaults, X-ray equipment, dental supplies, orthopedic braces, ball bearings, appliances, scientific equipment, chemicals, and railroad cars. Chicago-O'Hare International Airport, just outside of the city, has greatly aided the city's industrial development.

● **DE WITT COUNTY,** Central Illinois; Area 399 square miles; Pop. 16,516; Seat Clinton; Agricultural region, mainly corn-producing.

● **DIETERICH,** Village, Effingham County; Pop. 568; Area Code 217; Zip Code 62424; SE Illinois; 10 miles ESE of Effingham in an agricultural area noted for livestock, corn, wheat, and dairying.

● **DIVERNON,** Village, Sangamon County; Pop. 1,178; Area Code 217; Zip Code 62530; Central Illinois; 15 miles S of Springfield in an agricultural and bituminous coal mining area.

● **DIXMOOR,** (alt, DIXMORE), Village, Cook County; Pop. 3,647; Area Code 312; Zip Code 6M06; NE Illinois; S of Chicago.

Dixmoor, incorporated in 1922, is mainly a residential community with a few commercial establishments. Its main manufactures are metal roof decking and gutters.

● **DIXON,** City, Lee County Seat; Pop. 15,144; Area Code 815; Zip Code 61021; Elev. 659; N Illinois; 35 miles SW of Rockford.

Dixon was founded in 1830 by John Dixon, a trader who opened a tavern on the site. Being located on the Rock River, the settlement attracted homesteaders early on, as well as factories who benefited from the water power. A ferry was established which served the militia during the Black Hawk War of 1832. Abraham Lincoln, as a young captain, was stationed there for a short time, and a statue of him stands on the "site of the Dixon Blockhouse" (known also as the Lincoln Monument State Memorial, q.v.).

Many riverfront factories, descendants of the 1800s, sprawl along the banks of the Rock River. The city is a manufacturing and trade center for livestock, grain, wire, cement, burial vaults, plastics, shoes, screw machine products, millwork, and pipe specialties. Sand and gravel are taken out of nearby quarries. The city boasts eight grain elevators and maintains six other sites for storage of surplus grain.

Of note is the John Deere Historic Site, which contains the restored house, gardens, and workshops where John Deere produced the first self-scouring steel plow in 1837.

An annual event is the Petunia Festival (July 4th), with a parade, carnival, and national drum and bugle competition.

POINTS OF INTEREST:

- John Deere Historic Site. 6 miles NE on IL 2 in Grand Detour.
- Old Settlers' Memorial Log Cabin. Lincoln Statue Drive, on N bank of river near Galena Avenue bridge.
- Ronald Reagan's Boyhood Home. 816 S Hennepin.
- Site of Fort Dixon. Lincoln Statue Drive, on N bank of river between Galena & Peoria Avenues.

● **DOLTON,** Village, Cook County; Pop. 23,930; Area Code 312; Zip Code 60419; NE Illinois; 17 miles S of Chicago.

Dolton was incorporated in 1892 and has flourished as a leading truck farming and manufacturing center for the area. Products include bakery equipment, brass castings, shipping containers, insulating cement, wood furniture, agricultural equipment, steel tanks, and chemicals. Industrial development has been greatly aided by the dredging of the Little Calumet River which is known as "the barge channel to America's great inland waterways throughout the Mississippi Valley."

● **DONGOLA,** Village, Union County; Pop. 728; Area Code 618; Zip Code 62926; S Illinois; 25 miles N of Cairo.

Dongola has light industry (wood millwork, meat processing, printing) and is located in the rich fruit and truck belt of the Illinois Ozarks (q.v.).

●**DONOVAN,** Village, Iroquois County; Pop. 361; Area Code 815; Zip Code 60931; Elev. 667; E Illinois; SE of Kankakee in an agricultural area noted for corn, oats, and soybeans. Donovan has one sawmill.

●**DOUGLAS COUNTY,** E Central Illinois; Area 420 square miles; Pop. 19,464; Zip Code 62401; Seat Tuscola. The first settler was John Richmond in 1829. The Kaskaskia River flows through the western part of county. It has been the settlement of the Amish since the 1860s.

●**DOWELL,** Village, Jackson County; Pop. 465; Area Code 618; Zip Code 62927; Elev. 400; SW Illinois; 15 miles NW of Herrin in a bituminous coal and agricultural area.

● **DOWNERS GROVE,** Village, Du Page County; Pop. 43,858; Area Code 312; Zip Code 605 ; Elev. 717; NE Illinois; 20 miles W of Chicago in an agricultural area noted for dairying, poultry, and truck crops.

Downers Grove was established at the crossroads of two Indian trails in 1832 and became incorporated as a village on March 31, 1873. It is a quiet commuting suburb of Chicago with a wealth of parks and tree-lined streets. Beyond the village limits lies the famous Morton Arboretum, a 700-acre parkland devoted to plant research. It contains several ponds, nature trails, and a prairie restoration. Over 4,500 species of plants and trees are represented at the arboretum.

The largest industry in Downers Grove is Pepperidge Farms, Inc., a nationally known bakery which, at this site, employs 600 people. Other commercial establishments produce a diversified number of items including tools, portable buildings, electrical hoists, cabinets, electrical switching equipment, chemicals, pulleys, scientific instruments, store fixtures, and telephone communication equipment.

The village boasts two specialty schools; the George Williams College trains students for work with the YMCA and the Avary Conley School (1911) teaches children of superior intelligence.

POINTS OF INTEREST:

    ● Historical Museum (1892). 831 Maple Avenue.
    ● Morton Arboretum. 3 miles W on US 34 to Lisle, then 1 mile N on IL 53.

● **DOWNS,** Village, McLean County; Pop. 620; Area Code 309; Zip Code 61736; Central Illinois; 8 miles SE of Bloomington in an agricultural area noted for livestock.

● **DUNDEE,** Village, Kane County; Pop. 3,314; Area Code 312; Zip Code 60118; NE Illinois; N of Elgin in a rich agricultural area; Separated geographically by the Fox River into East Dundee and West Dundee; Carpenterville has also been included in the Dundee municipal district, but all three villages were settled and incorporated at different times.

Dundee's most famous citizen was Allan Pinkerton (1819- 1884), cooper turned private detective and later, bodyguard for Abraham Lincoln. The old cooperage where Pinkerton made barrel staves is now a favorite tourist attraction.

Dundee is a trade center for crystal glassware, pottery and ceramics, asphalt, animal feed formulas, and railroad car hand brakes. The Haeger Potteries has been making ceramics for over 100 years and is the world's largest pottery factory. Hand-thrown pottery is continuously being made and demonstrations of the craft are given daily. Dundee is also the home of D. Hill Nurseries, the nation's largest evergreen nursery.

POINTS OF INTEREST:

● Industrial Tour. Haeger Outlet Complex. Van Buren St., 2 blks S of IL 72.

● Racing Rapids Action Water Park. IL 25 at IL 72.

● Santa's Village Theme Park. At jct. IL 25, 72.

● **DUPO,** Village, St. Clair County; Pop. 3,164; Area Code 618; Zip Code 62239; Elev. 422; SW Illinois; 6 miles S of East St. Louis.

Dupo is located on the Mississippi River but was named after a nearby small creek crossed by a bridge. The name is contracted from Prairie du Pont, French for "meadow of the bridge."

Dupo had a minor oil boom in 1928, but the resource proved to be limited and the village subsequently turned to manufacturing, limestone quarrying, and train servicing.

The scenic Mississippi bluffs can be seen from Dupo, but the sight is somewhat marred by the great number of railroad tracks that radiate from town.

● **DU QUOIN,** City, Serry County; Pop. 6,697; Area Code 618; Zip Code 62832; Elev. 468; SW Illinois; 35 miles S of Centralia.

Du Quoin, although settled at an earlier time, was actually founded in 1853 when the first settlement was moved to the site of a new railroad. It was named after Jean Baptiste du Quoigne, a French-Indian chief of the Kaskaskia whose village was nearby.

Du Quoin is a leading bituminous coal mining center, having sunk its first shaft in 1856. A cheap fuel supply attracted industries and soon several mining companies staked their claims in the city. The Freeman United Coal Mining Company alone employs 190 miners. Although mining is the mainstay, agriculture and manufacturing have both aided the economy.

Manufactures include beverages, clothing, cable and wire, playground equipment, explosives, cigars, and drugs.

● **DURAND,** Village, Winnebago County; Pop. 1,100; Area Code 815; Zip Code 61024; N Illinois; 17 miles NW of Rockford in an area noted for dairying and feed grains.

● **DWIGHT,** Village, Livingston County; Pop. 4,230; Area Code 815; Zip Code 60420; Elev. 641; NE Illinois; 30 miles W of Kankakee in an agricultural and bituminous coal mining area.

Dwight was founded in 1854 with the building of the railroad. It was the site of the Keeley Institute, a renowned center for the treatment of alcoholism and drug abuse. The center was closed in 1966 due to lack of personnel. There are several institutions in Dwight which renders it somewhat unique among small towns. The Oakdale Women's Prison teaches its inmates elementary and secondary education and instructs them in various occupational trades. The William Fox Children's Center provides therapy for retarded youngsters.

● **EARLVILLE,** City, La Salle County; Pop. 1,435; Area Code 815; Zip Code 60518; N Illinois; 16 miles NNW of Ottawa.

Earlville was named after the first postmaster's nephew. It grew slowly as a farm trading center, with agriculture still the main source of income of the population.

The principal industry is the Marathon Electric Manufacturing Corporation which has been expanding at the edge of the city limits. Marathon employs 1,500 people and is a national manufacturer of electric motors for oil burners and fans.

● **EAST ALTON,** Village, Madison County; Pop. 7,063; Area Code 618; Zip Code 62024; Elev. 438; SW Illinois; 4 miles E of Alton and on the Mississippi River.

East Alton is part of the Alton-Wood River Metroplex, an industrial conglomeration of cities within the St. Louis Metropolitan Area.

East Alton was first settled in 1800 and developed as a river port. It became incorporated in 1894 and later, the Olin Corporation, one of the nation's largest chemical manufacturers, established two of its plants in the city. The plants employ a total of 5,000 people. Olin Brass has become the world's largest and most efficient brass sheet and strip mill.

Other manufactures include ammunition, explosives, and assorted brass products. A spectacular plant is the geodesic dome of the Union Tank Car Company. The white dome houses a repair shop for railroad tank cars.

In 1804, the Meriwether Lewis and William Clark expedition to explore the wilderness from Louisiana Territory to the Pacific Northwest proved to be one of the biggest and most ambitious undertakings in U.S. history. A memorial to the explorers stands at nearby Lewis and Clark State Park (q.v.) at a point near the confluences of the Mississippi and Missouri river systems.

● **EAST DUBUQUE,** City, Jo Daviess County; Pop. 1,914; Area Code 815; Zip Code 61025; Elev. 615; NW Illinois; Opposite Dubuque, Iowa on the east bank of the Mississippi River.

East Dubuque grew up as a bustling ferrytown in the 1800s but declined after the construction of a highway bridge in 1887. The city is today, mainly a commuter town with a large segment of the population employed at Dubuque. There are a few small industries and manufactures include tractors, furniture, agricultural chemicals, boats, and iron castings.

The scenery around the city is enhanced by the Mississippi palisades and bluffs which provide panoramic views of the river from several vantage points. East Dubuque and its Iowa neighbor have consequently become favorite tourist spots.

● **EAST DUNDEE,** Village, Kane County; Pop. 2,721; Area Code 312; Zip Code 60118; Elev. 739; NE Illinois, 35 miles WNW of Chicago.

East Dundee, along with West Dundee, comprise the municipal area of the city of Dundee. Located in a rich agricultural area, East Dundee is a trading center for dairy products, livestock, and feed grains.

● **EAST GALESBURG,** Village, Knox County; Pop. 813; Area Code 309; Zip Code 61W1;,NW Illinois; E of Galesburg in an agricultural and bituminous coal mining area.

● **EAST HAZELCREST,** Village, Cook County; Pop. 1,570; Area Code 312; Zip Code 60429 NE Illinois; S of Chicago.

East Hazelcrest, a commuter suburb of Chicago, was incorporated in 1918. Although many of the residents work in Chicago, the village has light industry. Products include chain slings, transfer tape, and machine shop parts.

● **EAST MOLINE,** City, Rock Island County; Pop. 20,147; Area Code 309; Zip Code 61244; Elev. 576; NW Illinois; Near Moline.

East Moline, an industrial offshoot of Moline and Rock Island, was incorporated in 1907. Along with those communities, it shares the distinction of being one of the world's largest manufacturing centers for agricultural equipment. The International Harvester plant employs 3,500 people and is a world-noted producer of farm implements and harvesting-planting machines. Other industries include a steel plant, several printing offices, a packing company, foundry, and sheet metal plants. Manufactures are diversified and the city is a trade center for goods such as aluminum products, castings, marine pulleys, machine tools, air compressors, and porch enclosures.

The East Moline State Hospital has facilities for several thousand patients and is one of the state's leading medical centers. Just west of the hospital is Campbell's Is land State Park (q.v.), site of an Indian battle that took place during the War of 1812.

● **EASTON,** Village, Mason County; Pop. 351; Area Code 309; Zip Code 62633; Central Illinois, 31 miles NNW of Springfield in an agricultural area.

●**EAST PEORIA,** City, Tazewell County; Pop. 21,378; Area Code 309; Zip Code 616 ; Elev. 478; Central Illinois, near Peoria.

East Peoria was settled in 1884 and was then known as Blue Town. The name stems from the fact that the residents, many of whom were French, wore blue smocks which were unique to their native Alsace-Lorraine. The settlement spread out along the flood plain of the Illinois River, many of the houses having been built on pilings to support their weight on the soft, swampy soils. Although it was under constant threat of floods, Blue Town prospered as a farming center due to its rich bottomland soils. The name was changed to East Peoria in 1889, and in 1919, the village was incorporated as a city. Ten years earlier, a caterpillar tractor plant was built there, but the present Caterpillar Tractor Company became located within the city limits of adjacent Peoria.

The industry, however, spurred East Peoria's own growth as a manufacturing center and today the city is a leader in the production of janitorial supplies, generator switch gear, brick, tile, irrigation systems, brass and aluminum castings, and snow- making equipment.

● **EAST ST. LOUIS,** City, St. Clair County; Pop. 40,944; Area Code 618; Zip Code 622; Elev. 418; SW Illinois; Across from St. Louis, Missouri on the Mississippi River.

Early on, the area around East St. Louis became noted for its wealth of natural resources. Fertile bottom-lands of the Mississippi flood plain yielded abundant crops, the river itself offered a natural transport route (one of the main reasons settlements sprang up rapidly), and vast coal deposits provided a cheap source of fuel both for local residences and industry.

A village was established as early as 1699 by French missionaries who hoped to civilize local Indian tribes. The settlement, known as Cahokia, flourished briefly, then declined as a result of frequent floods which threatened to destroy it. A new village was platted in 1818, shortly after a ferry service had been established there which helped bring in homesteaders. The chief function of the new village which was named Illinoistown, was to ferry coal and other staple goods to other towns along the river. It was not until 1859 that the state legislature presented Illinoistown with a new charter incorporating it as a city and renaming it East St. Louis.

East St. Louis has been under constant threat of floods since its early beginnings, and the worst one occurred in 1844 when the entire American Bottom, on which the city rested, was inundated. Levees were subsequently constructed to check flood waters, but even those have proven to be insufficient at times. East St. Louis has seen its streets flooded many times since the 1844 disaster. To make matters worse, the city is also located in a tornado belt. A twister that struck in 1896, demolished the business district and killed in excess of 100 people. A $90,000 relief fund contributed by neighboring communities helped East St. Louis get back on its feet, and it entered the 20th century with a new lease on life.

Strategic location, abundance of resources, and nearness to St. Louis contributed to the city's ensuing swift expansion as an important industrial and railroad center and as a livestock market. In the suburb of National City are the Nation Stock Yards, reputed to be the largest in the United States. Several meat processing and packing plants have their headquarters nearby. Diversified manufactures include steel, chemicals, packaging materials, incinerators, fish nets, petroleum products, automobile parts, fertilizers, aircraft parts, air brakes, and agricultural implements.

Unfortunately, rapid expansion and a large, low-income population segment, have contributed to pollution, noise, and widespread slums. Several urban renewal projects have been attempted, many have failed, some have not, but the blight remains.

A noted tourist attraction is Cahokia Mounds State Park (q.v.) six miles to the east. This park is the site of eight well-preserved prehistoric Indian mounds believed to have been constructed in the 11th century. The mounds probably had a dual function: to prevent flooding and to serve as areas of worship in great ceremonies. The park contains a museum and facilities for camping and picnicking.

POINTS OF INTEREST:

  ● Frank Holten State Park. 7 miles SE off US 50.

  ● Katherine Dunham Museum. 1005 Pennsylvania, 1 mile
  NE via I-64.

●EDGAR COUNTY, E Illinois; Area 628 square miles; Pop. 19,595; Seat Paris; Lincoln spoke here in 1856; His cousin, Dennis Hanks, was killed at the county fair in 1853 by runaway horses; Agricultural area.

● EDGEWOOD, Village, Effingham County; Pop. 502; Area Code 217; Zip Code 62426; SE Central Illinois, 15 miles SSW of Effingham in an agricultural region.

● EDINBURGH, Village, Christian County; Pop. 982; Area Code 217; Zip Code 62531; Central Illinois, 15 miles SE of Springfield. Edinburgh, incorporated in 1872, is basically a farming town which reaps abundant harvests of grain and soybeans. It is a livestock center and has two grain elevators. The only industry is the Herman Vault Company which manufactures burial vaults.

●EDWARDS COUNTY, SE Illinois; Area 225 square miles; Pop. 7,440; Seat Albion; Agricultural, wooded region first settled in 1818 by Englishmen. The Little Wabash River flows along the western border. The area was named for Governor Ninian Edwards (1809-1818) of Illinois.

● EDWARDSVILLE, City, Madison County seat; Pop. 14,579; Area Code 618; Zip Code 620 ; Elev. 554; SW Illinois; 17 miles NE of East St. Louis.

Edwardsville, founded in 1813, was named for Ninian Edwards, governor of Illinois Territory from 1809 to 1818 and one of the local landowners. The community developed slowly and was not incorporated until 1837. Edwardsville early on became a commuter city with much of the population working in cities from Alton to St. Louis but preferring the scenic city, located on bluffs 136 feet above the Mississippi River, as their home.

Edwardsville does have some manufacturing (machine tools, sand castings, septic tanks, brick), and a flourishing coal mining industry which began in the 1800s. One of its newest titles is college town with the establishment of a branch of Southern Illinois University. The campus sprawls over 2,600 acres of rolling bluffs. There are five modern classroom buildings but no dormitories as it is basically a commuter school. Approximately 10,000 students attend classes with a future projected enrollment of 20,000.

POINTS OF INTEREST:

- Madison County Historical Museum. 715 N Main Street.
- Southern Illinois University at Edwardsville (1957).

●**EFFINGHAM,** City; Effingham County seat; Pop. 11,851; Zip Code 62401; SE Central Illinois; 26 miles SSW of Mattoon.

Effingham was designated the county seat in 1852 after the building of the Illinois Central Railroad. The seat had formerly been at Ewington, 3 miles to the west. Incorporation came in 1861, and 10 years later, a courthouse was built there. In addition to being a farm trade center (dairy products, corn, wheat, livestock) and a manufacturing city (machine parts, church fixtures, golf clubs, air conditioners, gloves, chemicals, wood products), Effingham is also a tourist gateway to the scenic Illinois Ozarks.

Location on a geological transition zone between the fertile prairie and hilly, forested uplands has given Effingham a decided advantage over the other farmtowns located entirely on the level prairie. Several tourist accommodations and nearby parks and lakes have brought added income to the flourishing city. Lakes Sara and Kanaga provide excellent camping, boating, and picnicking facilities.

●**EFFINGHAM COUNTY,** SE Central Illinois; Area 481 square miles; Pop. 31,704; Seat Effingham; Former seat, Ewington; Rolling, hilly land cut through by the Little Wabash River; Agriculture and lumber are the main industries.

●**ELBURN,** Village, Kane County; Pop. 1,275; Area Code 312; Zip Code 60119; Elev, 848; NE Illinois; 12 miles NW of Aurora in an agricultural area noted for corn and livestock.

Elburn was founded in 1854 with the construction of the Galena and Chicago Union Railroad. The village flourished early on as a farm trading center and has also gained some light industry including a meat-packing plant. Manufactures include trailers, toys, cabinets, and playground equipment.

●**ELDORADO,** City, Saline County; Pop. 4,536; Area Code 615; Zip Code 62930; Elev. 388; 7 miles NE of Harrisburg.

Eldorado, incorporated in 1873, began as a farm center, then became a mining town. Vast bituminous coal deposits discovered underneath the city brought miners from around the state and although the shaft mines have been closed down, the strip mines are still active. Fifty years of coal mining and more recently, oil drilling, have lured new industry into the city. A nearby source of fuel and strategic location to transport routes have aided Eldorado's rise as a manufacturing center. Products are diversified and include flags, industrial coils, diesel engine parts, stone monuments, agricultural chemicals, glass and clothing.

Recreational facilities are numerous as the scenic Shawnee National Forest lies only 10 miles south of the city. Hilly uplands, forests, and lakes provide hiking, swimming, mountain- climbing, and camping facilities unequalled anywhere in the state. Within easy driving time are Garden of the Gods, Pounds Hollow Recreation Area, Saline County Conservation Area, and Cave-In-Rock State Park (q.v.).

●**ELGIN,** City, Cook-Kane County line; Pop. 77,010; Area Code 312; Zip Code 601 ; Elev. 717; NE Illinois; 36 miles WNW of Chicago.

Elgin was founded in 1835 by James and Hezekiah Gifford, two settlers from New York. The Giffords cleared some land along the Fox River and laid out a road to Belvidere. This road became part of the Chicago-Galena stage route and was partially responsible for Elgin's rapid settlement. A dam was built to provide power for the grist and sawmills and the river has since been a link to the city's business. Elgin shipped milk to Chicago as early as 1832, a task which became sufficiently easier when the Galena and Chicago Union Railroad laid its tracks there in 1847. Gail Borden patented the condensed milk process in Elgin in 1856, and the enterprise soon became world famous.

Although Elgin lies in the heart of rich agricultural lands, farming plays only a secondary role to industry. The Elgin Watch Company, established in 1866, became a great rival to the flourishing dairy industry and essentially initiated Elgin's rise as an industrial center. The watch com pany was a great economic asset until it was transferred out of the state in 1970.

Diversified manufactures now include electric metal working equipment, burial vaults, conveying equipment, pesticides, cams, packaging materials, industrial diamond products, light fixtures, plastics and molds, fiberglass products, transformers, and steel trusses. In addition, there are several food processing plants in the city. Raw building materials are provided by nearby sand and gravel pits, and local attractions have added a new source of income. Trout Park contains a botanical garden, the Fox River provides recreational boating, Wing Park has picnicking facilities, and the Audubon Museum of Natural Science provides an educational experience for its visitors.

Elgin boasts of one of the oldest preparatory schools in the Midwest. The Elgin Academy was chartered in 1839 and opened in 1856. Since then more educational institutions have made Elgin their home. Next to the Academy is the Laura Davidson Sears Academy of Fine Arts. Elgin Community College opened its doors in 1949 and Judson College, a Baptist school, was established there in 1963.

POINTS OF INTEREST:

- Forest Preserves. Burnidge. Coombs Road.
- Fox River Trolley Museum. S on IL 31 in South Elgin.
- Lord's Park. Park Avenue.

● **ELIZABETH,** Village, Daviess County; Pop. 641; Area Code 815; Zip Code 61028; Elev. 790; NW Illinois; 25 miles ESE of Dubuque, Iowa.

Situated on the banks of the Apple River, Elizabeth was founded in 1832. The village was once the site of a fort which was attacked by 200 hostile Indians on June 24, 1832. An historical marker commemorates the battle which turned out to be a victory for the defending white settlers. The village was named in honor of Elizabeth Armstrong, the woman who rallied the residents of the fort to a successful defense. Elizabeth is basically a farming and lead mining community but has some light manufacturing. Products include steel trusses, transformers, chokes, and battery chargers. There is also a meat packing plant and weekly newspaper.

● **ELIZABETHTOWN,** Village, Hardin County seat; Pop. 427; Area Code 618; Zip Code 62931; Extreme SE Illinois; 23 miles SSE of Harrisburg.

Elizabethtown was founded around 1812 when Captain James McFarland of the Big Creek Militia constructed a hotel on a picturesque site overlooking the Ohio River. The Rose Hotel, although it has limited services, is still in operation and remains a favorite stopping place for visitors who flock to this busy tourist, mining, and farming community. Mining of lead, fluorospar, and zinc has long been a leading economic activity, but Elizabethtown flourishes primarily as a tourist mecca. It is the gateway to Shawnee National Forest and in the vicinity are numerous scenic attractions. Fossil beds, caves, and rock formations provide a haven for rockhounds, the Ohio River is a favorite with boaters and fishermen, and the heavily wooded knobs and hills of the Illinois Ozarks provide miles of trails for hikers, backpackers, and campers. The biggest attraction nearby is Cave-ln-Rock State Park (q.v.), a 64-acre scenic area noted for its cavern and spectacular rock formations.

Fertile bottomlands support farming, and Elizabethtown is a shipping plant for dairy products, wheat, corn, and poultry. Of minor importance is manufacturing. The two main products are metal purifiers and wood millwork.

● HISTORICAL PLACES: (See Hist. Pl. Sect. for Details.)

Rose Hotel (McFarlan's Tavern).

● **ELK GROVE VILLAGE,** Village, Cook County; Pop. 33,429; Area Code 312; Zip Code 60007; NE Illinois; NW of Chicago.

Elk Grove Village, until 1960, was little more than a cornfield with scattered houses. That year Centrex Construction Company, a community planning enterprise, laid out a new town. Industrial parks, subdivisions, recreational areas, schools, underground utilities, and shopping centers were built and industry flocked to the area. Thirteen parks grace the environs of the village and strategic location to major transportation routes, including nearby O'Hare International Airport, has aided industrial development. Although a large portion of the population commutes to Chicago, many residents are employed in the village's 700 diversified businesses. Manufactures include tools and dies, communication equipment, glass products, magnets, packing materials, scientific apparatus, parking meters, gears, springs and coils, foods, plastics, water softeners, transformers, dental supplies, metal alloys products, and chemicals.

● **ELKHART,** Village, Logan County; Pop. 475; Area Code 217; Zip Code 62634; Elev. 592; Central Illinois; 17 miles NNE of Springfield in an agricultural area noted for feed grains and livestock. Bituminous coal mining is also important and strip mines are nearby. It is the burial place of Richard J. Oglesby (1824-1899), soldier, U.S. Senator, and three times governor of Illinois.

● **ELKVILLE,** Village, Jackson County; Pop. 958; Area Code 618; Zip Code 62932; Elev. 400; SW Illinois; 13 miles NW of Herrin in a bituminous coal mining and agricultural area.

● **ELMHURST,** City, DuPage County; Pop. 42,029; Area Code 312; Zip Code 60126; Elev, 681; NE Illinois; 8 miles E of Wheaton.

Elmhurst was founded in 1843 and was named for the area's stately elms, many of which still line the city's boulevards. It remains one of Chicago's most desirable suburbs with magnificent homes, good transportation links, and excellent facilities for shopping, education, and recreation.

Although Elmhurst is mainly a residential city, increased movement of industry outward from Chicago has added a new dimension to the economy. Light manufacturing has kept a large portion of the population, which previously commuted to jobs in Chicago, in Elmhurst. Products include stainless steel, garage door openers, sprinklers, machine tools, conveyors, crackers and biscuits, packaging materials, paper items, and metal springs.

Elmhurst was once the home of Carl Sandburg, noted poet, Rosamond du Jardin, novelist, and Jens Christian Bay, author and former head of Chicago's John Crerar Library.

One of Elmhurst's finest attractions is the Lizzadro Museum of Lapidary Arts. It houses one of the nation's finest collections of inlaid gem dioramas, Japanese jade, gems, and stone carvings. Also located in the city are Elmhurst College (1871) and the DuPage County Memorial Hospital. Recreational facilities are available at six city parks and at nearby York Forest Preserve.

POINTS OF INTEREST:

- Elmhurst Historical Museum. 120 E Park Avenue.
- Lizzadro Museum of Lapidary Art. 220 Cottage Hill Avenue, in Wilder Park.

● **ELMWOOD,** City, Peoria County; Pop. 1,841 Area Code 309; Zip Code 61529; Elev. 626; Central Illinois; 19 miles WNW of Peoria.

Elmwood was founded in 1864 after the discovery of a rich coal deposit on the site of the present city. The first mines were of the shaft type, but eventually that type of mining became unprofitable and all the present mines are strip operations. The city is also a major manufacturer of granite monuments.

Laredo Taft (1860-1936), nationally known sculptor, was born in Elmwood. His bronze statue "Pioneers of the Prairies" stands in Central Park and is reputed to be a tribute to his parents.

● **ELMWOOD PARK,** Village, Cook County; Pop. 23,206; Area Code 312; Zip Code 60635; NE Illinois; W of Chicago.

Elmwood Park grew as a commuter suburb of Chicago after its incorporation in 1914. It is generally a residential community with very little industry. The only important manufactures are transformers, sealants, tools and dies, floodlights, electronic parts, and clothing.

Of note are the forest preserves bordering the Des Plaines River, which historically were sites of intertribal Indian councils. A monument in one of them marks a chipping station where the Indians made stone tools and weapons.

● **EL PASO,** City, Woodford County; Pop, 2,291; Area Code 309; Zip Code 61738; Elev. 749; N Central Illinois; 30 miles E of Peoria.

El Paso, a leading agricultural center, was founded in 1854 by a land promoter who hoped to develop El Paso as a leading manufacturing center. The city was the birthplace of Lester Pfister, developer of a remarkable hybrid corn, which also bears his name. Encouraged by an Iowa farm editor, Pfister experimented with the hybrids between 1925 and 1935. His reward came in 1935 and his initial efforts spurred the city's growth as a leader in agricultural experimentation. The Pfister Hybrid Corn Company, Inc. employs

750 people in the busy season and ships agricultural seeds and hybrids all over the country.

Other enterprises produce agricultural chemicals, fertilizers, and farm supplies. El Paso is also a shipping point for poultry, livestock, coal, grain, tile, concrete, petroleum, and modular steel buildings.

● **ELSAH,** Town, Jersey County; Pop. 851; Area Code 618; Zip Code 62028; Elev. 429; SW Illinois; 10 miles WNW of Alton in an agricultural area.

Located on the Mississippi River, Elsah was founded in 1847 by a woodchopper who settled there in hopes of selling wood to the steamboats. The tiny settlement which attracted more woodchoppers, was first known as Jersey Landing, but the name was changed in 1853 (when it was platted as a town) by the first postmaster and later U.S. Senator, James Semple. Semple named the town Elsah, a derivation of Ailsea, after his ancestral home in Scotland.

Elsah prospered for a time as a successful shipping port and had a distillery and two gristmills. The town ceased as a river port with the coming of the railroads. The economy dwindled rapidly and the present town is now a college community. Principia College (Christian Scientist denomination) is a four- year, coeducational liberal arts school, which moved here from St. Louis in 1935. Picturesquely located on high bluffs overlooking the river, the campus has accommodations for 700 students. Of note is the School of Nations Museum which houses an excellent display of international arts and crafts.

● HISTORICAL PLACES: (See Hist. Pl. Sect. for Details.)

Elsah Historic District.

● **ELWOOD,** Village, Will County; Pop. 951; Area Code 815; Zip Code 60421 Elev. @6; NE Illinois; 9 miles S of Joliet in an agricultural area noted for livestock and corn production.

Athough Elwood is mainly a farming community, it also manufactures loader tractors and farm tractor axles. It is the home of the Joliet Army Ammunition Plant which manufactures explosives.

● **EMBARRAS RIVER,** (alt. EMBARRASS); River, E Illinois; Flows 185 miles S and SE from rising point in Champaign County to mouth at Wabash River near Lawrenceville. Named by French explorers because of the difficulty of crossing the stream at flood time, when the river turned into a lake at its mouth. It was used for many years to operate gristmills.

● **EMDEN,** Village, Logan County; Pop. 459; Area Code 217; Zip Code 62635; Central Illinois; 20 miles SSE of Pekin in an agricultural and bituminous coal mining area. Home of BB Milling Company which produces feed, farm chemicals, and fertilizers for the local area.

● **ENERGY,** Village, Williamson County; Pop. 1,106; Area Code 618; Zip Code 62933; S Illinois; S of Herrin in an agricultural and coal mining area; Light industry and manufactures include metal culvert pipe and stencil brushes.

● **ENFIELD,** Village, White County; Pop. 764; Area Code 683; Zip Code 62835; Elev. 422; SE Illinois; 26 miles NNE of Harrisburg.

Enfield was settled in 1813 and spread out in the valley of the Little Wabash River. The area was rich in wild game and quickly attracted settlers, including Ann Rutledge, Abraham Lincoln's one-time sweetheart.

Today, the village profits as an agricultural shipping point and as a manufacturing center for clothing, machine tools, and lumber products.

● **EQUALITY,** Village, Gallatin County; Pop. 732; Area Code 618; Zip Code 60519; SE Illinois; 10 miles E of Harrisburg. A farming center, manufacturing ornamental iron products.

● HISTORICAL PLACES: (See Hist. Pl. Sect. for Details.)

Saline Springs.

● **ERIE,** Village, Whiteside County; Pop. 1,572; Area Code 815; Zip Code 61250; NW Illinois; 25 miles ENE of Moline and near the Rock River.

Erie is located on the site of an old Indian crossroad. The town triangle shows the pattern of intersection of the historic trails. The village was incorporated in 1872 and developed as a farm center. Agriculture remains the economic mainstay. Two plants manufacture chemical fertilizers and the Erie Casein Company is a noted processor of dairy products.

● **ESSEX,** Village, Kankakee County; Pop. 482; Area Code 815; Zip Code 60935; NE Illinois; 16 miles WNW of Kankakee in an agricultural area noted for feed grains.

● **EUREKA,** City, Woodford County seat; Pop. 4,435; Area Code 309; Zip Code 61530; Elev. 738; Central Illinois; 17 miles E of Peoria.

Eureka was founded in 1830 and became the county seat in 1896. Eureka is a college town, having developed around Eureka College (1848), a coeducational school which originally was a seminary of the Christian Church. President Ronald Reagan of California graduated from the college in 1932.

The city is a trading center for the prosperous agricultural hinterland. It is a major grower of corn, wheat, oats, soybeans, and truck crops and has a canning and meat processing plant. Light industry supplements the farm economy, and manufactures include livestock feeding equipment, car wash equipment, and earth moving machinery.

● **EVANSTON,** City, Cook County; Pop. 73,233; Area Code 312; Zip Code 602 ; Elev. M3; NE Illinois; 15 miles N of Chicago.

Evanston existed as a settlement as early as 1674 when Pere Marquette and his Indian companions landed in the natural harbor on Lake Michigan. Ephemeral encampments came and went until 1826 when the first permanent dwelling was built there. Evanston proper was not platted, however, until 1854, the year before the opening of Northwestern University. The university became the focus of the new town, and Evanston remained small for the next 25 years as it channeled all its energies into the development of the school.

Cheap transportation, which became increasingly available after the turn of the century, changed all that, and Evanston came into the spotlight as a desirable residential community. Before long, it was one of Chicago's leading commuter suburbs.

Evanston attracted several notables in its rise to independency, among them Sewell Avery, president of United States Gypsum and Montgomery Ward; Major Lenox Lohr, head of the Museum of Science and Industry; James W. Good, President Hoover's Secretary of War; A.N. Marquis, first publisher of *Who's Who in America*; and Charles Gates Dawes (1865-1951), vice president of the U.S. from 1925-1929. Dawes' mansion is now headquarters for the Evanston Historical Society.

Evanston is a manufacturing and trade center for a prosperous agricultural and industrial hinterland. It has in excess of 200 business enterprises, some of which make their main headquarters in the city (American Hospital Supply Corporation, Tinker Toys, General Finance Corporation, Rustoleum Corporation, American Photocopy Equipment Company). Diversified manufactures include steel products, foods, hospital equipment, photographic supplies, chemicals, furniture, packaging machinery, beverages, paper products, pharmaceuticals, scales, rust preventatives, microphones, soil testing equipment, laboratory instruments, tools and dies, and seismographs.

Although Evanston's 8.2 square miles offer numerous opportunities for employment, most workers commute to nearby Chicago, and the city remains first and foremost a college community. Evanston is also "dry," a result of the revision of the Northwestern University charter which prohibits the sale of liquor within four miles of the campus. Although the revision was made when the charter was only two years old, the ruling remains unchanged.

Northwestern University, member of the "Big Ten," is one of the nation's leading schools. It has excellent facilities in the fields of law, medicine, education, science, and theology. The Deering Library, also open to the general public, contains 90,000 books and periodicals. Points of interest on campus are Dyche Stadium, home of fall football games; the Technological Institute, one of the world's largest scientific research buildings; and the Lindheimer Astronomical Research Center. Besides Northwestern, Evanston has several other educational institutions, among them Garrett Biblical Institute (1855); Seabury-Western Theological Seminary (1936); the National College of Education (1886); Kendall College; and Evanston Collegiate Institute.

Recreational facilities are numerous. Sandy beaches along the Lake Michigan shore lure swimming and sunbathing enthusiasts, and boating and fishing activities are plentiful. Three separate park districts as well as the city operate 58 parks. Of historic interest is the Grosse Pointe

Lighthouse, built in the 1800s on a high bluff overlooking the lake. The maritime setting earned Evanston the title of "the finest New England village in the Midwest." Other favorite visitors' attractions are Ladd Arboretum, Dearborn Observatory, Shakespeare Garden, and the Merrick Rose Garden.

POINTS OF INTEREST:

- Evanston Historical Society, Dawes House. 225 Greenwood Street off Sheridan Road.
- Grosse Point Lighthouse. Sheridan Road & Central Street.
- Ladd Arboretum. McCormick Blvd. between Emerson and Green Bay Roads.
- Merrick Rose Garden. Lake Avenue & Oak Street.
- Mitchell Indian Museum. Kendall College. 2408 Orrington Avenue, 1 blk. W of Sheridan Road.
- Northwestern University (founded 1851, opened 1855). 633 Clark street.

- HISTORICAL PLACES: (See Hist. Pl. Sect. for Details.)

   Carter, Frederick B. Jr., House; Willard, Frances, House.

- **EVANSVILLE,** Village, Randolph County; Pop. 863; Area Code 618; Zip Code 62242; SW Illinois; 38 miles SSE of East St. Louis in an agricultural area. It was founded by Cadwell Evans in 1837, and was incorporated in 1869. By the time the latter took place, the town had been built up to include a flour mill, stores, a hotel, a brewery, and a Catholic Church. The area's first electric company appeared in 1927. Agriculturally, the village produces and trades wheat, corn, and soybeans. Its manufactures include ice machinery.

- **EVERGREEN PARK,** Village, Cook County; Pop. 20,874; Area Code 312; Zip Code 60642; NE Illinois; SW of Chicago in an agricultural and industrial area.

   Evergreen Park was incorporated in 1893 and developed as a residential suburb of Chicago. Some light manufacturing and products include machine tools, reconditioning products, grave monuments, and millwork.

- **FAIRBURY,** City, Livingston County; Pop. 3,643; Area Code 815; Zip Code 61739; Elev. 686; NE Illinois; 33 miles NE of Bloomington in an agricultural and bituminous coal mining area.

The city is an agricultural trade center and ships corn, wheat, soybeans, livestock, and poultry to other parts of the Midwest. It had several coal mines in the early 1900s, but they were closed before World War II. Today, manufacturing supplements the farming economy, and two grain elevators, one steel plant, and a garment factory employ a large portion of the population. Nearby gravel pits supply building materials to construction companies. Fairbury was incorporated in 1895.

● **FAIRFIELD,** City, Wayne County seat; Pop. 5,439; Area Code 618; Zip Code 62837; Elev. 451; SE Illinois; 30 miles E of Mount Vernon.

Fairfield was settled in 1819 when a group of pioneers arrived with their wagons and declared "there was no fairer field for farms." The name was derived from this epitaph. Fairfield has thrived on farming and is a major producer of feed grains and dairy products. It is also a shipping center for poultry and livestock.

More recently, oil was discovered in the vicinity, and the city has become a market for petroleum products. In addition, manufacturing is important and products include clothing, automobile parts, ready-mix concrete, millwork, and magnetic slate for bulletin boards.

Of historic interest is the monument in the business district which proclaims that the Wayne County Republicans, on March 31, 1860, were the first to endorse Abraham Lincoln for President of the United States.

● **FAIRMONT CITY,** Village, St, Clair County; Pop. 2,140; Area Code 618; Zip Code 62201; Elev. 420; SW Illinois, 5 miles NE of East St. Louis.

The village was founded in 1910 when a roundhouse for the Pennsylvania Railroad was built there. It developed as an industrial offshoot of East St. Louis and in its early years, flourished as a leading trade center for zinc. Present manufactures include industrial chemicals and fertilizer.

● **FAIRMOUNT,** Village, Vermillion County; Pop 785; Area Code 217; Zip Code 61841; SW Illinois; 12 miles WSW of Danville in an agricultural area noted for feed grains and livestock. In the vicinity are several limestone rock quarries that provide building materials such as concrete, crushed stone and fieldstone to the surrounding area. Material Service

Corporation is one of the largest suppliers. Some manufacturing includes the production of sheet metal ducts and fittings, and portable sawmills.

● **FARINA,** Village, Fayette County; Pop. 575; Area Code 618; Zip Code 62838; S Central Illinois; 20 miles ESE of Vandalia.

Farina is a farming town and a local supplier of nursery products. Brown Products Company processes eggs.

● **FARMER CITY,** City, De Witt County; Pop. 2,252; Area Code 309; Zip Code 61842; Central Illinois; 23 miles SE of Bloomington.

Farmer City, as the name implies, bases its economy on agriculture. It had its beginnings in 1830 when a white settler built a log cabin at nearby Salt Creek. By the time 19 more families had moved in, the town was ready to be platted.

Farmer City has been variously known as Mount Pleasant, Hurley's Grove, and Santa Ana, but acquired its present name in 1869 just before the railroad laid its tracks through the settlement. Since the entire population consisted of farmers, the present name was adopted.

The city remains a farming community with grain elevators next to the railroad tracks and several agricultural retail businesses and cooperatives. A local plant supplies farm chemicals and fertilizers. Agricultural produce includes corn, wheat, soybeans, oats, livestock, and cheese. Manufactures include cabinetry and trucking.

● **FARMERSVILLE,** Village, Montgomery County; Pop. 698; Area Code 217; Zip Code 62533; S Central Illinois; 23 miles S of Springfield.

Farmersville, above all, is an agricultural trade center for livestock feeds and processed meats. Supplementary to the economy is bituminous coal strip mining.

● **FARMINGTON,** City, Fulton County; Pop. 2,535; Area Code 309; Zip Code 61531; Elev. 742; W Central Illinois; 21 miles W of Peoria.

Farmington was laid out in 1834 after coal was discovered in the vicinity. Mining is still vital although agriculture is the second most important activity. The city has a potato chip factory and has one plant which supplies hydraulic equipment for sawmills and the lumbering industry. Other products include processed meats, paper goods, and burial vaults.

● **FAYETTE COUNTY,** S Central Illinois; Area 719 square miles; Pop. 20,893; Seat Vandalia; Named for the Marquis de LaFayette, the French solider who served in the American Revolution. Established February 12, 1821. Kaskaskia River cuts through this agricultural area, once the site of the state capital.

● **FILLMORE,** Village, Montgomery County; Pop. 326; Area Code 217; Zip Code 62032; S Central Illinois; 20 miles ESE of Litchfield in an agricultural and coal mining area; One plant manufactures agricultural equipment.

● **FINDLAY,** Village, Shelby County; Pop. 787; Area Code 217; Zip Code 62534; Central Illinois; 24 miles SSE of Decatur in an agricultural and bituminous coal mining region.

● **FISHER,** Village, Champaign County; Pop. 1,525; Area Code 217; Zip Code 61843; E Illinois; 14 miles NNW of Champaign in an agricultural area.

Fisher, located in a rich farm belt, is a major grower of corn and soybeans. There is some light manufacturing, including the production of motorcycle fairing frames and industrial steel teeming valves. Fisher was founded in 1876 and incorporated in 1896.

● **FITHIAN,** Village, Vermilion County; Pop. 512; Area Code 217; Zip Code 61844; E Illinois; 12 miles W of Danville in an agricultural and bituminous coal mining region. Named for Dr. William Fithian, early Danville settler and friend of Abraham Lincoln.

● **FLANAGAN,** Village, Livingston County; Pop. 987; Area Code 815; Zip Code 61740; N Central Illinois; 11 miles W of Pontiac in an agricultural area noted for feed grains, poultry, and livestock.

● **FLAT ROCK,** Village, Crawford County; Pop. SM; Area Code 421; Zip Code 62427; SE Illinois; 16 miles NNW of Vincennes, Indiana in an agricultural area noted for feed grains, wheat, and poultry. Light manufactures include barrel staves and racing apparel.

● **FLORA,** City, Clay County; Pop. 5,054; Area Code 618; Zip Code 62839; Elev. 490; S Central Illinois, 36 miles ENE of Centralia.

Flora, named for the daughter of one of the founders, grew with the coming of the railroad in 1854. It is considered the chief industrial, manufacturing, and trade center for Clay County. Oil was discovered in the vicinity, and the refining of petroleum products shares the limelight with agriculture and industry as the economic mainstay.

Flora has several large manufacturing outlets, and the major products include radio and TV parts, record albums, clothing, shoes, concrete, drilling bits, transmission cables, mine roof bolts, and automobile accessories.

● **FLOSSMOOR,** (alt. FLOSSMORE), Village, Cook County; Pop. 8,651; Area Code 312; Zip Code 60422; NE Illinois; S of Chicago.

Flossmoor, a suburb of Chicago, was incorporated in 1924 and has become one of Cook County's most desirable residential communities. The name of the village is of Scotch derivation. It means "gently rolling countryside," an apt description for this golfer's paradise. Seven country clubs surround Flossmoor and other recreational pursuits are likewise plentiful. Of note are the Washington Park Race Track and Flossmoor Park.

Aside from the retail trades, the only manufactures in the village are a hammer factory and sheet metal plant. Most of the residents commute to work in Chicago.

● **FORD COUNTY,** NE Central Illinois; Area 488 square miles; Pop. 14,275; Seat Paxton; Named for Governor Thomas Ford of Illinois (1842-46); Established February 17, 1859. Agricultural region produces corn and soybeans.

● **FOREST PARK,** Village, Cook County; Pop. 14,918; Area Code 312; Zip Code 60130; Elev. 620; W of Chicago and on the Des Plaines River.

Forest Park originally was the site of an historic Indian burial ground, and has remained a virtual burial ground since its founding in 1835. The phrase "more dead than alive" has aptly been applied to the village since nearly half of its corporate area is occupied by cemeteries. Woodlawn Cemetery contains a monument, exemplified by five granite elephants, leased by the Showmen's League of America. The site is the resting place of 68 circus performers killed in a train wreck in 1918. Since then, in

257

creased numbers of circus performers have been buried in this cemetery.

Forest Park is mainly residential with some industry. Noted manufactures are torpedo parts, burial vaults, steel ladders, cranes, monorails, resins, hospital equipment, pens, loose-leaf binders, wheelchair lifts, packaging materials, and tools.

● **FOREST VIEW,** Village, Cook County; Pop. 743; Area Code 312; Zip Code 60638; NE Illinois; W of Chicago; Mainly a commuter suburb of Chicago, but has some light manufacturing. Products include Mexican foods, concrete blocks, packaging materials, and plastic bottles. Incorporated in 1924.

● HISTORICAL PLACES: (See Hist. Pl. Sect. for Details.)

Chicago Portage National Historic Site.

● **FORREST,** Village, Livingston County; Pop. 1,756; Area Code 815; Zip Code 61741; Elev. 688; E Central Illinois; 14 miles SE of Pontiac in an agricultural area.

The land that eventually became Forrest was bought by Charles Jones in 1836, and named after a businessman from New York. It was platted in 1866, and incorporated in 1890. The area owed its growth to the construction of the railroad. German- Amish immigrants arrived in the 1860s and the town became a center for this religious sect.

Forrest is based on a farming economy but has some light manufacturing. Agriculturally, the area produces corn, soybeans, beef, and hogs. Industry includes sealing products, mowers, electrical coil windings, wood pallets, concrete tile, and chairs.

● **FORRESTON,** Village, Ogle County; Pop. 1,361; Area Code 815; Zip Code 61030; Elev. 931; N Illinois; 26 miles WSW of Rockford in a fertile dairying region. Besides farming, Forreston has some manufacturing, including the production of concrete roofing tiles, plastic molds and tools, and concrete. Nearby gravel pits supply raw materials.

● **FOX LAKE,** Village, Lake County; Pop, 4,511; Area Code 312; Zip Code 60020; Elev, 745; NE Illinois; 17 miles W of Waukegan. Fox Lake, a leading resort center, was founded in 1839, incorporated in 1906, and has thrived since its beginnings on the tourist trade. Sprawled out along the shores of Fox, Pistakee, and Grass lakes, all of which belong to

Chain-O'-Lakes State Park, the area is a mecca for the boater, swimmer, and fisherman. Because of its attractive location and nearness to Chicago, Fox Lake has become a popular residential community. Light industry includes dairy products, plastics, grinding wheels, beverages, but tourism dominates the economy.

●**FOX RIVER,** River, NE Illinois; Approx. 220 miles long; Flows S from point in SE Wisconsin to mouth at Illinois River at Ottawa in LaSalle County. The area around the river is fertile and used for extensive corn raising. Sauk and Fox Indians lived in the surrounding region until early 1800s, when many white Quakers settled here. Passes through town of Geneva.

● **FOX RIVER GROVE,** Village, McHenry County; Pop. 3,551; Area Code 815; Zip Code 60021; Elev. 771; NE Illinois; 11 miles NNE of Elgin.

Located on the Fox River, the village was incorporated in 1919 and became a noted summer and winter resort community. It boasts Illinois' first ski jump (1906), which is the site of annual jumping contests. The nationally known Norge Ski Club has sponsored several international tournaments at the ski hill. Aside from recreational income, Fox River Grove bases its economy on dairying and manufacturing. Diverse products include insulation, tools, dies, molds, paper goods, and wood cabinets.

● **FRANKFORT,** Village, Will County; Pop. 7,180; Area Code 815; Zip Code 62896; NE Illinois; 11 miles E of Joliet.

Frankfort was named for its counterpart, Frankfort-am-Main, in West Germany. It was platted in 1855 although there was a settlement here as early as 1845. The oldest building (1845), still stands and served as a rest stop for pioneers migrating westward on the Sauk Trail.

Frankfort is a small industrial center. Its largest industries, a foam plastics plant and a mechanical seals factory, employ, respectively, 300 people. Other manufacturers produce chemicals, electrical control assemblies, cabinets, ornamental iron products, packaging materials, and building stone.

● **FRANKLIN,** Village, Morgan County; Pop, 634; Area Code 217; Zip Code 62638; Central Illinois; 12 miles SE of Jacksonville in an agricultural area noted for feed grains.

●**FRANKLIN COUNTY,** S Illinois; Area 434 square miles; Pop. 403,191; Seat Benton; Named for Benjamin Franklin; Established January 2, 1818; Coal mining and farming region at the foothills of the Illinois Ozarks.

●**FRANKLIN GROVE,** Village, Lee County; Pop. 968; Area Code 815; Zip Code 61031; N Illinois; 9 miles E of Dixon in a fertile agricultural area noted for feed grains and livestock; Sole commercial enterprise is a stone aggregate plant.

● **FRANKLIN PARK,** Village, Cook County; Pop. 18,485; Area Code 312; Zip Code 60131; NE Illinois; WNW of Chicago.

Franklin Park was incorporated in 1892, but the area around the village was inhabited in the 1670s after Pere Marquette and Louis Joliet declared the Des Plaines River Valley "most suitable for settlement." Franklin Park, located along the Des Plaines River, is one of the major industrial and commercial centers of NE Illinois. Motorola is the largest of over 500 plants located in the village. Diversified manufactures include molds, paints, automatic screw machinery, steel products, cheese, tubular rivets, sports equipment, thermocouples, plastic containers, housewares, adhesives, amusement games, resonant reed relays and oscillators, loudspeakers, plumbing fixtures, and X- ray equipment.

●**FREEBURG,** Village, St. Clair County; Pop, 2,495; Area Code 618; Zip Code 62243; SW Illinois; 18 miles SE of East St. Louis.

Freeburg was founded in 1836 and grew initially because of the discovery of rich coal deposits in the vicinity. At its height, the village boasted seven shaft mines, but the deeper deposits eventually dwindled out. A solitary mine now ships coal to nearby East St. Louis. Farming (dairy products, corn, livestock), and manufacturing dominate the economy. Noted manufactures include brass and bronze castings, electronics equipment, fire apparatus, and aluminum products.

● **FREEMAN SPUR,** Village, Franklin-Williamson County line; Pop. 290; Area Code 618; Zip Code 62841; 4 miles NNE of Herrin in an agricultural and bituminous coal mining area.

● **FREEPORT,** City, Stephenson County seat; Pop. 25,840; Area Code 815; Zip Code 61032; Elev. 781; N Illinois; 26 miles W of Rockford.

Freeport was founded in 1835 by a group of unsuccessful miners from Galena's lead-mining district. Mineral deposits were discovered around Freeport which eventually aided its development. After the construction of the railroad, the city grew quickly, and today Freeport is a successful trade and industrial center with over 40 businesses. Main manufactures include water softening equipment, hardware, brass and aluminium castings, packaging materials, foods, dairy products, windmills, and patent medicines.

Freeport was the site of the second Lincoln-Douglas Debate in 1858; a boulder commemorates the event. Historians agree that the Freeport debate helped Lincoln's cause and also hastened the outbreak of the Civil War.

POINTS OF INTEREST:

● Freeport Art Museum/Arts Council. 121 N Harlem Avenue.

● Krape Park. Park Blvd.

● Stephenson County Historical Museum. 1440 S Carroll Avenue.

● **FULTON,** City, Whiteside County; Pop. 3,698; Area Code 815; Zip Code 61252; Elev. 597; NW Illinois; On the Mississippi River; NNE of Clinton, Iowa.

Fulton, an old river town founded in 1839, was named for the inventor of the steamboat, Robert Fulton (1765-1815). Fulton was incorporated in 1859 and grew to be a leading river port and terminus for the Diamond Joe Steamboat Line. Today, Fulton is a modern manufacturing, farming, and trading center. Noted manufactures include agricultural chemicals, novelties, tanks, and boilers. Acres of greenhouses grow tomatoes and cucumbers which are shipped to big city markets all over Illinois. The city is also a shipping point for livestock, wheat, corn, and poultry.

Recreational activities are plentiful and Mississippi Palisades State Park, 19 miles to the north, is one of Illinois' leading tourist areas.

● **FULTON COUNTY,** W Central Illinois; Area 874 square miles; Pop. 38,080; Seat Lewiston; Established January 28,

1823. Named for Robert Fulton, inventor of the steamboat. Bordered to the SE by the Illinois River. The area was part of the Military Tract, set aside for veterans of the War of 1812 by the government. It is the site of Dickson Mound State Park, where prehistoric Indians and artifacts lie buried.

● **GAGES LAKE,** Town and small lake, Lake County; Pop. 5,337; Area Code 312; Zip Code 60030; NE Illinois; Town at the NE corner of Gages Lake, approximately 6 miles N of Mundelein. In summer, the grounds surrounding the lake are managed by students from the University of Illinois.

● **GALATIA,** Village, Saline County; Pop. 983; Area Code 618; Zip Code 62935; SE Illinois; 48 miles SE of Mount Vernon.

● **GALENA,** City, Jo Daviess County Seat; Pop. 3,647; Area Code 815; Zip Code 61036; Elev. 603; NW corner of Illinois; 4 miles from the Mississippi River. Located at an altitude of 603 ft., Galena is picturesquely situated on the many terraces cut by the Galena River (formerly the Fever River), which is bridged here. Houses cling dizzyingly to the hillsides whose different levels are connected by steep flights of steps. Galena has been called the "city where time stood still." Its many stately buildings, some in part restored, enable one to envision Galena as it was in its 19th-century heyday as an industrial and mining center.

In about 1700, a Frenchman, Le Sueur, discovered that the local Indians were mining lead on the site. In 1807 the mines were placed under U.S. government protection. In 1818 the site was called Fever River. In 1826, by which time it had become more than a lead-mining camp, the town was laid out and named Galena, which is also the name for the sulphide lead ore extracted from the bedrock of the district. The new town had a post office and a school, as well as 15 log houses. By 1827, there were 115 houses and stores, and Galena became the county seat of the newly-organized Jo Daviess County.

While the peak of the Galena rush occurred in 1828-29, commercial lead mining had begun in 1823, when the yearly output was 210 tons of metal. By 1845, lead production was up to 27,000 tons, after which Galena went on to produce 83 percent of the country's lead supply.

In the 1820s, Galena also developed as a river port. At times as many as 14 to 16 steamboats were docked on

Galena's levee. Trading was vigorous, and the incoming stream of new settlers stimulated business. Families from the South arrived in droves, and some of them erected stately mansions of stone and brick, at a time when other new towns in the vicinity were still building log houses. With prosperity came churches, schools, and a library. After the boom, however, a gradual decline set in during the 1840s and '50s. The lead in the surface veins was exhausted, and the mines began to lose money. Galena's supremacy as a market center vanished when the railroad was completed in 1855, diverting traffic from the river. In addition, the river silted up, so that heavily-laden cargo boats could no longer navigate the channel. Dairy farming slowly became predominant. The California gold rush of 1849 drew off the last of the adventurers and miners.

With the outbreak of the Civil War (1861-65) Galena suffered from divided allegiances. There was much political wrangling between Union supporters and the strong Southern faction. The Union prevailed, and two local companies were formed in response to President Lincoln's appeal for troops. Ulysses S. Grant, who had recently come to Galena from St. Louis, volunteered as drillmaster for the new troops. He accompanied them to Springfield, and the Galena company became part of the 11th Illinois volunteer infantry. In August, 1865, General Grant returned to Galena to be greeted by 25,000 visitors, after which he was presented with a $16,000 house.

Galena has changed little since the Civil War, and stands as a symbol of life a century ago. By 1970 it had become a leading tourist center in the region, and a large section of it was designated as an Illinois historic site. Notable buildings include the restored home of Ulysses S. Grant, an excellent example of Mid-Victorian architecture; the John Dowling House, the oldest (1828) structure still standing; and the Market House (1845), in the Greek revival style, the oldest remaining market house in the Midwest. The Old Stockade on Main Street was built in 1832 and used during the Black Hawk War of the same year. It is built of logs and has an underground shelter, carved from the solid bedrock, where many of the pioneers sought refuge from attacking Indians.

The Galena Historical Society Museum houses memorabilia of the lead mining days, as well as a Civil War collection. The town thrives mainly on the tourist trade, and antique shops conduct a profitable business. Some marble and granite works are nearby.

POINTS OF INTEREST:

- The Belvedere (1857). 1008 Park Avenue.
- Dowling House (ca. 1826). 220 N Diagonal Street.
- Galena-Jo Daviess County History Museum. 211 S Bench Street.
- Grace Episcopal Church (1848). Hill & Prospect Streets.
- Grant Hills Auto Museum. 1 mile E on US 20.
- Lolly's Toy & Doll Museum. 225 Magazine Street.
- Old General Store Museum. 233 S. Main Street.
- Stockade (1832) and Underground Refuge. 208 Perry Street at N Main.
- Turney House (ca. 1835). 612 Spring Street.
- Vinegar Hill Lead Mine & Museum. 6 miles N on IL 84, then E on Furlong Road.

- HISTORICAL PLACES: (See Hist. Pl. Sect. for Details.)

Galena Historic District; Grant, Ulysses S., House; Old Market House; Washburne, Elihu Benjamin, House.

- **GALESBURG,** City, Knox County seat; Pop. 35,305; Area Code 309; Zip Code 614 ; Elev. 788; W Illinois; 45 miles WNW of Peoria. Founded in 1836 by a group of Congregationalist parishioners (and a small group of Presbyterians), led by George Washington Gale, the minister. Original settlement consisted of a temporary town known as Log City and was located at the grove which bordered Henderson Creek.

Galesburg is one of the few communities in Illinois developed from a preconceived plan rather than having sprung haphazardly from a group of cabins. The plan had been laid out prior to the arrival of the settlers. After the first inhabitants came in 1836, a proposal was made for a college, and in 1837 a charter was granted for the Knox Manual Labor College whose chief function was to be the training of ministers. It was renamed Knox College in 1857, and in 1870, women were admitted to the full college program for the first time. The college has the only preserved site (at "Old Main") of the fifth Lincoln- Douglas Debate on the slavery issue of 1858.

Galesburg was incorporated as a town in 1841 and grew rapidly with the coming of the railroad in 1854; it was incorporated as a city in 1876.

Among the most illustrious of Galesburg's early families were the Ferrises. Olmsted Ferris experimented with popcorn and introduced it to England. Yet another Ferris invented the Ferris Wheel, exhibited at the 1893 Columbian Exposition in Chicago.

In 1856, the city was a division point for the Burlington Railroad, and has become one again, as they have modernized their large classification yards.

Galesburg is the birthplace of poet-historian Carl Sandburg, who also attended Knox College. His restored three-room cottage, designated as an Illinois Historical Site, can be seen at Third Street and contains interesting memorabilia of his life and works. His burial place, known as Remembrance Rock, is behind the cottage.

Modern Galesburg's economy centers mainly on agriculture and manufacturing. The rich, rolling farmlands contribute to its prosperity, and the countryside around the city is dotted with lofty grain elevators. Several surrounding agricultural villages, which were founded in the 1850's, parallel the railroad.

Galesburg manufactures iron, and steel products as well as appliances, industrial hoses, paint, sanitary supplies, and candy. Numerous coal mines, clay, and gravel pits, can be found in the vicinity and although this phase of Galesburg's economy flourished in the middle 1850's, the industry has been on a steady decline. Lake Storey is nearby. In October of 1986, the Henry C. Hill Correction Center, a minimum security prison, was opened.

@SMALL1 = POINTS OF INTEREST:
- Carl Sandburg State Historical Site (1874). 331 E 3rd Street.
- Knox College (1837). Cherry & South Streets. 2 blks S of Public Square.
- Lake Storey Recreational Area. 1/4 mile N on US 150, then 1/2 mile W on S Lake Storey Road.

- HISTORICAL PLACES: (See Hist. Pl. Sect. for Details.)

  Old Main, Knox College.

GALLATIN COUNTY, SE Illinois; Area 328 square miles; Pop. 6,909; Seat Shawneetown; Named for Albert Gallatin, Secretary of the Treasury (1801-14). Established September 14, 1812. One of the oldest-settled regions in the state, it was a major salt-mining area in the early 1800's. Bounded to the west by the Wabash River and Indiana State line, the area is at the eastern edge of the Illinois Ozarks (q.v.).

● **GALVA,** City, Henry County; Pop. 2,742,; Area Code 815; Zip Code 61434; Elev. 849; NW Illinois; 35 miles SE of Rock Island; Name is the Anglicized form of Gefle, a Swedish seaport. Founded in 1854 as an offshoot of the Swedish religious community of Bishop Hill (q.v.) which is located NE of the town.

● **GARDNER,** Town, SE corner Grundy County; Pop. 1,237; Area Code 815; Zip Code 60424; Elev. 590; NE Illinois; Approximately 2 miles from the East Fork of the Mazon River, in a primarily agricultural region.

● **GENESEO,** City, Henry County; Pop. 5,990; Area Code 815; Zip Code 61254; Elev. 639; NW Illinois; 24 miles E of Rock Island; Settled in 1836 by colonists from Bergen and Geneseo, N.Y. Located in a mainly agricultural section, the city is a farm trade center, and has a cannery and a bandage factory. Nearby is the Geneseo State Fish Hatchery (q. v.) and Lock No. 24 of the Illinois and Mississippi Canal.

POINTS OF INTEREST:

● Johnson 1910 Farm. E on US 6, midway between Geneseo and Atkinson exits of I-80.

● **GENEVA,** City, Kane County Seat; Pop, 9,115; Area Code 312; Zip Code 60134; Elev. 720; NE Illinois; 36 miles W of Chicago; Located on both sides of the Fox River, Geneva was founded in 1835 and sprung up indirectly as a result of the Black Hawk War of 1832. It was incorporated as a city in 1887.

The charm of this riverside city is reflected in the many mid-nineteenth century homes, among them the Mill Race Inn which contained the city's first blacksmith shop. Geneva manufactures auto parts and foundry products, is a center for livestock and houses the State Training School for Girls, a correctional institution.

● **GENOA,** City, De Kalb County; Pop. 3,083; Area Code 815; Zip Code 60135; NE Illinois, E of the Kishwaukee River. Industries include sound systems, paper products, garden equipment, and machine tools.

● **GEORGETOWN,** City, SE Vermilion County; Pop. 3,678; Area Code 217; Zip Code 61846; Elev. 676; E Illinois; 10 miles S of Danville. Founded in 1827, Georgetown's first settlers included Quakers who emigrated from Tennessee and North Carolina.

The historical Star Mill on Mill Street was built in 1850 and operated until 1929. The city is located in an agricultural and coal-mining region.

● **GERMANTOWN,** City, Clinton County; Pop. 1,167; Area Code 618; Zip Code 62245; SW Illinois; 27 miles E of Belleville. The Southern Railroad passes through the city.

● **GERMANTOWN HILLS,** Village, E Woodford County; Pop. 1,195; Area Code 309; Zip Code 61601; N Central Illinois; 9 miles N of E Peoria.

● **GIBSON CITY,** City, SE Ford County; Pop. 3,396; Area Code 217; Zip Code 60936; NE central Illinois; 32 miles E of Bloomington.

● **GIFFORD,** Village, Champaign County; Pop. 845; Area Code 217; Zip Code 61847; E central Illinois; 7 miles E of Rantoul in an agricultural area.

● **GILLESPIE,** City, SE Macoupin County; Pop. 3,645; Area Code 217; Zip Code 62033; W Illinois; S of Gillespie Lake in an agricultural area. Gillespie manufactures steel tubing, cabinets, and chemicals.

● **GILMAN,** City, Iroquois County; Pop. 1,816; Area Code 815; Zip Code 60938; Elev. 654; E Illinois; 27 miles S of Kankakee.

Gilman is the birthplace of James Robert Mann (1856-1922) the Illinois Representative who sponsored the Mann Act. The city is located in a gently rolling, fertile agricultural region noted for grains, livestock, poultry, and swine. Oil fields are nearby.

● **GIRARD,** City, Macoupin County; Pop, 1,881; Area Code 217; Zip Code 62640; SW Central Illinois; 22 miles SSW of Springfield. Located in a sparsely wooded, gently rolling to level terrain, based on an agricultural economy.

● **GLADSTONE,** Village, Henderson County; Pop. 270; Area Code 309; Zip Code 61437; Elev. 543; W Illinois; 21 miles W of Monmouth. Platted in 1856 and the early settlers included Irish, Swedish, and German immigrants. Many of the bridge piers of the Upper Mississippi Valley have been constructed from the limestone quarried along Henderson Creek.

Nearby is a 100 year-old covered bridge made of oak beams and held together by wooden pegs.

● **GLASFORD,** Town, Peoria County; Pop. 1,115; Area Code 309; Zip Code 61539; NW Central Illinois just north of the Illinois River in an agricultural and bituminous coal mining area. Glasford has a grain elevator and is a petroleum supplier for the surrounding area.

● **GLENCOE,** Village, Cook County; Pop. 8,499; Area Code 312; Zip Code 60022; Elev. 673; NE Illinois; 22 miles N of Chicago. Founded in 1836 and incorporated as a village in 1869. The name is a composite of "glen" suggestive of the site, and "coe" the maiden name of the wife of one of the founders, Walter S. Gurnee.

● **GLENDALE HEIGHTS,** City, Du Page County; Pop. 27,973; Area Code 312; Zip Code 60139; NE Illinois; 20 miles W of Chicago in an agricultural area noted for feed grains and livestock.

● **GLEN ELLYN,** Village, Du Page County; Pop. 24,738; Area Code 312; Zip Code 60137; Elev. 766; NE Illinois; 23 miles W of Chicago. Originally a stagecoach stop, the area was founded in 1834, and has had several different names including Babcock's Grove, DuPage Center, Stacy's Corners, Newton's Station, Danby, and Prospect Park. The village was officially platted with the name of Danby in 1855, and soon after, was given the name Glen Ellyn by Thomas Hill, the village president, who chose it in honor of his wife Ellyn.

By that time, the town had experienced a large population growth, and the area not only had the Galena and Chicago Union Railroad, but later, in the 1860's, had two branches of the Underground Railroad operating there. This now thriving village houses the Andrew Carnegie Library, and was given a "Beautiful Place" award.

POINTS OF INTEREST:

● Stacy's Tavern (1846). 577 Geneva Road at Main Street.

● HISTORICAL PLACES: (See Hist. Pl. Sect. for Details.)

Stacy Tavern.

● **GLENVIEW,** Village, Cook County; Pop, 24,880; Area Code 312; Zip Code 60025; NE Illinois; 18 miles NNW of Chicago; Site of a U.S. Naval Air Station. Light manufacturing is the basis of Glenview's economy and products include electrical components, car wash equipment, wood products, piping systems, rubber goods, printed circuit boards, educational teaching materials, gourmet foods, and formica tops.

One of the largest research labs of the Kraftco Corporation is located in town. It employs 360 people and deals with food research and container products.

POINTS OF INTEREST:

● The Grove National Historic Landmark. 1421 N Milwaukee Avenue, just S of Lake Avenue.

● Hartung's Automotive Museum. 3623 W Lake Street, W of Glenview Naval Air Station.

● HISTORICAL PLACES: (See Hist. Pl. Sect. for Details.)

Kennicott's Grove.

● **GLENWOOD,** Village, Cook County; Pop. 9,289; Area Code 312; Zip Code 60425; NE Illinois; South of town is the Glenwood Woods Forest Preserve.

Glenwood is mainly a residential community but has some manufacturing. Products include chemicals, patio door locks, kitchen cabinets, and store fixtures.

● **GODFREY,** Village, Madison County; Pop. 1,225; Area Code 618; Zip Code 620 ; Elev. 438; SW Illinois; 2 miles N of Alton; Named after Benjamin Godfrey, a retired Cape Cod sea captain, the community was founded in 1835.

Godfrey is the site of the Monticello College and Preparatory School for Girls. It has a four year preparatory program and a two year junior college. Nearby is the Godfrey Mansion which houses a 12,000 piece collection of Indian relics, among them axes, peace pipes, and ceremonial objects.

● **GOLCONDA,** City, Pope County Seat; Pop. 960; Area Code 618; Zip Code 62938; SE Illinois; On the Ohio River and 35 miles S of Harrisburg; Originally called Sarahsville, the area was founded in 1796 by Major James and Sarah Lusk, who operated the first ferry on the Ohio River. It was incorporated in 1816. The location was pertinent as a site of the infamous Trail of Tears crossing (1838), during which Native Americans were removed from their homelands and forced to migrate westward.

Situated in a rich agricultural area, the town is a center for fruit, corn, wheat, hay, and livestock. Nearby in the Shawnee National Forest, is the Steamboat Hill--Ohio River

Recreation Area (q.v.). Golconda is also the location of the Smithland Lock & Dam, the largest in the United States.

● **GOLDEN,** Village, Adams County; Pop. 565: Area Code 217; Zip Code 62339; W Illinois; 24 miles ENE of Quincy. It is located in agricultural region and produces mainly corn, wheat, and oats. Its manufactures include seed sowers, and it is close to the Northwestern and Burlington Northern railroads.

● **GOLF,** Village, Cook County; Pop. 454; Area Code 312; Zip Code 60029; NE Illinois; N of Morton Grove.

● **GOOD HOPE,** Town, McDonough County; Pop. 416; Area Code 309; Zip Code 61438; Elev. 714; W Illinois; 6 miles N of Macomb.

Naming Good Hope was a project in itself. It was platted as Sheridan in 1866 by J. E. Morris. The following year, W. F. Blandin built a rival town bordering it to the west and called it Milan. The local post office, however, was already called Good Hope. Confusion set in as railway tickets went by the name Sheridan, conductors called out Milan, and all mail was addressed to Good Hope. To top it all off, some local residents went by the original name which was Clarkesville. The name Good Hope was finally agreed upon by all, and today the town can be spotted by the lofty grain elevator next to the railroad tracks. It is basically an agricultural and farming community.

● **GOREVILLE,** Town, Johnson County; Pop. 872; Area Code 618; Zip Code 62939; S Illinois; In the Shawnee National Forest. One and a half miles from town is Ferne Clyffe State Park (q. v.) noted for its scenic high bluffs and wooded surroundings.

● **GORHAM,** Village, Jackson County; Pop. 290; Area Code 618; Zip Code 62940; SW Illinois; NW edge of the Shawnee National Forest and 9 miles W of Murphysboro.

● **GRAFTON,** Town, Jersey County; Pop, 1,108; Area Code 618; Zip Code 62037; Elev. 446; SW Illinois; On the confluence of the Mississippi and Illinois rivers.

In 1834 the town consisted of a post office, store, tavern, and a few family dwellings. It grew rapidly with the coming of river commerce, and it flourished for a short time as a main river port. Its decline followed rapidly, and it turned for its existence to fishing and rock quarrying.

Today, tourism plays a large part in its economy. Nearby rock quarries yield some of the finest specimens of trilobites (extinct, joint-legged marine arthropods) in the country.

West of Grafton on Highway 100, a stone cross marks the place where Marquette, Joliet, and their companion explorers entered Illinois in 1673. Pere Marquette State Park, just north of Grafton, is dedicated to the explorer, who described its scenic bluffs as "frightful for their height and length." From their summits, the Illinois and Mississippi rivers appear as tiny streams winding their way through fields of green. The park has one of the finest lodges in the Illinois state park system.

● **GRAND DETOUR,** Village, Ogle County; Pop. n.a,; Area Code 815; NW Illinois; On the banks of the Rock River; Named by the French for the great horseshoe bend in the Rock River by which it is located.

The charming old village retains many relics of its age. Several of the buildings, such as St. Peter's Episcopal Church (1850), are over a century old.

In 1837, John Deere from Vermont, settled in Grand Detour, and in the same year, built the first successful steel plow using an abandoned saw from a lumber mill. The John Deere Historic Site (q.v.) contains the restored homestead and memorabilia of his life in Grand Detour.

● HISTORICAL PLACES: (See Hist. Pl. Sect. for Details.)

Deere, John, House and Shop.

● **GRAND RIDGE,** Village, La Salle County; Pop. 560; Area Code 815; Zip Code 61325; N Illinois; 8 miles S of Ottawa; North of Grand Ridge is the La Salle County Conservation Area (q.v.).

● **GRAND TOWER,** Town, Jackson County; Pop. 775; Area Code 618; Zip Code 62942; Elev. 367; SW Illinois; On the E bank of the Mississippi River.

The town was named for Tower Rock (q.v.), a natural stone sentinel 60 feet in height, in the Mississippi River. For many years it was used as a checkpoint for local riverboat captains. Crossing the river is the world's longest pipeline suspension bridge. The Grand Tower Toll Ferry carries passengers to the Missouri side of the river.

● **GRANDVIEW,** Village, Edgar County; Pop. 1,647; Area Code 217; Zip Code 62701; E Illinois; Approx. 20 miles E of Charleston; Located in a fertile agricultural region noted for grain, soybeans, and hybrid Indian corn.

● **GRANITE CITY,** City, Madison County; Pop. 32,862; Area Code 618; Zip Code 62040; Elev. 431; SW Illinois; 7 miles N of East St. Louis; Became an important city at the turn of the century, and was named for granite ware, its first product.

Settled in 1815 as a farming community, Granite City began its industrial career with the construction of the National Enameling and Stamping Company in 1892. More industry followed, and the city incorporated in 1896. Located in town are the Vocational Training School, Granite City Steel Works, and the Commonwealth Steel Mills. Main products of the city are sheet steel, tin plate, and granite ware.

●**GRANT PARK,** Village, NE Kankakee County; Pop. 1,024; Area Code 815; Zip Code 60940; NE Illinois; Approx. 19 miles NE of Kankakee in an agricultural region devoted to grain, hay, livestock, poultry, and swine.

● **GRANVILLE,** City, Putnam County; Pop. 1,407; Area Code 815; Zip Code 61326; N central Illinois; 5 miles S of the Illinois River in rolling, fertile farm country. Businesses include printing, publishing, production machining, and tool and die making. There are also two farm feed and seed companies.

●**GRAYSLAKE,** City, Lake County; Pop. 7,388; Area Code 312; Zip Code 60030; Elev. 799; NE corner of Illinois; In a recreational lake region; Named for the lake at its western edge. Industries include cement plants, planning mills, and a gelatin factory.

● **GRAYVILLE,** City, Edwards White County Line; Pop. 2,043; Area Code 618; Zip Code 62844; SE Illinois; On the Wabash River.

Just west of the town is Burnt Prairie, site of the old Morrison Mill where corn meal is still ground, as in the old days.

● **GREENE COUNTY,** W. Illinois; Area 543 square miles; Pop. 15,317; Seat Carrollton; Named for General Nathaniel Greene, Revolutionary War hero; Established January 20,

1821; Bounded to W by Illinois River; Farming and coal mining area.

● **GREENFIELD,** City, Greene County; Pop. 1,162; Area Code 217; Zip Code 62044; W Illinois; Approx. 30 miles N of Alton on the Burlington Northern railway route.

● **GREEN OAKS,** Village, Lake County; Pop. 2,101; Area Code 312; Zip Code 60048; NE Illinois; E of Libertyville.

● **GREEN ROCK,** City, Henry County; Pop. 2,615; Area Code 309; Zip Code 61241; NW Illinois; On the Rock River just E of Moline.

● **GREENUP,** City, Cumberland County; Pop. 1,616; Area Code 217; Zip Code 62428; Elev. 554; E Illinois; 18 miles S of Charleston; Named for William C. Greenup, first clerk of the Illinois Territorial Legislature. Incorporated in 1836.

Former seat of Cumberland County, Greenup is a relic of a past era of prosperity. The Conzet Hotel was a stopping place for merchants who displayed and sold their wares in a special room set aside for that purpose. Today's economy is based on agriculture.

● **GREEN VALLEY,** Village, Tazewell County; Pop. 745; Area Code 309; Zip Code 61534; N central Illinois; 20 miles S of Peoria in an agricultural area noted for feed grains and livestock. A manufacturer of concrete vaults, septic tanks, and farm feeds.

● **GREENVIEW,** Village, Menard County; Pop. 848; Area Code 217; Zip Code 62642; central Illinois; 20 miles NW of Springfield.

● **GREENVILLE,** City, Bond County Seat; Pop. 4,806; Area Code 618; Zip Code 62246; Elev. 563; 47 miles ENE of East St. Louis.

Settled in 1815, it is primarily a manufacturing city and has the nation's oldest evaporated milk plant. Other products include steel balls for crushing concrete, lodge and circus uniforms, and gloves.

Greenville College (1892; coed) and Almira College (1855; women) are in town.

POINTS OF INTEREST:

● Bock Museum. Greenville College, College Avenue.

●**GRIDLEY,** Town, McLean County; Pop. 1,304; Area Code 217; Zip Code 61744; Elev. 752; Central Illinois; 35 miles E of Peoria. Named for Asahel Gridley (1810-1881), a Civil War brigadier general from New York.

Gridley was at first mainly a farming town. Later it became a trade center for dairy products, welding equipment, and freezer meats.

● **GRIGGSVILLE,** Town, Pike County; Pop. 1,218; Area Code 217; Zip Code 62340; W Illinois; 5 miles W of the Illinois River.

The town earned its claim to fame due to its unique program of natural insect control. A serious mosquito problem led the town to take advantage of its location along the Brazil-Illinois migration route of the purple martin, America's largest swallow. A voracious insect eater, the purple martin is able to consume huge amounts of mosquitoes each day. Martin houses were installed throughout the town and a forty foot tower with 504 nesting units in the main business district have provided a home for thousands of the birds. The town is now virtually mosquito-free. Griggsville has been referred to as the "purple martin capital of the world."

●**GROSSE POINT,** Point, NE Illinois; 25 foot bluff on SW Lake Michigan at city of Evanston, an early name for that city.

Pere Marquette and his Indian companions landed in 1674 at the natural harbor formed by this bluff. Marquette's diary has an account of the incident and a sketch of his fleet of 10 canoes drawn up on the sands. In pioneer days, as lake traffic increased, Grosse Point assumed some importance as a port, and a village grew up around it, settled by those who traveled the inland seas. A number of families here today trace their descent from the early Great Lakes captains.

● **GRUNDY COUNTY,** Seat Morris; Pop. 32,337; Area 432 square miles; NE Illinois; Named for Felix Grundy, Senator and Attorney General from Tennessee, (1829-40). Established February 17, 1841. A rural area, the Illinois River flows across the northern part of the county.

● **GULFPORT,** Village, W Henderson County; Pop. 209; Area Code 309; Zip Code 61469; NW Illinois; Across the

Mississippi River from Burlington, Iowa. Consisting of a scattering of small houses and cottages, it is all that remains of the original (1855) ferry port of East Burlington which was abandoned when the Burlington Bridge was built. The toll bridge connects the village with Burlington, Iowa.

● **GURNEE,** Village, Lake County; Pop, 11,000; Area Code 312; Zip Code 60031; NE Illinois; On the shore of Lake Michigan and just N of Waukegan. Earlier names for this area included Wentworth, O'Plain, and Gurnee Station. Incorporated in 1928, it was later given its current name in honor of Walter S. Gurnee, one of the city's founders, and a one time mayor of Chicago.

Agriculturally, the area produces corn, soybeans, wheat, and oats. It is also a sizable manufacturing and trade center for such products as glass containers, metal fabricators, electronic equipment, automobile and truck hardware, chemicals, plastics, lubricants, fluorescent lighting equipment, telephone attachments, silkscreen and engravings, video games, refrigeration equipment, and furniture, among several others.

POINTS OF INTEREST:

● Six Flags Great America. On Grand Avenue, off I- 94, exit IL 132.

● **HAGARSTOWN,** Village, Fayette County; Pop. 100; Area Code 618; Zip Code 62247; Elev. 529; S Central Illinois; 6 mi. W of Vandalia in a coal mining and farming center.

● **HAINESVILLE,** Town, Lake County; Pop. 142; Area Code 312; Zip Code 60030; Elev. 800; NE Illinois; Near Grayslake; Reached by US 12 and Ill. Highway 59; 3 miles east of Holiday Park, a recreation ground.

● **HALDANE,** Town, Ogle County; Pop. 75; Area Code 815; Zip Code 61030; N Central Illinois; Near Forreston.

● **HALF DAY,** Town, Lake County; Pop, 400; Area Code 312; Zip Code 60069; NE Illinois; Near Prairie View; Reached by I-294, Ill. Highway 21, and US 45. Founded in 1836 by trappers or traders, the name is the English translation of the Potawatomi chief, Aptakisic, who lived here.

The village was once a half day's journey from the Chicago Loop. It was an early crossroads settlement where Adlai E. Stevenson voted when his country place in Lake County was his legal residence.

● **HAMBURG,** Town, Calhoun County; Pop. 162; Area Code 618; Zip Code 62045; Elev. 445.

● **HAMILTON,** Town, Hancock County; Pop. 3,001; Area Code 217; Zip Code 62341; Elev. 637; W Illinois; Reached by U.S. 67; On Mississippi River 33 miles north of Quincy; Near Keokuk hydroelectric dam (1913) and Lake Cook, created by the dam; Founded 1852 by Artois Hamilton; Incorporated 1854.

Site of D. Dadant and Sons, world's largest manufacturer of bee products. Shipping point for fruit and farming area. Principal industry: stock farms.

● **HAMILTON COUNTY,** SE Illinois; Area 435 sq. miles; Pop. 8,665; Seat McLeansboro; Named for Alexander Hamilton, first Secretary of U.S. Treasury, 1789-95; Drained by creeks flowing into the Wabash River, which constitutes its SE boundary.

Timber abounds and there are numerous sawmills in the county, along with some coal industry. Principal crops are corn, tobacco, fruit, oats, winter wheat, potatoes, and sorghum. Among pioneer settlers were Auxier (1815) and Adam Crouch (1818). Most important town is McLeansboro.

● **HAMLETSBURG,** Town, Pope County; Pop. 79; Area Code 618; Zip Code 62944; Elev. 324; S Illinois.

● **HAMMOND,** Town, Piatt County; Pop. 502; Area Code 217; Zip Code 61929; Elev. 678; Central Illinois; Reached by US 36; 6 miles south of Cerro Gordo; Settled 1855.

● **HAMPSHIRE,** Town, Kane County; Pop. 1,611; Area Code 312; Zip Code 60140; Elev. 900; NE Illinois. Founded in 1875 when the Chicago, Milwaukee, St. Paul, and Pacific Railroad reached here. It was once called Henpeck.

● **HANCOCK COUNTY,** Western Illinois; Area 797 sq. miles; Pop. 23,664; Seat Carthage; Named for John Hancock, first signer of the Declaration of Independence; Established January 13, 1825; Bounded on west by Mississippi River.

Its early history includes establishment of a ferry across the Mississippi River at Montebello in 1829, and the birth of Black Hawk, the famous Indian chief. Fort Edwards was erected on present site of Warsaw. The Mormon city of Nauvoo is located here. County is among the wealthiest in the state.

● **HANOVER,** Town, Jo Daviess County; Pop. 1,243; Area Code 815; Zip Code 61041; Elev. 630; NW Illinois; Reached by Ill. Highway 84; Just north of Mississippi Palisades State Park; Founded 1828 by Daniel Fowler and Charles Ames, named for Hanover, New Hampshire; Originally a mining town, now a center for farm products.

● **HANOVER PARK,** City, Cook and DuPage counties; Pop. 24,000; Area Code 312; Zip Code 60103; Elev. 800; NE Illinois; Near Bartlett; 27 miles WNW of Chicago; Incorporated 1958. Commuter town bordered by Streamwood on the north, Bartlett on the south, Schaumburg on the east, and on the west again by Bartlett.

● **HARDIN,** Town, Calhoun County Seat; Pop. 1,035; Area Code 618; Zip Code 62047; Elev. 436; W Illinois; Reached by US 67; Wheat raising center. Named to honor Col. John J. Hardin, killed leading a charge of the First Illinois Volunteers at Buena Vista during the Mexican War.

● **HARDIN COUNTY,** SE Illinois; Area 183 sq. miles; Pop. 4,914; Seat Elizabethtown; Named for a county in Kentucky which had been named for Col. John Hardin; Established March 2, 1839; Bounded on the east and south by the Ohio River.

The surface of the land, which is very timbered, is broken by ridges and deep gorges. Principal crops are corn, wheat, and oats. Minerals found here include iron, coal, lead, and carboniferous limestone.

● **HARMON,** Town, Lee County; Pop. 205; Area Code 815; Zip Code 61042; Elev. 675; N Central Illinois.

● **HARRISBURG,** City, Saline County Seat; Pop. 9,289; Area Code 618; Zip Code 62946; Elev. 403; SE Illinois; Reached by Ill. Highway 13; 22 miles east of Marion; Platted 1853; The area was first settled by a sawmill proprietor, James Harris. The first coal mines opened in 1885.

Industries include coal mining, flour and lumber mills. Site of Southeastern Illinois College (1961). Gateway to Shawnee National Forest.

● **HARTFORD,** Village, Madison County; Pop. 1,887; Area Code 618; Zip Code 62048; Elev. 420; SW Illinois; Reached by US 67 and Ill. Highway 287; South of Alton and north of Granite City and East St. Louis, near conflux of Missis sippi and Missouri rivers. The area was incorporated on May 1, 1920.

Agriculturally, Hartford produces soybeans, corn, and wheat. It is part of an industrial complex of oil refineries, power plants, and petrochemical distilleries on the east bank of Mississippi, and also has access to three major railroads.

Nearby is the Lewis & Clark Site, a small state park and monumental rock, where on May 14, 1804, the Lewis and Clark expedition began their trek to the Pacific Northwest.

●HARTLAND, Town, McHenry County; Pop. 50; Area Code 815; Zip Code 60098; Near Woodstock; NE Illinois.

●HARVARD, City, McHenry County; Pop. 5,156; Area Code 815; Zip Code 60033; Elev. 966; NE Illinois; Reached by US 14, the Northwest Highway; 28 miles ENE of Rockford; 70 miles SE of Chicago; Town platted by Chicago and Northwestern Railroad men in 1856; Incorporated 1869.

Near a group of small lakes created by glaciers, Harvard is the site of several winter and summer resorts. Principal industries are television and electronic devices, refrigerator doors, outdoor furniture, screw-machine products, barn equipment, and fiber barrels.

● HARVEY, City, Cook County; Pop. 33,500; Area Code 312; Zip Code 60426; Elev. 600; Reached by Ill. Highway 1; Industrial city 18 miles south of Chicago; Founded 1890 by Turlington W. Harvey, a Chicago land developer; Incorporated 1894.

A mile north is Calumet Sag Channel and 6 miles NE is Lake Calumet Harbor, 6 miles west of the Illinois-Indiana line. Companies located here include Allis-Chalmers, Bliss and Laughlin, Whiting, Fahralloy, Sinclair Research, Harris Hat Co. Industries are diesel engines, railroad equipment, steel castings, and gears.

● HARWOOD HEIGHTS, City, Cook County; Pop. 8,837; Area Code 312; Zip Code 60656; Elev. 650; NE Illinois; Reached by US 14, the Northwest Highway; NW suburb of Chicago incorporated 1947; 3 miles east of O'Hare Airport, 1 mile south of Kennedy Expressway; Name contrived from the "Har" of Harlem and the "wood" of Norwood Park Township.

● **HAVANA,** City, Mason County Seat; Pop. 4,376; Area Code 309; Zip Code 62644; Elev. 470; Central Illinois; Reached by Ill. Highway 78; On Illinois River 38 miles SW of Peoria, 190 miles from Chicago. Founded 1822 by Maj. Ossian M. Ross, a veteran of the War of 1812. In 1836, 36 steamboats called on schedule at this port. Barge docks still handle grain, coal and building materials.

Once called "Catfish Riviera of the Corn Belt," Havana is downstream from Chantauqua Lake National Wildlife Refuge, a 4,474-acre feeding area for 1 million ducks and geese, and 5 miles south of Dickson Mounds State Memorial, where the skeletons of 200 aborigines are displayed in the positions in which they were found by excavators. Principal industries: flour, farm implements, gasoline engines.

POINTS OF INTEREST:

    ● Chautauqua National Wildlife Refuge. 9 miles NE on Manito Road.

    ● Dickson Mounds State Museum. 2 miles NW off IL 78, 97, in the Spoon River Valley.

● **HAZEL CREST,** City, Cook County; Pop. 14,000; Area Code 312; Zip Code 60429; Elev. 650; NE Illinois; Reached by Ill. Highway 1; NNW of Chicago Heights; 23 miles south of Chicago Loop; Residential commuter community served by I-80; Incorporated 1912; Site of 250-bed South Suburban Hospital.

●**HAZEL DELL,** Town, Cumberland County; Pop. 100; Area Code 217; Zip Code 62430; Elev. 600; SE Central Illinois.

●**HAZEL GREEN,** Town, Cook County; Pop. (included with Alsip) 17,100; Area Code 312; Zip Code 60482; NE Illinois; Near Worth.

● **HEBRON,** Town, McHenry County; Pop. 781; Area Code 815; Zip Code 60034; Elev. 930; NE Illinois.

● **HENNEPIN,** Town, Putnam County Seat; Pop. 628; Area Code 815; Zip Code 61327; Elev. 500; N Central Illinois; Reached by I-80; 109 miles from Chicago Loop. Founded 1817 as a trading post by a family named Beaubien. Named for Father Louis Hennepin (1860-1701), a Flemish missionary who was among the first Europeans to explore the region.

Site of a $150 million Jones and Laughlin mill (1966), Buel Institute (the first farmers' organization in the West), and historic Putnam County Courthouse.

●**HENNING,** Town, Vermilion County; Pop. 307; Area Code 217; Zip Code 61848; Elev. 685; E Illinois.

● **HENRY,** Town, Marshall County; Pop. 2,655; Area Code 309; Zip Code 61537; Elev. 495; N Central Illinois; Reached by I-80; On Illinois River 30 miles north of Peoria midway between it and LaSalle; Settled 1833; Named for Gen. James D. Henry of Black Hawk War fame.

A shipping point for a productive agricultural region, Henry's principal industries include steel, meat packing, and fertilizer. Site of a large boating marina and facilities for duck hunting.

●**HENRY COUNTY,** NW Illinois; Area 826 sq. miles; Pop. 53,217; Seat Cambridge; Named for Revolutionary War hero Patrick Henry, famed orator and governor of Virginia; Established January 20, 1841.

One of the middle tier of counties of Northern Illinois. Pioneer of the region was Dr. Baker, who located in 1835 on what became Colona. First county court was at Dayton, subsequent seats were Richmond (1837), Geneseo (1840), Morristown (1842), and finally Cambridge (1843).

●**HERALD,** Town, White County; Pop. 100; Area Code 618; Zip Code 62845; Elev. 420; SE Illinois.

● **HEROD,** Town, Pope County; Pop. 60; Area Code 618; Zip Code 62947; Elev. 426.

●**HERRIN,** City, Williamson County; Pop. 9,623; Area Code 618; Zip Code 62948; Elev. 420; S Central Illinois; 5 miles NE of Marion.

Herrin, a trading center in a coal-mining section, was scene of Herrin Massacre during a miner's strike in 1922. Principal industries are real estate, washing machines, women's clothes, automobile trim and upholstery, staplers.

● **HERSCHER,** Town, Kankakee County; Pop. 1,127; Area Code 815; Zip Code 60941; Elev. 660; NE Illinois.

● **HEYWORTH,** Town, McLean County; Pop. 1,441 ; Area Code 309; Zip Code 61745; Elev. 749; Central Illinois; Reached by US 5I; 10 miles south of Bloomington. Former

Kickapoo Indian encampment settled by whites in 1825. Village was platted in 1855 when the first trains ran through here on the Illinois Central Railroad. Named for Laurence Heyworth, former member of Parliament, and one of a group of English stockholders in the railroad.

● **HICKORY HILLS,** City, Cook County; Pop. 13,989; Area Code 708; Zip Code 60457; Elev. 675; NE Illinois; 15 miles SW of Chicago, near Bridgeview and Justice. In the early days, the area was inhabited by Indians, and later on, other groups that resided there included traders, explorers, and French trappers, as well as French and British soldiers. In 1883, the first one-room schoolhouse was built, serving about 50 students. Around 1834, a number of farmers began settling there. The area, which originally held the names of North Palos, and the Village of Hickory Hills, incorporated as a village in 1951, and as a city in 1967.

● **HIDALGO,** Town, Jasper County; Pop. 171; Area Code 618; Zip Code 62432; Elev. 580.

● **HIGH LAKE,** Town, DuPage County; Pop. 750; Area Code 312; Zip Code 60185; NE Illinois; Near West Chicago.

● **HIGHLAND,** City, Madison County; Pop. 6,652; Area Code 618; Zip Code 62249; Elev. 545; SW Illinois; Reached by US 40, I-270, and I-70; 27 miles ESE of East St. Louis; Settled 1804 by families from Kentucky and North Carolina, with many Swiss among them.

Site of a large organ company and of a Dow-Jones Printing plant, which prints the Wall Street Journal for southern Illinois, Missouri, and Kentucky. Evaporated milk industry was born here from a formula brought from Switzerland by John Mayenard in 1884. Site of granite monument to Swiss poet Heinrich Bosshard, who died here in 1877. Industries include electronic equipment, transformers.

● **HIGHLAND HILLS,** Town, DuPage County; Pop. 1,600; Area Code 312; Zip Code 60148; NE Illinois; Near Lombard.

● **HIGHLAND PARK,** City, Lake County; Pop. 32,100; Area Code 312; Zip Code 60035; Elev. 690; NE Illinois; Deluxe residential suburban city on Lake Michigan 25 miles north of Chicago and immediately north of Cook-Lake County line; First settled in 1847 as Port Clinton and Saint Johns; Named by Walter Gurnee, mayor of Chicago (1852-53) who bought the site in 1854.

Site of five first-class golf courses in the valley of the Skokie River, and of 36-acre Ravinia Park, which presents summer concerts by performers of international repute. Town has been dry by ordinance since 1869.

POINTS OF INTEREST:

- Francis Stupey Log Cabin (1847). 1750 Block of St. Johns Avenue.
- Highland Park Historical Society. Headquarters in Jean Butz James Museum, 326 Central Avenue.

● **HIGHWOOD,** City, Lake County; Pop. 4,973; Area Code 312; Zip Code 60040; Elev. 685; NE Illinois; Reached by Sheridan Rd. and Ill. Highway 42; On Lake Michigan 12 miles south of Waukegan and 27 miles north of Chicago; Bounded by Lake Forest and Highland Park.

Fort Sheridan is located here. The first camp of U.S. Army contingents called to Chicago by the Haymarket Riot of 1886 was also located here.

POINTS OF INTEREST:

- Ft. Sheridan. N on Sheridan Road.

● **HILLSDALE,** Town, Rock Island County; Pop. 539; Area Code 309; Zip Code 61257; Elev. 587; NW Illinois.

● **HILLSIDE,** City, Cook County; Pop. 9,500; Area Code 312; Zip Code 60162; Elev. 650; NE Illinois; Reached by US 20 and I-90; WSW of Oak Park, 14 miles west of the Loop; Settlement of German farmers in 1837; Named by railroad, 1905; Industries: large shopping center, stone quarry, casting, and heavy machinery.

● **HINCKLEY,** Town, DeKalb County; Pop. 1,053; Area Code 815; Zip Code 60520; Elev. 750; N Central Illinois. Settled 1854 by DeKalb County's first settlers, Mr. and Mrs. John S. Sebree. Laid out 1872 when Chicago, Burlington, and Quincy Railroad built its line from Aurora to Rochelle. Platted by F. E. Hinckley, an officer of the railroad company, who named the town for himself.

● **HINDSBORO,** Town, Douglas County; Pop. 418; Area Code 217; Zip Code 61930; Elev. 649; E Illinois.

● **HINSDALE,** City, DuPage and Cook counties; Pop. 16,726; Area Code 312; Zip Code 60521; Elev. 725; NE Illinois; Reached by US 34; NE Illinois, 17 miles west of Chicago on the Cook-DuPage county line; Boundaries: 39th and 55th Streets on north and south, Tri-State Tollway and

Ill. Highway 83 on east and west. Originally called Brush Hill, the area was founded by William Robbins in 1865, and was platted that same year by a noted landscaper, H. W. G. Cleveland, on 800 acres of morainic hills. Incorporated in 1873, it was named for Henry W. Hinsdale.

POINTS OF INTEREST:

- Robert Crown Center for Health Education. 21 Salt Creek Lane.

- **HODGKINS,** Town, Cook County; Pop. 2,270; Area Code 312; Zip Code 60525; Elev. 600; NE Illinois; Reached by US 66 and I-55; 15 miles SW of the Loop, between the Des Plaines River and Joliet Rd. Explored by Father Marquette and Louis Joliet (1673), and settled by laborers who dug a canal from a local tributary of the Mississippi to Lake Michigan, 1836-48. The town was incorporated in 1896, and is a major producer of dolomite limestone from a 500-acre quarry.

- **HOFFMAN,** Town, Clinton County; Pop. 458; Area Code 618; Zip Code 62250; Elev. 457; SW Central Illinois.

- **HOLBROOK,** Town, Cook County; Pop. 500; Area Code 312; Zip Code 60411; Near Chicago Heights.

- **HOLDER,** Town, McLean County; Pop. 100; Area Code 309; Zip Code 61746; Elev. 838; Central Illinois.

- **HOLIDAY HILLS,** Town, McHenry County; Pop. 764; Area Code 815; Zip Code 60050; Elev. 750; NE Illinois.

- **HOLLYWOOD HEIGHTS,** Town, St. Clair County; Pop. 1,200; Area Code 618; Zip Code 62232; Near Casyville; SW Illinois.

- **HOMETOWN,** City, Cook County; Pop. 6,729; Area Code 312; Zip Code 60456; Elev. 620; NE Illinois; SW suburb of Chicago; Village in the NW corner of Oak Lawn between Cicero Ave, and Pulaski Rd.; Developed 1948 as a subdivision by J. E. Merrion; Incorporated 1953; Struck by a tornado on April 21, 1967, and since rebuilt.

- **HOMEWOOD,** City, Cook County; Pop. 20,700; Area Code 312; Zip Code 60430; Elev. 650; NE Illinois; 22 miles SE of Chicago; Reached by Ill. Highway 1, or I-80, and Dan Ryan Expressway; Settled in 1834 by German, Dutch, and Yankee homesteaders, it was incorporated in 1893. Almost exclusively residential, it borders on Washington Park Race Track.

● **HOOKDALE,** Town, Bond County; Pop. 100; Area Code 618; Zip Code 62284; Near Smithboro.

● **HOOPESTON,** City, Vermillion County; Pop. 60.942; Area Code 217; Zip Code 60942; Elev. 718; E Illinois, 25 miles north of Danville, 110 miles from the Loop; Reached by Ill. Highway 1; Platted by three land companies in 1871 on the farm of Thomas Hoopes.

"The Sweet Corn Capital of the World," Hoopeston has two canneries with an annual output of 110 million cans of corn. Other principal industries are cable and wire.

● **HOOPPOLE,** Town, Henry County; Pop. 227; Area Code 309; Zip Code 61258; Elev. 620; Reached by Ill. Highway 78; On the Green River; Received its name from the practice of coopers who cut hickory bands for their barrels in a nearby grove.

A. A. Haff dehorned his Texas Longhorns here in 1880 to keep them from injuring each other in the feeding pens, and was arrested and charged with cruelty to animals. His acquittal established a precedent in Illinois for a practice now common.

● **HOPEDALE,** Town, Tazewell County; Pop. 923; Area Code 309; Zip Code 61747; Elev. 630; Central Illinois.

● **HORATIO GARDENS,** Town, Lake County; Pop. 400; Area Code 312; Zip Code 60069; NE Illinois; Near Prairie View.

● **HORD,** Town, Clay County; Pop. 100; Area Code 618; Zip Code 62858; Near Louisville.

● **HOYLETON,** Town, Washington County; Pop. 457; Area Code 618; Zip Code 62803; Elev. 520; S Central Illinois.

● **HULL,** Town, Pike County; Pop. 585; Area Code 217; Zip Code 62343; Elev. 469; W Illinois.

● **HUNTLEY,** Town, McHenry County; Pop. 1,432; Area Code 312; Zip Code 60142; Elev. 900; NE Illinois. Founded 1851 by Thomas Stilwell Huntley as a station for the new Chicago and Northwestern Railway.

In a dairy-farming area, Huntley is the site of a large egg hatchery, a milk-processing plant, and factories making industrial sewing machines, plastic and foil wrappings, computer tape, and plastic packaging.

● **HUTSONVILLE,** Town, Crawford County; Pop. 544; Area Code 618; Zip Code 62433; Elev. 451; SE Illinois; Reached by Ill. Highway 1; On the Wabash River.

● **ILLINOIS CITY,** Town, Rock Island County; Pop. 220; Area Code 309; Zip Code 61259; Elev. 768; NW Illinois; Name derived from Indian word *ininiok*, meaning "men." It's located on the Mississippi River.

● **ILLIOPOLIS,** Town, Sangamon County; Pop. 1, 122; Area Code 217; Zip Code 62539; Elev. 602; W Central Illinois.

● **IMBS,** Town, St. Clair County; Pop. rural; Area Code 618; Zip Code 62240; Near East Carondelet; SE Illinois.

● **INA,** Town, Jefferson County; Pop. 333; Area Code 618; Zip Code 62846; Elev. 433; S Central Illinois.

● **INDIAN CREEK,** Town, Lake County; Pop. 270; Area Code 312; Zip Code 60060; Elev. 750; NE Illinois; Located on creek of same name, which is a tributary of the Des Plaines River near Half Day.

● **INDUSTRY,** Town, McDonough County; Pop. 558; Area Code 309; Zip Code 61440; Elev. 660; W Illinois.

● **INGALLS PARK,** Town, Will County; Pop. 3,500; Area Code 815; Zip Code 60431; Near Joliet; NE Illinois.

● **INGRAHAM,** Town, Clay County; Pop. 150; Area Code 618; Zip Code 62946; Elev. 480; SE Illinois.

● **INVERNESS,** Town, Cook County; Pop. 2,427; Area Code 312; Zip Code 60067; Elev. 853; Exclusive real estate development since 1847.

Incorporated 1962; 2.5 miles west of Palatine and 3 miles SE of Barrington.

● **IOLA,** Town, Clay County; Pop. 163; Area Code 618; Zip Code 62847; Elev. 524; SE Illinois.

● **IPAVA,** Town, Fulton County; Pop. 608; Area Code 309; Zip Code 61441; W Central Illinois.

● **IROQUOIS,** Town, Iroquois County; Pop. 226; Area Code 815; Zip Code 60945; Elev. 660; E Illinois; Name derived from Iroquois River, which was named because of an ancient battle that took place on its banks between the Iroquois and Illinois Indians; Name is probably an Algonquin word meaning "snakes." The once county seat was called Bunrum.

●**IRVING,** Town, Montgomery County; Pop. 599; Area Code 217; Zip Code 62051; Elev. 656; SW Central Illinois.

● **IRVINGTON,** Town, Washington County; Pop. 489; Area Code 618; Zip Code 62848; Elev, 550; Center of a strawberry- raising area; S Central Illinois.

●**ISLAND LAKE,** Town, Lake and McHenry Counties; Pop. 1,973 ; Area Code 312; Zip Code 60042; Elev. 780; NE Illinois; Reached by Ill, Highway 176, which is about 2 miles NW of US 12 at Wauconda; 45 miles NW of the Loop and 8 miles south of Fox Lake; On a small lake created by damming Cotton Creek in 1936; Incorporated 1954.

●**ITASCA,** Village, DuPage and Cook Counties; Pop. 7,129; Area Code 312; Zip Code 60143; Elev. 686; NE Illinois, 20 miles WNW of Chicago; Reached by I-290; Suburb surrounded by golf links; Settled 1870s by farmers; Originally founded by Dr. Elijah J. Smith, a Boston physician. Industries include cosmetics, tractor parts, and other light manufacturing.

● **IUKA,** Town, Marion County; Pop. 343; Area Code 618; Zip Code 62849; Elev. 518; S Central Illinois; Once named Middleton, the name was changed by the legislature in 1867 at the request of soldiers who had been in the Battle of Iuka in the Civil War. The name is from Choctaw Indian word *i yuk hana*, meaning "where two roads cross."

● **IVESDALE,** Town, Champaign and Piatt Counties; Pop. 357; Area Code 217; Zip Code 61851; Elev. 694.

● **JACKSON COUNTY,** SW Illinois; Area 604 sq. miles; Pop. 55,008; Seat Murphysboro; Mississippi River principal western boundary; Named for Andrew Jackson; Established January 10, 1816.

Crossed by a range of hills regarded as a branch of the Ozarks. The county is the site of one of the richest beds of bituminous coal in the state, and there is also an abundance of timber and saline springs. Principal crops are wheat, tobacco, and fruit. Major towns are Murphysboro, Carbondale, and Grand Tower.

●**JACKSONVILLE,** City, Morgan County Seat; Pop. 19,600; Area Code 217; Zip Code 62650; Elev. 613; W Illinois; 35 miles west of Springfield on US 36 and 54; Settled 1819 by brothers Seymour and Elisha Kellogg, veterans of the War of

1812; Incorporated 1867. Named for Gen. Andrew Jackson (1767-1845), seventh president of the U.S.

Site of oldest home of higher education in the state - Beecher Hall, on the campus of Illinois College (1829), the first college in Illinois to graduate a class. It's also the site of MacMurray College, founded in 1846 by two Methodist ministers, and of Jacksonville State Hospital, which holds 3,000 psychiatric patients.

Called by the local Chamber of Commerce the "Book Binding Capital" and the "Ferris Wheel Town," because of the presence here of the Eli Bridge Co., the Ferris Wheel maker since 1906. Other industries include men's clothing, margarine, shortening, salad dressing, and polyethylene film and bags.

POINTS OF INTEREST:

- Lake Jacksonville. 4 1/2 miles SE off US 67.

- HISTORICAL PLACES: (See Hist. Pl. Sect. for Details.)

    Beecher Hall, Illinois College; Duncan, Joseph, House (Elm Grove).

- **JAMAICA,** Town, Vermilion County; Pop. 70 Area Code 217; Zip Code 61841; E Illinois; Near Fairmont; Named for island in the West Indies; Name may also be derived from that of an Arawakarn tribe, Yamaye, which inhabited the island.

- **JAMESBURG,** Town, Vermilion County; Pop. rural; Area Code 217; Zip Code 61865; Near Potomac.

- **JASPER COUNTY,** SE central Illinois; Area 495 sq. miles; Pop. 10,741; Seat Newton; Named for Sgt. William Jasper, Revolutionary hero at Charleston and Savannah. Established February 15, 1831.

- **JERSEY COUNTY,** Western Illinois; Area 376 sq. miles; Pop. 18,492; Seat Jerseyville; Borders on Illinois and Mississippi rivers; Named for New Jersey; Settled in 1816 by emigrants from New Jersey; Established February 28, 1839; Originally part of Greene County, the area has a mild climate. Its principal crops are fruits.

- **JERSEYVILLE,** City, Jersey County Seat; Pop. 7,432; Area Code 718; Zip Code 62052; Elev. 663; W Illinois; 60 miles SW of Springfield; Settled by James Faulkner of Pennsylvania in 1827. Called Hickory Grove until a post office was established in 1834. Named, like the county, for New Jersey, former home of many of the settlers. Town was platted in 1834 when lots cost $20 each.

A one-industry town: lime-fertilizer spreaders and other self-loading equipment. Also has two elevators which store soybeans and wheat.

● **JEWETT,** Town, Cumberland County; Pop. 211 ; Area Code 217; Zip Code 62436; Elev. 584; E Illinois; Village developed from the former town of Pleasantville, a stagecoach stop.

● **JOHNSON COUNTY,** Southern Illinois; Area 345 sq. miles; Pop. 7,550; Seat Vienna; One of smallest counties; Divided in half, east to west by a ridge, forming a sort of watershed; Drained by Cache, Bay, Big Muddy, and Saline rivers; Named for Colonel Richard M. Johnson, reputed to have killed the Indian chief Tecumseh, and who was U.S. Vice President, 1837-41; Established September 14, 1812.

Abundant sandstone and limestone, some coal and salt-peter. Soil is rich, producing principal crops of tobacco, corn, wheat, and cotton.

● **JOHNSTON CITY,** Town, Williamson County; Pop. 3,928; Area Code 618; Zip Code 62951; Elev. 432; S Central Illinois; 8 miles north of Marion and 5 miles east of Herrin; First city in the county; Platted 1893, when work in nearby coal mines was at its peak; On an approach to I-57, the Chicago-Cairo route, north of Crab Orchard Lake.

Site of an annual Billiard Tournament. Principal industries are coal and wheat.

● **JOLIET,** City, Will County Seat; Pop. 77,956; Area Code 815; Zip Code 60431; Elev. 564; NE Illinois; 43 miles SW of Chicago; Reached by I-55 and I-80; On the Des Plaines River 10 miles upstream from where it meets the Kankakee to become the Illinois River. It was discovered by Father Marquette and Louis Joliet in 1673. The first permanent settler, Charles Reed, came to the area in 1833, the same year the post office was established. Originally called Juliet, the name was changed in 1845 by the legislature.

The area was incorporated in 1852, and the first railroad, the Rock Island, appeared the same year. Industry grew rapidly, with mills and quarries, and steel and river industries. Several merchants set up shops as well. The town continued to grow around the turn of the century.

It is the site of Illinois Waterway, opened in 1838, which floats strings of barges through the city, as well as the state penitentiary, the College of St. Francis (1874), and Joliet Junior College (1902). There is some agriculture such as grains and soybeans, and principal industries include petroleum products, steel rods, wire, road construction machinery, wallpaper, chemicals, food products, and clothing.

Joliet is the location of the Stateville Federal Prison.

POINTS OF INTEREST:

  ● Bicentennial Park Theater/Bandshell Complex. Jefferson & Bluff Streets.

  ● Historic Districts. The South East Neighborhood Historic District is a Registered National Landmark District. On N Broadway & Hickory Streets.

  ● Pilcher Park. Off US 30.

  ● Rialto Square Theatre. 102 N Chicago Street.

● HISTORICAL PLACES: (See Hist. Pl. Sect. for Details.)

  Illinois and Michigan Canal (Locks and Towpath).

●JONESBORO, Town, Union County Seat; Pop. 1,676; Area Code 618; Zip Code 62952; Elev. 568; SE Illinois; 30 miles SW of Marion; First settled in 1803; Located in wooded hills near Shawnee National Forest and Union State Forest; Reached by I-57 and Ill. Highway 127.

Site of a 22-acre park commemorating the Lincoln-Douglas debate of September 15, 1858. Principal industries are lumber mills, limestone quarries.

●JOPPA, Town, Massac County; Pop. 531; Area Code 618; Zip Code 62593; Elev. 350.

●JOSLIN, Town, Rock Island County; Pop. 125; Area Code 309; Zip Code 61257; NW Illinois; Near Hillsdale.

●JOY, Town, Mercer County; Pop. 513; Area Code 309; Zip Code 61260; Elev. 688; NW Illinois.

● KAMPSVILLE, Town, Calhoun County; Pop, 439; Area Code 618; Zip Code 62053; Elev. 438; W Illinois; On west bank of Illinois River; Near Koster, site of Cahokia Mounds archaeological excavations.

● **KANE,** Town, Greene County; Pop. 432; Area Code 618; Zip Code 62054; Elev. 560.

● **KANE COUNTY,** NE Illinois; Area 520 sq. miles; Pop. 251,005; Seat Geneva; Named for Sen. Elias Kent Kane, first Secretary of State of Illinois; Fox River flows through county north to south; Immigration began 1833 and increased 1835 when the Potawatomi Indians were removed west of the Mississippi River; Established January 16, 1836.

Kane is one of the wealthiest and most progressive counties in the state. Its principal industries are farming, dairy products, livestock, and manufacturing.

● **KANEVILLE,** Town, Kane County; Pop. 400; Area Code 312 Zip Code 61044; Elev, 790; NE Illinois.

● **KANKAKEE,** City; Kankakee County Seat; Pop. 30,300; Area Code 815; Zip Code 60901; Elev. 663; NE Illinois; 32 miles SSE of Joliet; Reached by I-57, US 45, US 52, and US 54; Named for the river, word may be a corruption of a Potawatomi Indian word, *teh-yak-ki-ki*, meaning "swampy country"; Platted in 1835 as Bourbonnais, now a residential suburb of Kankakee; Incorporated 1854.

Former residents include Casey Stengel, Fred MacMurray, and Frank Waterman, fountain pen manufacturer. Site of Kankakee State Hospital, Kankakee Community College (1966), and Olivet Nazarene College (1970). Industries include home appliances, furniture, farm machinery, shipping grain and livestock, hosiery, office supplies, paint, and birdhouses.

POINTS OF INTEREST:

● Kankakee County Historical Society Museum. Water Street & 8th Avenue, in Small Memorial Park.

● Kankakee River State Park. 8 miles NW on IL 102.

● Olivet Nazarene University (1907). 3 miles N on US 45/52 at IL 102 in Bourbonnais.

● **KANKAKEE COUNTY,** NE Illinois; Area 678 sq. miles; Pop. 97,250; Seat Kankakee; Named after an Indian tribe; Created February 11, 1851, from Will and Iroquois counties.

First white settler in the county was Noah Vasseur, a Frenchman, and the first American, Thomas Durham. Owners of the site of present city of Kankakee contributed $5,000 toward the erection of county buildings.

●**KANSAS,** Town, Edgar County; Pop. 779; Area Code 217; Zip Code 61933; Elev. 710; E Illinois; Named for Kansas Indians, a tribe of Siouan stock.

●**KASKASKIA RIVER,** SW Illinois; About 320 miles long, partly navigable; Rises in Champaign County, flows SW into Mississippi River in SW central Randolph County; Named for the principal tribe of Illinois confederacy, whose large village on the Illinois River near Utica was visited by Father Marquette in 1673 and 1675.

●**KEENEYVILLE,** Town, DuPage County; Pop. 650; Area Code 312; Zip Code 60172; NE Illinois; Near Roselle.

●**KEITHSBURG,** Zip Code 61442; Elev. 549; NW Illinois.

●**KELL,** Town, Marion County; Pop. 173; Area Code 618; Zip Code 62853; Elev. 615; S Central Illinois.

●**KEMPTON,** Town, Ford County; Pop. 263; Area Code 815; Zip Code 60946; Elev. 740.

●**KENILWORTH,** Town, Cook County; Pop. 2,980; Area Code 312; Zip Code 60043; Elev. 615; NE Illinois; 17 miles NW of Chicago; High-income residential suburban community; Founded 1890; Incorporated 1896.

●**KENNEY,** Town, DeWitt County; Pop. 367; Area Code 217; Zip Code 61749; Elev. 650.

●**KERNAN,** Town, LaSalle County; Pop. 100; Area Code 815; Zip Code 61364, Near Streator; N Central Illinois.

●**KEWANEE,** City, Henry County; Pop. 14,500; Area Code 309; Zip Code 61443; Elev. 820; NW Illinois; 38 miles ESE of Rock Island; On the Burlington Railroad line, completed 1854; Reached by US 34 and Ill. Highways 81 and 78; Name derived from Ottawa Indian word, *ke-won-nee*, meaning "prairie hen."

Colony established here 1836 by a Connecticut association for promoting the education of Protestants in Illinois. Nicknamed "Hog Capital of America." Industries include coal mines, boilers, gloves, truck bodies, agricultural and mining machinery. Black Hawk College is located here.

● HISTORICAL PLACES: (See Hist. Pl. Sect. for Details.)

, Ryan Round Barn.

● **KEYESPORT,** Town, Clinton and Bond counties; Pop. 352; Area Code 618; Zip Code 62253; Elev. 453.

● **KILBOURNE,** Town, Mason County; Pop. 441; Area Code 309; Zip Code 62655; Elev. 493.

● **KILDEER,** Town, Lake County; Pop. 1,107; Area Code 312; Zip Code 60047; Elev. 780; NE Illinois near Lake Zurich.

● **KINCAID,** Town, Christian County; Pop. 1,424; Area Code 217; Zip Code 62540; Elev. 601; Central Illinois; 22 miles SE of Springfield; Platted and built by Peabody Coop. Mining Co., 1913; Named for James R. Kincaid of Springfield, a planner of the town; Site of Peabody mine which produces 4 million tons of coal a year.

● **KINCAID LAKE,** Lake, Christian County; Covers 4 sq. miles, near town of same name; Average depth 13 feet; Built by damming a creek; Supplies cooling water to a Commonwealth Edison plant that supplies electricity for the Chicago area.

● **KINMUNDY,** Town, Marion County; Pop. 759; Area Code 618; Zip Code 62854; Elev. 619; S Central Illinois.

● **KIRKLAND,** Town, DeKalb County; Pop. 1,138; Area Code 815; Zip Code 60146; Elev. 746; N Central Illinois.

● **KIRKWOOD,** Town, Warren County; Pop. 817; Area Code 309; Zip Code 62447; Elev. 758; NW Illinois.

● **KLONDIKE,** Town, Lake County; Pop. 400; Area Code 312; Zip Code 60002; Near Antioch.

● **KNOLLWOOD,** Town, Lake County; Pop. 1,400; Area Code 312; Zip Code 60044; Near Lake Bluff; NE Illinois.

● **KNOX COUNTY,** Western Illinois; Area 728 sq. miles; Pop. 60,939; Seat Galesburg; Named for Gen. Henry Knox, Revolutionary hero and Washington's Secretary of War; Established January 13, 1825.

A wealthy interior county west of the Illinois River, Knox is the site of Knox College (1837), Lombard University (1851), Episcopal Seminary, and Hedding College at Abingdon.

● **KNOXVILLE,** Town, Knox County; Pop. 2,930; Area Code 309; Zip Code 61484; Elev. 755; W Illinois; 5 miles ESE of

Galesburg in an agricultural region; Reached by US 150; Seat of county until it was moved to Galesburg in 1872; Stephen A. Douglas presided in the Circuit Court here from 1841 to 1843.

● **LA CLEDE,** Town, Fayette County; Pop. 160; Area Code 618; Zip Code 62437; Elev. 576.

● **LADD,** Village, Bureau County; Pop. 1,328; Area Code 815; Zip Code 61329; Elev. 651; N central Illinois; Founded 1890; In the upper Illinois River valley coal belt which boomed in the 1920s but declined in the '40s and '50s due to competition from strip mines. It is located about 3 miles south of Cherry, scene in 1909 of a mine explosion and fire that killed 270. Named for George D. Ladd of Peru, Illinois, who, in 1887, built a railroad from the Illinois River into the village known until then as Osgood.

Agriculturally, the area produces corn and soybeans. Its manufactures include polyethelene and rubber. The village celebrated their 100th anniversary in June of 1990.

● **LA GRANGE,** City, Cook County; Pop. 15,362; Area Code 708; Zip Code 60525; Elev. 650; NE Illinois; Suburb 15 miles west of Chicago; Settled 1862 when the Burlington Railroad was extended westward across the Des Plaines River; Chartered 1879 with a population of 500; Named for LaGrange, Tennessee, former home of city's first president, Franklin D. Cossitt; Industries: limestone quarries, aluminum products.

POINTS OF INTEREST:

> ● Historic District. Bordered by 47th Street on the S, Brainard Avenue on the W and 8th Avenue on the East.

● **LA GRANGE PARK,** Village, Cook County; Pop. 13,359; Area Code 708; Zip Code 60525; Elev. 625; NE Illinois; Western suburb of Chicago immediately north of older town of La Grange; Bounded by Brookfield, the Salt Creek Forest Preserve, and La Grange. It was founded around 1845 from five farms on Salt Creek, 15 miles SW of Chicago. The area really grew when people who were left homeless by the Great Chicago Fire began to settle here in 1871. It was incorporated on July 14, 1892.

● **LA HARPE,** Town, Hancock County; Pop. 1,240; Area Code 217; Zip Code 61450; Elev. 691; W Illinois; Reached by Ill. Highways 9 and 94. Founded by and named for Benard de la Harpe, who headed a band of French explorers who tried to cross the 100 miles of trail from Fort Creve Coeur, at Peoria, to the Mississippi River and were stopped here by storms in the mid- 1700s. Settled in 1834 by William Smith and Marvin Tryon, veterans of the Black Hawk War. The post office was established in 1836. A 30-minute drive east is Western Illinois University at Macomb.

● **LAKE BLUFF,** Village, Lake County; Pop. 4,434; Area Code 312; Zip Code 60044; Elev. 671; NE Illinois; Summer resort on Lake Michigan, eight miles south of Waukegan, 33 miles from the Loop. Northernmost of Chicago's North Shore residential suburbs on a bluff overlooking a sandy beach, a location which was originally a summer resort on Lake Michigan. Settled 1836 by farmers who built cabins along the old Green Bay military road.

● **LAKE COUNTY,** NE corner of Illinois; Area 457 sq. miles; Pop. 382,638; Seat Waukegan; Named because 40 small lakes are found within its limits; Cut off from McHenry County and separately organized March 1, 1839.

Pioneers arrived 1839 and located along the Des Plaines River. The land is equally divided among sand, prairie, and timber. Is the site of Glen Flora medicinal spring.

● **LAKEMOOR,** Town, McHenry County; Pop. 797; Area Code 815; Zip Code 60050; Elev. 750; N Central Illinois; Near McHenry.

● **LAKE VILLA,** Town, Lake County; Pop. 1,081; Area Code 312; Zip Code 60046; Elev. 800; NE Illinois; 13 miles west of Waukegan, 7 miles west of the Tri-State Tollway, and 49 miles from the Loop; Reached by Ill. Highways 59 and 83; Encompasses Cedar Lake; Lies east of Fox Lake, south of Deep Lake, and west of Crooked Lake and Sand Lake; Incorporated 1900; Site of Allendale Farm School, founded 1897 to help homeless boys acquire skills.

● **LAKEWOOD,** Town, McHenry County; Pop. 1,185; Area Code 312; Zip Code 60014; Elev. 894; NE Illinois; Near Crystal Lake.

● **LAKE ZURICH,** City, Lake County; Pop. 7,550; Area Code 312; Zip Code 60047; Elev. 860; NE Illinois; Lake resort 18 miles SW of Waukegan, 37 miles NW of Chicago on Rand Rd. (US 12); Settled 1836 by Daniel Wright, a veteran of War of 1812; Incorporated 1896.

A summer resort for over 100 years, now a sizable city and center of a complex of small towns and resorts in wooded hills just north of western Cook County. Industries include concrete products, tools.

● **LA MOILLE,** Town, Bureau County; Pop. 669; Area Code 815; Zip Code 61330; Elev. 800: N Central Illinois.

● **LANARK,** Town, Carroll County; Pop. 1,495; Area Code 815; Zip Code 61046; Elev. 851; In the hills of NW Illinois at the "T" junction of north-south Ill. Highways 72 and 73 with east-west US 52 and Ill. Highway 64; Founded 1861 when Milwaukee Railroad was built; Described in many poems by Glenn Ward Dresbach, who lived here most of his life.

● **LANCASTER,** Town, Wabash County; Pop. 200; Area Code 618; Zip Code 62855; Elev. 490.

● **LANSING,** City, Cook County; Pop. 29,400; Area Code 312; Zip Code 604388; Elev. 630; NE Illinois, on Indiana border, 24 miles south of Chicago; Reached by I-80; Adjacent to the Little Calumet River, Thorn Creek, and Cook County forest preserves; Founded 1864 by brothers John and Henry Lansing; Industries: farming, brickmaking, steel mills, oil refineries.

● **LA SALLE COUNTY,** Northern Illinois; Area 1,150 sq. miles; Pop. 111,409; Seat Ottawa; Named for Sieur de La Salle; Established January 15, 1821.

County's early history includes establishment of a mission by Marquette in 1675 at an Indian village where Utica now stands, 8 miles west of Ottawa. First American settlers arrived in 1816, the time of Captain Long's survey of a canal route.

One of the wealthiest counties in the state, it is also the second largest and second most populous. The soil is rich, producing much timber. Minerals found here include coal and calciferous building stone. County is site of Starved Rock, where Illinois Indians were exterminated by starvation, and a prominent base of military operations during Black Hawk War.

● **LATHAM,** Town, Logan County; Pop. 361; Area Code 217; Zip Code 62543; Elev. 610.

● **LATHAM PARK,** Town, Winnebago County; Pop. 250; Area Code 815; Zip Code 61103; Near Rockford.

●**LEE COUNTY,** Northern Illinois; Area 725 sq. miles; Pop. 37,947; Seat Dixon; Named for Richard Henry Lee, orator and statesman of the Revolution; One of the third tier of counties south of the Wisconsin line, and created from part of Ogle County; Established February 27, 1839.

Lee County was first settled in 1828 when a half-breed, Ogee, built a cabin and established a ferry across the Rock River. In 1832 it was the scene of several battles during the Black Hawk War. First courthouse was built in 1840, and the first commissioners were Charles F. Ingals, Nathan Whitney, and James Dixon.

Agriculture is the principal industry of the county, and there are stone quarries at Ashton.

● **LEMONT,** City, Cook and DuPage counties; Pop. 5,197; Area Code 312; Zip Code 6043939; Elev. 606; NE Illinois; On Illinois River 25 miles SW of Chicago, just south of Argonne National Laboratory; Name is French word meaning "mountain"; The post office was established May 30, 1850; Incorporated June 9, 1873.

Lemont is an industrial city served by the Chicago Sanitary and Ship Canal, Calumet Sag Channel, and the Santa Fe Railroad. Its principal industries are steel, aluminum, petroleum plants, and limestone quarries.

●**LENA,** Town, Stephenson County; Pop. 1,722; Area Code 815; Zip Code 61048; Elev. 950; N Central Illinois, 10 miles south of the Wisconsin line, 4 miles south of Le-Aqua-Na State Park; Reached by Ill. Highway 73; Post office established July 1, 1853; Incorporated March 30, 1869; Known for output of Camembert and Brie cheeses.

● **LEXINGTON,** Town, McLean County; Pop. 1,615; Area Code 309; Zip Code 61753; Elev. 754; Central Illinois; Between Bloomington and Pontiac, reached by US 66; First white settlers arrived 1828, post office established May 10, 1837; Incorporated February 25, 1867; Market outlet for farm produce in the corn belt.

● **LIBERTY,** Town, Saline County; Pop. 200; Area Code 217; Zip Code 62946; Near Harrisburg.

● **LIBERTYVILLE,** City, Lake County; Pop. 14,730; Area Code 312; Zip Code 60048; Elev. 700; NE Illinois; Post office established April 16, 1838; Incorporated March 28, 1882; Site of Samuel Insull's 4,445-acre farm.

POINTS OF INTEREST:

   ● David Adler Cultural Center. 1700 N Milwaukee Avenue.

   ● The Lambs. Jct. I-94 & IL 176 exit.

   ● Safari Resort. 12 miles NW via US 45, W on IL 120, 134; 1/2 mile E on US 12.

● **LILY CACHE,** Town, Will County; Pop. (included with Lily Cache Acres) 600; Area Code 815; Zip Code 60544; NE Illinois; Near Plainfield.

● **LIMA,** Town, Adams County; Pop. 125; Area Code 217; Zip Code 62348; Elev. 659; Post office established March 12, 1836; Incorporated September 28, 1847.

● **LINCOLN,** City, Logan County seat; Pop. 17,100; Area Code 217; Zip Code 62656; Elev. 591; W Illinois; 30 miles NNE of Springfield; Founded 1853; Post office established October 6, 1854; Incorporated February 18, 1857.

Site of 12 historical landmarks associated with Abraham Lincoln. Also site of Lincoln College (1865) and Lincoln Christian College (1944). Industries include shipping of dairy products, glassware, clothing, and electrical equipment.

POINTS OF INTEREST:

   ● Mt. Pulaski Court House State Historic Site (1848). 12 miles SE on IL 121.

   ● Postville Court House State Historic Site. 914 5th Street, I-55 Business on the W side of town.

● HISTORICAL PLACES: (See Hist. Pl. Sect. for Details.)

   University Hall.

● **LINCOLN ESTATES,** Town, Will County; Pop. 700; Area Code 815; Zip Code 60423; NE Illinois; Near Frankfort.

● **LINCOLNSHIRE,** Town, Lake County; Pop. 4,076; Area Code 312; Zip Code 60015; Elev. 675; NE Illinois; 25 miles NW of Chicago on the Des Plaines River; Incorporated 1957; Short distance north is the estate of Adlai E. Stevenson (1900-65), governor of Illinois (1949-53) and later U.S. Ambassador to the UN.

● **LINCOLNWOOD,** Village, Cook County; Pop. 11,940; Area Code 708; Zip Code 60645; Elev. 600; NE Illinois; North of Chicago; Originally called Tessville, the area was founded in 1795 and incorporated on September 29, 1911. It was settled mostly by German farmers who had migrated from Michigan. Lincolnwood has shifted from a farming community to a residential one with light industry.

● **LINDENHURST,** City, Lake County; Pop. 4,789; Area Code 312; Zip Code 60046; Elev. 800; NE Illinois; 50 miles from the Loop, 10 miles west of Waukegan, near Lake Villa; Incorporated October 1, 1956; Developed from the 1,100-acre Lindenhurst farm, owned by E. J. Lehmann, a State Street merchant.

●**LINDENWOOD,** Town, Ogle County; Pop. 250; Area Code 815; Zip Code 61049; Elev. 770; N Central Illinois; Post office established April 18, 1846.

● **LISBON,** Town, Kendall County; Pop. 261; Area Code 815; Zip Code 60541; Elev. 675; Near Newark; Reached by US 30 and Ill. Highway 38; Post office established September 17, 1836; Incorporated December 15, 1883; Once called Holderman's Grove.

● **LISLE,** Village, DuPage County; Pop. 18,618; Area Code 708; Zip Code 60532; Elev. 682; NE Illinois; About 5 miles south of Wheaton on Des Plaines River; Reached by US 34. The area was settled by two brothers, Luther and James Hatch in 1832. A farming community quickly evolved, and the county's first frame schoolhouse was built in 1835. The CB & O Railroad reached Lisle in 1864, and the latter quarter of the century saw an increase in the dairy and brick-making industries.

Originally called DuPage, the name was changed in 1850, taken from the township of Lisle, which according to the more accepted theory, was named in 1835 by Alonzo B. Chatfield, originally of Lisle, New York. The post office was established on June 15, 1854, and Lisle was incorporated on June 26, 1856. St. Procopius College was opened in 1887. 1900 was marked by the opening of St. Procopius Abbey, and the Morton Arboretum was founded in 1922. Lisle remained primarily agricultural until the post World War II boom when it began a transformation into a residential community and became part of the Corporate Corridor.

Today, only two working farms remain within village limits. Manufactures include commercial printing, computer systems and software design, fiber optics, plastic products, and telecommunications.

●LITCHFIELD, City, Montgomery County; Pop. 7,190; Area Code 217; Zip Code 62056; Elev. 680; S Central Illinois; 45 miles south of Springfield; Reached by US 24; Post office established March 23, 1855; Incorporated February 16, 1859. Founded by and named for Electus Bachus Litchfield, born in Delphi, New York in 1813. Principal industries are dairy farming and manufacture of clothing, aluminum windows and doors, and paper products.

● LITTERBERRY, Town, Morgan County; Pop. 120; Area Code 217; Zip Code 62660; Elev. 602; Post office established January 29, 1886.

● LITTLE YORK, Town, Warren County; Pop. 297; Area Code 309; Zip Code 61453; Elev. 620; Post office established February 15, 1840; Incorporated May 11, 1894.

● LIVINGSTON, Town, Madison County; Pop. 916; Area Code 618; Zip Code 62058; Elev. 600; SW Illinois; Post office established December 23, 1904; Incorporated November 15, 1905.

● LOAMI, Town, Sangamon County; Pop. 818; Area Code 217; Zip Code 62661; Elev. 630; W Central Illinois; Post office established April 30, 1855; Incorporated July 29, 1875.

● LOCKPORT, City, Will County; Pop. 8,488; Area Code 815; Zip Code 60441; Elev. 604; NE Illinois; 35 miles SW of Chicago; Platted by the Illinois and Michigan Canal Commission in 1837; Post office established March 21, 1837; Incorporated February 12, 1853 as a village, and 1904 as a city.

The first permanent settler in Lockport Township was Armstead Runyon who came in 1830 with his family. The north part of what became Lockport was named Runyontown. November, 1837 saw the first sale of town lots by the Canal Commission, and Runyontown settlers relocated there. The Canal opened in 1848. During those early years, Lockport had boat building yards, grain elevators, and mills. It was also the site of the first oil refinery built in the northern states, with oil refining being its major industry from 1912 to 1981; its closing was a blow to the local economy. In 1833, John Lane invented the first steel plow, which was manufactured here.

The city continues to use the locks that reverse the flow of the Chicago River, and the device that raises the water level so that shipping can clear the divide between the Mississippi and St. Laurence valleys. It is also the site of a lock and dam marking the end of the Chicago Sanitary and Ship Canal in the Illinois Waterway.

Agriculturally, the city produces corn and wheat. Manufactures include concrete products, grain elevators, and computer data acquisitions systems. It is the site of Lewis College (1930).

POINTS OF INTEREST:

- Illinois and Michigan Canal Museum. 803 S State Street.

- HISTORICAL PLACES: (See Hist. Pl. Sect. for Details.)

    Will County Historical Society Headquarters (Illinois and Michigan Canal Office Building).

●**LODA,** Town, Iroquois County; Pop. 525; Area Code 217; Zip Code 60948; Elev. 781; E Illinois; Post office established March 10, 1880; Incorporated March 13, 1869.

●**LODGE,** Town, Piatt County; Pop. 150; Area Code 217; Zip Code 61856; Near Monticello; Post office established September 15, 1874; Incorporated August 16, 1910; Once called Woods.

●**LOGAN COUNTY,** Central Illinois; Area 622 sq. miles; Pop. 33,538; Seat Lincoln; Named for Dr. John Logan, pioneer physician and father of Gen. John A. Logan; Created 1839 from part of Sangamon County; Portion of Tazewell County added in 1840, and in 1845, a section of DeWitt was added.

First county seat was Postville, changed in 1847 to Mt. Pulaski, later Elkhart. Principal crops and products are corn, wheat, oats, hay, cattle, and pork.

●**LOMAX,** Town, Henderson County; Pop. 565; Area Code 217; Zip Code 61454; Elev. 550; W Illinois; Post office established March 1, 1870; Incorporated November 4, 1913.

●**LOMBARD,** City, DuPage County; Pop. 37,000; Area Code 312; Zip Code 60148; Elev. 700; NE Illinois; 20 miles west of Chicago; Reached by US 30; Post office established April 7, 1868; Incorporated March 29, 1869.

First white settler was Winslow Churchill (1834). City was named for Josiah Lombard, who platted the town in the early 1860s. Principal industries are plastics, dairy farms. Site of Lilacia Park, and noted for annual Lilac Festival and Parade.

●**LONDON MILLS,** Town, Fulton and Knox counties; Pop. 610; Area Code 309; Zip Code 61544; Elev. 534; W Central Illinois; Post office established February 3, 1875; Incorporated November 27, 1883.

● **LONG CREEK,** Town, Macon County; Pop. 250; Area Code 217; Zip Code 62521; Near Decatur.

● **LONG POINT,** Town, Livingston County; Pop. 310; Area Code 815; Zip Code 61333: Elev. 638; Post office established November 2, 1847; Incorporated July 27, 1889.

● **LONGVIEW,** Town, Champaign County; Pop. 224; Area Code 217; Zip Code 61852; Elev. 680; Post office established August 3, 1889.

● **LORAINE,** Town, Adams County; Pop. 372; Area Code 217; Zip Code 62349; Elev. 648; Post office established May 15, 1871; Incorporated June 20, 1881.

● **LOSTANT,** Town, LaSalle County; Pop. 46S; Area Code 815; Zip Code 61334; Elev. 700; Post office established October 16, 1861; Incorporated February 16, 1865.

● **LOTUS WOODS,** Town, Lake County; Pop. 350; Area Code 815; Zip Code 60081; Near Spring Grove.

● **LOUISVILLE,** Town, Clay County seat; Pop. 1,020; Area Code 618; Zip Code 62858; Elev. 480; SE Central Illinois; Post office established July 1, 1839; Incorporated March 1, 1867; Named for a man called Lewis who owned a gristmill on the Little Wabash River; Principal industry: oil wells.

● **LOVES PARK,** City, Winnebago County; Pop. 12,198; Area Code 815; Zip Code 61111; Elev. 740; N Central Illinois; NE of Rockford; Incorporated April 30, 1947; Named for Malcolm Love, who bought a 9,236-acre farm on the Rock River just north of Rockford; Industries: machine tools, governors, clutches.

●**LOXA,** Town, Coles County; Pop. 70; Area Code 217; Zip Code 61938; Near Mattoon; Post office established July 22, 1862.

● **LYNDON,** Town, Whiteside County; Pop. 673; Area Code 815; Zip Code 61261; Elev. 615; NW Illinois; Post office established June 18, 1838; Incorporated March 3, 1874.

● **LYNWOOD,** Town, Cook County; Pop. 1,042; Area Code 312; Zip Code 60411; NE Illinois; Near Chicago Heights; Reached by US 30; Incorporated December 23, 1959.

● **LYNWOOD,** Town, Kendall County; Pop. 400; Zip Code 60543; Near Oswego.

●**LYONS,** City, Cook County; Pop. 11,124; Area Code 312; Zip Code 60534; Elev. 625; NE Illinois; 8 miles west of Chicago; Post office established February 29, 1848; Incorporated July 18, 1888; On the Chicago portage between the valleys of the St. Laurence and Mississippi rivers.

Lyons is a residential village located at an old portage between the Des Plaines River and the Chicago River, which was used by Marquette and other early French explorers and by the Indians. It is the site of Hofmann Tower, on a dam built (1908) by George Hofmann to generate electricity for a beer garden.

●**McCORMICK,** Town, Pope County; Pop. rural; Area Code 618; Zip Code 62987; Near Stonefort; Post office established September 16, 1889.

● **MACEDONIA,** Town, Hamilton and Franklin counties; Pop. 86; Area Code 618; Zip Code 62860; Elev. 480; Post office established August 27, 1861; Incorporated March 3, 1894.

●**McHENRY,** City, McHenry County; Pop. 8,459; Area Code 815; Zip Code 60050; Elev. 761; NE Illinois; On the Fox River, reached by Ill. Highway 120; Platted 1837; Post office established June 27, 1837; Incorporated February 15, 1855.

McHenry is the western gateway to the Chain 0' Lakes. The first settler was Dr. Christy Wheeler in 1836. City was named for an army officer in the War of 1812 and the Black Hawk War of 1832.

POINTS OF INTEREST:

  ● Moraine Hills State Park. 914 S River Road.

  ● Old Volo Museums and Village. 5 miles E on IL 120 in Volo.

● **MACKINAW,** Town, Tazewell County; Pop. 1,444; Area Code 309; Zip Code 61755; Elev. 680; Central Illinois;

Reached by Ill. Highway 9; Platted 1827; Post office established May 14, 1827; Incorporated January 21, 1840; Name is an Ojibway Indian word meaning "turtle."

● **McLEAN,** Town, McLean County; Pop. 820; Zip Code 61754; Elev. 700; Central Illinois; Reached by US 66 and I-55; Post office established February 29, 1856; Incorporated January 23, 1873.

● **MACOMB,** City, McDonough County seat; Pop. 23,100; Area Code 309; Zip Code 61455; Elev. 700; W Illinois; 37 miles SSW of Galesburg, midway between the Mississippi and the Illinois rivers; Reached by US 136 and US 67; First settled 1830 as Washington, later named for Alexander Macomb, Commander-in- Chief of the U.S. Army, 1828-41; Post office established November 4, 1831; Incorporated January 27, 1841.

Industries include Illinois license plates, pottery, clay, and steel products, ball bearings, coal mines, electric fencing, and agriculture. Site of Western Illinois University (1899).

POINTS OF INTEREST:

● Argyle Lake State Park. 7 miles SW on US 136, then 1 1/2 miles North.

● Clarence Watson/Wiley Schoolhouse Museum. 301 W Calhoun.

● Spring Lake Park. 3 miles N on US 67, then 2 miles W, then 1 mile North.

● Western Illinois University (1899). 900 W Adams Street, NW edge of city.

● HISTORICAL PLACES: (See Hist. Pl. Sect. for Details.)

McDonough County

● **MACON,** Town, Macon County; Pop. 1,249; Area Code 217; Zip Code 62544; Elev. 721; Central Illinois; Reached by US 51; Founded 1835; Post office established August 16, 1864; Incorporated April 15, 1869,

Macon is the site of a 5-million-bushel grain elevator and of a sanitarium for women run by the Order of the Eastern Star of Illinois.

● **MADISON,** City, Madison County; Pop. 7,042; Area Code 618; Zip Code 62060; Elev. 410; SW Illinois; Across the Mississippi River from St. Louis, reached by US 67; Post office established May 17, 1841; Platted 1889; Incorporated

November 2, 1891; First settlers called the site Venice because the river came to their doors every spring.

● **MAEYSTOWN,** Town, Monroe County; Pop. 109; Area Code 618; Zip Code 62256; Elev. 500; Post office established June 1, 1860; Incorporated March 28, 1904.

●**MAKANDA,** Town, Jackson County; Pop. 176; Area Code 618; Zip Code 62958; Elev. 437; Post office established January 11, 1870; Incorporated February 7, 1888.

● **MALDEN,** Town, Bureau County; Pop. 262; Zip Code 61337; Elev. 704; Post office established February 19, 1857; Incorporated April 22, 1882.

● **MANCHESTER,** Town, Scott County; Pop. 335; Area Code 217; Zip Code 62663; Elev. 696; Post office established May 30, 1832; Incorporated February 21, 1861.

●**MANHATTAN,** Town, Will County; Pop. 1,530; Area Code 815; Zip Code 60442; Elev. 690; NE Illinois; 47 miles from Loop, on US 52 between Joliet and Kankakee; Platted 1880 when the Wabash Railroad reached here; Post office established September 10, 1880; Incorporated December 20, 1886; Reached by US 52; Named for New York Island.

● **MANITO,** Town, Mason County; Pop. 1,334: Area Code 309; Zip Code 61546; Elev. 500; Central Illinois; 17 miles SW of Pekin: Gateway to Mason State Forest (5,000 acres) and to the Spring Lake Conservation Area; Platted 1858; Post office established November 4, 1861; Incorporated April 20, 1876; Name is Algonquin Indian word meaning "the Great Spirit"; A trade center for farmers producing wheat, corn, soybeans, melons, and Christmas trees.

● **MANLIUS,** Town, Bureau County; Pop. 402; Area Code 815; Zip Code 61338; Elev. 710; N Central Illinois; Post office established May 22, 1871; Incorporated June 21, 1905.

● **MANSFIELD,** Town, Piatt County; Pop. 870; Area Code 217; Zip Code 61854; Elev. 727; E Central Illinois; Post office established July 27, 1870; Incorporated March 3, 1876.

● **MANTENO,** Town, Kankakee County; Pop, 2,864; Area Code 815; Zip Code 60950; Elev. 680; E Illinois; 10 miles north of Kankakee; Reached by US 45, Post office established April 25, 1854; Incorporated April 20, 1878; Named for half- Indian daughter of Francois Bourbonnais, Jr., a nineteenth- century French scout for whom a Kankakee River village is named.

Once a French settlement, it was a trading post until the Illinois Central Railroad reached here in 1853. It is 12 miles NE of 2,121-acre Kankakee River State Park.

● **MAQUON,** Town, Knox County; Pop. 374; Area Code 309; Zip Code 61458; Elev. 627; Post office established May 15, 1837; Incorporated April 19, 1873.

● **MARINE,** Town, Madison County; Pop. 882; Area Code 618; Zip Code 62061; Elev. 528; SW Illinois; Post office established September 15, 1851; Incorporated March 8, 1867.

● **MARION HILLS,** Town, DuPage County; Pop. (included with Darien) 12,257; Area Code 312; Zip Code 60559; NE Illinois.

● **MARISSA,** Village, St. Clair County; Pop. 2,568; Area Code 618; Zip Code 62257; Elev. 448; SW Illinois. The original post office was established in 1841 by James Wilson, Jr, and in 1846, he was appointed postmaster by President James K. Polk. The area, which was incorporated on May 26, 1882, was named by Wilson, who chose it from his copy of *Antiquities of the Jews.*

Agriculturally, the area produces soybeans, corn, and wheat. Its manufactures include coal mining.

● **MARKHAM,** City, Cook County; Pop. 15,987; Area Code 312; Zip Code 60426; Elev. 615; NE Illinois; Southern suburb of Chicago reached by US 6; Incorporated October 23, 1925; Named for a former president of the Illinois Central Railroad.

● **MARLEY,** Town, Will County; Pop. 100; Area Code 312; Zip Code 60448; Near Mokena; Post office established August 13, 1880.

● **MAROA,** Town, Macon County; Pop. 1,467; Area Code 217; Zip Code 61756; Elev. 710; Central Illinois; 13 miles north of Decatur, reached by US 51; Post office established March 30, 1855; Incorporated March 7, 1867; Named when members of the town council pulled letters from a hat.

● **MARSEILLES,** Town, LaSalle County; Pop. 4,320; Area Code 815; Zip Code 61341; Elev. 504; N Central Illinois; Reached by I-80; Post office established November 9, 1835;

Incorporated February 21, 1861; Name, pronounced "Marsales," is taken from the old Mediterranean port.

Marseilles is situated in a moraine caused by a glacier. At the turn of the century, it was an active port shipping grains, paper, flour, and lumber. Principal industries today are paper boxes, steel assembly, and clothing.

● **MARSHALL,** Town, Clark County Seat; Pop. 3,468; Area Code 217; Zip Code 62441; Elev. 641; E Illinois; 3 miles north of Lincoln Trail State Park; Reached by US 40; Post office established August 31, 1837; Incorporated February 10, 1853; Named for John Marshall.

● **MARSHALL COUNTY,** North central Illinois; Area 391 sq. miles; Pop. 13,302; Seat Lacon; Settlers arrived 1827; Established January 19, 1839; Named for John Marshall, Chief Justice of U.S. Supreme Court.

Bisected by the Illinois River and drained by Sugar Creek, the county's fertile soil produces crops of corn, wheat, hay, oats. Other industries are hogs and coal.

● **MARTINSVILLE,** Town, Clark County; Pop. 1,374; Area Code 217; Zip Code 62442; Elev. 574; E Illinois; Reached by US 40 and I-70; Platted 1833 by Joseph Martin on the north fork of the Embarras River; Post office established April 14, 1834; Incorporated June 13, 1905.

● **MARTINTON,** Town, Iroquois County; Pop. 278; Area Code 815; Zip Code 60951; Elev. 625; Reached by Ill. Highway 1; Post office established September 8, 1873; Incorporated September 27, 1875.

● **MARYVILLE,** Town, Madison County; Pop. 1,703; Area Code 618; Zip Code 62062; Elev. 582; SW Illinois; Reached by US 40 and I-70; Incorporated June 4, 1902; Post office established June 19, 1903.

● **MASCOUTAH,** City, St. Clair County; Pop. 5,045; Area Code 618; Zip Code 62258; Elev. 424; SW Illinois; 23 miles ESE of East St. Louis; Post office established August 6, 1838; Incorporated February 16, 1839; Name is Algonquin Indian word meaning "prairie."

● **MASON,** Town, Effingham County; Pop. 415; Area Code 618; Zip Code 62443; Elev. 594; Reached by I-57 and US 45; Post office established August 5, 1857; Incorporated February 15, 1865.

● **MASON CITY,** Town, Mason County; Pop. 2,611; Area Code 217; Zip Code 62664; Elev. 570; Central Illinois; 28 miles north of Springfield; Platted 1857 on land owned by George Straut, a director of the Tonica, Petersburg and Jacksonville Railroad; Post office established September 22, 1858; Incorporated March 4, 1869. Trading center for the corn belt and site of two grain elevators.

● **MASON COUNTY,** Central Illinois; Area 541 sq. miles; Pop. 16,180; Seat Havana; Established January 20, 1841; Named for a county in Kentucky.

A little NW of the center of the state, the county's western and southern boundaries are formed by the Illinois and Sangamon rivers, An American pioneer of the county was Major Ossian B. Ross, who settled in Havana in 1832. County seat was Bath until 1851. Corn is the chief crop.

● **MASSAC COUNTY,** Southern Illinois; Area 541 sq. miles; Pop. 13,889; Seat Metropolis; Established January 8, 1843; Named for Fort Massac.

One of the smallest counties in Illinois, Massac's natural resources consist largely of timber--oak, walnut, poplar, hickory, cypress, and cottonwood--and sawmills are found in almost every town. Land is hilly toward the north, bottom lands along the Ohio River are swampy and subject to frequent overflows.

Original settlers were largely from Ohio, Kentucky, and North Carolina. Ruins of an early French fort can be found at Massac City.

● **MATTESON,** City, Cook County; Pop. 8,350; Area Code 312; Zip Code 60443; Elev. 701; NE Illinois; 26 miles south of Chicago; Founded by German settlers in the 1850s; Post office established November 29, 1856; Incorporated March 20, 1889; Named for Gov. Joel A. Matteson.

● **MATTOON,** City, Coles County; Pop. 19,293; Area Code 217; Zip Code 61938; Elev. 726; E central Illinois; 40 miles SE of Decatur; Immediately north of the most southerly advance of the last glacier; Reached by US 45, Ill. Highway 16, and I-57; Founded in 1855 on the site where the Illinois Central Railroad and Terre Haute & Alton Railroad crossed. Named for the engineer in charge of construction, William Mattoon, the post office was established on July 14, 1855, and the area was incorporated on February 22, 1859.

In 1986, when the Statue of Liberty was undergoing a refurbishing, the lights used to relight Lady Liberty were made in Mattoon. Also that year, the world's largest bagel factory opened in the city, and more than 2 million bagels are made there each day.

Agriculturally, the area produces soybeans and corn. Its industry includes cement blocks, baby shoes, road-building equipment, flashbulbs, quartz lamps, pet food, frozen onion rings, springs, flexible hose, heat-transfer equipment, castings, printing, and brooms. Mattoon is the site of Lake Land College (1966).

● **MAYWOOD,** Village, Cook County; Pop. 27,998; Area Code 312; Zip Code 60163; Elev. 626; NE Illinois; 12 miles west of Chicago, on west bank of Des Plaines River; Reached by Eisenhower Expressway. The area was founded in the late 1860s by a group of New Englanders headed by Colonel W. T. Nichols, who named the settlement for his daughter May. The post office was established on April 29, 1870, and the village was incorporated on October 31, 1881. Industry in the early days was agricultural. The Chicago Union Railroad, passing through Maywood, was used to transport wheat. The city now has light manufacturing and retail.

Maywood served as an early home to poet Carl Sandburg, and was the location of one of the first airports in the United States to be used by aviator Charles Lindbergh. The airport, Checkerboard Field, was also utilized in the inauguration of the first United States airmail flights.

● **MAZON,** Town, Grundy County; Pop. 727; Area Code 815; Zip Code 60444; Elev. 586; NE Illinois; Post office established November 30, 1837; Incorporated April 30, 1895.

● **MEADOWBROOK,** Town, Madison County; Pop. 1,900; Area Code 618; Zip Code 62010; SW Illinois; Near Bethalto and Moro.

● **MECHANICSBURG,** Town, Sangamon County; Pop. 490; Area Code 217; Zip Code 62545; Elev. 595; Post office established May 7, 1838; Incorporated March 26, 1869; Once called Clear Creek.

● **MEDINAH,** Town, DuPage County; Pop. 1,200; Area Code 312; Zip Code 60157; Elev. 717; NE Illinois; Post office established March 7, 1924.

● **MEDORA,** Town, Macoupin County; Pop. 505; Area Code 618; Zip Code 62063; Elev. 600; SW Central Illinois; Reached by US 67; Post office established July 9, 1866; Incorporated January 10, 1874; Once called Delaware, Rhoades Point, and Trumbull.

● **MELROSE PARK,** City, Cook County; Pop. 19,900; Area Code 312; Zip Code 60160; Elev. 640; NE Illinois; Industrial suburb 12 miles west of Chicago with a large Italian population; Reached by US 20; Founded 1860 when road NW from Chicago toward Galena was cut; Post office established January 28, 1893; Incorporated March 13, 1893; Industries: plastics, metal products, structural steel, cosmetics, store fixtures, paints, and food products.

● **MELVIN,** Town, Ford County; Pop. 492; Area Code 217; Zip Code 60952; Elev. 800; Post office established February 12, 1872; Incorporated March 12, 1889.

● **MENARD COUNTY,** Central Illinois; Area 312 sq. miles; Pop. 9,685; Seat Petersburg; Near geographical center of the state, originally a part of Sangamon County; Established February 15, 1839; Named for Pierre Menard, first lieutenant governor of Illinois.

Among early American settlers were Matthew Rogers, Amor Batterton, Solomon Pruitt, and William Gideon. The town of Salem was, for some years, the home of Abraham Lincoln, who was once its postmaster, and who marched to the Black Hawk War as captain of a company. Three veins of bituminous coal underlie the county.

● **MENDOTA,** City, LaSalle County; Pop. 6,902; Area Code 815; Zip Code 61342; Elev. 740; N Central Illinois; 12 miles north of LaSalle, 20 miles NW of Ottawa; Reached by US 51, US 52, and Ill. Highway 92; Name comes from Dakota Indian word, *mdote,* meaning "mouth" or "junction of one river with another."

Birthplace of cartoonist Helen Hokinson. Principal industries: farm machinery, building materials, feed, livestock farms.

● **MEPPEN,** Town, Calhoun County; Pop. 50; Area Code 618; Zip Code 62064; Elev. 470; Post office established September 29, 1876.

● **MEREDOSIA,** Town, Morgan County; Pop. 1,178; Area Code 217; Zip Code 62665; Elev. 446; W Central Illinois;

At mouth of Meredosia Lake, 257 miles from Chicago, 107 miles from St. Louis; Post office established January 19, 1832; Incorporated February 25, 1867; Name said to be a corruption of the French *marais d'osier,* meaning "swamp of basket reeds"; Industries: power station, synthetic resins and polymers, fertilizer.

● **MERNA,** Town, McLean County; Pop. 55; Area Code 309; Zip Code 61738; Elev. 809; Post office established October 5, 1883.

● **MERRIONETTE PARK,** Town, Cook County; Pop. 2,303; Area Code 312; Zip Code 60655; Elev. 620; NE Illinois; Residential subdivision 16 miles SW of the Loop; Reached by Ill. Highway 1; Incorporated February 18, 1947.

● **METAMORA,** Town, Woodford County; Pop. 2,338; Area Code 309; Zip Code 61548; Elev. 821; N Central Illinois; Reached by Ill. Highways 89 and 116; First settled 1824 as Hanover; Incorporated February 21, 1845; Post office established August 23, 1845.

Once called Black Partridge and Hanover, the final name was coined by playwright John Stone, as the name for King Philip, son of Chief Massasoit, killed 1676, in a popular play called "Metamora, or the Last of the Wampanoags." Home of Adlai Stevenson before he moved to Bloomington, where his grandson, later governor of Illinois, was born.

● **METCALF,** Town, Edgar County; Pop. 269; Area Code 217; Zip Code 61940; Elev. 663; Post office established December 15, 1874; Incorporated February 16, 1885.

● **METROPOLIS,** City; Massac County Seat; Pop. 6,940; Area Code 618; Zip Code 62960; Elev. 345; On Ohio River NW of Paducah, Kentucky, SE Illinois tip; Reached by US 45; Settled 1796; Platted 1839 by William A. McBane, an engineer and merchant from New Orleans; Incorporated February 18, 1859; Post office established December 12, 1904; Called "City of Roses"; Industries; chemicals, gloves, agriculture.

● HISTORICAL PLACES: (See Hist. Pl. Sect. for Details.)

Fort Massac Site.

● **METTAWA,** Town, Lake County; Pop. 285; Zip Code 60048; Elev. 675; Near Libertyville; Incorporated January 25, 1960; Name is that of a Potawatomi chief.

● **MIDDLETOWN,** Town, Logan County; Pop. 626; Area Code 217; Zip Code 62666; Elev. 583; Central Illinois; Reached by US 66 and I-55; Post office established February 7, 1837; Incorporated November 17, 1900.

●**MIDLAND CITY,** Town, DeWitt County; Pop. rural; Area Code 217; Zip Code 61727; Near Clinton; Post office established August 5, 1875.

● **MIDLOTHIAN,** City, Cook County; Pop. 14,241; Area Code 312; Zip Code 60445; Elev. 615; NE Illinois; 18 miles south of Chicago, reached by Ill. Highways 50 and 83 and I-57; Named for a golf club built here in 1898 by George R. Thorne, then head of Montgomery Ward, and named for a shire in Scotland.

● **MILAN,** Town, Rock Island County; Pop. 6,036; Area Code 309; Zip Code 61264; Elev. 570; NW Illinois; 4 miles south of Rock Island on south bank of Rock River below a promontory in Black Hawk State Park; Reached by US 67 and Ill. Highway 287; Platted 1843 by New Yorker William Dickson; Post office established December 21, 1870; Incorporated March 13, 1893; Name pronounced Mee'-lan.

Located at the conflux of the Rock and Mississippi rivers and is served by the Hennepin Canal. Principal industries are quarries, gravel pits, industrial pumps, and agriculture.

● **MILDRED,** Town, Sangamon County; Pop. 1,900; Area Code 217; Zip Code 62707; Near Springfield; Central Illinois.

●**MILFORD,** Town, Iroquois County; Pop. 1,656; Area Code 815; Zip Code 60953; Elev. 670; E Illinois; Reached by Ill. Highway 1; Post office established March 13, 1840; Incorporated March 16, 1874; Once called Driftwood, Pickerell's Mill; Named for a mill near a ford at the Hubbard Trail crossing of Sugar Creek; Trade center for a cattle-raising area and site of a vegetable-canning factory.

● **MILLBURN,** Town, Lake County; Pop. 50; Area Code 312; Zip Code 60046; Near Lake Villa and Wadsworth; Post office established January 24, 1848; Once called Strong's Neighborhood.

● **MILLEDGEVILLE,** Town, Carroll County; Pop. 1,130; Area Code 815; Zip Code 61051; Elev. 749; NW Illinois; Reached by US 52; Post office established February 22,

1844; Incorporated May 24, 1887; Name derived from the sawmill built in 1834 by Jesse Kester, an early settler, at the edge of the "ville"; Boasts the largest Swiss Cheese factory in the world.

● **MILLER CITY,** Town, Alexander County; Pop. 50; Area Code 618; Zip Code 62962; Elev. 335; Post office established October 27, 1911.

● **MILLSTADT,** Town, St. Clair County; Pop. 2,332; Area Code 618; Zip Code 62260; Elev. 620; SW Illinois; Reached by Ill. Highways 158 and 163; Platted 1836 as Centerville; Name translated into German by residents because Illinois already had a post office of that name; Post office established June 7, 1843; Incorporated January 16, 1878.

● **MILTON,** Town, Pike County; Pop. 337; Area Code 217; Zip Code 62352; Elev. 660; Post office established August 15, 1837; Incorporated February 21, 1861.

● **MINIER,** Town, Tazewell County; Pop. 986; Area Code 309; Zip Code 61759; Elev. 630; Central Illinois; Post office established November 26, 1867; Incorporated July 17, 1872.

●**MINONK,** Town, Woodford County; Pop. 2,267; Area Code 309; Zip Code 61760; Elev. 750; N Central Illinois; 33 miles ENE of Peoria; Reached by US 51; Town began when a boarding house was erected 1854 for track workers of Illinois Central Railroad; Post office established December 22, 1854; Incorporated March 7, 1867; Name derived from Algonquin words, *mino,* meaning "good," and *onk,* meaning "place"; Industries: dairy products, grain, and livestock farms.

● **MINOOKA,** Town, Grundy and Will counties; Pop. 1,192; Area Code 815; Zip Code 60447; Elev. 590; NE Illinois; Post office established February 21, 1854; Incorporated March 27, 1869; Name is a corruption of Delaware Indian words *mino* ("good") and *oki* ("land").

● **MITCHELL,** Town, Madison County; Pop. 1,500; Area Code 618; Zip Code 62040; Elev. 427; SW Illinois; Reached by US 67; Post office established March 10, 1892.

● **MITCHELLSVILLE,** Town, Saline County; Pop. 100; Zip Code 62917; Near Carriers Mills; Post office established December 22, 1854.

● **MOKENA,** Town, Will County; Pop. 3,121; Area Code 312; Zip Code 60448; Elev. 700; NE Illinois; Reached by I-80 and I-57; Post office established February 10, 1853; Incorporated May 24, 1880; Name is a variation of the Algonquin word for "turtle."

Situated 1 mile north of the Van Horn Woods. Site of grave of Charles Denny, a veteran of the American Revolution who died in 1839. Industries include wallpaper and a foundry.

● **MOLINE,** City, Rock Island County; Pop. 42,000; Area Code 309; Zip Code 61265; Elev. 580; NW Illinois; Post office established March 13, 1844; Settled 1847; Incorporated February 14, 1855.

One of the Quad Cities, Moline is an industrial city on the Mississippi River just above Rock Island. Its industries include agricultural machinery, tools, ventilators, and furniture. It is the site of Black Hawk College (1946).

POINTS OF INTEREST:

  ● Center for Belgian Culture. 712 18th Avenue.
  ● Ziabi Zoo. 10 miles SE on US 6.

● **MONEE,** Town, Will County; Pop. 400; Area Code 312; Zip Code 60449; Elev. 800; NE Illinois; Reached by Ill. Highway 1; Post office established October 3, 1853; Incorporated November 9, 1874; Name is Indian pronunciation of name of Marie Lefevre (1783-1866), Indian wife of Joseph Bailly, a French trader.

● **MONROE COUNTY,** SW Illinois, bordering on the Mississippi River; Area 382 sq. miles; Pop. 18,831; Seat Waterloo; Established June 1, 1816; Named for President James Monroe.

First American settlers arrived in 1781. County is heavily timbered, accounting for its chief industry being the manufacture and shipping of lumber. Agriculture is also important.

● **MONTGOMERY,** Town, Kane and Kendall counties; Pop. 3,311; Area Code 312; Zip Code 60538; Elev. 642; NE Illinois; Industrial suburb 41 miles south of Aurora; Reached by US 34 and Ill. Highways 25 and 31; Post office established January 20, 1848; Incorporated September 26, 1894.

Montgomery was settled in 1840 by immigrants from Montgomery County in New York. Its major industries are soap and steel equipment.

● **MONTICELLO,** City; Piatt County Seat; Pop. 4,360; Area Code 217; Zip Code 61856; Elev. 675; E Central Illinois; 25 miles NE of Decatur; Reached by I-57 and US 45; Founded with a barbecue and auction sale of lots on July 4, 1837; Post office established December 18, 1837; Incorporated January 27, 1841; Named by land promoters for the home of Thomas Jefferson.

Monticello is the center of a 50-mile Grand Heritage tour in Piatt County. Also the site of the former estate of hog-cattle baron Robert H. Allerton (1873-1964).

● **MORRIS,** City; Grundy County Seat; Pop. 8,563; Area Code 815; Zip Code 60450; Elev. 531; NE Illinois; 20 miles SW of Joliet; Reached by US 6 and Ill. Highway 47; Post office established September 16, 1842; Incorporated February 12, 1853; Named for Isaac N. Morris, a canal commissioner for the Illinois and Michigan Canal (1848).

On west edge of city is Gebhard Woods State Park (33 acres). Principal industries are vending machines, carpet padding, egg cartons, limestone quarries, and dairy farms.
POINTS OF INTEREST:

● Gebhard Woods State Park. W edge of town.

● **MORRISON,** Town, Whiteside County Seat; Pop. 4,387; Area Code 815; Zip Code 61270; Elev. 716; NW Illinois; 40 miles NE of Rock Island on the Rock River 50 miles NE of the Quad Cities and 130 miles west of Chicago; Reached by Ill. Highway 78 and US 30; Post office established June 5, 1857; Incorporated February 27, 1867; Industries: furniture, electrical appliances, stock farms.

● **MORRISONVILLE,** Town, Christian County; Pop. 1,178; Area Code 217; Zip Code 62546; Elev. 625; Central Illinois; Reached by US 48; Post office established July 14, 1849; Incorporated October 19, 1872; Founded by and named by Col. J. L. D. Morrison, a veteran of the Civil War and son-in-law of Thomas Carlin, sixth governor of Illinois (1838-42); Industries: grain elevator and farm-machinery sales.

● **MORTON,** City, Tazewell County; Pop. 13,243; Area Code 309; Zip Code 61550; Elev. 710; N Central Illinois; 10 miles SE of Peoria; Reached by Ill. Highway 74; Post office established November 2, 1842; Incorporated August 18, 1877; Named for Marcus Morton, governor of Massachusetts (1840-

44); Principal industries: tractors, canning, pottery, washing machines.

●**MORTON GROVE,** City, Cook County; Pop. 26,300; Area Code 312; Zip Code 60053; Elev. 625; NE Illinois; Residential suburb 15 miles north of Chicago on north branch of Chicago River; Reached by Ill. Highways 43 and 58; Post office established July 2, 1874; Incorporated September 24, 1895; Named for Levi Parsons Morton (1824-1920), an official of the Chicago, Milwaukee, and St. Paul Railroad when it was built in 1872, and later Vice-President of the U.S. under President Benjamin Harrison.

First settled in 1831 by immigrant farmers from England. Primarily rural area until after WWII. Industries include pharmaceuticals, cosmetics, heating and air-conditioning equipment, industrial equipment.
POINTS OF INTEREST:

● Bradford Museum of Collector's Plates. 2 miles NW, just
S of Golf Road at 9333 Milwaukee Avenue in Niles.

●**MOSSVILLE,** Town, Peoria County; Pop. 600; Area Code 309; Zip Code 61552; Elev. 471; Post office established April 19, 1855; Named for William Moss.

● **MOULTRIE COUNTY,** Central Illinois; Area 345 sq. miles; Pop. 13,263; Seat Sullivan since 1845; In the eastern section of the middle tier of the state; Established February 16, 1843; Named for Gen. William Moultrie, successful defender of Fort Moultrie at Charleston during the Revolution; Earliest immigrants were from the SW; Contains a vein of bituminous coal.

● **MOUND CITY,** City; Pulaski County Seat; Pop. 1,177; Area Code 618; Zip Code 62961; Elev. 327; S Illinois; On Ohio River, 8 miles south of confluence with Mississippi River; Union Army used Mound City Marine Ways for gunboat repair during Civil War; Flood in 1937 covered town.

● HISTORICAL PLACES: (See Hist. Pl. Sect. for Details.)

Mound City Civil War Naval Hospital.

● **MOUNDS,** Town, Pulaski County; Pop. 1,718; Area Code 618; Zip Code 62964; Elev. 423; S Illinois; 10 miles north of confluence of Ohio and Mississippi rivers; Post office established October 15, 1903; Incorporated July 11, 1908; Named for Indian burial mounds nearby; Once called Beechwood Junction, and Mound City Junction.

● **MOUNT ERIE,** Town, Wayne County; Pop. 149; Area Code 618; Zip Code 62446; Elev. 500; SE Illinois; Post office established October 18, 1854; Incorporated March 26, 1895; Once called Ramsey's Grove.

● **MOUNT MORRIS,** Town, Ogle County; Pop, 3,173; Area Code 815; Zip Code 61054; Elev. 916; N Central Illinois; 25 miles SW of Rockford; 8 miles NE of White Pines Forest State Park (385 acres), and 6.5 miles SE of Oregon, on the western edge of the Rock River Valley; Reached by Ill. Highway 64; Post office established March 31, 1841; Incorporated February 13, 1857.

Rock River Methodist Seminary established 1839, two years before town was platted by Germans who migrated west from Pennsylvania and Maryland. Originally a college town, now a printing and publishing center.

● **MOUNT OLIVE,** Town, Macoupin County; Pop. 2,288; Area Code 217; Zip Code 62069; Elev. 681; SW Central Illinois; Reached by US 66; Post office established January 27, 1852; Incorporated October 1874.

The first settlers came in 1826, but growth was established by German immigrants during mid-1840s. Wabash Railroad built through here in 1870. Home of Mother Jones (1830-1930) and site of monument to United Mine Workers killed at the Virden Massacre and buried at Edwardsville. Industries: slide rules and lithographed business forms.

● HISTORICAL PLACES: (See Hist. Pl. Sect. for Details.)

Union Miners Cemetery.

● **MOUNT PROSPECT,** City, Cook County; Pop. 51,600; Area Code 312; Zip Code 60056; Elev. 675; NE Illinois; 21 miles NW of Chicago; Reached by US 12 and Ill. Highway 83; Post office established December 31, 1885; Incorporated February 3, 1917; Dominated by the Busse family, descendants of Friedrich Busse, a German immigrant who came here in 1848; Site of Randhurst shopping center (1962).

● **MOUNT PULASKI,** Town, Logan County; Pop. 1,677; Area Code 217; Zip Code 62548; Elev. 650; Central Illinois; 23 miles NE of Springfield; Reached by Ill. Highway 21 and US 54; Platted 1836; Post office established March 2, 1838; Incorporated January 4, 1893; Name changed from Scroggin.

Abraham Lincoln practiced law here while riding the Eighth Judicial Circuit. Home of Kickapoo Indians when the first settlers explored the Salt Creek Valley early in the nineteenth century. Now a farm marketing center.

● **MOUNT STERLING,** City; Brown County Seat; Pop. 2,182; Area Code 217; Zip Code 62353; Elev. 706; W Illinois; 34 miles east of Quincy; Reached by US 52 and Ill. Highway 99; Settled in 1830 by Robert Curry, who named the town for the sterling quality of the soil; Post office established March 26, 1833; Incorporated February 10, 1837.

Agriculturally, the area produces corn and beans, and its main industry is cheese; it is also the site of 2 grain elevators. The rural areas produce pottery as their industry. Mount Sterling is 11 miles from Siloam Springs State Park.

● **MOUNT VERNON,** City; Jefferson County Seat; Pop. 15,700; Area Code 618; Zip Code 62864; Elev. 500; S Central Illinois; 20 miles SE of Centralia; Reached by Ill. Highways 37, 148, and 15 and US 460; Settled 1819; Post office established March 29, 1827; Incorporated February 10, 1837.

Near $43 million Rend Lake. Site of largest coal mine in Illinois, Orient No. 3. Industries: shoes, iron castings, locomotive crankshafts, electrical equipment, furnaces, women's clothing, and agriculture.

POINTS OF INTEREST:

    ● Mitchell Museum. Richview Road.

● HISTORICAL PLACES: (See Hist. Pl. Sect. for Details.)

    Appellate Court, 5th District.

● **MOUNT ZION,** City, Macon County; Pop. 4,066; Area Code 217; Zip Code 62549; Elev. 681; Central Illinois; Post office established November 2, 1866; Incorporated April 13, 1881.

● **MOWEAQUA,** Town, Shelby and Christian Counties; Pop. 1,687; Area Code 217; Zip Code 62250; Elev. 620; Central Illinois; 16 miles from Decatur; Reached by US 51; Platted along the Illinois Central Railroad in 1852 near Flat Branch Creek; Post office established October 6, 1853; Incorporated May 26, 1877.

Moweaqua was scene of a 1932 Christmas mining disaster in which 54 men working in a local mine were entombed and fatally burned by a gas explosion. Name is Potawatomi Indian word meaning "weeping woman" or "wolf woman."

317

● **MULBERRY GROVE,** Town, Bond County; Pop. 697; Area Code 618; Zip Code 62262; Elev. 559; S Central Illinois; Reached by US 40 and I-70; Post office established October 15, 1834; Incorporated February 7, 1857; Once called Bucktown, Houston, and Shakerag; Sand is shipped from large deposits in nearby Hurricane Creek.

● **MUNDELEIN,** Village, Lake County; Pop. 17,053; Area Code 708; Zip Code 60060; Elev. 750; NE Illinois; Reached by US 45 and Ill. Highway 83. The first settler was Peter Shaddle in 1835. Through the years there have been several names for the area, including Mechanics Grove, Holcomb, Rockefeller, and Area, the latter being an acronym for Ability, Reliability, Endurance, and Action. Its current name was chosen in honor of Chicago's Cardinal George Mundelein. While the area was called Rockefeller, it was incorporated on July 12, 1909. The post office was established on May 1, 1925. At the time it was called Holcomb, members of the Diamond Lake Methodist Episcopal Church helped make the area a part of the intricate system that was the Underground Railroad, both during and after the Civil War.

In the 1920's, Samuel Insull, a Chicago business magnate, helped to develop the area for commuters. Like most of America, the village had to ride out the Great Depression and then rebuild until it was a thriving community once again. Industries include stamped dies, glassware, plastics, label machines, electro- plating, and scientific and medical equipment.

● **MURPHYSBORO,** City; Jackson County Seat; Pop. 9,629; Area Code 618; Zip Code 62966; Elev. 396; SW Illinois; 24 miles west of Marion; Reached by Ill. Highways 13 and 149; Founded 1843; Post office established December 23, 1843; Incorporated March 5, 1867.

Birthplace of Gen. John A. Logan, hero of the Civil War. Situated just north of Shawnee National Forest and Lake Murphysboro State Park, and 7 miles NW of Southern Illinois University at Carbondale. Principal industries are shoes, feed, and fertilizer.

● **MURRAYVILLE,** Town, Morgan County; Pop. 712; Area Code 217; Zip Code 62668; Elev. 687; W Central Illinois; Post office established February 16, 1863; Incorporated February 22, 1867.

● **NAPERVILLE,** City, DuPage and Will Counties; Pop. 29,300; Area Code 312; Zip Code 60540; Elev. 700; NE Illinois; 28 miles west of Chicago; Reached by US 34; Post office established March 1, 1836; Incorporated February 7, 1857; Named for Joseph Naper, who built a sawmill and platted the townsite in 1832.

The first settlers arrived here in 1831 and fled to Chicago's Fort Dearborn at the outbreak of the Black Hawk War in 1832. Major industries include laboratories, furniture, boilers, precision products, ice cream, and dietetic gum. Site of North Central College (1861), College of DuPage (1966), and Martin- Mitchell Museum.

POINTS OF INTEREST:

> ● Naper Settlement. Aurora Avenue, between Webster & Porter Streets.

● **NASHVILLE,** Town; Washington County Seat; Pop. 3,133; Area Code 618; Zip Code 62263; Elev. 532; S Central Illinois; 20 miles SW of Centralia; Reached by US 460 and Ill. Highway 127; Post office established October 31, 1831; Incorporated February 12, 1853; Named by Tennesseeans who platted town in 1830. Industries include loading machines and shovels for coal and phosphate mines. Situated 6 miles north of Washington County Conservation Area.

● **NAUVOO,** Town, Hancock County; Pop. 1,047; Area Code 217; Zip Code 62354; Elev. 659; W Illinois; On Mississippi River 45 miles north of Quincy; Reached by Ill. Highway 96; Post office established April 21, 1840; Incorporated February 1, 1841.

Occupied by Mormons under Joseph Smith (1838-39). Abandoned by Mormons who migrated to Utah in 1846 after Smith was killed by a mob in 1844. Was made site of a Utopian communistic society established 1849 by a group of French Icarians under leadership of Etienne Cabet. Settlement broke up in 1846 because of internal factional disagreements.

Major industry is cheese making. Site of 148-acre State Park and of St. Mary's Priory, motherhouse of Benedictine Sisters in the U. S.

POINTS OF INTEREST:

> ● Joseph Smith Historic Center. Water Street, 1 block W of IL 96.

- Nauvoo Restoration, Inc. Visitor Center. Young & Partridge Streets or N Main Street.
- Nauvoo State Park. S on IL 96.
- Old Carthage Jail (1839-41). 307 Walnut Street in Carthage; 12 miles S on IL 96, then 14 miles E on US 136.
- HISTORICAL PLACES: (See Hist. Pl. Sect. for Details.)

Nauvoo Historic District.

●**NEBO,** Town, Pike County; Pop. 454; Area Code 217; Zip Code 62355; Elev. 521; Post office established September 16, 1857; Incorporated August 3, 1885.

● **NEOGA,** Town, Cumberland County; Pop. 1,597; Area Code 217; Zip Code 62447; Elev. 650; E Central Illinois; Farm trading center between Mattoon and Effingham; Reached by I- 57; 2 miles south of Lake Mattoon on the Little Wabash River; Settled 1855 as a station on the Illinois Central Railroad; Post office established January 7, 1857; Incorporated April 5, 1930; Name derived from Iroquois Indian words, *new* ("supreme being"), and *oga* ("place").

●**NEW ATHENS,** Town, St. Clair County; Pop. 2,000; Area Code 618; Zip Code 62264; Elev. 429; SW Illinois; On the Kaskaskia River; 15 miles south of Belleville; Reached by Ill. Highway 13; Settled 1836 by French settlers who named town for city in Greece; Post office established April 10, 1866; Incorporated March 29, 1869; Industries: stove works and shoes.

●**NEW BADEN,** Town, Clinton and St. Clair counties; Pop. 2,278; Area Code 618; Zip Code 62265; Elev. 462; SW Illinois; 16 miles east of Belleville, near Scott AFB; Reached by Ill. Highway 160 and I-64; Incorporated February 28, 1867; Post office established March 26, 1867.

Once a coal-mining center called Looking Glass. Settled in 1855 by immigrants from Germany who named town for the spa in their homeland.

● **NEW BOSTON,** Town, Mercer County; Pop. 706; Area Code 309; Zip Code 61272; Elev. 577; NW Illinois; Post office established August 27, 1835; Incorporated February 21, 1859; Once called Dennison's Landing and Upper Yellow Banks.

● **NEW HAVEN,** Town, Gallatin County; Pop. 606; Area Code 618; Zip Code 62867; Elev. 370; SE Illinois; Post office established January 25, 1819; Incorporated February 15, 1839.

●**NEW LENOX,** City, Will County; Pop. 4,862; Area Code 815; Zip Code 60451; Elev. 675; NE Illinois; 6 miles east of Joliet; Reached by US 30; Settled in the 1820s by two fur traders, Aaron Friend and Joseph Brown; Post office established October 21, 1851; Incorporated May 25, 1946; Once called Tracy, Van Horne's Point, and Young Hickory.

●**NEWMAN,** Town, Douglas County; Pop. 1,018; Area Code 217; Zip Code 61942; Elev. 646; E Central Illinois; Reached by US 16 and US 36; First settled 1830 along Bushy Ford Creek; Founded 1857 and named for B. Newman, son-in-law of the Methodist circuit rider, Peter Cartwright.

● **NEWTON,** Town; Jasper County Seat; Pop. 3,188; Area Code 618; Zip Code 62448; Elev. 536; SE Illinois; 20 miles north of Olney; Reached by Ill. Highways 33 and 130; Incorporated February 15, 1831; Post office established March 20, 1833; Named for Sgt. John Newton, hero of the Revolutionary War; Industries: shoes, wood veneer, brooms, women's clothing, beverages. Trading center for farmers in the Embarras River valley.

● **NILES,** City, Cook County; Pop. 30,900; Area Code 312; Zip Code 60648; Elev. 650; NE Illinois; 14 miles north of Chicago; Post office established May 23, 1850; Incorporated August 24, 1899.

Once called Dutchman's Point and Lyttleton's Point, it derived its present name from pioneer newspaper owner William Ogden Niles. Once the site of a Civil War gristmill on the north branch of the Chicago River. City boasts 140 registered industries, including printing and lithography, typesetting, plate making, and binding and is the site of two major shopping centers.

● **NOBLE,** Town, Richland County; Pop. 719; Area Code 618; Zip Code 62868; Elev. 478; SE Illinois; Reached by US 50; Post office established February 13, 1854; Incorporated March 27, 1869.

●**NOKOMIS,** Town, Montgomery County; Pop. 2,532; Area Code 217; Zip Code 62075; Elev. 670: S Central Illinois; Reached by Ill. Highway 16; Post office established July 25, 1856; Incorporated March 9, 1867; Named for the grandmother of Hiawatha in Longfellow's poem. Industries: manufacture of skis and sleds, woodwork, and novelty items.

●**NORMAL,** City, McLean County; Pop. 26,396; Area Code 309; Zip Code 61761; Elev. 790; Central Illinois; Sister city of Bloomington; Named for the first state Normal School, opened here, 1857.

When the Normal School opened in North Bloomington, citizens shortly changed the town name to Normal. Situated in the midst of cornfields today, the city was once the focus of several Indian trails in a huge forest. A few trappers had a party here with Indians in the early 1800s, and the site was called Keg Grove when the first English settlers arrived in 1822.

Although this area is generally referred to as Bloomington- Normal. Normal residents have their own city government and public departments. The Normal School is now known as Illinois State University at Normal.

●**NORRIS CITY,** Town, White County; Pop. 1,515; Area Code 618; Zip Code 62869; Elev. 443; SE Illinois; 25 miles from Shawneetown, in an area called Little Egypt because of the confluence of the Ohio and Wabash rivers; Reached by US 45 and Ill. Highway 1. The town was platted in 1871, organized in 1874, and named after the Norris family who owned the largest portion of acreage in the area at that time. The post office was established on May 15, 1871, and the town was incorporated on November 6, 1901. Agriculturally, the area produces corn, wheat, and soybeans, and is the site of a grain elevator. Manufactures include metal fabrication, farm implements, and gas refinery.

●**NORTH BARRINGTON,** Town, Lake County; Pop. 1,411; Area Code 312; Zip Code 60010; Elev. 780; NE Illinois; 3 miles north of Barrington; Incorporated November 2, 1959.

●**NORTHBROOK,** Village, Cook County; Pop. 33,300; Area Code 708; Zip Code 60062; Elev. 650; NE Illinois; NW suburb of Chicago; Reached by I-94 and US 41. Founded by a German settler named Schermer, the area was originally called Shermerville; the named was changed to Northbrook in 1923. Some of the first settlers of Northbrook were French traders and trappers. The area was incorporated in 1901, and the post office was established on February 1, 1923.

Industries include Underwriters Laboratories, bakery equipment, and water-softening equipment.

POINTS OF INTEREST:

- Chicago Botanic Garden. 1/2 miles E of US 41 Lake-Cook exit on Lakecook Road in Glencoe.
- River Trail Nature Center. 3120 N Milwaukee Avenue, 1/2 mile S of Willow Road.

●**NORTH CHICAGO,** City, Lake County; Pop. 32,300; Area Code 312; Zip Code 60064; Elev. 650; NE Illinois; Industrial city in NE Illinois on Lake Michigan, 5 miles south of Waukegan and 37 miles north of the Loop; Reached by Ill. Highway 176; Post office established April 11, 1895; Incorporated February 18, 1909; Annexed Great Lakes Naval Training Center in 1960; Industries: automobile parts, chemicals, generators, steel, pharmaceuticals, hospital supplies.

●**NORTHFIELD WOODS,** Town, Cook County; Pop. 1,000; Area Code 312; Zip Code 60025; NE Illinois; Near Glenview.

● **NORTHLAKE,** City, Cook County; Pop. 14,191; Area Code 312; Zip Code 60164; Elev. 650; NE Illinois; NE suburb of Chicago astride North Ave. (Ill Highway 64) and Lake St. (US 20), west of Mannheim Rd. (US 12); Tri-State Tollway forms western city limits; Reached by US 20 and I-90; Incorporated April 23, 1949. Industries: telephones and electronic equipment, chemicals, paper, bakery goods, bearings, construction, food; Site of Triton College (1964).

● **OAK BROOK,** Town, DuPage and Cook counties; Pop. 4,800; Area Code 312; Zip Code 60521; Elev. 660; NE Illinois, 16 miles west of Chicago; Reached by I-294 and Ill. Highways 190 and 83; Incorporated February 21, 1958.

Elegant residential suburb, which started as a polo club, is site of Oak Brook Shopping Center, a tennis and polo club, two golf clubs, a stable, a fox hunt club, a soccer field, an archery course, an air strip, and a shooting preserve.

POINTS OF INTEREST:

- Fullersburg Woods Environmental Center. 3609 Spring Road.
- Old Graue Mill and Museum. York & Spring Roads.

● **OAKBROOK TERRACE,** Town, DuPage County; Pop. 1,692; Area Code 312; Zip Code 60181; NE Illinois; Near Villa Park; Elev. 700; Incorporated June 24, 1958; 1 sq. mile in area on the north border of the plush Oak Brook development; Bounded by Roosevelt Rd. on the north, Cermak Rd.

on the south, Midwest Rd. on the west, and Salt Creek and the Kingery Highway (Ill. Highway 83) on the east.

● **OAKDALE,** Town, Cook County; Pop. 200; Area Code 312; Zip Code 62268; Elev. 500; Post office established April 3, 1872.

● **OAKFORD,** Town, Menard County; Pop. 272; Area Code 217; Zip Code 62673; Elev. 495; Post office established July 17, 1874; Incorporated March 22, 1892.

● **OAK FOREST,** City, Cook County; Pop. 22,600; Area Code 312; Zip Code 60452; Elev. 660; NE Illinois, 20 miles south of Chicago; Reached by Ill. Highway 50, US 6, and I-80; Post office established November 21, 1912; Incorporated May 10, 1947; Residential community with no industry; Traversed by Midlothian Creek; Site of Cook County forest preserves and 2,464- bed Oak Forest Hospital.

● **OAK HILLS,** Town, St. Clair County; Pop. 1,000; Area Code 309; Zip Code 62232; SW Illinois; Near Caseyville.

● **OAKLAND,** Town, Coles County; Pop. 1,012; Area Code 217; Zip Code 61943; Elev. 656; SE Central Illinois; Post office established July 26, 1833; Incorporated February 9, 1855; Once called Independence and Pinhook.

● **OAK LAWN,** City, Cook County; Pop. 65,400; Area Code 312; Zip Code 60453; Elev. 615; NE Illinois, 12 miles SW of Chicago, one of the largest suburbs of Chicago in Cook County; Reached by US 66, Ill. Highway 50, and I-55; Settled 1842; Post office established March 22, 1895; Incorporated 1909.

Composed largely of individual homes, Oak Lawn has little industry. It is bounded by 87th St. on the north, 111th St. on the south, Pulaski on the east, and Harlem Ave. on the west.

● **OAKLEY,** Town, Macon County; Pop. 150; Zip Code 62552; Elev. 685; Post office established August 5, 1850.

● **OAK PARK,** City, Cook County; Pop. 58,000; Area Code 312; Zip Code 60302; Elev. 620; NE Illinois, 10 miles west of Chicago; Founded 1833; Post office established March 6, 1866; Incorporated November 13, 1901; Initially called Oak Ridge because of a slight, tree-covered rise which has since disappeared due to grading and building.

The first settler was Joseph Kettlestrings, who came from Maryland in 1833. The city is noted for the 25 structures, public and private, designed by Frank Lloyd Wright, including his own home and studio and the Unitarian Universalist Church. It is also the site of Emmaus Bible College (1941), and Freedom Hall, a free museum of historical documents founded in 1959 by I. M. Fixman and Philip D. Sang to illustrate man's eternal struggle for freedom.

City has council manager form of government. Sale of liquor has been prohibited by law.

POINTS OF INTEREST:

- Oak Park Visitors Center. 158 N Forest Avenue and Lake Street.

- HISTORICAL PLACES: (See Hist. Pl. Sect. for Details.)

Frank Lloyd Wright-Prairie School of Architecture Historic District; Gale, Mrs. Thomas H., House; Gale, Walter, House; Pleasant Home (Mills House, Farson House; Thomas, Frank, House; Unity Temple; Wright, Frank Lloyd, House and Studio.

●OBLONG, Town, Crawford County; Pop. 1,860; Area Code 618; Zip Code 62449; Elev. 524; In the Wabash River valley of SE Illinois 10 miles west of Robinson, the county seat.

●ODELL, Town, Livingston County; Pop. 1,076; Area Code 815; Zip Code 60460; NE Illinois; Near Streator.

●ODIN, Town, Marion County; Pop. 1,263; Area Code 618; Zip Code 62870; Elev. 527; S Central Illinois; Near Centralia; Mining and farming town.

● O'FALLON, Town, St. Clair County; Pop. 7,268; Area Code 618; Zip Code 62269; Elev. 550; SW Illinois; Near St. Louis and Mississippi River; Named for town site owner; settled, 1854; Residential area.

● OGDEN, Town, Champaign County; Pop. 543; Area Code 217; Zip Code 61859; W. Central Illinois; 10 miles east of Champaign.

● OGLE COUNTY, Northern Illinois; Area, 757 square miles; Pop. 42,867; Seat, Oregon; Named for Joseph Ogle, early Illinois settler and soldier; Established January 16, 1836 from a section of Jo Daviess County.

●OGLESBY, Town, La Salle County; Pop, 4,175; Area Code 815; Zip Code 61358; Elev. 465; N Central Illinois; Near La

Encyclopedia of Illinois

Salle; On Vermillion River; Named for Governor Richard J. Oglesby.

● **OHIO RIVER,** Southern Illinois; Forms border between Kentucky and state; Flows through Pulaski, Massac, Pope, Hardin and Gallatin Counties in southwesterly direction; source at junction of Allegheny and Monongahela Rivers; Mouth at Mississippi River near Cairo, Illinois; Used to transport coal, stone, cement, iron, steel, oil and timber; Major transportation route for early settlers, Indians; Prone to flooding the land around it.

● **OLNEY,** Town; Richland County seat; Pop. 8,974; Area Code 618; Zip Code 62450; Elev. 484; SE Illinois; 31 miles west of Vincennes, Indiana; Named for John Olney, lawyer and Civil War lieutenant. In 1858, the Olney *Times* became first U.S. newspaper to endorse Abraham Lincoln for President. Industries include shipping and shoes.

POINTS OF INTEREST:

● Bird Haven-Robert Ridgway Memorial. N on East Street to Miller's Grove.

● **OLYMPIA FIELDS,** Town, Cook County; Pop. 3,478; Area Code 312; Zip Code 60461; NE Illinois; suburb of Chicago; Developed, 1926; Residential community.

● **ONARGA,** Town, Iroquois County; Pop. 1,436; Area Code 815; Zip Code 60955; Elev. 657; NE Illinois; 30 miles south of Kankakee.

● **OQUAWKA,** Town, Henderson County seat; Pop. 1,352; Area Code 309; Zip Code 61469; Elev. 548; NW Illinois; On Mississippi River; 30 miles west of Galesburg; Established, 1827 as small trading post; Name derived from the Indian word, *Ozaukee,* meaning "yellow banks"; Industries include lumber and shell buttons.

● **OREGON,** Town, Ogle County seat; Pop. 3,539; Area Code 815; Zip Code 61061; Elev. 702; NW Illinois; 26 miles southwest of Rockford; On Rock River; Artistic Community.

POINTS OF INTEREST:

● Castle Rock State Park. 5 miles SW on IL 2.

● Ogle County Historical Museum. Corner of N 6th & Franklin.

● Lowden Memorial State Park. N on River Road, E side of Rock River.

● Oregon Public Library Art Gallery. 300 Jefferson Street.

- Soldiers Monument. Courthouse lawn.
- Stronghold Castle. 2 miles N on IL 2.
- White Pines Forest State Park. 9 miles W on Pines Road.

● **ORIENT,** Town, Franklin County; Pop. 502; Area Code 618; Zip Code 62874; Southern Illinois.

● **ORION,** Village, Henry County; Pop. 2,100; Area Code 309; Zip Code 61273; NW Illinois; 15 mi. S of Moline. The area was platted on December 26, 1853 by Charles Wesley Dean, who named it Deanington. The name was changed to Orion in 1865, and the area was incorporated in 1873. Orion was first settled by Quakers from Pennsylvania in the early 1840's, and Swedish immigrants came to the area in the early 1850's. In the 1870's, the railroad brought new industry into the town, including brick yards, furniture, a creamery, and a flour mill.

Today, Orion's agricultural products include corn, hay, soybeans, and hogs, and its main manufactures are tool and die, and fertilizer.

● **OTTAWA,** City; La Salle County seat; Pop. 18,716; Area Code 815; Zip Code 61350; Northern Illinois; At junction of Fox and Illinois Rivers; Settled, 1830; Incorporated, 1858; Site of first Lincoln-Douglas debate, August 21, 1858; Wheat farming center; Industries include glass, clay products, agricultural equipment; Nearby is Starved Rock State Park.

POINTS OF INTEREST:

- Buffalo Rock State Park. 5 miles W off US 6.
- Fox River Marina. US 6 at Fox River bridge.
- Starved Rock State Park. 10 miles W on IL 71.
- William Reddick Mansion. 100 W Lafayette Street.

● HISTORICAL PLACES: (See Hist. Pl. Sect. for Details.)

Hossack, John, House; Old Kaskaskia Village; Starved Rock; Washington Park Historic District

● **OZARK RANGE,** Southern Illinois; Elev. 700- 1,000; Continuation of chain of mountains through Missouri; Sandstone and metamorphic rock; From the Mississippi to Ohio Rivers, the belt of highlands is 70 miles long; Site of fruit orchards.

● **PALATINE,** Town, Cook County; Pop. 25,904; Area Code 312; Zip Code 60067; Suburb of Chicago; Named for a division in Germany by that name.

● **PALESTINE,** Town, Crawford County; Pop. 1,640; Area Code 618; Zip Code 62451; Elev. 450; SE Illinois; South of Terre Haute, Indiana; On Wabash River.

●**PALOS HEIGHTS,** Town, Cook County; Pop. 9,915; Area Code 312; Zip Code 60463; Suburb of Chicago.

● **PALOS HILLS,** City, Cook County; Pop. 16,654; Area Code 708; Zip Code 60465; NE Illinois; 22 SW of Chicago. Originally called North Palos. According to the area's lore, settlers during the 1840's selected the township name of "Palos," which means "little sticks" in Spanish. Another theory was that one of the settlers had an ancestor who sailed with Columbus from a Spanish port named "Palos." In the early years, there were Indian sites and reputed forts in Palos Hills, believed by some to have been built by the French in the 1730's. The building of the Illinois-Michigan Canal in 1835 brought the first permanent settlers to Palos Hills. Between 1880 and 1890, the area had a population of 1,209, and agriculturally, there were mostly dairy farms. Palos Hills was incorporated on October 25, 1958.

It took until after World War II for the area to recover from the Great Depression, but the city is now thriving and has won several Governor's Hometown awards for it's beauty.

● **PANA,** Town, Christian County; Pop. 6,326; S Central Illinois; 33 miles north of Vandalia; Coal and rose culture important.

●**PARADISE LAKE,** Lake, Coles County, 6 miles southwest of Mattoon; site of Mattoon fish hatchery.

● **PARIS,** City; Edgar County seat; Pop. 9,885; Area Code 217; Zip Code 61944; Elev. 739; SE Illinois; 36 miles south of Danville; The area, named for Paris, Kentucky, was settled in 1853, and incorporated in 1869. Lincoln spoke here in 1856 and 1858.

Agriculturally, products include corn and soybeans. Manufactures include metal fabrication, finished hardwood furniture, printing, farm and industrial truck bodies, and pet food supplements.

● **PATOKA,** Town, Marion County; Pop. 562; Area Code 618; Zip Code 62875; S Central Illinois; 17 miles north of Centralia; Named for an Indian chief.

● **PAWNEE,** Town, Sangamon County; Pop. 1,936; Area Code 217; Zip Code 62875; W Central Illinois; Near Springfield.

● **PAW PAW,** Town, Lee County; Pop. 846; Area Code 815; Zip Code 61353.

● **PAXTON,** Town; Ford County seat; Pop. 4,373; Area Code 217; Zip Code 60957; E Central Illinois; Near Champaign; settled, 1853, by Swedish immigrants.

● **PAYSON,** Town, Adams County; Pop. 589; Area Code 217; Zip Code 62360; W Central Illinois; Near Quincy.

● **PEARL CITY,** Town, Stephenson County; Pop. 535; Area Code 815; Zip Code 61062; Northern Illinois.

● **PECATONICA,** Town, Winnebago County; Pop. 1,781; Area Code 815; Zip Code 61063; Northern Illinois; Near Rockford.

● **PEKIN,** City; Tazewell County seat; Pop. 31,375; Area Code 309; Zip Code 61554; Elev. 479; N Central Illinois; Near Peoria,

POINTS OF INTEREST:

> ● The Dirksen Congressional Center. Broadway & 4th Street.
>
> ● Spring Lake State Conservation Area. 1 mile S on IL 29, then 9 miles SW on Manito blacktop; 3 miles W on Spring lake blacktop.

● **PEORIA,** City; Peoria County seat; Pop. 126,963; Area Code 309; Zip Code 61601; Elev. 608; N Central Illinois; On northwest bank of Illinois River at widened point, Lake Peoria. (See article on page 156.)

POINTS OF INTEREST:

> ● Detweiller Marina. End of Caroline Street, on Lower Peoria Lake.
>
> ● Eureka College (1855). 18 miles E on US 24 in Eureka.
>
> ● Flanagan House (ca. 1837). 942 NE Glen Oak Avenue.
>
> ● Glen Oak Park. Prospect Road & McClure Avenue.
>
> ● Jubilee College State Park. 15 miles NW on US 150.
>
> ● Lakeview Museum of Arts and Sciences. 1125 W Lake Avenue at University Street North.
>
> ● Metamore Courthouse State Historic Site. 10 miles NE on IL 116, 89 at 113 E Partridge in Metamora.
>
> ● Pettengill-Morron House (1868). 1212 W Moss Avenue.

● Wheels O'Time Museum. 8 miles N via IL 88 at 11923 Knoxville Avenue in Dunlap.

● Wildlife Prairie Park. 10 miles W via I-74, Edwards exit 82, then 3 miles S on Taylor Road.

● HISTORICAL PLACES: (See Hist. Pl. Sect. for Details.)

Peoria City Hall.

● **PEORIA COUNTY,** N Central Illinois; Area, 624 square miles; Pop. 299,800; Seat, Peoria; Named for Indian tribe; Established, 1825 from part of Fulton County.

● **PEOTONE,** Town, Will County; Pop. 2,345; Area Code 815; Zip Code 60468; NE Illinois; 20 miles southeast of Joliet.

● **PERCY,** Town, Randolph County; Pop. 967; Area Code 618; Zip Code 62272; Southern Illinois; Near Mississippi River.

● **PERRY COUNTY,** Southern Illinois; Area 443 square miles; Pop. 19,184; Seat Pickneyville; Named for Cmdr. Oliver H. Perry, leader in Battle of Lake Erie, 1812; Established 1827 from portions of Jackson and Randolph Counties; Near Mississippi River.

● **PERU,** City, La Salle County; Pop. 10,886; Area Code 815; Zip Code 61354; Elev. 459; N central Illinois; Near Ottawa; On Illinois River. The area, named after the city in South America, was settled in 1835, and incorporated in 1851. According to some sources, Peru is an Incan word meaning "wealth," or "plenty of everything." Settlers initially emigrated to Peru to either work on the Illinois- Michigan Canal, or to work in the coal mines. In addition, with it's location being a major port on the Illinois River, there were merchants, traders, ice harvesters, boat-builders, and farmers.

Now a thriving city, its agriculture entails corn and soybeans, and its manufactures include prefinished metals, foam for insulation, corrugated boxes, books, nails, and automation controls.

Located amidst three state parks, Starved Rock, Buffalo Rock, and Matthiesson, Peru is the perfect setting for hiking, photography, camping, and nature walks. The Illinois and Vermillion Rivers are here for boating, water-skiiing, and fishing, and in the winter, snowmobiling, cross-country skiing, and ice-skating are favorite pastimes.

POINTS OF INTEREST:

- La Salle County Historical Museum and Blacksmith Shop (1848). 5 miles E on I-80, 1 1/2 miles S on US 178, at Canal & Mill Streets in Utica.
- Lake De Pue. 6 miles W on IL 29.
- Matthiessen State Park. 9 miles SW via I-80E, IL 178S in Utica.
- Starved Rock State Park. 6 miles E on I-80, Utica exit, S on IL 178, then E on Dee Bennett Road, E of Utica.
- Time Was Village Museum. 11 miles N on US 52, IL 251, 4 miles S of Mendota.

- **PESOTUM,** Town, Champaign County; Pop. 536; Area Code 217; Zip Code 61863; Elev. 720; E Central Illinois; Farming, grain storage center; 15 miles south of Champaign-Urbana.

- **PETERSBURG,** Town; Menard County seat; Pop. 2,632; Area Code 217; Zip Code 62675; Elev. 524; W Central Illinois; 30 miles northwest of Springfield; site of Ann Rutledge grave.

POINTS OF INTEREST:

- Edgar Lee Masters Memorial Home. Jackson & 8th Streets.
- Menard County Courthouse. 102 S 7th Street.
- Oakland Cemetery. Oakland Avenue.

- HISTORICAL PLACES: (See Hist. Pl. Sect. for Details.)

Lincoln's New Salem State Historic Site.

- **PHILO,** Town, Champaign County; Pop. 1,022; Area Code 217; Zip Code 61864; suburb of Champaign-Urbana.

- **PIATT COUNTY,** E Central Illinois; Area 437 square miles; Pop. 14,960; Seat Monticello; Named for Piatt family, early settlers in region; Established 1841, from portions of Macon and De Witt counties; Sangamon River runs through northwest part of county.

- **PIKE COUNTY,** Western Illinois; Area 829 square miles; Pop. 20,552; Seat Pittsfield; Named for Zebulon M. Pike, explorer; Established 1821, from portions of Madison, Bond, and Clark counties; Other county seats were: Coles Grove, 1821; Atlas, 1824; Mississippi River forms Western border.

- **PINCKNEYVILLE,** Town; Perry County seat; Pop. 3,377; Area Code 618; Zip Code 62274; Southern Illinois.

- **PIPER CITY,** Town, Ford County; Pop; 817; Area Code 815; Zip Code 60959; Elev. 688; NE Illinois; Near Pontiac.

- **PITTSBURG,** Town, Williamson County; Pop. 509; Area Code 618; Zip Code 62974; Elev. 419; Southern Illinois.

- HISTORICAL PLACES: (See Hist. Pl. Sect. for Details.)

    Pittsfield East School.

- **PITTSFIELD,** Town; Pike County seat; Pop. 4,244; Area Code 217; Zip Code 62363; Elev. 725; Western Illinois; In between Mississippi and Illinois Rivers; Founded, 1833 by settlers from Pittsfield, Massachussetts; Former home of John Hay, Lincoln's private secretary and co-author of *Abraham Lincoln: A History*; Lincoln spoke here, 1858.

- **PLAINFIELD,** Town, Will County; Pop. 2,928; Area Code 815; Zip Code 60544; Elev. 601; NE Illinois; Near Joliet; Named for prairie topography; On Des Plaines River; Originally an Indian village; Trading Post, 1790-1829; Known as Walker's Grove, after first settler Jesse Walker, in early nineteenth century.

- **PLANO,** Town, Kendall County; Pop. 4,664; Area Code 815; Zip Code 60545; Elev. 649; NE Illinois; 50 miles south west of Chicago; Settled, 1835.

- **PLEASANT HILL,** Town, Pike County; Pop. 1,064; Area Code 217; Zip Code 62366; Western Illinois.

- **PLEASANT PLAINS,** Town, Sangamon County; Pop. 644; Area rode 217; Zip Code 62677; W Central Illinois; Near Springfield.

- HISTORICAL PLACES: (See Hist. Pl. Sect. for Details.)

    Clayville Tavern.

- **PLYMOUTH,** Town, Hancock County; Pop. 740; Area Code 217; Zip Code 62367; Western Illinois.

- **POCAHONTAS,** Town, Bond County; Pop. 764; Area Code 618; Zip Code 62275; Elev. 515; SW Illinois; 30 miles west of Vandalia; Once a stage station on Cumberland Road.

- **POLO,** Town, Ogle County; Pop. 2,542; Area Code 815; Zip Code 61064; Elev. 836; Livestock Center.

- HISTORICAL PLACES: (See Hist. Pl. Sect. for Details.)

    Barber, Henry D., House.

●**PONTIAC,** City; Livingston County seat; Pop. 9,031; Area Code 815; Zip Code 61764; Elev. 647; NE Illinois; 57 miles southwest of Joliet; Named for Ottawa Indian chief; Founded, 1837.

●**POPE COUNTY,** Southern Illinois, Area 381 square miles; Pop. 4,061; Seat Golconda; Named for Nathaniel Pope, Illinois Secretary of the Territory (1809-16); Established 1816, from parts of Johnson and Gallatin counties; Bordered at south by Ohio River.

●**POPLAR GROVE,** Town, Boone County; Pop. 607; Area Code 815; Zip Code 61065; Elev. 908; Northern Illinois; Near Rockford.

●**POSEN,** Town, Cook County; Pop. 5,498; Area Code 312; Zip Code 60469; Elev. 605; 20 miles south of Chicago.

● **POTOMAC,** Town, Vermillion County; Pop. 909; Area Code 217; Zip Code 61865; Eastern Illinois; Near Indiana border.

● **PRAIRIE CITY,** Town, McDonough County; Pop. 630; Area Code 309; Zip Code 61470; NW Illinois; Near Macomb.

● **PRAIRIE DU ROCHER,** Town, Randolph County; Pop. 658; Area Code 618; Zip Code 62277; Elev. 396; Southern Illinois; On bluffs overlooking Mississippi River; Founded, 1722; French settlement.

● HISTORICAL PLACES: (See Hist. Pl. Sect. for Details.)

  Creole House; Fort De Chartres; French Colonial Historic District; Kolmer Site (Michigamea Village).

● **PRINCETON,** Town; Bureau County seat; Pop. 6,959; Area Code 815; Zip Code 61356; N Central Illinois; Settled, 1833; Strong abolitionist community before Civil War; Farming and orchards center.

POINTS OF INTEREST:

  ● Bureau County Historical Museum. 109 Park Avenue West.

● HISTORICAL PLACES: (See Hist. Pl. Sect. for Details.)

  Lovejoy, Owen, Homestead.

● **PRINCEVILLE,** Town, Peoria County; Pop. 1,455; Area Code 309; Zip Code 61559; E Central Illinois.

● **PROPHETSTOWN**, Town, Whiteside County; Pop. 1,915; Area Code 815; Zip Code 61277; Elev. 627; NE Illinois; Near Rock Falls, on Rock River; Site of White Cloud's village, which was destroyed in 1832. White Cloud was an Indian prophet.

● **PULASKI COUNTY**, Southern Illinois; Area 204 square miles; Pop. 10,490; Seat Mound City; Named for General Casimir Pulaski, Polish count and American Revolutionary War general; Established 1843, from portions of Fulton and Edgar Counties; Southeasterly border is Ohio River; Cache River flows through western part of county.

● **PUTNAM COUNTY**, Central Illinois; Area 166 square miles; Pop. 4,570; Seat Hennepin; Named for General Israel Putnam, Revolutionary War hero; Established, 1825, from portions of Johnson and Alexander counties; Site of Senachwine Lake.

● **QUINCY**, City; Adams County seat; Pop. 45,288; Area Code 217; Zip Code 62301; Elev. 602; Western Illinois; 132 miles southwest of Peoria; On Mississippi River bluffs; Named for John Quincy Adams, President at time of founding, 1825; Originally, Sauk Indian Village; Abolitionist center before Civil War; Incorporated, 1840; Second largest Illinois city during nineteenth century; River port today.

POINTS OF INTEREST:

  ● Quincy Museum of Natural History & Art. 16th & Main Streets.

● HISTORICAL PLACES: (See Hist. Pl. Sect. for Details.)

  Wood, John, Mansion.

● **RAMSEY**, Town, Fayette County; Pop. 830; Area Code 618; Zip Code 62080; S Central Illinois; Near Vandalia.

●**RANDOLPH COUNTY**, Southern Illinois; Area 594 Square miles; Pop. 29,988; Seat Chester; Named after Edmund Randolph, early American statesman; Established 1795, from a portion of St. Clair County; Second County formed in state; Former County seat, Kaskaskia; Site of Fort Kaskaskia State Park; Fort erected, 1736.

●**RANKIN**, Town, Vermillion County; Pop. 727; Area Code 217; Zip Code 60960; Eastern Illinois.

● **RANTOUL**, City, Champaign County, Pop. 25,562; Area Code 217; Zip Code 61866; Elev. 758; W Central Illinois;

Near Champaign-Urbana; Chanute Air Force Base at southeast city limits; Named after Robert Rantoul, early railroad executive.

●**RAPIDS CITY**, Town, Rock Island County; Pop. 656; Area Code 309; Zip Code 61278; Elev. 444; NW Illinois.

● **RAYMOND**, Town, Montgomery County; Pop. 890; Area Code 217; Zip Code 62560; S Central Illinois.

● **RED BUD**, Town, Randolph County; Pop. 2,559; Area Code 618; Zip Code 62278; Southern Illinois; Named for red- bud trees which once grew near village site.

●**REND LAKE**, Reservoir, Jefferson County; S Central Illinois; Formed by a damming of the Big Muddy River; 24,800 acres, with 219 miles of shoreline; 10 miles S of Mount Vernon; Completed, 1970.

● **REYNOLDS**, Town, Rock Island County; Pop. 610; Zip Code 61279; NW Illinois.

●**RICHLAND COUNTY**, Southeast Illinois; Area 364 square miles; Pop. 16,829; Seat Olney; Named after an Ohio county; Established 1842, from portions of Clay and Lawrence counties.

● **RICHMOND**, Town, McHenry County; Pop. 1,153; Area Code 312; Zip Code 60071; Elev. 819; Northern Illinois; 80 miles northwest of Chicago.

● **RIDGE FARM**, Town, Vermillion County; Pop. 1,015; Area Code 217; Zip Code 61870; E Central Illinois.

●**RIDGWAY**, Town, Gallatin County; Pop, 1,160; Area Code 618; Zip Code 62979; Southern Illinois; Named for Dr. Robert Ridgway, naturalist.

● **RIVERGROVE**, City, Cook County; Pop. 11,465; Area Code 312; Zip Code 60171; NW suburb of Chicago.

● **RIVERSIDE**, City, Cook County; Pop. 10,432; Area Code 312; Zip Code 60546; Elev. 430; Designed as a Chicago residential suburb, 1866.

● HISTORICAL PLACES: (See Hist. Pl. Sect. for Details.)

Coonley, Avery, House; Riverside Landscape Architecture District.

● **RIVERTON**, Town, Sangamon County; Pop. 2,090; Area Code 217; Zip Code 62561; Suburb of Springfield.

● **ROANOKE,** Town, Woodford County; Pop. 2,040; Area Code 309; Zip Code 61561; 25 miles north of Bloomington.

● **ROBBINS,** City, Cook County; Pop. 9,641; Area Code 312; Zip Code 60472; Elev. 602; Chicago suburb; Near Blue Island.

●**ROBERTS,** Town, Ford County; Pop. 506; Area Code 217; Zip Code 60962.

● **ROBINSON,** Town; Crawford County seat; Pop. 7,178; Area Code 618; Zip Code 62454.

●**ROCHELLE,** Town, Ogle County; Pop. 8,594; Area Code 815; Zip Code 61068; Elev. 793; Northern Illinois; 27 miles south of Rockford; Farming center.

● HISTORICAL PLACES: (See Hist. Pl. Sect. for Details.)

Flagg Township Public Library; Holcomb, William H., House.

●**ROCHESTER,** Town, Sangamon County; Pop. 1,667; Area Code 217; Zip Code 62563; Suburb of Springfield.

● **ROCK FALLS,** Town, Whiteside County; Pop. 10,287; Area Code 815; Zip Code 61071; Elev. 646; Settled 1837; Important port on Rock River.

●**ROCKFORD,** City; Winnebago County seat; Pop. 147,287; Area Code 815; Zip Code 61101; Elev. 742.

(See article on page 159.)
POINTS OF INTEREST:

● Burpee Museum of Natural History. 813 N Main Street.
● John Erlander Home. 404 S 3rd Street.
●Midway Village/Rockford Museum Center. 6799 Guilford Road.
● Rockford Art Museum. 711 Main Street.
● Rock Cut State Park. NE via US 51, W on IL 173.
● Sinnissippi Park. 1300-1900 N 2nd Street.
● Time Museum. 7801 E State Street.
● Trailside Center. 5209 Safford Road.
● Zitelman Scout Museum. 708 Seminary Street.

● HISTORICAL PLACES: (See Hist. Pl. Sect. for Details.)

Tinker Swiss Cottage.

● **ROCKFORD COLLEGE,** Rockford, Winnebago County; Four-year institution; Co-educational; Liberal arts emphasis; Founded 1847; Chartered, 1892; Originally, for women only.

● **ROCK ISLAND,** City; Rock Island County seat; Pop. 50,166; Area Code 309; Zip Code 61201; Elev. 563; NW Illinois; Surrounded by the Mississippi River at the only point that it runs due west in Illinois; Across from Davenport, Iowa; Originally Illinois Indian village; Settled by eastern immigrants, 1828; Important river port, railroad center; Industries include agricultural implements and vehicles.

POINTS OF INTEREST:

    ● Black Hawk State Historic Site. On S edge of town.

● HISTORICAL PLACES: (See Hist. Pl. Sect. for Details.)

    Denkmann-Hauberg House (Hauberg Civic Center); Rock Island Arsenal.

● **ROCK ISLAND COUNTY,** NW Illinois; Area 420 square miles; Pop. 150,991; Seat Rock Island; Named for Rock Island in the Mississippi; At mouth of Rock River; Established, 1831, taken from a portion of Jo Daviess County.

● **ROCK RIVER,** Northern Illinois; Runs south- southwest through NW part of State; Rises at point 50 miles west of Lake Michigan in State of Wisconsin; Flows into Mississippi River at Rock Island; Length, 330 miles; Some boat transportation; There are many rapids, and a shallow ford near Rockford.

● **ROCKTON,** Town, Winnebago County; Pop. 2,099; Area Code 815; Zip Code 61072; Northern Illinois; On Rock River.

● **ROME,** Town, Peoria County; Pop. 1,919; Area Code 309; Zip Code 61562; Suburb of Peoria.

● **ROODHOUSE,** Town, Greene County; Pop. 2,357; Area Code 217; Zip Code 62082; Elev. 650; SW Illinois; 20 miles south of Jacksonville; Named for founder, John Roodhouse; Railroad center for coal mining region.

● **ROSCOE,** Town, Winnebago County; Pop. 800; Area Code 815; Zip Code 61073; Northern Illinois.

● **ROSELLE,** Village, DuPage County; Pop. 19,603; Area Code 708; Zip Code 60172; NW Illinois; 30 mi. NW of Chicago. Named for Roselle Hough, a land developer and railroad promoter, who, in 1836, settled in the area, which was originally Bloomingdale Township. In 1874, property owned by Bernard Beck, a neighbor of Roselle Hough, was platted and recorded as the town of Roselle, which for years, remained a part of Bloomingdale Township.

The earliest settlers that arrived at Bloomington came from Vermont, and were mostly made up of German immigrants. After the Civil War, Roselle Hough started the Illinois Linen Factory which manufactured rope and linen, and by the end of the century, it was turned into a tile and brick manufacturing company. Roselle began to outdistance Bloomingdale in business and in population, and in 1922, with its citizens voting for the area to become independent, the village was incorporated.

There is light industry in Roselle, and it is the location of the award-winning Lynfred Winery, which produces over 50,000 bottles annually.

● **ROSEVILLE,** Town, Warren County; Pop. 1,111; Area Code 309; Zip Code 61473; Elev. 736; NW Illinois; Agricultural center.

● **ROSICLARE,** Town, Hardin County; Pop. 1,421; Area Code 618; Zip Code 62982; On Ohio River.

● HISTORICAL PLACES: (See Hist. Pl. Sect. for Details.)

Illinois Iron Furnace.

● **ROSSVILLE,** Town, Vermillion County; Pop. 1,420; Area Code 217; Zip Code 60963; Elev. 700; Named for Jacob Ross, early settler; Founded, 1857.

● **ROUND LAKE,** Town, Lake County; Pop. 1,531; Area Code 312; Zip Code 60073.

● **ROXANA,** Town, Madison County; Pop. 1,882; Area Code 618; Zip Code 62084; Near Alton.

● **ROYALTON,** Town, Franklin County; Pop. 11,166; Area Code 618; Zip Code 62983; Southern Illinois.

● **RUSHVILLE,** Town, Schuyler County seat; Pop. 3,300; Area Code 217; Zip Code 62681; Elev. 683; Named for Philadelphia physician, Dr. William Rush; Founded, 1825; Lincoln spoke here, 1858.

● **ST. ANNE,** Town, Kankakee County; Pop. 1,271; Area Code 815; Zip Code 60964; Elev. 678; NE Illinois; Near

Kankakee; Founded, 1852 by Friar Charles Chinquay of France.

● **ST. CHARLES,** Town, Kane County; Pop. 12,928; Area Code 312; Zip Code 60174; Elev. 802; NE Illinois; 33 miles northwest of Chicago; On Fox River.

POINTS OF INTEREST:

● Dunham-Hunt Museum (1840). 304 Cedar Avenue in Century Corners.

● Garfield Farm Museum. W via IL 64, S on Randall Road, W on IL 38 to Garfield Road, near La Fox.

● Pottawatomie Park. On 2nd Avenue, 1/2 mile North, just off IL 64.

● St. Charles Historical Museum. Municipal Center, 2 E Main Street.

● **ST. CLAIR COUNTY,** SW Illinois; Area 673 square miles; Pop. 285,199; Seat Belleville; Named for Arthur St. Clair, Revolutionary War veteran; Established 1790, first county in Illinois territory; Former county seats: Kaskaskia, 1790; Cahokia, 1795; Across Mississippi River from St. Louis, Missouri area.

● **ST. DAVID,** Town, Fulton County; Pop. 773; Area Code 309; Zip Code 61563; W. Central Illinois.

● **ST. ELMO,** Town, Fayette County; Pop. 1,676; Area Code 618; Zip Code 62458; Elev. 618; Southern Illinois; Near Vandalia; Settled, 1830.

● **ST. FRANCISVILLE,** Town, Lawrence County; Pop. 997; Area Code 618; Zip Code 62460; SE Illinois.

● **ST. JACOB,** Town, Madison County; Pop. 659; Area Code 618; Zip Code 62281; Elev. 508; SW Illinois; Site of Fort Chilton, circa. 1812.

● **ST. JOSEPH,** Town, Champaign County; Pop. 1,554; Area Code 217; Zip Code 61873.

● **SALEM,** Town; Marion County seat; Pop. 6,187; Area Code 618; Zip Code 62881; Elev. 544; S Central Illinois; Founded, 1813; Incorporated, 1837; Birthplace of William Jennings Bryan.

POINTS OF INTEREST:

● Ingram's Log Cabin Village. 12 miles N via 37 in Kinmundy.

● One-Room Schoolhouse. N on IL 37.

- Stephen A. Forbes State Park. 8 miles E on US 50, then 2 miles N on 1900E, 4 miles N on 1950E.
- William Jennings Bryan Birthplace/Museum. 408 S Broadway.

- **SALINE COUNTY,** SE Illinois; Area 383 square miles; Pop. 25,721; Seat Harrisburg; Named for salt springs in the region; Established 1847 from portions of Gallatin County; Large coal producing region.

- **SALINE RIVER,** SE Illinois; Flows southeasterly from Ohio River near Cave-in-Rock to McLeansboro, in Hamilton County, approx. 45 miles long; Named for numerous salt springs in region, used by Indians and early settlers in early nineteenth century.

- **SANDOVAL,** Town, Marion County; Pop. 1,332; Area Code 618; Zip Code 62882; Elev. 509; S central Illinois; Railroad and mining center.

- **SANDWICH,** Town, DeKalb County; Pop. 5,056; Area Code 815; Zip Code 60548; Elev. 657; NE Illinois; Named for Sandwich, Massachusetts by early settlers; 55 miles west of Chicago.

- **SANGAMON COUNTY,** W Central Illinois; Area 879 square miles; Pop. 161,335; Seat Springfield; Name from an Indian word; Established 1821, from portions of Madison and Bond counties; Courthouse here was focal point for Lincoln's law activities; The 16th President lived in Springfield as well as New Salem; Sangamon River flows through northeast area of county.

- **SANGAMON RIVER,** Central Illinois; 225 miles long from rising point at Ellsworth, McLean County, to its mouth at the Illinois River in northern Cass County; Flows southwest and west; Marshy, with numerous lakes and sloughs.

- **SAN JOSE,** Town, Mason county; Pop. 681; Area Code 309; Zip Code 62682; Central Illinois.

- **SAVANNAH,** Town, Carroll County; Pop. 4,942; Area Code 815; Zip Code 61074; NW Illinois; Elev. 592; On Mississippi River; Named for grassy plains upon which it sits; Founded, 1828.

POINTS OF INTEREST:

- Mississippi Palisades State Park. N on IL 84.

● **SAVOY**, Town, Champaign County; Pop. 592; Area Code 217; Zip Code 61874.

● **SAYBROOK**, Town, McLean County; Pop. 814; Area Code 309; Zip Code 61770.

● **SCHUYLER COUNTY**, Western Illinois; Area 434 square miles; Pop. 8,135; Seat Rushville; Named for Gen. Phillip J. Schuyler, French and Indian War and Revolutionary soldier; Established 1825 from unorganized territory and portions of Pike and Fulton counties; Former county seat: Beardstown, 1825-26; Mining and farming area.

● **SCOTT COUNTY**, W Illinois; Area 251 square miles; Pop. 6,096; Seat Winchester; Named for a Kentucky county; Established 1839, from portions of Morgan County.

● **SECOR**, Town, Woodford County; Pop. 508; Area Code 309; Zip Code 61771.

● **SENECA**, Town, LaSalle County, Pop. 1,781; Area Code 815; Zip Code 61360; Elev. 521; N Central Illinois; On bluffs overlooking the Illinois-Michigan Canal.

● **SESSER**, Town, Franklin County, Pop. 2,125; Area Code 618; Zip Code 62884; Southern Illinois.

● **SHABBONA**, Town, DeKalb County; Pop. 730; Area Code 815; Zip Code 60550; NE Illinois; Named for Potawatomi Indian Chief who befriended early settlers in region; Site of Shabbona State Park.

● **SHANNON**, Town, Carroll County; Pop. 848; Area Code 815; Zip Code 61078; NW Illinois.

● **SHAWNEETOWN**, City; Gallatin County seat; Pop. 1,742; Area Code 618; Zip Code 62984; Elev. 350; Southern Illinois; On Ohio River; Named for Indian tribe; Center of coal mines, oil wells, prehistoric Indian mounds; Area plagued by floods in early twentieth century.

● **SHELBY COUNTY**, Central Illinois; Area 772 square miles; Pop. 22,589; Seat Shelbyville; Named for General Isaac Shelby, Revolutionary War soldier; Established 1827, from portions of Fayette County.

● **SHELBYVILLE**, Town; Shelby County seat; Pop. 4,597; Area Code 217; Zip Code 62565; Central Illinois; 32 miles southeast of Decatur.

● **SHELBYVILLE MORAINE,** SE Illinois; Long ridge and valley region of land marking the maximum advance of recent glaciation; Entire area between Mattoon and Norris City, from east of the Indiana state line to central Illinois; Named for town of Shelbyville, built upon moraine.

● **SHELBYVILLE LAKE,** Reservoir, Shelby and Moultrie Counties; Central Illinois; Formed by a damming of the Kaskaskia River; 11,000 acres, with an irregular shoreline of 110 miles between Allenville and Shelbyville; Completed in 1969.

● **SHELDON,** Town, Iroquois County seat; Pop. 1,455; Area Code 815; Zip Code 60966; Elev. 685.

● **SHERIDAN,** Town, LaSalle County; Pop. 724; Area Code 815; Zip Code 60551.

● **SHERRARD,** Town, Mercer County; Pop. 808; Area Code 309; Zip Code 61281.

● **SHILOH CEMETERY,** Coles County; E Central Illinois; Site of Sarah and Thomas Lincoln graves; Near Lincoln Log Cabin State Park.

● **SIDELL,** Town, Vermillion County; Pop. 645; Area Code 217; Zip Code 61876; Eastern Illinois.

● **SIDNEY,** Town, Champaign County; Pop. 915; Area Code 217; Zip Code 61877; E Central Illinois.

● **SILVIS,** Town, Rock Island County; Pop. 5,907; Area Code 309; Zip Code 61282; Elev. 576; NE Illinois; near Rock Island and Moline.

● **SKOKIE,** City, Cook County; Pop. 68,627; Area Code 312; Zip Code 60001; NE Illinois; 15 miles north of Chicago; Industries include aluminum, plastic, electronic components, sports equipment; Site of Hebrew Theological College, established 1922.

POINTS OF INTEREST:

    ● Centre East for the Arts. 7701-A Lincoln Avenue.

● **SMITHTON,** Town, St. Clair County; Pop. 847; Area Code 618; Zip Code 62285.

● **SOMONAUK,** Town, DeKalb County; Pop, 1,112; Area Code 815; Zip Code 60552; NE Illinois.

● **SORENTO,** Town, Bond County; Pop. 625; Area Code 618; Zip Code 62086; SW Illinois.

● **SOUTH BELOIT,** Town, Winnebago County; Pop. 3,804; Area Code 815; Zip Code 61080; Elev. 742; Northern Illinois; Suburb of Beloit, Wisconsin.

● **SOUTH ELGIN,** Town, Kane County; Pop. 4,289; Area Code 312; Zip Code 60177; NE Illinois; Suburb of Elgin.

● **SOUTH HOLLAND,** City, Cook County; Pop. 23,931; Area Code 312; Zip Code 60473; Elev. 600; NE Illinois; 10 miles south of Chicago; Settled, 1840 by Dutch farmers.

● **SOUTHERN ILLINOIS UNIVERSITY,** Carbondale, Jackson County; Four-year public institution; Co-educational; Founded, 1874 as a teachers college.

● **SOUTH PEKIN,** Town, Tazewell County; Pop. 955; Area Code 309; Zip Code 61564; W Central Illinois; Suburb of Pekin.

● **SOUTH ROXANA,** Town, Madison County; Pop. 2,200; Area Code 618; Zip Code 62087.

● **SOUTH WILMINGTON,** Town, Grundy County; Pop. 725; Area Code 815; Zip Code 60474; NE Illinois; 25 miles west of Kankakee.

● **SPARLAND,** Town, Marshall County; Pop. 585; Area Code 309; Zip Code 61565; N Central Illinois.

● **SPARTA,** Town, Randolph County; Pop. 4,307; Area Code 618; Zip Code 62286; Southern Illinois.

● **SPOON RIVER,** NW and W Central Illinois; Flows southwest-southeast from north Stark County to Illinois River at Havana, Mason County; Approx. 80 miles long; Made famous by poet Edgar Lee Masters in his *Spoon River Anthology*; Stone from River Valley used on many local houses.

● **SPRINGFIELD,** Capital City of Illinois; Sangamon County seat; Pop. 91,753; Area Code 217; Zip Code 62701; W Central Illinois. (See article on page 162.)
POINTS OF INTEREST:

> ● Clayville Rural Life Center and Museum. 14 mi NW, IL 97 to IL 125, near Pleasant Plains.
>
> ● Dana-Thomas House State Historic Site. 301 E Lawrence Ave.

- Daughters of Union Veterans National Headquarters. 503 S Walnut St.
- Edwards Place (1833). 700 N 4th St.
- Executive Mansion. 5th & Jackson Sts.
- Henson Robinson Zoo. 1100 E Lake Dr, 4 mi SE.
- Lincoln Depot. Monroe St between 9th & 10th Sts.
- Lincoln-Herndon Building. 6th & Adams Sts.
- Lincoln Home National Historic Site. 426 S 7th St.
- Lincoln Memorial Garden & Nature Center. 2301 E Lake Dr, 8 mi S on E bank of Lake Springfield.
- Lincoln's Tomb State Historic Site. Oak Ridge Cemetery. End of Monument Ave.
- Old State Capitol State Historic Site. City Square, between Adams, Washington, 5th & 6th Sts.
- Oliver P. Parks Telephone Museum. 529 S 7th St.
- Thomas Rees Memorial Carillon. Washington Park, Fayette Ave & Chatham Rd.
- Vachel Lindsay Home (1846). 603 S 5th St.

- HISTORICAL PLACES: (See Hist. Pl. Sect. for Details.)

  Dana, Susan Lawrence, House; Edwards Place; Lincoln Home National Historic Site; Lincoln Tomb; Lindsay, Vachel, House; Old State Capitol.

- **SPRING VALLEY,** Town, Bureau County; Pop. 5,605; Area Code 815; Zip Code 61362; Elev. 465; N Central Illinois; Across Illinois River from LaSalle.

- **STANFORD,** Town, McLean County; Pop. 657; Area Code 309; Zip Code 61774; Central Illinois.

- **STARK COUNTY,** NW Central Illinois; Area, 291 square miles; Pop. 8,152; Seat, Toulon; Named for Gen. John Stark, Revolutionary War leader (1775-80); Established 1839, from an area out of Putnam and Knox Counties; Spoon River runs through central region of county.

- **STAUNTON,** Town, Macoupin County; Pop. 4,396; Area Code 618; Zip Code 62088; Elev. 622; SW Central Illinois; Founded, 1817; Important trading post in early nineteenth century.

- **STEELEVILLE,** Town, Randolph County; Pop. 1,957; Area Code 618; Zip Code 62288; SW Illinois.

- **STEGER,** Town, Cook County; Pop. 8,104; Area Code 312; Zip Code 60465; Elev. 712; 30 miles south of Chicago.

● **STEPHENSON COUNTY,** N Illinois; Area 568 square miles; Pop. 46,207; Seat Freeport; Named for Benjamin Stephenson, colonel in War of 1812 and Illinois territorial delegate to Congress (1814-16); Established March 4, 1837.

Courthouse at Freeport is site of two monuments: one commemorates Civil War veterans, erected 1869; the other is a tablet in honor of Colonel Stephenson, who in 1816 negotiated a treaty bringing 10,000,000 more acres into Illinois.

● **STERLING,** City, Whiteside County; Pop. 16,113; Area Code 815; Zip Code 61081; Elev. 645; NW Illinois; 95 miles west of Chicago; Across Rock River from town of Rock Falls; Founded, 1836, by Captain Daniel Harris of Galena; Outgrowth of two settlements, Chatham and Harrisburg.

● **STEWARDSON,** Town, Shelby County; Pop. 729; Area Code 217; Zip Code 62463; Central Illinois.

● **STILLMAN VALLEY,** Village; Ogle County; Pop. 961; Area Code 815; Zip Code 61084; Elev. 707; N Illinois; 20 miles south of Rockford. The area was founded by Joshua White in 1874, and the first settlement was originally called Hale. The current name was in honor of Major Stillman, leader of the Battle of Stillman's Run, which took place here on May 14, 1832; it was this battle that started the Black Hawk War. The Stillman Valley Monument was dedicated here in 1902 in honor of the soldiers killed in battle.

Stillman Valley was incorporated in 1911. Agriculturally, its products include corn and soybeans, and the village also has several small businesses.

● **STOCKTON,** Town, Jo Daviess County; Pop. 1,930; Area Code 815; Zip Code 61085; Elev. 1,000; NE Illinois; 50 miles west of Rockford; Named by early settler, Alanson Parker, who envisioned the area as a stock raising center; Hilly region.

● **STONINGTON,** Village, Christian County; Pop. 1,100; Area Code 217; Zip Code 62567; Central Illinois; 30 mi. E of Springfield. Originally called Covington, the area was founded by Ellington Adams, and incorporated in 1836. The town was surveyed and platted, along with a post office being established, in 1870, and a year later, it had a population of 150.

The community has continued to grow, and along with the producing of such agriculture as corn and beans, its manufactures include both seed and fertilizer companies.

● **STREATOR,** City, La Salle and Livingston Counties; Pop. 15,600; Area Code 815; Zip Code 61364; Elev. 625; 50 miles northeast of Peoria; N Central Iliinois; Named for owner of early coal company, 1872.

Center of important clay-producing area along Vermillion River. Great shale, clay, sand deposits at south end of city helped develop glassmaking and coal industries. Other industries include building materials, canned goods, and railroad shops. Birthplace and boyhood home (1870) of George "Honey Boy" Evans, actor and author of "In the Good Old Summertime."

● **STRONGHURST,** Town, Henderson County; Pop. 836; Area Code 309; Zip Code 61480; W Illinois.

● **SUGAR GROVE,** Town, Kane County; Pop. 1,230; Area Code 312; Zip Code 60554; Elev. 740; NE Illinois; Near Aurora.

● **SULLIVAN,** City; Moultrie County seat; Pop. 4,112; Area Code 217; Zip Code 61951; Central Illinois; 25 miles southeast of Decatur; Industries include shoes, concrete, agriculture.

● **SUMMIT,** Village, Cook County; Pop. 10,110; Area Code 708; Zip Code 60501; Elev. 602; NE Illinois; 12 miles SW of Chicago; on Des Plaines River at crest of watershed between the Great Lakes and Mississippi drainage systems; Frs. Marquette and Jolliet explored the area around 1673; The name is derived from the fact that the village straddles the "summit" of a continental shelf; Corn refining important; Manufactures include shipping and trucking.

● **SUMNER,** Town, Lawrence County; Pop. 1,201 : Area Code 6l8; Zip Code 62466; SE Illinois.

● **SYCAMORE,** City; DeKalb County seat; Pop. 7,843; Area Code 815; Zip Code 60178; N Illinois; 30 miles east of Elgin; Industries include brass, canned goods, wire.

● **TALLULA,** Town, Menard County: Pop. 643: Area Code 217: Zip Code 62688; W Central Illinois.

Dictionary of Places

●**TAMORA,** Town, Perry County; Pop. 799; Area Code 618; Zip Code 62888; Elev. 510; Southern Illinois; Named for Indian tribe that inhabited region.

● **TAMMS,** Town, Alexander County; Pop. 645; Area Code 618; Zip Code 62988; SW Corner of Illinois; On Cache River.

●**TAMPICO,** Town, Whiteside County; Pop. 838; Area Code 309; Zip Code 61283; NW Illinois.

●**TAYLOR SPRINGS,** Town, Montgomery County; Pop. 620; Area Code 217; Zip Code 62089; S Central Illinois.

●**TAYLORVILLE,** City; Christian County seat; Pop. 10,644; Area Code 62568; S Central Illinois; 25 miles southeast of Springfield; Industries include cigars, tools, paper, clothing, coal, dairy products.

● **TAZEWELL COUNTY,** Central Illinois; Area 653 square miles; Pop. 99,789; Seat Pekin; Named for Littleton W. Tazewell, Virginia governor, and for the county in Virginia by the same name; Established, January 31, 1827.

First Amish in Illinois settled here along Illinois River, 1850; Other county seats were: Mackinaw, 1827; Tremont, 1836-49.

● **TEMPLE MOUND,** Prehistoric Indian burial mound; St. Clair County; Near Cahokia; Named for its shape; In Cahokia Mounds State Park.

●**TEUTOPOLIS,** Town, Effingham County; Pop. 1,249; Area Code 217; Zip Code 62467; Elev. 602; Established, 1839 by a group from Cincinnati, Ohio.

● **THAYER,** Town, Sangamon County; Pop. 616; Area Code 217; Zip Code 62689; Near Springfield.

● **THOMASBORO,** Town, Champaign County; Pop. 806; Area Code 217; Zip Code 61878.

● **THOMSON,** Town, Carroll County; Pop. 617; Area Code 815; Zip Code 61285; Elev. 606; NW Illinois; Near Fulton; Melon Day celebrated here with a carnival each Labor Day.

●**THORNTON,** Town, Cook County; Pop. 3,714; Area Code 312; Zip Code 60476; NE Illinois.

● **TILDEN,** Town, Randolph County; Pop. 909; Area Code 618; Zip Code 62292; Southern Illinois.

● **TINLEY PARK,** Village, Cook and Will Counties; Pop. 35,700; Area Code 708; Zip Code 60477; NE Illinois; 26 mi. SW of Chicago. The area was founded in 1835 when the John Fulton family came from New York and established a homestead at the northern edge of Tinley. Early names of the town included "The English Settlement," Yorktown, and New Bremen; its current name came from the last name of three brothers, Sam, Charles, and Edward Tinley, who had been prominent in the construction and running of the Rock Island Railroad. The area was incorporated in 1892.

Although agriculture and farming was once a large industry here, today it's almost non-existent. Manufactures include plastics, ink, batteries, cleaning products, and brooms.

● **TISKILWA,** Town, Bureau County; Pop. 973; Area Code 815; Zip Code 61368; N Central Illinois.

● **TOLEDO,** Town; Cumberland County seat; Pop. 1,068; Area Code 217; Zip Code 62468; SE Central Illinois.

● **TOLONO,** Town, Champaign County; Pop. 2,027; Area Code 217; Zip Code 61880; Elev. 736; Near Champaign-Urbana; Name coined by J. B. Calhoun of the Illinois Central Railroad; Lincoln last spoke in Illinois here in February, 1861.

● **TOLUCA,** Town, Marshall County; Pop. 1,319; Area Code 309; Zip Code 61369; N Central Illinois; Near Illinois River.

● **TONICA,** Town, La Salle County; Pop. 821; Area Code 815; Zip Code 61370; N Central Illinois; Midpoint between LaSalle and Streator.

● **TOULON,** City; Stark County seat; Pop. 1,207; Area Code 309; Zip Code 61483; NW Central Illinois.

● **TOWANDA,** Town, McLean County; Pop. 578; Area Code 309; Zip Code 61776; Elev. 787; Central Illinois; Indian name meaning, "where we bury the dead"; Settled, 1826, by John Smith; Incorporated, 1854, as first railroad passed through.

● **TOWER HILL,** Town, Shelby County; Pop. 683; Area Code 217; Zip Code 62571; Near Shelbyville.

● **TOWER ROCK,** Rock, Jackson County near town of Grand Tower; NW Illinois; On Mississippi River; 60 feet high; one acre in extent; Nicknamed "smallest national park in America."

● **TREMONT,** Town, Tazewell County; Pop, 1,942; Area Code 309; Zip Code 61568; N Central Illinois; Near Pekin.

●**TRENTON,** Town, Clinton County; Pop. 2,328; Area Code 618; Zip Code 62293; Elev. 498; SW Illinois; Incorporated, 1865; Borders on "Looking Glass Prairie."

●**TROY,** City, Madison County; Pop. 2,144; Area Code 618; Zip Cide 62294; Elev. 549; SW Illinois; Near Edwardsville, St. Louis; Established, 1819; Named for New York town by land speculators; Incorporated as a city in 1892.

● **TUSCOLA,** City; Douglas County seat; Pop. 3,917; Area Code 217; Zip Code 61953; Elev. 653; E Illinois; 23 miles south of Champaign-Urbana; Settled, 1857 with railroad entry into region; Industries include chemicals, fertilizer, plastics.

●**ULLIN,** Town, Pulaski County; Pop. 546; Area Code 618; Zip Code 62992; Southern Illinois.

● **UNION,** Town, McHenry County; Pop. 579; Area Code 815; Zip Code 60180; NE Illinois.

> ● Illinois Railway Museum. Olson Rd.
> ● McHenry County Historical Museum. 6422 Main St.
> ● Seven Acres Antique Village and Museum. US 20 & S Union Rd.

● **UNION COUNTY,** SW Illinois; Area 410 square miles; Pop. 17,645; Seat Jonesboro; Named in commemoration of a union revival meeting held in 1816 in the area by a Dunkard preacher, George Wolf; County seal bears their effigies; Established, January 2, 1818; Mississippi River forms western border; Cache River flows through central region.

●**UNIVERSITY OF CHICAGO,** Cook County; Private, non-sectarian institution; Founded, 1891; Coeducational; Bachelor's and Master's degree programs; Enrollment, 7,781.

John D. Rockefeller, under the encouragement of first university president William Rainey Harper, donated initial gift of $600,000 in 1891; Land donated by Marshall Field; Graduate divisions include biological sciences, humanities, physical sciences and social sciences as well as seven professional schools; National historical landmarks on campus: Robie House, designed by Frank Lloyd Wright; Site of first nuclear chain reaction; The Midway Studios; George H.

Jones Laboratory, where plutonium was first weighed; U. of Chicago Press is most prolific university press in U.S.

● **UNIVERSITY OF ILLINOIS,** Champaign-Urbana, Champaign County and Chicago Circle, Cook County; Founded, 1867 as Illinois Industrial University; Women first admitted, 1870; State university and land grant college; Bachelor's, Master's, and Doctoral programs; Total enrollment, 53,000.

Champaign-Urbana opened March 2, 1868, with three faculty members and 50 students near present Champaign-Urbana communities; Enrollment, Fall 1978, 25,400 undergraduate; 7,300 graduate.

Chicago-Circle opened, February 22, 1965; Enrollment, Fall 1978, 17,998 undergraduates; 2,770 graduates; University Medical Center in Chicago offers studies in nursing, medicine, dentistry, and pharmacy as well as research facilities.

● **URBANA,** City; Champaign County seat; Pop. 32,800; Area Code 217; Zip Code 61801; Elev. 750; E Central Illinois; Near Champaign; Settled, 1822; Incorporated, town, 1833; City, 1855; Site of University of Illinois, chartered, 1867; Named for town in Ohio.

Divided from Champaign by a street; U. of Illinois is partly in both cities; Center of agricultural region; Lincoln spoke here, 1853 and 1854.

● HISTORICAL PLACES: (See Hist. Pl. Sect. for Details.)

Altgeld Hall, University of Illinois; Morrow Plots, University of Illinois.

● **UTICA,** Town, LaSalle County; Pop. 974; Area Code 815; Zip Code 61373; Elev. 486; NE Illinois; Near Ottawa and LaSalle; Recreation area for Starved Rock State Park Recreational Area.

● **VALIER,** Town, Franklin County; Pop. 628; Area Code 618; Zip Code 62891.

● **VALMEYER,** Town, Monroe County; Pop, 733; Area Code 618; Zip Code 62295.

● **VANDALIA,** City; Fayette County seat; Pop. 5,160; Area Code 618; Zip Code 62471; Elev. 503; S Central Illinois; 30 miles N of Centralia; Second capital of Illinois (1819-39); On Kaskaskia River.

State legislature, in 1819, laid out the new state capital, 60 miles east of Mississippi River; In 1837 the "Long Nine," a coalition including Abraham Lincoln, obtained legislation removing capital to Springfield; State House erected here, 1836.

● HISTORICAL PLACES: (See Hist. Pl. Sect. for Details.)

Little Brick House; Vandalia Statehouse.

● Little Brick House Museum. 621 St Clair St.

● Ramsey Lake State Park. 12 Mi N on US 51, then W on unnumbered road.

● Vandalia Statehouse State Historic Site. 315 W Gallatin St.

● **VENICE**, City, Madison County; Pop. 4,680; Area Code 618; Zip Code 62090; Elev. 410; SW Illinois; S miles east of Mississippi River and St. Louis; Settled, 1804; Incorporated, 1873; named because streets were often flooded by the river before levees were constructed; Oldest and smallest of the Tri-Cities, which include Granite City and Madison.

● **VERMILLION RIVER**, N Central Illinois; 50 miles NW from its rising point in eastern Vermillion County the Illinois River at La Salle; Named for fine, red soil in river valley, which Indians used for facepainting.

● **VERMILLION COUNTY**, E Illinois, Area 898 square miles; Pop. 96,176; Seat Danville; Named for Vermillion River; Established January 18, 1826; Farming, dairying, coal mining area; Lands ceded to the Federal government, 1819 by Kickapoo Indians; Large salt mining area in nineteenth century.

● **VERMONT**, Town, Fulton County; Pop. 947; Area Code 309; Zip Code 61484; W Central Illinois.

● **VICTORIA**, Town, Knox County; Pop. 782; Area Code 309; Zip Code 61485.

● **VIENNA**, Town; Johnson County seat; Pop. 1,325; Area Code 618; Zip Code 62995; Elev. 405; Southern Illinois.

● **VILLA GROVE**, City, Douglas County; Pop. 2,707; Area Code 217; Zip Code 61956; Central Illinois; 25 mi. S of Champaign-Urbana. When pioneers first came to the area, they settled on the Embarrass River near the Villa in the Grove. This home had been built by George Warren Henson in 1852, who along with his wife Eliza, and other settlers such as Tom Duncan and Jim Richman, had come from Kentucky looking for land to farm. The name Villa Grove was used for the town that grew around this home.

Villa Grove was incorporated in 1904. Around that time, the city was one of the stops on a railroad line because it was the perfect division point for shipping grain due to its location, which was situated exactly between Chicago and St. Louis. Today, the city's agricultural products are corn and beans.

● **VILLA PARK,** City, DuPage County; Pop, 25,891; Area Code 312; Zip Code 60181.

● **VIOLA,** Town, Mercer County; Pop. 946; Area Code 309; Zip Code 61486; Elev. 797; NW Illinois; Near Iowa River.

● **VIRDEN,** City, Macoupin County; Pop. 3,405; Area Code 217; Zip Code 62690; Elev. 674; SW Central Illinois; 30 miles south of Springfield; Site of Virden Riot, October 12, 1989, when coal miners went on strike in protest of pay reductions; 10 miners and six armed guards were killed in fight with local coal company.

● **VIRGINIA,** City; Cass County seat; Pop. 1,814; Area Code 217; Zip Code 62691; W Central Illinois; 40 miles northeast of Springfield; Elev. 619; Settled, 1836, by Dr. Henry Hall, former British Navy surgeon; It was incorporated as a village in 1842, and as a city in 1872.

● **WABASH COUNTY,** SE Illinois; Area 221 square miles; Pop. 14,047; Seat Mount Carmel; Named for the Wabash River, which forms its eastern boundary between the state and Indiana; Established December 27, 1824. Farming region; Prehistoric Indian settlements.

● **WABASH RIVER,** SE Illinois border; 475 miles long; Flows from Darke County in Western Ohio in a west- southwesterly direction across Indiana to Illinois state-line at Mount Carmel, Wabash County; Continues southwest to empty into Ohio River at southwest corner of Indiana; Piankashaw Indians lived along its banks; Prone to flooding before deepened and leveed in nineteenth century; Some areas provided an abundance of mussels, used for pearls; Lincoln Memorial Bridge, commemorating the Lincoln family's trek into Illinois territory, 1830, spans river between Vincennes, Indiana and Illinois at a point near Lawrenceville.

●**WADSWORTH**, Town, Lake County; Pop. 756; Area Code 312; Zip Code 60083; NE Illinois, Suburb of Chicago; On Des Plaines River.

●**WALNUT**, Village; Bureau County; Pop. 1,500; Area Code 815; Zip Code 61376; N Central Illinois; NW Illinois; 50 mi. W of Moline. Early names were Walnut Grove and Brewersville; the current name was derived from the many walnut trees in the area. It was founded in 1837 by Greenburg Triplett and A. H. Jones, who, according to Walnut lore, pilfered land claims previously staked by other settlers. They later sold the land to Truman Culver. The area was incorporated in 1872.

Agriculturally, products include corn, beans, wheat, beef, hogs, sheep, and dairy farming. Some of its manufactures are pre-fab housing, wooden crafts, pizza, cheese, and heavy-duty conveyor equipment, among others. Walnut has been officially named the Rocking Horse Capital of Illinois.

● **WAMAC**, Town, Washington and Marion Counties; Pop. 1,347; Area Code 618; Elev. 497; Southern Illinois; Near Centralia.

●**WAPELLA**, Town, De Witt County; Pop. 572; Area Code 217; Zip Code 61777; Central Illinois.

● **WARREN**, Town, Jo Daviess County; Pop. 1,523; Area Code 815; Zip Code 61087; Elev. 1,005; NE Illinois corner; 2 miles south of Wisconsin border; Settled, 1843, by Alexander Burnett; Organized as town of Courtland, 1850; Renamed, 1853, in honor of town's founder's son, Warren.

● **WARREN COUNTY**, W Illinois; Area 542 square miles; Pop. 21,587; Seat Monmouth; Named for Gen. Joseph Warren, physician and soldier in the Battle of Bunker Hill; Established January 13, 1825; Cattle raising region; Many tributaries of the Mississippi River flow through area.

●**WARRENSBURG**, Town, Macon County; Pop. 738; Area Code 217; Zip Code 62573; Central Illinois; Near Decatur.

●**WARRENVILLE**, Town, DuPage County; Pop. 3,854; Area Code 312; Zip Code 60555; Elev. 693; NE Illinois; 30 miles southwest of Chicago; On DuPage River.

●**WARSAW**, Town, Hancock County; Pop. 1,758; Area Code 217; Zip Code 62397.

●**WASHINGTON,** City, Tazewell County; Pop. 6,790; Area Code 309; Zip Code 61571; Elev. 766; Central Illinois; 12 miles east of Peoria.

●**WASHINGTON COUNTY,** SW Illinois; Area 565 square miles; Pop. 13,569; Seat Nashville; Named for George Washington; Established January 2, 1818; Former county seat was Covington (1818-31); Kaskaskia River, flows through county, forming its northwestern border.

●**WATAGA,** Town, Knox County; Pop. 570; Area Code 309; Zip Code 61488.

●**WATERLOO,** City; Monroe County seat; Pop. 4,546; Area Code 618; Zip Code 62298; Elev. 717; SW Illinois; Near St. Louis; Industries include feed, dairy products.

●**WATERMAN,** Town, De Kalb County; Pop. 990; Area Code 815; Zip Code 60556; Northern Illinois.

●**WATSEKA,** City; Iroquois County seat; Pop. 5,294; Area Code 815; Zip Code 60970; Elev. 634; E Illinois; 27 miles south of Kankakee; Incorporated, 1860 as South Meddleport; Renamed, 1865, in honor of *Watch-e-kee* (pretty woman), Potawatomi Indian and wife of Gurdon Hubbard, an early settler.

●**WAUCONDA,** City, Lake County; Pop, 5,460; Area Code 312; Zip Code 60084; Elev. 800; NE Illinois; 44 miles north of Chicago; Settled, 1836 on Bangs Lake by Justus Bangs; Named by Bangs for a fictional Indian character.

●**WAUKEGAN,** City; Lake County seat; Pop. 65,269; Area Code 312; Zip Code 60085; Elev. 669; NE Illinois; 10 miles south of Wisconsin state line on Lake Michigan.

Site of Indian village known to seventeenth century explorers; Named for Indian word meaning "fort or trading post"; French fur trading post and fort in mid-eighteenth century; Settled by Americans, 1836; Incorporated as a village in 1849, and a city in 1859; Lincoln spoke here, 1860; Industries include wire, pharmaceuticals, outboard motors; Near Great Lakes Naval Training Center.

　　● Great-Lakes Naval Training Center. 3 mi E off I- 94.

　　● Illinois Beach State Park. 3 mi N & E.

●**WAVERLY,** Town, Morgan County; Pop. 1,442; Area Code 217; Zip Code 62692; W Central Illinois.

• **WAYNE**, Town, Du Page County; Pop. 572; Area Code 312; Zip Code 60184; NE Illinois.

• **WAYNE CITY**, Town, Wayne County; Pop. 985; Area Code 618; Zip Code 62895; SE Illinois.

• **WAYNE COUNTY**, SE Illinois; Area 715 square miles; Pop. 19,008; Seat Fairfield; Named for General "Mad" Anthony Wayne, Revolutionary and early territorial soldier; Established March 26, 1819; Little Wabash and Skillet Fork, tributaries of the Wabash River, flow through county; Auto parts manufacturing area.

• **WAYNESVILLE**, Town, DeWitt County; Pop. 522; Area Code 217; Zip Code 61778; W. Central Illinois.

• **WELDON**, Town, De Witt County; Pop. 553; Area Code 217; Zip Code 61882; W. Central Illinois.

• **WENONA**, Town, Marshall County; Pop. 1,080; Area Code 309; Zip Code 61377; Elev. 696; N. Central Illinois; Near Streator; Marketing center for soybeans and corn.

• **WEST CHICAGO**, City, Du Page County; Pop. 10, 111; Area Code 312; Zip Code 60185; NE Illinois; Near Wheaton.

• **WESTERN SPRINGS**, City, Cook County; Pop. 12,147; Area Code 312; Zip Code 60558; Elev. 668; NE Illinois; 15 miles south of Chicago Loop; Residential; Incorporated by Quakers, 1866; Named for local mineral springs believed to be medicinal, which have since dried up.

• **WESTFIELD**, Town, Clark County; Pop. 678; Area Code 217; Zip Code 62474; Elev. 686; Eastern Illinois; Farming region.

• **WEST FRANKFORT**, City, Franklin County; Pop. 8,836; Zip Code 62896; Area Code 618; Southern Illinois.

• **WESTMONT**, City, Du Page County; Pop. 8,482; Zip Code 312; Zip Code 60559; NE Illinois; Elev. 740; Near Hinsdale.

• **WEST SALEM**, Town, Edwards County; Pop. 979; Area Code 618; Zip Code 62476; SE Illinois.

• **WESTVILLE**, City, Vermillion County; Pop. 3,655; Area Code 217; Zip Code 61883; Elev. 671; E. Illinois; Settled, 1873, by W. P. and E. A. West.

● **WHEATON,** City, Du Page County seat; Pop. 31,138; Area Code 312; Zip Code 60187; Elev. 753; NE Illinois; 25 miles west of Chicago; Settled, 1838 by Warren and Jesse Wheaton; Incorporated, 1853.

The Wheaton family donated land for the Wheaton College campus, established 1853; City became county seat, 1868, when Wheaton residents descended upon the seat at that time, Naperville, and stole a wagonload of public records; Judge Elbert Gary, steel entrepreneur, was born here, 1846; Residential community in agricultural region.

- ● Billy Graham Center Museum.
- ● Cantigny. W on IL 38.
- ● Cosley's Animal Farm & Museum. 1356 N Gary Ave.
- ● Du Page Heritage Gallery. 421 County Farm Rd.
- ● DuPage County Historical Museum. 102 E Wesley St.
- ● Marion E. Wade Collection. Housed in the Wheaton College Library.
- ● Wheaton College (1860). (2,500 students) 501 E Seminary Ave.

●**WHEATON COLLEGE,** Wheaton, Du Page County; Established, 1853 as Illinois Institute by Wesleyan Methodists; Reorganized, 1860, as Wheaton College under the Congregational Church; Named for Warren Wheaton, who donated large plots of land for the campus; Today, college is non-denominational, co- educational and liberal arts oriented.

●**WHEELING,** City, Cook County; Pop. 14,746; Area Code 312; Zip Code 60090; Elev. 650; NE Illinois; 20 miles NW of Chicago; Settled, 1830, as a country store.

● **WHITE COUNTY,** SE Illinois; Area 501 square miles; Pop. 19,373; Seat Carmi; Named for Leonard White, state senator, 1820-24; Established December 9, 1815; Hilly farmland region; Bounded to the east by the Wabash River; Tributaries run through central county.

● **WHITE HALL,** City, Greene County; Pop. 2,979; Area Code 217; Zip Code 62092; Elev. 585; SE Illinois; 23 mi. S of Jacksonville; Originally called Loafer's Grove, the area was founded in 1832 by David Barrow. The current name was due to a small house on Main Street that was whitewashed--an unusual sight back then--and some people in the town called it "the White Hall." Soon after, the post office was given that name, and then the town. The area was incorporated as a town in 1837, and as a city in 1884.

The downtown area is now listed in the National Register of Historical Places, and other points of interest include the Annie Keller Monument, plus the gravesite of the Little Drummer Boy, Edward L. Hager, who was wounded at Shiloh on April 7, 1862, and died later at his home in White Hall.

Agriculture includes corn, soybeans, and wheat, and manufactures include clay and tilemaking, coffee filters, and pharmaceuticals.

● **WHITESIDE COUNTY,** NW Illinois; Area 690 square miles; Pop. 59,887; Seat Morrison; Named for Gen. Samuel Whiteside, who commanded the Illinois militia in the War of 1812, as well as the Black Hawk War; Established January 16, 1836; Eastern border formed by Mississippi River; Rock River flows through southeast area of county; Hilly, wooded region.

●**WILL COUNTY,** NE Illinois; Area 845 square miles; Pop. 191,617; Seat Joliet; Named for Conrad Will, pioneer in Illinois; Established January 12, 1836; Hilly, moraine valley region; Illinois and Kankakee Rivers flow through west and southwest region; Site of McKinley Woods and Fisher Mounds, prehistoric Indian burial grounds.

● **WILLIAMSFIELD,** Town, Knox County; Pop, 552; Area Code 309; Zip Code 61489; W. Illinois.

● **WILLIAMSON COUNTY,** S. Illinois; Area 441 square miles; Pop. 46,117; Seat Marion; Established February 28, 1839; Hilly coal mining region; Crab Orchard Lake situated here; Big Muddy River flows through northwest boundary.

● **WILLIAMSVILLE,** Town, Sangamon County; Pop. 923; Area Code 923; Area Code 217; Zip Code 62693; Central Illinois.

●**WILLISVILLE,** Town, Perry County; Pop. 659; Area Code 618; Zip Code 62997; SW Illinois.

●**WILLOWSPRINGS,** Town, Cook County; Pop. 3,318; Area Code 312; Zip Code 60480.

● **WILMETTE,** Residential village, Cook County; Pop. 32,134; Area Code 312; Zip Code 60091; Elev. 614; NE Illinois; Suburb of Chicago; On Lake Michigan; Settled, 1829; Named for first white settler, Antoine Ouilmette, a French Canadian whose Indian wife gained the land under a government treaty; Site of Mallinckrodt College, established 1918.

● HISTORICAL PLACES: (See Hist. Pl. Sect. for Details.)

Baker, Frank J., House
● Baha'i House of Worship. Sheridan Rd & Linden Ave.
● Gillson Park. Washington & Michigan Aves.
● Historical Museum. 565 Hunter Rd.

● **WILMINGTON,** City, Will County; Pop. 60481; Area Code 815; Zip Code 60481; Elev. 549; NE Illinois; 17 miles south of Joliet; Incorporated, 1854; Coal and agricultural business center.

●**WILSONVILLE,** Town, Macoupin County; Pop. 691; Area Code 618; Zip Code 62093; SW Illinois.

●**WINCHESTER,** City, Scott County seat; Pop. 1,788; Area Code 217; Zip Code 62694; Elev. 546; Settled, gristmill opened, 1824; Founded, 1830; Named by a Kentucky settler who gained the honor from surveyors in exchange for a jug of whiskey; Stephen A. Douglas lived here, 1833-34; Near Illinois River.

●**WINDSOR,** Town, Shelby County; Pop. 1,126; Area Code 217; Zip Code 61957; Central Illinois.

● **WINFIELD,** Town, Du Page County; Pop. 4,285; Area Code 312; Zip Code 60190.

●**WINNEBAGO,** Town, Winnebago County; Pop. 1,285; Area Code 815; Zip Code 61088; N Central Illinois.

● **WINNEBAGO COUNTY,** N, Central Illinois; Area 520 square miles; Pop. 209,765; Seat Rockford; Named for Indian tribe; Established January 16, 1836; Rock River cuts through eastern area of county; Agricultural region; Courthouse built, 1878.

● **WINNETKA,** Village, Cook County; Pop. 14,131; Area Code 312; Zip Code 6@93; Elev. 651; NE Illinois; 20 miles north of Chicago; Incorporated, residential village, 1869; on Lake Michigan.

● HISTORICAL PLACES: (See Hist. Pl. Sect. for Details.)

Lloyd, Henry Demarest, House (The Wayside).
● Woodstock Opera House.

●**WINTHROP HARBOR,** Town, Lake County; Pop. 4,795; Area Code 312; Zip Code 60096; Elev. 598; NE Illinois Corner, 1 mile south of Wisconsin state line; On Lake Michigan; Incorporated, 1892 by Winthrop Harbor and Dock

Company, which planned to develop a harbor and establish an industrial town; Dairying is chief industry here.

● **WITT**, Town, Montgomery County; Pop. 1,040; Area Code 217; Zip Code 62094.

● **WONDER LAKE**, Town, McHenry County; Pop. 4,806; Area Code 815; Zip Code 60097.

● **WOOD DALE**, Town, Du Page County, Pop. 8,831; Area Code 312; Zip Code 60191.

● **WOODFORD COUNTY**, N. Central Illinois; Area 537 square miles; Pop. 24,579; Seat Eureka; Named for a county in Kentucky; Established February 27, 1841; Former county seats: Versailles, 1841, Hanover, 1843-94; Area settled by Amish in mid- nineteenth century along Illinois River; River forms western boundary of county.

● **WOODHULL**, Town, Henry County; Pop. 898; Area Code 309; Zip Code 61490; NW Illinois.

● **WOOD RIVER**, City, Madison County; Pop. 13,186; Area Code 618; Zip Code 62095; Elev. 430; SW Illinois; Along Mississippi River; Standard Oil Refinery built, 1907 because of rail and water transportation convenience; Town grew around oil industry.

● **WOODSTOCK**, City, McHenry County seat; Pop. 10,226; Area Code 815; Zip Code 60098; Elev. 943; NE Illinois; 50 miles NW of Chicago; Named for Vermont town of early settlers in 1830s and 40s; Industries include typewriters, dairy products, and agriculture.

● HISTORICAL PLACES: (See Hist. Pl. Sect. for Details.)

  Old McHenry County Courthouse; Woodstock Opera House.

● **WORDEN**, Town, Madison County; Pop. 1,091; Area Code 618; Zip Code 62097.

● **WORTH**, Residential Village, Cook County; Pop. 11,999; Area Code 312; Zip Code 60482; NE Illinois; Chicago suburb.

● **WYANET**, Town, Bureau County; Pop. 1,005; Area Code 815; Zip Code 61379; Elev. 656; N. Central Illinois; On Illinois and Mississippi Canal.

● **WYOMING**, Town, Stark County; Pop. 1,563; Area Code 309; Zip Code 61491; NW Central Illinois.

●**YATES CITY,** Town, Knox County; Pop. 840; Area Code 309; Zip Code 61572; W. Illinois; Named for Gov. Richard Yates (1861-65).

● HISTORICAL PLACES: (See Hist. Pl. Sect. for Details.)

Wolf Covered Bridge.

● **YORKVILLE,** Town, Kendall County seat; Pop. 2,049; Area Code 815; Zip Code 60560; Elev. 584; NE Illinois; On Fox River.

●**ZEIGLER,** Town, Franklin County; Pop. 1,940; Area Code 618; Zip Code 62999; Southern Illinois; On Big Muddy River.

● **ZION,** City, Lake County; Pop. 17,268; Area Code 312; Zip Code 60099; Elev. 633; NE Illinois; 3 miles south of Wisconsin state line; Founded by a man who believed the world to be flat even though he had taken a trip around it.

Guide to Criteria for Selection
The National Register of Historic Places
(Illinois Section)

The quality of significance in American history, architecture, archeology, engineering and culture is present in districts, sites, buildings, structures, and objects that possess integrity of location, design, setting, materials, workmanship, feeling, and association and:

A. that are associated with events that have made a significant contribution to the broad patterns of our history; or
B. that are associated with the lives of persons significant in our past; or
C. that embody the distinctive characteristics of a type, period, or method of construction, or that represent the work of a master, or that possess high artistic values, or that represent a significant and distinguisable entity whose components may lack individual distinction; or
D. that have yielded, or may be likely to yield, information important in prehistory or history.

Criteria considerations:

a. a religious property deriving primary significance from architectural or artistic distinction or historical importance; or
b. a building or structure removed from its original location but which is significant primarily for architectural value, or which is the surviving structure most importantly associated with a historic person or event; or
c. a birthplace or grave of a historical figure of outstanding importance if there is no other appropriate site or building directly associated with his productive life; or
d. a cemetery that derives its primary significance from graves of persons of transcendent importance, from age, from distinctive design features, or from association with historic events; or
e. a reconstructed building when accurately executed in a suitable environment and presented in a dignified manner as part of a restoration master plan, and when no other building or structure with the same association has survived; or
f. a property primarily commemorative in intent if design, age, tradition, or symbolic value has invested it with its own historical significance; or
g. a property achieving significance within the past 50 years if it is of exceptional importance.

ENTRY REFERENCES

(NHL) indicates National Historic Landmark. Eight-character numbers at the end of each entry is the computer reference number for obtaining detailed information from The National Park Service.

HISTORIC PLACES IN ILLINOIS

(See page 403 for Alphabetical Listing)

ADAMS COUNTY

DOWNTOWN QUINCY HISTORIC DISTRICT, Roughly bounded by Hampshire, Jersey, 4th and 8th Sts., Ouincy, 4/07/83, A,C, 83000298

EBENEZER METHODIST EPISCOPAL CHAPEL AND CEMETERY, NW of Golden, Golden, 6/04/84, A,C,a, 840009211

EXCHANGE BANK, Quincy St., Golden, 2/12/87, A, 86003714

GARDNER, ROBERT W., HOUSE, 613 Broadway St., Quincy, 6/20/79, B, 79000812

LEWIS ROUND BARN, {Round Barns in Illinois TR}, NW of Clayton, Clayton vicinity, 8/16/84, C, 84000916

MORGAN-WELLS HOUSE, 421 Jersey St., Quincy, 11/16/77, B.C, 77000471

NEWCOMB, RICHARD F., HOUSE, 1601 Maine St., Quincy, 6/03/82, B.C, 82002516

ONE THIRTY NORTH EIGHTH BUILDING, 130 N. 8th St., Quincy, 2/09/84, C, 84000918

QUINCY EAST END HISTORIC DISTRICT, Roughly bounded by Hampshire, Twenty-fourth, State, and Twelfth Sts., Quincy, 11/14/85, C, 85002791

ROY, JOHN, SITE, Address Restricted, Clayton vicinity, 5/22/78, D, 78001109

STATE SAVINGS LOAN AND TRUST, 428 Maine Quincy, 3/23/79, B,C, 79000813

ST. THOMAS, F. D., HOUSE, 321 N. Ohio St., Camp Point, 7/28/83, C.c, 83000299

U.S. POST OFFICE AND COURTHOUSE, 200 N. 8th St., Quincy, 12/02/77, C, 77000472

ILLA DE KATHRINE, 5325. 3rd, Quincy, 12/08/78, C, 78001110

WARFIELD, WILLIAM 5., HOUSE, 1624 Maine St., Ouincy, 3/21/79, B.C, 79000814

WOOD, ERNEST M., OFFICE AND STUDIO, 126 N. 8th St., Quincy, 8/12/82, C, 82002517

WOOD, JOHN, MANSION, 425 S. 12th St., Quincy, 4/17/70, B.b, 70000228

ALEXANDER COUNTY

CAIRO HISTORIC DISTRICT, Roughly bounded by Park, 33rd, Sycamore, 21st, Cedar, and 4th Sts. and the Ohio River, Cairo, 1/26/79, A,B,C,g, 79000815

CHICAGO AND EASTERN ILLINOIS RAILROAD DEPOT, Front St., Tamms, 11/06/86, A, 86003168

DOGTOOTH BEND MOUNDS AND VILLAGE SITE, Address Restricted, Willard vicinity, 5/23/78, D, 78001111

MAGNOLIA MANOR, Washington Ave., Cairo, 12/17/69, C, 69000053

OLD CUSTOMHOUSE, Washington and 15th St., Cairo, 7/24/73, C, 73000689

THEBES COURTHOUSE, OFF IL 3. THEBES, 12/26/72, A,C, 72000447

BOND COUNTY

OLD MAIN, ALMIRA COLLEGE, 315 E. College St., Greenville, 4/21/75, A,C, 75000638

BOONE COUNTY

PETTIT MEMORIAL CHAPEL, 1100 N. Main St., Belvidere, 12/01/78, C,a,f, 78001112

BROWN COUNTY

DEWITT, BENJAMIN, HOUSE, Address Restricted, Versailles vicinity, 7/28/83, B.C, 83000300

MOUNT STERLING COMMERCIAL HISTORIC DISTRICT, Roughly bounded by Brnwn Co. Courthouse, Alley E of Capitol, South St., and Alley W of Capitol, Mount Sterling, 5/08/87, A.C, 87000724

BUREAU COUNTY

FIRST STATE BANK OF MANLIUS, N side of Maple St., Manlius, 5/12/75, C, 75000639

GREENWOOD COTTAGE, 543 E. Peru St., Princeton, 5/09/83, A,C, 83000301

HENNEPIN CANAL HISTORIC DISTRICT, W To Molineen N to Rock Falls vic., Hennepin vicinity, 5/22/78, A.C, 78003433

LOVEJOY, OWEN, HOMESTEAD, Peru St. (U.S. 6), Princeton, 5/24/73, B, 73000690

OLD DANISH CHURCH, SE corner of Cook and Washington Sts., Sheffield, 10/02/73, A,C,a, 73000691

PRINCETON CHAPTER HOUSE, {American Woman, 5 League Chapter Houses TR}, 1007 N. Main St., Princeton, 11/28/80, A.B,C, 80001338

RED COVERED BRIDGE, 2 mi. N of Princeton off IL 26 on Old Dad Joe Trail, Princeton vicinity, 4/23/75, A.C, 75000640

SKINNER, RICHARD M., HOUSE, 627 E. Peru St. Princeton, 2/10/83, C, 83000302

CALHOUN COUNTY

GOLDEN EAGLE TOPPMEYER SITE, Adress Restricted, Brussels vicinity, 6/14/79, D, 79000816

KAMP MOUND SITE ADDRESS RESTRICTED KAMPSVILLE VICINITY, 8/24/78, D, 78001114

KLUNK, MICHAEL FARMSTEAD, Address Restricted, Michael vicinity, 6/23/82, C, 82002518

SCHUDEL NO. 2 SITE, Address Restricted, Hamburg vicinity, 6/15/79, D, 79000817

CARROLL COUNTY

HALDERMAN, NATHANIEL, HOUSE, 728 E. Washington St., Mount Carroll, 11/24/80, B,C, 80001339

MARK, CAROLINE, HOUSE, 222 E. Lincoln St., Mount Carroll, 8/11/83, A,B,C, 83000303

MOUNT CARROLL HISTORIC DISTRICT, IL 64 and IL 78, Mount Carroll, 11/26/80, C, 80001340

STEFFENS, JOSEPH, HOUSE, Off of Elkhorn Rd., Milledgeville vicinity, 4/10/85, C, 85000771

CASS COUNTY

CUNNINGHAM, ANDREW, FARM, 2.5 mi. E of Virginia off Gridley Rd., Virginia vicinity, 5/12/75, C, 75000641

PARK HOUSE, 200 W. 2nd St., Beardstown, 2/10/83, C, 83000304

CHAMPAIGN COUNTY

ALTGELD HALL, University of Illinois {University of Illinois Buildings by Nathan Clifford Ricker TR (AD)j, University of Illinois campus, corner of Wright and John Sts., Urbana, 4/17/70, A,C, 70000229

BURNHAM ATHENAEUM, 306 W. Church St, Champaign, 6/07/78, C, 78001115

CATTLE BANK, 102 E. UNIVERSITY AVE., Champaign, 8/19/75, A, 75000642

CHEMICAL LABORATORY, {University of Illinois Buildings by Nathan Clifford Ricker TR}, 1305 W. Green St., Urbana, 11/19/86, A,B,C, 86003148

GREEK REVIVAL COTTAGE, 300 W. University Ave., Urbana, 10/20/77, C,b, 77000473

GRIGGS, CLARK R., HOUSE, 505 W. Main St., Urbana, 11/30/78, B.C, 78001116

MAHOMET GRADED SCHOOL, Main St., Mahomet, 12/02/87,A,C, 87002035

METAL SHOP, {University of Illinois Buildings by Nathan Clifford Ricker TR, 102 S. Burril Ave., Urbana, 11/19/86, B,C, 86003141

MILITARY DRILL HALL AND MEN'S GYMNASIUM, {University of Illinois Buildings by Nathan Clifford Ricker TR}, 1402-1406 W. Springfield, Urbana, 11/19/86, A,B,C, 86003144

MORROW PLOTS, University of Illinois, Gregory Dr. at Matthews Ave., Urbana, 5/23/68, A, NHL, 68000024

STONE ARCH BRIDGE, Springfield Ave. and 2nd St., Champaign, 81, A,C. 81000210

U.S. POST OFFICE, Randolph and Church Sts., Champaign, 8/17/76, C, 76000684

UNIVERSITY OF ILLINOIS ASTRONOMICAL OBSERVATORY, 901 S. Mathews Ave., Urbana, 11/06/86, A, 86003155

VRINERS CONFECTIONERY, 55 Main St., Champaign, 5/09/83, A,C, 83000305

CHRISTIAN COUNTY

ILLINOIS STATE BANK BUILDING, 201 N. Chestnut St., Assumption, 8/16/84, A,C, 84000923

TAYLORVILLE CHAUTAUQUA AUDTITORIUM, Manners Park, Taylorville, 1/21/88, A,b, 87002519

TAYLORVILLE COURTHOUSE SQUARE HISTORIC DISTRICT, Roughly bounded by Vine, Walnut, Adams, and Webster Sts., Taylorville, 12/02/85, A,C, 85003058

CLARK COUNTY

ARCHER HOUSE HOTEL, 717 Archer Ave., Marshall, 3/16/76, B, 76000685

LEWIS, JOHN W., HOUSE, 503 Chestnut St., Marshall, 2/26/82, B,C, 82002519

MANLY-MCCANN HOUSE, 402 S. 4th St., Marshall, 3/05/82, A, 82002520

MILLHOUSE BLACKSMITH SHOP, Main and Poplar Sts., Clarksville, 5/12/87, A, 86003156

OLD STONE ARCH BRIDGE, E of Clark Center off U.S. 40, Clark Center vicinity, 11/28/78, A,C, 78001117

OLD STONE ARCH, National Road, Archer St., Marshall vicinity, 2/20/75, A,C, 75000643

CLAY COUNTY

PAINE HOUSE, Rt. 1, Box 19 A, Xenia, 11/14/85, B, 85002843

SHRIVER HOUSE, 117 E. 3rd. St., Flora, 5/09/83, C, 83000306

CLINTON COUNTY

GENERAL DEAN SUSPENSION BRIDGE, E of Carlyle over the Kaskaskia River, Carlyle vicinity, 4/03/73, A,C, 73000693

COLES COUNTY

AIRTIGHT BRIDGE, {Coles County River TR}, NE of Charleston, Charleston vicinity, 11/30/81, A,C, 81000211

BLAKEMAN BRIDGE, {Coles County Highway Bridges Over the Embarras River TRj, SE of Charleston, Charleston vicinity, 11/30/81, A,C, 81000212

BRIGGS, ALEXANDER, HOUSE, 210 Jackson St., Charleston, 5/31/80, B,C, 80001341

CLEVELAND, CINCINNATI, Chicago and St. Louis Railroad Station, 1632 Broadway St., Mattoon, 1/30/86, A, 86000135

COLES COUNTY COURTHOUSE, Charleston Public Sq., Charleston, 11/28/78, A,C, 78001118

HARRISON ST. BRIDGE, {Coles County Highway Bridges Over the Embarras River TR}, E of Charleston, Charleston vicinity, 11/30/81, A,C, 81000213

OLD MAIN, LINCOLN AVE. AND 7TH ST., Charleston, 6/16/81, A,C 81000214

PEMBERTON HALL AND GYMNASIUM, Lincoln Ave. and 4th St., Charleston, 8/26/82, A, 82002521

RUTHERFORD, DR. HIRAM, HOUSE AND OFFICE, 14 S. Pike St., Oakland, 6/03/82, B,C, 82002523

STONE QUARRY BRIDGE, {Coles County Highway Bridges Over the Embarras River TR}, NE of Charleston, Charleston vicinity, 11/30/81, A,C, 81000215

U. S. POST OFFICE, 1701 Charleston Ave., Mattoon, 12/06/79, C, 79000818

UNITY CHURCH, 220 Western Ave., Mattoon, 3/19/82, A,C,a, 82002522

WILL ROGERS THEATRE AND COMMERCIAL BLOCK, 705-715 Monroe Ave., Charleston, 1/12/84, C, 84001066

COOK COUNTY

AVR 661, CALUMET HARBOR, CHICAGO, 11/19/80, A b,g, 80001342

ABBOTT, ROBERT S., HOUSE, 4742 Martin Luther King, Jr. Dr., Chicago, 12/08/76, B,g, NHL, 76000686

ADLER PLANETARIUM, 1300S. Lake Shore Dr., Chicago, 2/27/87, A, NHL, 87000819

ALTA VISTA TERRACE HISTORIC DISTRICT, Block bounded by W. Byron, W. Grace, N. Kenmore, and N. Seminary Sts., Chicago, 3/16/72, A,C, 72000448

ANDRIDGE APARTMENTS, {Suburban Apartment Buildings in Evanston TRj, 1627-1645 Ridge Ave., 1124-1136 Church St., Evanston, 3/15/84, A,C, 84000927

AUDITORIUM BUILDING, ROOSEVELT UNIVERSITY, 430 Michigan Ave. and Congress St., Chicago, 4/17/70, C: NHL, 70000230

AUSTIN HISTORIC DISTRICT, Roughly bounded by W. Ohio St., N. Waller, Parkside, W. West End & N. Mayfield Aves. & W. Corcoran Pl., Chicago, 8/08/85, C, 85001741

BACH, EMIL, HOUSE, 7415 N. Sheridan Rd., Chicago 1/23/79, C, 79000821

BAHAI TEMPLE, 100 Linden Ave., Wilmette, 5/23/78, A,C,a,g, 78001140

BAILEY-MICHELET HOUSE, 1028 Sheridan Rd., Wilmette, 8/12/82, C, 82002533

BAKER, FRANK J., House, 507 Lake Ave., Wilmette, 11/08/74, C, 74000759

BALABAN & KATZUPTOWN THEATRE, 4814-4816 N. Broadway, Chicago, 11/20/86, A,C, 86003181

BALABAN AND KATZ CHICAGO THEATRE, 175 N. State St., Chicago, 6/06/79, A ,C, 79000822

BALDWIN, HIRAM, HOUSE, 205 Essex Rd., Kenilworth, 7/28/83, C, 83000307

BARRINGTON HISTORIC DISTRICT, Roughly bounded by Chicago & Northwestern RR, S. Spring and Grove Sts., E. Hillside and W. Coolidge, and Dundee Aves., Barrington, 5/16/86, C, 86001047

BELMONT-SHEFFIELD TRUST AND SAVINGS BANK BUILDING, 1001 W. Belmont Ave. and 3146 N. Sheffield Ave., Chicago, 3/01/84, A,C, 84000931

BEST BREWING COMPANY OF CHICAGO BUILDING, 1315-1317 W. Fletcher, Chicago, 7/30/87, A,C, 87001263

BIOGRAPH THEATER BUILDING, 2433 N. Lincoln Ave., Chicago, 5/17/84, A, 84000934

BLACKSTONE HOTEL, 80 E. Balbo Dr., Chicago, 5/08/86, A,C, 86001005

BLOOM TOWNSHIP HIGH SCHOOL, 10th St., Dixie Hwy. and Chicago Heights St., Chicago Heights, 6/03/82, C,g, 82002527

BUENA PARK HISTORIC DISTRICT, Roughly bounded by Graceland Cemetery, Marine Drive, Irving Park Road, & Montrose Ave., Chicago, 7/13/84, A,C, 84000937

BUILDING AT 1101-1113 MAPLE AVENUE, {Suburban Apartment Buildings in Evanston TR}, 1101-1113 Maple Ave., Evanston, 3/15/84, A,C, 84000960

BUILDING AT 1209-1217 MAPLE AVENUE, {Suburban Apartment Buildings in Evanston TR}, 1209-1217 Maple Ave., Evanston, 3/15/84, A,C, 84000964

BUILDING AT 1301-1303 JUDSON AVENUE, {Suburban Apartment Buildings in Evanston TR}, 1301-1303 Judson Ave., Evanston, 4/27/84, A,C, a 84000968

BUILDING AT 1305-1307 JUDSON AVENUE, {Suburban Apartment Buildings in Evanston TR}, 1305-1307 Judson Ave., Evanston, 4/27/84, A,C, 84000966

BUILDING AT 1316 MAPLE AVENUE, (Suburban Apartment Buildings in Evanston TR}, 1316 Maple Ave., Evanston, 3/15/84, A,C, 84000969

BUILDING AT 14-16 PEARSON STREET, 14-16 Pearson Street, Chicago, 5/08/80, C, 89001343

BUILDING AT 1401-1407 ELMWOOD AVENUE, {Suburban Apartment Buildings in Evanston TR}, 1401-1407 Elmwood Ave., Evanston, 3/15/84, A,C, 84000973

BUILDING AT 1505-1509 OAK AVENUE, {Suburban Apartment Buildings in Evanston TR}, 15051509 Oak Ave., Evanston, 3/15/84, A,C, 84000976

BUILDING AT 1929-1931 SHERMAN AVENUE, {Suburban Apartment Buildings in Evanston TR}, 1929-1931 Sherman Ave., Evanston, 3/15/84, A,C, 84000978

BUILDING AT 2517 CENTRAL STREET, {Suburban Apartment Buildings in Evanston TRI, 2517 Central St., Evanston, 3/15/84, A,C, 84000980

BUILDING AT 2519 CENTRAL STREET, {Suburban Apartment Buildings in Evanston TR}, 2519 Central St., Evanston, 3/15/84, A,C, 84000982

BUILDING AT 2523 CENTRAL STREET, {Suburban Apartment Buildings in Evanston TR}, 2523 Central St., Evanston, 3/15/84, A,C, 84000983

BUILDING AT 257 EAST DELAWARE, 257 E. Delaware, Chicago, 6/26/87, C, 87001113

BUILDING AT 417-419 LEE STREET, {Suburban Apartment Buildings in Evanston TR}, 417-419 Lee St., Evanston, 3/15/84, A,C, 84000942

BUILDING AT 548-606 MICHIGAN AVENUE, {Suburban Apartment Buildings in Evanston TR}, 548-606 Michigan Ave., Evanston, 3/15/84, A,C, 84000945

BUILDING AT 813-815 FOREST AVENUE, {Suburban Apartment Buildings in Evanston TR}, 813-815 Forest Ave., Evanston, 3/15/84, A,C, 84000950

BUILDING AT 923-925 MICHIGAN AVENUE, {Suburban Apartment Buildings in Evanston TR}, 923-925 Michigan Ave., Evanston, 3/15/84, A,C, 84000953

BUILDING AT 999 MICHIGAN, 200 Lee {Suburban Apartment Buildings in Evanston TR}, 999 Michigan Ave., 200 Lee St., Evanston, 3/15/84, A,C, 84000958

BUILDINGS AT 1104-1110 SEWARD, {Suburban Apartment Buildings in Evanston TR}, 1104-1110 Seward, Evanston, 9/02/86, A,C, 86001743

BUILDINGS AT 815-817 BRUMMEL AND 819-821 BRUMMEL, {Suburban Apartment Buildings in Evanston TR}, 815-817, and 819-821 Brummel, Evanston, 3/15/84, A,C, 84000952

BUILDINGS AT 860880 LAKE SHORE DRIVE, 860-880 Lake Shore Drive, Chicago, 8/28/80, C,g, 80001344

BURLINGHAM BUILDING, 104 W. Oak St., Chicago, 2/14/85, C, 85000264

CALUMET PLANT, R. R. Donnelly & Sons Company, 350 E. 22nd St., Chicago, 2/17/83, A,C, 83000308

CARSON, PIRIE, SCOTT AND COMPANY, 1 S. State St., Chicago, 4/17/70, C, NHL, 70000231

CARTER, FREDERICK B., JR., HOUSE, 1024 Judson Ave., Evanston, 7/30/74, A, 74000758

CASTLE TOWER APARTMENTS, {Suburban Apartment Buildings in Evanston TR}, 2212-2226 Sherman Ave., Evanston, 3/15/84, A,C, 84000985

CHAPIN AND GORE BUILDING, 63 E. Adams St., Chicago, 6/27/79, C, 79000823

CHARNLEY, JAMES, HOUSE, 1365 N. Astor St., Chicago, 4/17/70, C, 70000232

CHICAGO AVENUE WATER TOWER AND PUMPING STATION, Both sides of N. Michigan Ave. between E. Chicago and E. Pearson Sts., Chicago, 4/23/75, C, 75000644

CHICAGO BEACH HOTEL, {Hyde Park Apartment Hotels TR}, 5100-5100 S. Cornell Ave., Chicago, 5/14/86, A,C, 86001193

CHICAGO BEE BUILDING, {Black Metropolis TR}, 3647 3655 S. State Ave., Chicago, 4/30/86, A,C, 86001090

CHICAGO BOARD OF TRADE BUILDING, 141 W. Jackson Blvd., Chicago, 6/16/78, A,g, NHL, 78003181

CHICAGO HARBOR LIGHTHOUSE, {U.S. Coast Guard Lighthouses and Light Stations on the Great Lakes TR}, N Breakwater, Chicago, 7/19/84, A, 84000986

CHICAGO PORTAGE NATIONAL HISTORIC SITE, S. Harlem Ave.

at Chicago Sanitary and Ship Canal, Forest View, 10/15/66, A, 66000108

CHICAGO PUBLIC LIBRARY, CENTRAL BUILDING, 78 E. Washington St., Chicago, 7/31/72, C, 72000449

CHICAGO SAVINGS BANK BUILDING, 7 W. Madison St., Chicago, 9/05/75, A,C, 75000645

CHICAGO AND NORTHWESTERN DEPOT, 1135-1141 Wilmette Ave., Wilmette, 4/24/75, A,C,b, 75000658

CLARKE, HENRY B., HOUSE, 4526 S. Wabash Ave., Chicago, 5/06/71, C,a, 71000290

CLAYSON, GEORGE, HOUSE, 224 E. Palatine Rd., Palatine, 3/21/79, C, 79000835

CLUEVER, RICHARD, HOUSE, 601 1st Ave., Maywood, 11/17/77, C, 77000482

COLONNADE COURT, {Suburban Apartment Buildings in Evanston TR}, 501-507 Main St., 904-908 Hinman Ave., Evanston, 3/15/84, A,C, 84000987

COMPTON, ARTHUR H., HOUSE, 5637 Woodlawn Ave., Chicago, 5/11/76, B,g, NHL, 76000687

CONWAY BUILDING, 111 W. Washington St., Chicago, 2/09/84, B,C, 84000988

COOK COUNTY CRIMINAL COURT BUILDING, 54 W. Hubbard St., Chicago, 11/13/84, A,C, 84000281

COONLEY, AVERY, HOUSE, 290 and 300 Scottswood Rd., 281 Bloomingbank Rd., and 336 Coonley St., Riverside, 12/30/70, C, NHL, 70000243

DAWES, CHARLES GATES, HOUSE, 225 Greenwood St., Evanston, 12/08/76, B, NHL, 76000706

DAWSON BROTHERS PLANT, 517-519 N. Halsted St., Chicago, 2/14/85, A,C, 85000265

DE PRIEST, OSCAR STANTON, HOUSE, 4536-4538 S. Dr. Martin Luther King, Jr. Dr., Chicago, 5/15/75, B,g, NHL, 75000646

DEARBORN STATION, 47 W. Polk St., Chicago, 3/26/76, A,C, 76000688

DELAWARE BUILDING, 36 W. Randolph St., Chicago, 7/18/74, C, 74000749

DEWES, FRANCIS J., HOUSE, 503 W. Wrightwood Ave., Chicago, 8/14/73, C, 73000694

DOUGLAS TOMB STATE MEMORIAL, 636 E. State St. Chicago, 5/28/76, B,C,c,f, 76000689

DRAKE HOTEL, 140 E. Walton St., Chicago, 5/08/80, C, 89001345

DRUMMOND, WILLIAM E. HOUSE, 559 Edgewood Pl., River Forest 3/05/70, C, 79000241

DRYDEN, GEORGE B., HOUSE, 1314 Ridge Ave., Evanston, 12/18/78, A,C, 78001135

DU SABLE, JEAN BAPTISTE POINT, Homesite, 401 N. Michigan Ave., Chicago, 5/11/76, B,f, NHL, 76000690

DUNHAM, ARTHUR J., HOUSE, 3131 S. Wisconsin Ave., Berwyn, 2/11/82, C, 82002524

EAST PARK TOWERS, {Hyde Park Apartment Hotels TR}, 5236- 5252 S. Hyde Park Blvd., Chicago, 5/14/86, A,C, 86001197

EIGHTH REGIMENT ARMORY, {Black Metropolis TR}, 3533 S. Giles Ave., Chicago, 4/30/86, A, 86001096

EMMEL BUILDING, 1357 N. Wells St., Chicago, 11/13/84, C, 84000283

EVANSTON LAKESHORE HISTORIC DISTRICT, Roughly bounded by Northwestern University, Lake Michigan, Calvary Cemetery, and Chicago Ave., Evanston, 9/29/80, A,C, 80001353

EVANSTON RIDGE HISTORIC DISTRICT, Roughly bounded by Main, Asbury, Ashland, Emerson, Ridge and Maple Ave., Evanston, 3/03/83, A,C, 83000309

EVANSTON TOWERS, {Suburban Apartment Buildings in Evanston TR}, 554-602 Sheridan Sq., Evanston, 3/15/84, A,C, 84000990

FAIRBANKS, MORSE AND COMPANY BUILDING, 900 S. Wabash Ave., Chicago, 11/16/88, A, 88002233

FIELD MUSEUM OF NATURAL HISTORY, E. Roosevelt Rd. at S. Lake Shore Dr., Chicago, 9/05/75, C, 75000647

FIRST CONGREGATIONAL CHURCH OF AUSTIN, 5701 W. Midway Pl., Chicago, 11/17/77, C,a, 77000474

FIRST SELF-SUSTAINING NUCLEAR REACTION, Site of, S. Ellis Ave. between E. 56th and 57th Sts., Chicago, 10/15/66, A,B,f,g, NHL, 66000314

FISHER BUILDING, 343 S. Dearborn St., Chicago, 3/16/76, C, 76000691

FLAMINGO-ON-THE-LAKE APARTMENTS, {Hyde Park Apartment Hotels TR}, 5500-5520 S. Shore Dr., Chicago, 5/14/86, A,C, 86001194

FOLEY, JENNIE, BUILDING, 626-628 S. Racine Ave., Chicago, 6/19/85, A,C, 85001274

FORD AIRPORT HANGER, Glenwood-Lansing Rd. and Burnahn Ave., Lansing, 5/09/85, A,C, 85001009

FOREST, THE, AND ANNEX, {Suburban Apartment Buildings in Evanston TR}, 901-905 Forest Ave., Evanston, 3/15/84, A,C, 84000991

FORT DEARBORN HOTEL, 401 S. LaSalle St., Chicago, 11/12/82, A,C, 82000390

FOUNTAIN PLAZA APARTMENTS, {Suburban Apartment Buildings in Evanston TR}, 830-856 Hinman Ave., Evanston, 3/15/84, A,C, 84000992

FOURTH PRESBYTERIAN CHURCH OF CHICAGO, 126 E. Chestnut St., Chicago, 9/05/75, C,a, 75000648

FRANK LLOYD WRIGHT-PRAIRIE SCHOOL OF ARCHITECTURE HISTORIC DISTRICT, Bounded roughly by Harlem Ave., Division, Clyde, and Lake Sts., Oak Park, 12/04/73, C, 73000699

GAGE GROUP ASCHER, KEITH, AND GAGE BUILDINGS, 18-30 S. Michigan Ave., Chicago, 11/14/85, C, 85002840

GALE, MRS. THOMAS H., HOUSE, 6 Elizabeth Ct., Oak Park, 3/05/70, C, 70000239

GALE, WALTER, HOUSE, 1031 W. Chicago Ave., Oak Park, 8/17/73, C, 73000700

GAULER, JOHN, HOUSES, 5917-5921 N. Magnolia Ave., Chicago, 6/17/77, C, 77000475

GERMANIA CLUB, 108 W. Germania Pl., Chicago, 10/22/76, A,C, 76000692

GETTY TOMB, GRACELAND CEMETERY, N. Clark St. and W. Irving Park Rd., Chicago, 2/15/74, C,c, 74000750

GLESSNER, JOHN J., HOUSE, 1800 S. Prairie Ave., Chicago, 4/17/70, C, NHL, 70000233

GOLD COAST HISTORIC DISTRICT, Roughly bounded by North Ave., Lake Shore Dr., Clark and Oak Sts., Chicago, 1/30/78, A,B,C,g, 78001121

GREENWOOD, The (Suburban Apartment Buildings in Evanston TR}, 425 Greenwood St., Evanston, 3/15/84, A,C, 84000993

GRIFFITHS, JOHN W., MANSION, 3806 S. Michigan Ave., Chicago, 3/05/82, B,C, 82002528

GROSSDALE STATION, 8820 1/2 Brookfield Ave., Brookfield, 6/15/82, A,C,b, 82004912

GROSSE POINT LIGHTHOUSE, 2535 Sheridan Rd., Evanston, 9/08/76, A,C, 76000707

GUYON HOTEL, 4000 W. Washington Blvd., Chicago, 5/09/85, B,C, 85000966

HALSTED, ANN, HOUSE, 440 Belden St., Chicago, 8/17/73, C, 73000695

HARRER BUILDING, 8051 Lincoln Ave., Skokie, 2/17/83, A,C, 83000310

HELLER, ISADORE H., HOUSE, 5132 S. Woodland Ave., Chicago, 3/16/72, C, 72000450

HERMITAGE APARTMENTS, 4606 N. Hermitage Ave., Chicago, 2/14/85, C, 85000266

HILLCREST APARTMENT, {Suburban Apartment Buildings in Evanston TR}, 1509-1515 Hinman Ave., Evanston, 3/15/84, A,C, 84000994

HINMAN APARTMENTS, {Suburban Apartment Buildings in Evanston TR}, 1629-1631 Hinman Ave., Evanston, 3/15/84, A,C, 84000995

HITCHCOCK, CHARLES, HALL, 1009 E. 57th St., Chicago, 12/30/74 C 74000751

HOFMANN TOWER, 3910 Barry Point Rd., Lyons, 12/22/78, A, 78001139

HOLY TRINITY RUSSIAN ORTHODOX CATHERDRAL AND RECTORY, 1117- 1127 N. Leavitt, Chicago, 3/16/76, C,a, 76000693

HOTEL DEL PRADO, {Hyde Park Apartment Hotels TR}, 5307 S. Hyde Park Blvd., Chicago, 5/14/86, A,C, 86001195

HOTEL WINDERMERE EAST, {Hyde Park Apartment Hotels TR (AD)}, 1642 E. 56th St., Chicago, 10/19/82, A,C, 82000391

HULL HOUSE, 800 S. Halsted St., Chicago, 10/15/66, B,b, NHL, 66000315

HYDE PARK KENWOOD HISTORIC DISTRICT, Roughly bounded by 47th and 59th Sts., Cottage Groves and Lake Park Aves., Chicago, 2/14/79, A,B,C,g, 79900824

HYDE PARK KENWOOD HISTORIC DISTRICT, (Boundary Increase), 821-829 816-826 E. 49th St., Chicago, 8/16/84, C: 84900996

HYDE PARK-KENWOOD HISTORIC DISTRICT, (Boundary Increase 11), 825-833 and 837-849 E. Fifty second St., Chicago, 5/16/86, A,C, 86001041

IMMACULATA HIGH SCHOOL, 600 W. Irving Park Rd., Chicago, 8/30/77, C,a, 77000476

JACKSON PARK HISTORIC LANDSCAPE DISTRICT AND MIDWAY PLAISANCE, Jackson and Washington Parks and Midway Plaisance roadway, Chicago, 12/15/72, C, 72001565

JEFFERY-CYRIL HISTORIC DISTRICT, 7146-7148, 7128-7138 Cyril Ave., 7144-7148, 7147 and 7130 S. Jeffrey Blvd., and 1966-1974 E. Seventy-first Pl., Chicago, 5/05/86, C, 86001007

JEWELERS' BUILDING, 15-195. Wabash Ave., Chicago, 8/07/74, C, 74000752

JEWISH PEOPLE'S INSTITUTE, 3500 W. Douglas Blvd., Chicago, 11/15/78, A,C,a, 78001122

JUDSON, THE, (Suburban Apartment Buildings in Evanston TR}, 1243-1249 Judson Ave., Evanston, 3/15/84, A,C, 84000998

KEHILATH ANSHE MA'ARIV SYNAGOGUE, 3301 S. Indiana

Ave., Chicago, 4/26/73, C,a, 73000696

KENILWORTH CLUB, 410 Kenilworth Ave., Kenilworth, 3/21/79, C, 79000832

KENNICOTT'S GROVE, Milwaukee and Lake Aves., Glenview, 8/13/73, B, NHL, 73000698

KENT, SYDNEY, HOUSE, 2944 S. Michigan Ave., Chicago, 11/17/77, B,C,a, 77000477

KIMBALL, WILLIAM W., HOUSE, 1801 S. Prairie Ave., Chicago, 12/09/71, A,C, 71000291

KING, PATRICK J., HOUSE, 3234 W. Washington Blvd., Chicago, 2/10/83, B,C, 83000311

LA GRANGE VILLAGE HISTORIC DISTRICT, U.S. 12, La Grange, 8/08/79, C, 79000834

LAKE SHORE APARTMENTS, {Suburban Apartment Buildings in Evanston TR}, 470-498 Sheridan Rd., Evanston, 3/15/84, A,C, 84001000

LAKE-SIDE TERRACE APARTMENTS, 7425-7427 S. Shore Dr., Chicago, 11/13/84, C, 84000289

LAKESIDE PRESS BUILDING, 731 S. Plymouth Ct., Chicago, 6/23/76, A,C, 76000694

LAKEVIEW HISTORIC DISTRICT, Roughly bounded by Wrightwood, Lakeview, Sheridan, Belmont, Halsted, Wellington, Racine, and George Sts., Chicago, 9/15/77, C, 77000478

LAKEVIEW HISTORIC DISTRICT, (Boundary Increase), 701, 705, 711, 715-717, 721, 733, 735, 737, and 739 Belmont Ave., 3162 and 3164 N. Orchard, and 3171 Halsted Sts., Chicago, 5/16/86, A,C, 86001042

LATHROP, BRYAN, HOUSE, 120 E. Bellevue Pl., Chicago, 2/15/74, B,C, 74000753

LEGLER, HENRY E., Regional Branch of the Chicago Public Libraiy, 1155. Pulaski Rd., Chicago, 11/06/86, A,C, 86003169

LEITER II BUILDING, NF corner of S. State and E. Congress Sts., Chicago, 1/07/76, C, NHL, 76000695

LEMONT CENTRAL GRADE SCHOOL, 410 McCarthy Rd., Lemont, 3/07/75, C, 75000656

LEMONT METHODIST EPISCOPAL CHURCH, 306 Le St., Chicago, 5/11/76, B, NHL, 76000696

LINCOLN PARK, South Pond Refectory; 2021 N. Stockton Dr., Chicago, 11/20/86, A,C, 86003154

LINDEN AVENUE TERMINAL, 330 Linden Ave., Wilmette, 2/08/84, A,C, 84001002

LLOYD, HENRY DEMAREST, HOUSE, 830 Sheridan Rd., Winnetka, 11/13/66,,B, NHL,66000320

LOGAN SQUARE BOULEVARDS HISTORIC DISTRICT, W. Logan Blvd., Logan Sq., N. Kedzie Blvd., Palmer Sq., and N. Humbolt Blvd., Chicago, 11/20/85, C, 85002901

LOUCKS, CHARLES N., HOUSE, 3926 N. Keeler Ave.,; Chicago, 2/09/84, C, 84001006

LUDINGTON BUILDING, 1104 S. Wabash Ave., Chicago, 5/08/80, C, 80001347

LYONS TOWNSHIP HALL, 53 S. LaGrange Rd., Lai Grange, 11/30/78, C, 78001138

MADLENER, ALBERT F., HOUSE, 4 W. Burton St., Chicago, 10/15/70, C, 70000234

MAHER, GEORGE W., HOUSE, 424 Warwick Rd., Kenilworth, 3/21/79, C, 79000833

MALDEN TOWERS, 4521 N. Malden St., Chicago, 12/08/83, C, 83003560

MANHATTAN BUILDING, 431 S. Dearborn St., Chicago, 3/16/76, C, 76000697

MANOR HOUSE, 1021-1029 W. Bryn Mawr Ave.,; Chicago, 8/12/87, C, 87001290

MAPLE COURT APARTMENTS, {Suburban Apartment Buildings in Evanston TR}, 1115-1133 Maple Ave., Evanston, 3/15/84, A,C, 84001013

MARQUETTE BUILDING, 1405. Dearborn St., Chicago, 8/17/73, C, NHL, 73000697

MARSHALL FIELD COMPANY STORE, 111 N. State St., Chicago, 6/02/78, A, NHL, 78001123

MARSHALL FIELD AND COMPANY STORE, 1144 W.I Lake St., Oak Park, 1/21/88, A,C, 87002510

MASONIC TEMPLE BUILDING, 119-137 N. Oak Park Ave., Oak Park, 2/11/82, C, 820025322

MAYFAIR APARTMENTS, {Hyde Park Apartment Hotels TR}, 16501666 E. Fifty-sixth St., Chicago, 5/14/86, A,C, 86001198

MCCARTHY BUILDING, Washington and Dearborn Sts., Chicago, 6/16/76, C, 76000698

MCCLURG BUILDING, 2185. Wabash Ave., Chicago, 8/17/70, C, 70000235

MELWOOD APARTMENTS, {Suburban Apartment Buildings in Evanston TR}, 1201-1213 Michigan Ave. and 205207 Hamilton, Evanston, 3/15/84, A,C, 84001016

MICHIGAN-LEE APARTMENTS, {Suburban Apartment Buildings in Evanston TR}, 940-950 Michigan Ave., Evanston, 3/15/84, A,C, 84001018

MICHIGAN WACKER HISTORIC DISTRICT, Michigan Ave. and Wacker Dr. and environs, Chicago, 11/15/78, A,C, 78001124

MIDWEST ATHLETIC CLUB, 6 N. Hamlin Ave., Chicago, 10/18/84, A,C, 84000138

MILLIKAN, ROBERT A., HOUSE, 5605 Woodlawn Ave., Chicago, 5/11/76, B, NHL, 76000699

MONADNOCK BLOCK, 53 W. Jackson Blvd., Chicago, 11/20/70, C, 70000236

MONTGOMERY WARDCOMPANY COMPLEX, 619 W. Chicago Ave., Chicago, 6/02/78, A,C,g, NHL, 78001125

MORTON, J. STERLING, High School East Auditorium, 2423 S. Austin Blvd., Cicero, 5/09/83,1 A,C, 83000312

MULLER HOUSE, 500 N. Vail Ave., Arlington Heights, 3/26/79, B, 79000819

MUNDELEIN COLLEGE SKY-SCRAPER BUILDING, 63631 N. Sheridan Rd., Chicago, 5/31/80, A,C,a, 80001348

MUNICIPAL COURTS BUILDING, 116 5. Michigan Ave., Chicago, 8/29/85, A,C, 85001912

MUNICIPAL PIER, 200 Streeter Dr., Chicago, 9/13/79, A,C, 79000825

NEW MASONIC BUILDING AND ORIENTAL THEATER, 20 W. Randolph St., Chicago, 9/26/78, A,C, 78003401

NEW MICHIGAN HOTEL, 2135 S. Michigan Ave., Chicago, 12/08/83, C, 83003562

NICKERSON, SAMUEL, HOUSE, 40 E. Erie, Chicago, 11/07/76, C, North Wells Street Historic District, 1240-1260 N. Wells St., Chicago, 5/03/84, A,C, 84001021

NOTRE DAME DE CHICAGO, 1338 W. Flournoy St., Chicago, 3/07/79, C,a, 79000826

OAK RIDGE APARTMENTS, {Suburban Apartment Buildings in Evanston TR}, 1615-1625 Ridge Ave., Evanston, 3/15/84, A,C, 84001025

OAKTON GABLES, {Suburban Apartment Buildings in Evanston TR}, 900-910 Oakton and 439-445 Ridge, Evanston, 3/15/84, A,C, 84001024

OCTAGON HOUSE, 223 W. Main St., Barrington, 3/21/79, C, 79000820

OLD CHICAGO HISTORICAL SOCIETY BUILDING, 632 N. Dearborn St., Chicago, 11/28/78, A,C, 78001126

OLD COLONY BUILDINGS, 4075. Dearborn St., Chicago, 1/02/76, A,C, 76000701

OLD MAIN BUILDING, 3235 W. Foster Ave. on North Park College Campus, Chicago, 2/11/82, A, 82002529

OLD STONE GATE OF CHICAGO UNION STOCKYARDS, Exchange Ave., Chicago 12/27/72, A, NHL, 72000451

OLD TOWN TNANGLE HISTORIC DISTRICT, Roughly bounded by Armitage and North Aves., Clark and Mohawk Sts., Chicago, 11/08/84, A,C, 84000347

OLIVER BUILDING, 159 N. Dearborn St., Chicago, 12/08/83, A,C, 83003563

ORCHESTRA HALL, 2205. Michigan Ave., Chicago, 3/21/78, A,C, 78001127

ORTH HOUSE, 42 Abbotsford Rd., Winnetka 10/08/76, C, 76000708

OVERTON HYGIENIC BUILDING, {Black Metropolis TR}, 3619-3627 S. State St., Chicago, 4/30/86, A, 86001091

PAGE BROTHERS BUILDING, SE corner of Lake and State Sts., Chicago, 6/05/75, C, 75000649

PATTINGTON APARTMENTS, 660-700 Irving Park Rd., Chicago 3/08/80 A,C, 80001349

PEOPLES GAS BUILDING, 1225. Michigan Ave., Chicago, 11/13/84, A,C, 84000293

PERKINS, DWIGHT, HOUSE, 2319 Lincoln St., Evanston, 8/29/85, B,C, 85001908

PICKWICK THEATER BUILDING, 5 S. Prospect Ave., Park Ridge, 2/24/75, A,C,g, 75000657

PLEASANT HOME, 217 Home Ave., Oak Park, 6/19/72, A,C, 72000454

POINSETTA APARTMENTS, {Hyde Park Apartment Hotels TR}, 5528 S. Hyde Park Blvd., Chicago, 5/14/86, A,C, 86001199

PONTIAC BUILDING, 542 S. Dearborn St., Chicago, 3/16/76, C, 76000702

PRAIRIE AVENUE DISTRICT, Prairie Ave. on either side of 18th St., about 1 block in, Chicago, 11/15/72, A,C, 72000452

PULASKI PARK AND FIELD-HOUSE, 1419 W. Black-hawk St., Chicago, 8/13/81, C, 81000217

PULLMAN HISTORIC DISTRICT, Bounded by 103rd St., C.S.S. and S.B. Railroad spur tracks, 115th St. and Cottage Grove Ave., Chicago, 10/08/69, A,C, NHL, 69000054

QUINN CHAPEL OF THE A.M.E. CHURCH, 2401 S. Wabash Ave., Chicago, 9/04/79, A,a, 79000827

RAILWAY EXCHANGE BUILD-ING, 80 E. Jackson Blvd. and 224 S. Michigan Ave., Chicago, 6/03/82, A,B,C, 82002530

REEBIE MOVING AND STORAGE COMPANY, 2325-2333 N. Clark St., Chicago, 3/21/79, C, 79000828

REID MURDOCH BUILDING, 325 N. LaSalle St., Chicago, 8/28/75, A,C, 75000650

RELIANCE BUILDING, 32 N. State St., Chicago, 10/15/70, C, NHL, 70000237

RIDGE BOULEVARD APARTMENTS, {Suburban Apartment Buildings in Evanston TR}, 843-849 Ridge Ave. and 1014-1020 Main St., Evans ton, 3/15/84 A,C, 75000650

RIDGE GROVE, {Suburban Apartment Buildings in Evanston TR}, 1112 Grove St., Evanston, 3/15/84, A,C, 84001030

RIDGE HISTORIC DISTRICT, Roughly bounded by RR tracks, 87th, Prospects, Homewood, 115th, Lothair, Hamilton, and Western Sts., Chicago, 5/28/76, A,C, 76000703

RIDGE MANOR, {Suburban Apartment Buildings in Evanston TR}, 1603-1611 Ridge Ave. and 1125 Davis St., Evanston, 3/15/84, A,C,a,c, 84001034

RIDGELAND-OAK PARK HISTORIC DISTRICT, Roughly bounded by Austin Blvd., Harlem, Ridge land, and Chicago Aves., Lake and Madison Sts., Oak Park, 12/08/83, A,C, 83003564

RIDGEWOOD, 1703-1713 Ridge Ave., Evanston, 10/04/78, C, 78001136

RIVER FOREST HISTORIC DISTRICT, Between Harlem Ave. and Des Plaines River with 2 extensions N of Chicago Ave. and 2 extensions S of Lake St., River Forest, 8/26/77, C, 77000483

RIVERSIDE LANDSCAPE ARCHITECTURE DISTRICT, Bounded by 26th St., Harlem and Ogden Aves., the Des Plaines River, and Forbes Rd., Riverside, 9/15/69, A,C, NHL, 69000055

ROBIE, FREDERICK C., HOUSE, 5757 S. Woodlawn Ave., Chicago, 10/15/66, C, NHL, 66000316

ROLOSON, ROBERT, HOUSES, 3213-3219 Calumet Ave., Chicago, 6/30/77, C, 77000479

ROOKERY BUILDING, 209 S. LaSalle St., Chicago, 4/17/70, C, NHL, 70000238

ROOKWOOD APARTMENTS, {Suburban Apartment Buildings in Evanston TR}, 718-734 Noyes St., Evanston, 3/15/84. A,C, 84001043

ROOM 405, GEORGE HERBERT JONES LABORATORY, The University of Chicago, S. Ellis Ave. be tween E. 57th and 58th Sts., Chicago, 5/28/67, A,g, NHL, 67000005

ROPP-GRABILL HOUSE, 4132 N. Keeler Ave., Chicago, 4/15/85, C, 85000840

ROSEHILL CEMETERY ADMINISTRATION BUILDING AND ENTRY GATE, 5600 N. Ravenswood Ave., Chicago, 4/24/75, C,d, 75000651

ROSENWALD APARTMENT BUILDING, 47th St. and Michigan Ave., Chicago, 8/13/81, A,C, 81000218

ROYCEMORE SCHOOL, 60 Lincoln St., Evanston, 8/03/87, C, 87001256

S/S CLIPPER, Navy Pier 600 E. Grand Ave., Chicago, 12/08/83, A,C, 83003570

SCHOENHOFEN BREWERY HISTORIC DISTRICT, Roughly bounded by 16th, 18th, Canal, and Clinton Sts., Chicago, 12/27/78, A,C, 78001128

SCHULZE BAKING COMPANY PLANT, 40 E. Garfield Blvd., Chicago, 11/12/82, A,B,C, 82000393

SCHWEIKHER, PAUL, HOUSE AND STUDIO, 645 S. Meacham Rd., Schaumburg, 2/17/87, C,g, 87000098

SEARS, ROEBUCK AND COMPANY COMPLEX, 925 S. Homan Ave., Chicago, 6/02/78, A, NHL, 78001129

SECOND PRESBYTERIAN CHURCH, 1936 S. Michigan Ave., Chicago, 12/27/74, C,a, 74000754

SHAKESPEARE GARDEN, Northwestern University campus, Evanston, 11/16/88, A,C, 88002234

SHEDD PARK FIELDHOUSE, 3660 W. 23rd St., Chicago, 12/30/74, C, 74000755

SHEDD, JOHN G., AQUARIUM, 1200 S. Lake Shore Dr:, Chicago, 2/27/87, A, NHL, 87000820

SHEFFIELD HISTORIC DISTRICT, Bounded roughly by Fullerton, Lincoln, Larabee, Dickens, Burlin, Wisconsin, Clayburn, Lakewood, Belder, and Southport, Chicago, 1/11/76, C, 76000704

SHEFFIELD HISTORIC DISTRICT (BOUNDARY INCREASE), Montana, Alt geld Sts., and Southport Ave., Chicago, 2/17/83, C, 83000313

SHEFFIELD HISTORIC DISTRICT, (Boundary Increase II), Roughly bounded by W. Altgeld St., N. Lakewood, N. Fullerton, and N. Southport Aves., Chicago, 6/19/85, C,a, 85001333

SHEFFIELD HISTORIC DISTRICT, (Boundary Increase III), Roughly bounded by W. Wisconsin St. and Armitage Ave., N. Howe and N. Halsted Sts., N. Willow St., and N. Kenmore Ave. Chicago, 8/22/86, A,C, 86001474

SHERIDAN PARK HISTORIC DISTRICT, Roughly bounded by Lawrence, Racine, and Montrose Aves., and Clark St., Chicago, 12/27/85, C, 85003352

SHERIDAN PLAZA HOTEL, 4601-4613 N. Sheridan Rd., Chicago, 11/21/80, A,C, 80001350

SHERIDAN SQUARE APARTMENTS, {Suburban Apartment Buildings in Evanston TR}, 620-638 Sheridan Sq., Evanston, 3/15/84, A,C,84001050

SHORELAND HOTEL, {Hyde Park Apartment Hotels TR}, 5450-5484 S. Shore Dr., Chicago, 5/14/86: A,C, 86001201

SINGER BUILDING, 120 S. State St., Chicago, 120 S. State St, A,C, Chicago, 5/14/86 83000314

SMITH, J. P., SHOE COMPANY PLANT, 671-699 N. Sangamon Ave. and 901-921 W. Huron St., Chicago, 11/14/85, BC 85002842

SOLDIER FIELD, 425 E. 14th St., Chicago, 8/09/84, A,C, NHL, 84001052

SOUTH DEARBORN STREET-PRINTING HOUSE ROW HISTORIC DISTRICT, 343, 407, 431 S. Dearborn St. and 53 W. Jackson Blvd., Chicago, 1/07/76, C, NHL, 76000705

SOUTH LOOP PRINTING HOUSE DISTRICT, Roughly bounded by Taylor, Polk, Wells, Congress and State Sts., Chicago, 3/02/78, A,C, 78001130

SOUTH SHORE BEACH APARTMENTS, 7321 S. Shore Dr., Chicago, 6/09/78, C, 78001131

SOUTH SHORE COUNTRY CLUB, 71st St. and S. Shore Dr., Chicago, 3/04/75, A,C, 75000652

ST. IGNATIUS COLLEGE, 1076 W. Roosevelt Rd., Chicago, 11/17/77, A,C,a, 77000480

ST. JAMES CATHOLIC CHURCH AND CEMETERY, 106th St. and Archer Ave., Lemont vicinity, 8/16/84, A,C,a,d, 84001047

ST. LUKE'S HOSPITAL COMPLEX, 1435 S. Michigan Ave., 1400 Block S. Indiana Ave., Chicago, 11/24/82, A,C, 82000392

ST. PATRICK'S ROMAN CATHOLIC CHURCH, 718 W. Adams St., Chicago, 7/15/77, C,a, 77000481

Encyclopedia of Illinois

ST. THOMAS CHURCH AND CONVENT, 5472 S. Kimbark Ave., Chicago, 12/18/78, C,a, 78001132

STONELEIGH MANOR, {Suburban Apartment Buildings in Evanston TR}, 904-906 Michigan Ave. and 227-229 Main St., Evanston, 3/15/84, A,C, 84001057

STORY-CAMP ROWHOUSES, 1526-1528 W. Monroe St., Chicago, 5/08/80, A,C, 80001351

STUDEBAKER BUILDING, 410-418 S. Michigan Ave., Chicago, 8/11/75, A,C, 75000653

SWEDISH AMERICAN TELEPHONE COMPANY BUILDING, 5235-5257 N. Ravenswood, Chicago, 9/13/85, A,C, 85002286

SWEDISH CLUB OF CHICAGO, 125 8 N. LaSalle St., Chicago, 12/02/85, A,C, 85003031

SWIFT HOUSE, 4500 S. Michigan Ave., Chicago, 6/09/78, B,C, 78001133

SYLVAN ROAD BRIDGE, Sylvan Rd., Glencoe, 6/23/78, C, 78001137

TAFT, LORADO, MIDWAY STUDIOS, 60165. Ingleside Ave., Chicago, 10/15/66, B, NHL, 66000317

THEURER WRIGLEY HOUSE, 2466 N. Lake View Ave., Chicago, 7/28/80, B,C, 80001352

THOMAS, FRANK, HOUSE, 210 Forest Ave., Oak Park, 9/14/72, C, 72000455

TREE STUDIO BUILDING AND ANNEXES, 4 E. Ohio St., Chicago, 12/16/74, B,C, 74000756

TRI-TAYLOR HISTORIC DISTRICT, Roughly bounded by Claremont, Harrison, Oakley, Polk, Ogden, and Roosevelt Rds., Chicago, 3/03/83, A,C, 83000315

TRI TAYLOR HISTORIC DISTRICT, (Boundary Increase), Roughly bounded on the N by Oakley, Harrison and Clairmont Sts. and on SE by Tailor and Oakley Sts., Chicago, 2/03/88, A,C, 87002540

TUDOR MANOR, {Suburban Apartment Buildings in Evanston TRj, 524 Sheridan Sq., Evanston, 3/15/84, A,C, 84001058

TWIN TOWER SANCTUARY, 9967 W. 144th St., Orland Park, 11/16/88, C,a, 88002235

USS SILVERSIDES (SS 236) National Historic Landmark, S side of Navy Pier, Chicago, 10/18/72, A,g, NHL, 72001566

UNITY BUILDING, 127 N. Dearborn St., Chicago, 9/06/79, B,C, 79000829

UNITY HALL, {Black Metropolis TR}, 31405. Indiana Ave., Chicago, 4/30/86, A,a, 86001092

UNITY TEMPLE, 875 Lake St., Oak Park, 4/17/70, C,a, NHL, 70000240

UPTOWN BROADWAY BUILDING, 4703-4715 N. Broadway, Chicago, 11/06/86, C, 86003143

VICTORY SCULPTURE, {Black Metropolis TR}, Thirty-fifth St. at King Dr., Chicago, 4/30/86, A, 86001089

VILLA HISTORIC DISTRICT, Roughly bounded by Avondale, W. Addison, N. 40th and N. Hamlin Aves., Chicago, 9/11/79, A,C, 79000830

VILLA HISTORIC DISTRICT, (Boundary Increase), 3948-3952 and 3949-3953 W. Waveland Ave., Chicago, 3/10/83, A,C, 83000316

VOGT, KARL, BUILDING, 6811 Hickory St., Tinley Park, 1/21/88, C, 87002499

WABASH AVENUE YMCA, {Black Metropolis TR}, 3763 S. Wabash Ave., Chicago, 4/30/86, A, 86001095

WALLER, WILLIAM, HOUSE, 1012 N. Dearborn St., Chicago, 11/21/80, A,C, 80001346

WARNER, SETH, HOUSE, 631 N. Central Ave., Chicago, 6/03/82, B,C, 82002531

WARREN, EDWARD KIRK, HOUSE AND GARAGE, 2829 and 2831 Sheridan Pl., Evanston, 1/30/86, B,C,a, 86000136

WELLS-BARNETT, IDA B., HOUSE, 3624 S. Martin Luther King Dr., Chicago, 5/30/74, B, NHL, 74000757

WEST JACKSON BOULEVARD DISTRICT, Roughly bounded by Laflin, Ashland, Adams, and Van Buren Sts., Chicago, 5/19/78, C, 78001134

WESTERN METHODIST BOOK CONCERN BUILDING, 12 W. Washington St., Chicago, 9/11/7 5 A,C, 75000654

WESTERN SPRINGS WATER TOWER, 914 Hillgrove Ave., Western Springs, 6/04/81, C, 81000219

WESTMINSTER, {Suburban Apartment Buildings in Evanston TR}, 632-640 Hinman Ave., Evanston,3/15/84, A,C, 84001061

WICKER PARK HISTORIC DISTRICT, Roughly bounded by Wood, Crystal and N. Caton Sts., Claremont and North Aves., Chicago, 6/20/79, C, 79000831

WILD FLOWER AND BIRD SANCTUARY, in Mahoney Park Sheridan Rd., Kenilworth, 4/10/85, C, 85000772

WILLARD, FRANCES, HOUSE, 1730 Chicago Ave., Evanston, 10/15/66 NHL 66000318

WILLIAMS, DR. DANIEL HALE, HOUSE, 445 E. 42nd St., Chicago, 5/15/75, B, NHL, 75000655

WINSLOW, WILLIAM H., HOUSE AND STABLE, 515 Auvergne Pl., River Forest, 4/17/70, C, 70000242

WRIGHT, FRANK LLOYD, HOUSE AND STUDIO, 428 Forest Ave. (house), 951 Chicago Ave. (studio), Oak Park, 9/14/72, B,C, NHL, 72000456

YONDORF BLOCK AND HALL, 758 W. North Ave., Chicago, 11/13/84, A,C, 84000297

YOUNG, JOSHUA P., HOUSE, 2445 High St., Blue Island, 8/12/82, B,C, 82002525

CRAWFORD COUNTY

RIVERTON SITE, Address Restricted, Palestine vicinity, 12/18/78, D, 78001141

STONER SITE, Address Restricted, Robinson vicinity, 12/18/78, D, 78001143

SWAN ISLAND SITE, Address Restricted, Palestine vicinity, 12/18/78, D, 78001142

CUMBERLAND COUNTY

CUMBERLAND COUNTY COURTHOUSE, Court House Sq., Toledo, 6/11/81, A, 81000220

DE KALB COUNTY

BROWER, ADOLPHUS W., HOUSE, 705 DeKalb Ave., Sycamore, 2/14/79, C, 79003160

CHICAGO AND NORTHWESTERN DEPOT, Sacramento and DeKalb Sts., Sycamore, 12/08/78, A, 78003101

EGYPTIAN THEATRE, 135 N. 2nd St., De Kalb, 12/01/78, A,C,g, 78003100

ELLWOOD MANSION, 509 N. 1st St., DedKalb, 6/13/75, B, 75002075

ELMWOOD CEMETERY GATES, S. Cross and Charles Sts., Sycamore, 11/28/78, A, 78003102

GLIDDEN, JOSEPH F., House, 917 W. Lincoln Hwy., De Kalb, 10/25/73, B, 73002159

GURLER, GEORGE H., HOUSE, 205 Pine St., De Kalb, 3/21/79, B, 79003158

HAISH MEMORIAL LIBRARY, 309 Oak St., De Kalb, 10/09/80, C, 80004319

MARSH, WILLIAM W., HOUSE, 740 W. State St., Sycamore, 12/22/78, B,C, 78003103

NISBET HOMESTEAD FARM, Suydam Rd., Earlville vicinity, 5/31/84, A,C, 84001069

SANDWICH CITY HALL, 144 E. Railroad St., Sandwich, 12/06/79, A,C, 79003159

SYCAMORE HISTORIC DISTRICT, Irregular pattern along Main and Somonauk Sts., Sycamore, 5/02/78, C,a, 78003104

VON KLEINSMID MANSION, 218 W. Center, Sandwich, 5/09/85, C, 85000979

DE WITT COUNTY

MOORE, C. H., HOUSE, 219 E. Woodlawn St., Clinton, 3/23/79, B,C, 79003112

DOUGLAS COUNTY

MCCARTY, JOHN, ROUND BARN, {Round Barns of Illinois TR}, NW of Filson, Filson vicinity, 12/07/82, C, 82000394

DU PAGE COUNTY

ADAMS MEMORIAL LIBRARY, 9th St., Wheaton, 6/04/81, A,C, 81000675

ARDMORE AVENUE TRAIN STATION, 10 W. Park Ave., Villa Park, 11/21/80, A, 80004525

BLANCHARD HALL, Wheaton College campus, Wheaton, 11/14/79, A,B,C,a, 79000836

DU PAGE COUNTY COURTHOUSE, 200 Reber St., Wheaton, 6/07/78, A,C, 78003107

DUPAGE THEATRE AND DUPAGE SHOPPES, 101-109 S. Main St., Lombard, 11/20/87, C, 87002047

FIRST CHURCH OF LOMBARD, Maple and Main Sts., Lombard, 8/10/78, C,a, 78001144

GLEN ELLYN MAIN STREET HISTORIC DISTRICT, Main St. between Cottage Ave. and Hawthorne St., Glen Ellyn, 10/29/84, C, 84000204

GRAUE MILL, NW of jct. of Spring and York Rds., Oak Brook, 5/12/75. B,C, 75002077

GREGG, WILLIAM L., HOUSE, 115 S. Linden, Westmont, 10/03/80, A,B,b, 80004526

HAUPTGEBAUDE, 190 Prospect St., Elmhurst, 8/13/76, A,C,a, 76002162

MCAULEY SCHOOL DISTRICT NO. 27, Roosevelt Rd., West Chicago, 6/03/82, A,C, 82004890

MIDDAUGH, HENRY C., HOUSE, 66 Norfolk Ave., Clarendon Hills, 9/21/78, A,C,a, 78003105

NAPERVILLE HISTORIC DISTRICT, Roughly bounded by Juilian, Highland, Chicago, Jackson, Eagle, and 5th Sts., Naperville, 9/29/77, A,C,a, 77001516

PINE CRAIG, AURORA RD. (RTE. 65), Naperville, 8/15/75, B,C,75002076

STACY S TAVERN, Geneva Rd. and Main St., Glen Ellyn, 10/29/74, B, 74002195

TRINITY EPISCOPAL CHURCH, 130 N. West St., Wheaton, 1/09/78, C,a, 78003108

VILLA AVENUE TRAIN STATION, 220 S. Villa Ave., Villa Park, 8/22/86, A, 86001480

WAYNE VILLAGE HISTORIC DISTRICT, Irregular pattern along Army Trail Rd., Wayne, 12/29/78, A,a,b, 78003106

EDGAR COUNTY

EDGAR COUNTY COURTHOUSE, Main St., Paris, 6/04/81, A,C, 81000221

FRANCE HOTEL, 118 E. Court St., Paris, 8/03/87, A,C, 87001305

PARIS ELKS LODGE NO. 812 BUILDING, 111 E. Washington St., Paris, 8/06/87, A,C, 87001343

PINE GROVE COMMUNITY CLUB, NW of Paris, Paris vicinity, 3/30/84, A,a, 84001071

EFFINGHAM COUNTY

EFFINGHAM COUNTY COURT-HOUSE, 110 E. Jefferson St., Effingham, 9/11/85, A,C, 85002304

WRIGHT, DR. CHARLES M., HOUSE, 3 W. Jackson St., Altamont, 5/08/86, A,C, 86001018

FAYETTE COUNTY

FIRST PRESBYTERIAN CHURCH, 301 W. Main St., Vandalia, 3/24/82, A,C,a, 82002534

FOREHAND, CLARENCE, Round Barn {Round Barns of Illinois TR}, W of Vandalia off IL 185, Vandalia vicinity, 12/07/82, C, 82000395

LITTLE BRICK HOUSE, 621 St. Clair St., Vandalia, 6/04/73, A,B,C, 73000701

VANDALIA STATEHOUSE, 315 W. Gallatin St., Vandalia, 1/21/74, A, 74000760

FORD COUNTY

PAXTON FIRST SCHOOLHOUSE, 406 E. Franklin St., Paxton, 1/29/80, A,a, 80001354

PAXTON WATER TOWER AND PUMP HOUSE, 145 S. Market St., Paxton, 11/13/84, C, 84000302

FRANKLIN COUNTY

SESSER OPERA HOUSE, 106 W. Franklin St., Sesser, 3/12/82, A, 82002535

FULTON COUNTY

BABYLON BEND BRIDGE, {Metal Highway Bridges Fulton County TR}, SR 123, Ellisville vicinity, 10/29/80, A,C, 80001355

BERNADOTTE BRIDGE, {Metal Highway Bridges of Fulton County TR}, SR 2, Smithfield vicinity, 10/29/80, A,C, 80001360

BUCKEYE BRIDGE, {Metal Highway Bridges of Fulton County TR}, Spans Spoon River, Smithfield Vicinity, 10/29/80, A,C, 80001361

CARITHERS STORE BUILDING, Table Grove Village Sq., W of US 136, Table Grove, 8/03/87, A,C,a, 87001262

DICKSON MOUNDS, Off CR 4, Lewistown vicinity, 5/05/72, A,D: 72000457

DUNCAN MILLS BRIDGE, {Metal Highway Bridges of Fulton County TR}, W of Havanna, Lewistown vicinity, A,C, 80001356

ELROD BRIDGE, {Metal Highway Bridges of Fulton C TR}, Spans Spoon River SE of Smithfield, Smithfield vicinity, 10/29/80, A,C, 80001362

INDIAN FORD BRIDGE, {Metal Highway Bridges of Fulton County TR}, SR 20, London Mills vicinity, 10/29/80, A,C, 80001357

LARSON SITE, Address Restricted, Lewistown vicinity, 11/21/78 D, 78001145

LONDON MILLS BRIDGE, {Metal Highway Bndges of Fulton County TR}, SR 39, London Mills, 10/29/80, A,C, 80001358

OGDEN FETTIE SITE, S of Lewistown, Lewistown vicinity, 7/31/72, D, 72000458

ORENDORF SITE, Address Restricted, Canton vicinity, 9/13/77, D, 77000484

ORENDORFF, ULYSSES G., HOUSE, 345 W. Elm St., Canton, 12/09/71, C, 71000292

SEVILLE BRIDGE, {Metal Highway Bridges of Fulton County R}, Spans Spoon River in Seville, Seville, 10/29/80, A,C, 80001359

SHEETS SITE, Address Restricted, Lewistown vicinity, 12/22/78, D, 78001146

SLEETH SITE, Address Restricted, Liverpool vicinity, 5/17/79, D, 79000837

ST. JAMES EPISCOPAL CHURCH, NE corner of MacArthur and Broadway, Lewiston, 12/31/74, C,a, 74000761

TABLE GROVE COMMUNITY CHURCH, N. Broadway and W. Liberty Sts., Table Grove, 2/09/79, B,a, 79003783

TAMPICO MOUNDS, Address Restricted, Maples Mills vicinity, 5/14/79, D, 79000838

TARTAR'S FERRY BRIDGE, {Metal Highway Bridges of Fulton County TR}, Spans Spoon River SW of Smithfield, Smithfield vicinity, 10/29/80, A,C, 80001363

VERMONT MASONIC HALL, N. Main St., Vermont, 11/16/88, A,C, 88002236

GALLATIN COUNTY

CRENSHAW HOUSE, Off Rt. 1, Equality, 5/29/85, A,C, 85001164 Duffy Site, Address Restricted, New Haven vicinity, 8/26/77, D, 77000485

MARSHALL, JOHN, HOUSE SITE, Address Restricted, Old Shawneetown vicinity, 1/21/75, B,C, 75000659

PEEPLES, ROBERT AND JOHN MCKEE, HOUSES, Main St., Old Shawneetown, 2/24/83, A,B,C, 83000317

SALINE SPRINGS, Address Restricted, Equality vicinity, 5/24/73, A,D, 73000702

STATE BANK, Corner of Main St. and IL 13 Old Shawneetown, 4/19/72, A,C, 72000459

GREENE COUNTY

CARROLLTON COURTHOUSE SQUARE HISTORIC DISTRICT, Roughly bounded by S. Main, W. 5th, N. Main and W. 6th Sts., Carrollton, 8/01/85, A,C, 85001667

HODGES HOUSE, 532 N. Main St., Carrollton, 11/03/80, B,C, 80001364

KOSTER SITE, S of Eldred, Eldred vicinity, 6/19/72, A,D, 72000460

MOUND HOUSE SITE, Address Restricted, Hillview vicinity, 9/01/78, D, 78001148

RAINEY, HENRY T., Farm, RR 1, N side of IL 108, Carrollton vicinity, 5/12/87, B,C, 87000682

TILLERY, VIRGINIA, Round Barn {Round Barns in Illinois TR}, W of Whitehall on CR 728, Whitehall vicinity, 8/26/82, A 82002536

WHITE HALL FOUNDRY, 102 S. Jacksonville St., White Hall, 5/28/80, A,C, 80001365

WHITE HALL HISTORIC DIS-
TRICT, Roughly bounded by
Bridgeport, Jacksonville, Ayers, and
Main Sts., White Hall, 5/20/87, A,
86003145

HAMILTON COUNTY

CLOUD STATE BANK, 108 N.
Washington St., McLeansboro,
11/28/78, A,C, 78001149

CLOUD, AARON G., HOUSE,
1645. Washington St., McLeansboro,
4/15/78, C, 78001150

HANCOCK COUNTY

CAMBRE HOUSE AND FARM, SW
of Niota, Niota vicinity, 11/13/84,
A, 84000308

CARTHAGE   COURTHOUSE
SQUARE HISTORIC DISTRICT,
Roughly hounded by Main, Adams,
Wabash, and Madison Sts., Car-
thage, 8/13/86, A,C, 86001482

CARTHAGE JAIL, Walnut and N.
Fayette Sts., Carthage, 3/20/73,
73000703

FELT, CYRUS, HOUSE, 3 mi. N
of Hamilton, Hamilton vicinity,
3/18/80, A,C, 80001366

LAHARPE HISTORIC DISTRICT,
100-124 W. Main St., 100-122 and
101-129 E. Main Sts., 101-121 S.
Center St., and City Pk., LaHarpe,
4/30/87, A, 87000031

NAUVOO HISTORIC DISTRICT,
Nauvoo and its environs, Nauvoo,
10/15/66, A,B,a, NHL, 66000321

REIMBOLD,   WILLIAM   J.,
HOUSE, 950 White St., Nauvoo,
12/02/87, A,C, 87002033

WARSAW HISTORIC DISTRICT,
Roughly bounded by the Mississippi
River, Marion and 11th Sts., War-
saw, 12/16/77, C,a, 77000486

HARDIN COUNTY

ILLINOIS   IRON   FURNACE,
Shawnee National Forest, Rosiclare
vicinity, 3/07/73, A,C, 73000704

ORR-HERL MOUND AND VIL-
LAGE SITE, Address Restricted,
Rosiclare vicinity, 11/21/78, D,
78001151

ROSE HOTEL, S. Main St., Elizabethtown, 12/26/72, A, 72000461

HENDERSON COUNTY

OQUAWKA WAGON BRIDGE, 2.5
mi. S of Oquawka over Henderson
Creek, Oquawka vicinity, 2/24/75,
A, 75000660

PHELPS, ALEXIS, HOUSE, On
Mississippi River, Oquawka,
4/28/82, B, 82002537

SOUTH HENDERSON CHURCH
AND CEMETERY, E of Gladstone,
Gladstone vicinity, 10/14/76,
A,C,a,d, 76000709

HENRY COUNTY

ANDOVER CHAPTER HOUSE,
{American Woman s League Chapter
Houses TR}, Locust St., NW, An-
dover, 11/28/80, A,C, 80001367

ANNAWAN CHAPTER HOUSE,
{American Woman's League Chapter
Houses TR},206 S. Depot St., An
Francis, Frederick, Woodland Palace,
2.5 mi. NE of Kewanee on IL 34,
Kewanee vicinity, 4/14/75, C,g,
75000662

GALVA OPERA HOUSE, 334-348
Front St., Galva, 2/II/82, A,
82002538

JOHNSON, OLOF, HOUSE, 408
NW 4th St., Galva, 2/11/82, B,C,
82002539

LIND, JENNY, CHAPEL, SW
corner 6th and Oak Sts., Andover,
4/01/75, A,C,a, 75000661 n Round

Barn, 6 mi. N of Kewanee, Kewanee vicinity, 12/31/74, A,C, 74000762

SOUTH SIDE SCHOOL, 209 S. College Ave., Geneso, 5/06/75, A,C, 75002142

IROQUOIS COUNTY

OLD IROQUOIS COUNTY COURTHOUSE, Cherry St. at 2nd St., Watseka, 6/13/75, A,C, 75000663

JACKSON COUNTY

CLEIMAN MOUND AND VILLAGE SITE, Address Restricted, Gorliam vicinity, 10/18/77, D, 77000487

GIANT CITY STATE PARK LODGE AND CABINS, {Illinois State Parks Lodges and Cabins TR}, RR #1, Makanda, 3/04/85, C,g, 85002403

GRAND TOWER MINING, Manufacturing and Transportation Company Site, Devil's Backbone Park, Grand Tower, 4/13/79, A,D, 79000839

HAMILTON, ROBERT W., HOUSE, 203 S. 13th St., Murphysboro, 3/05/82, C, 82002540

MOBILE AND OHIO RAILROAD DEPOT, 1701 Walnut St., Murphysboro, 11/13/84, A,C, 84000317

REEF HOUSE, 411 S. Poplar St., Carbondale, 11/14/85, C, 85002839

WEST WALNUT STREET HISTORIC DISTRICT, Roughly bounded by W. Elm, S. Poplar, W. Main, and S. Forest Sts., Carbondale, 5/02/75, B,C, 75000664

WOODLAWN CEMETERY, 405 E. Main St., Carbondale, 12/19/85, A,B,d, 85003219

JEFFERSON COUNTY

APPELLATE COURT, 5th, 14th and Main Sts., Mount Vernon, 7/02/73, A,C, 73000705

JUDD,C.H., HOUSE, Ina-Belle River Rd. Belle vicinity, 12/08/83, C, 83003571

JERSEY COUNTY

DUNCAN FARM, Address Restricted, Grafton vicinity, 8/24/82, D, 82002542

ELSAH HISTORIC DISTRICT, N of McAdams Hwy., Elsah, 7/27/73, C,a, 73000706

JERSEY COUNTY COURTHOUSE, Public Sq., Jerseyville, 5/08/86, A,C, 86091008

JERSEYVILLE DOWNTOWN HISTORIC DISTRICT, Rough-bounded by Exchange Lafayette, Prairie and Jefferson Sts. Jerseyville, 12/29/86 A,C, 86003528

NEW PIASA CHAUTAUQUA HISTORIC DISTRICT, Off McAdams Pkwy., Chautauqua, 6/15/82, A,a, 82002541

NUTWOOD SITE, Address Restricted, Nutwood vicinity, 2/09/79, D, 79003784

PERE MARQUETTE STATE PARK LODGE AND CABINS, {Illinois State Parks Lodges and Cabins TRi, Box 158, Grafton, 3/04/85, C,g, 85002405

STONE ARCH BRIDGE, 760-800 E. Main St., Danville, 5/16/86, A, 86001087

JO DAVIESS COUNTY

EAST DUBUQUE SCHOOL, Montgomery Ave., East Dubuque, 11/12/82, A,C,g, 82000396

GALENA HISTORIC DISTRICT, Galena and environs, Galena, 10/18/69, A,C, 69000056

GRANT, ULYSSES S., HOUSE, 511 Bouthillier St., Galena, 10/15/66, B, NHL, 66000322

OLD MARKET HOUSE, Market Square-Commerce St., Galena, 7/16/73, A,C, 73000707

OLD STONE HOTEL, 110 W. Main St., Warren, 4/16/75, A,C, 75000665

WASHBURNE, ELIHU BENJAMIN, HOUSE, 908 3rd St., Galena, 7/05/73, B,C, 73000708

WENNER, CHARLES, HOUSE, Rocky Rd., Galena vicinity, 8/22/84, A,C, 84001073

KANE COUNTY

AURORA COLLEGE COMPLEX, 3475. Gladstone Ave., Aurora, 2/16/84, A,C, 84001126

AURORA ELKS LODGE NO. 705, 775, Stolp Ave., Aurora, 3/31/80, C, 80001369

AURORA WATCH FACTORY, 603-621 LaSalle St., Aurora, 5/08/86, A,C, 86001009

BATAVIA INSTITUTE, 333 S. Jefferson St., Batavia, 8/13/76, A,a, 76000712

BEITH, WILLIAM, HOUSE, 6 Indiana St., St. Charles, 12/07/83, C, 83003575

CAMPANA FACTORY, N of Batavia on N. Batavia Ave., Batavia vicinity, 4/06/79, A,C,g, 79000841

CAMPANA FACTORY, (Boundary Decrease), Roughly along SR 31 and Campana Rd., Batavia vicinity, 4/06/79, A,C,g, 79003760

CAMPTOWN TOWN HALL, W of Wasco at Town Hall Rd. and IL 64, Wasco vicinity, 11/24/80, A, 80001378

CENTRAL GENEVA HISTORIC DISTRICT, Roughly bounded by Fox River, South, 6th and W. State Sts., Geneva, 9/10/79, A,C,a, 79000845

CHICAGO, BURLINGTON, & QUINCY ROUNDHOUSE AND LOCOMOTIVE SHOP, Broadway and Spring Sts. Aurora, 2/16/78, C, 78001154

CHICAGO, BURLINGTON, AND QUINCY RAILROAD DEPOT, 155 Houston St., Batavia, 6/06/79, A,C,b,.79000842

CITY BUILDING, 15 N. 1st Ave., St. Charles, 3/21/79, A,C, 79000847

COPLEY, COL. IRA C., MANSION, 434 W. Downer Pl., Aurora, 3/29/78, BC, 78001155

DUNDEE TOWNSHIP HISTORIC DISTRICT, Both sides of Fox River, including sections of E. Dundeey, W. Dundee and Carpentersville, Dundee and Vicinity, 3/07/75, A,C,a,b,g, 75000666

DURANT HOUSE, NW of St. Charles off Dean St., St. Charles vicinity, 6/18/76, A, 76000714

DUTCH MILL, N of Batavia off IL 25, Batavia vicinity, 6/04/79, C,b, 79000843

ELGIN ACADEMY, 350 Park St., Elgin, 10/08/76, A, 76000713

ELGIN HISTORIC DISTRICT, Roughly bounded by Villa, Center, Park, N. Liberty, and S. Channing Sts., Elgin, 5/09/83, C,a, 83000318

ELGIN MILK CONDENSING CO./ILLINOIS CONDENSING CO., Brook and Water Sts., Elgin, 2/14/85, A,B, 85000267

FABYAN VILLA, 1511 S. Batavia Ave., Geneva, 2/09/84, C, 84001128

FIRST METHODIST CHURCH OF BATAVIA, 3551st St., Batavia, 3/19/82, A,C,a, 82002546

FIRST UNIVERSALIST CHURCH, 55 Villa St., Elgin, 11/07/80, C,a, 80001374

FOX RIVER HOUSE, 166 W. Galena, Aurora, 5/04/76, A, 76000710

GAR MEMORIAL BUILDING, 23 E. Downer Pl., Aurora, 8/23/84, A,C, 84001130

GARFIELD FARM AND TAVERN, W of St. Charles at IL 38 and Garfield Rd., St. Charles vicinity, 6/23/78, A,C, 78001156

GIFFORD-DAVIDSON HOUSE, 363-363 Prairie St., Elgin, 5/31/80, B,C, 80001375

GRAHAM BUILDING, 33 S. Stolp Ave., Aurora, 3/19/82, C, 82002543

GRAY-WATKINS MILL, 211 N. River St., Montgom ery, 12/17/79, A, 79000846

HEALY CHAPEL, 332 W. Downer Pl., Aurora, 2/28/85, A,C, 85000361

HOTEL AURORA, 2 N. Stolp Ave., Aurora, 6/03/82, A, 82002544

HOTEL BAKER, 100 W. Main St., St. Charles, 12/08/78, C, 78001157

HUNT HOUSE, 304 Cedar Ave., St. Charles, 11/12/82, 5,B,C 82000397

KEYSTONE BUILDING, 30 S. Stolp Ave., Aurora, 3/18/80, C, 80001370

LIBRARY HALL, 21 N. Washington St., Carpentersville, 8/14/73, A,B,C, 73000709

MASONIC TEMPLE, 104 S. Lincoln Ave., Aurora, 3/19/82, C, 82002545

MEMORIAL WASHINGTON REFORMED PRESBYTERIAN CHURCH, W of Elgin on W. Highland Ave. Rd., Elgin vicinity 11/19/80, A,C,a, 80001376

NORTH GENEVA HISTORIC DISTRICT, Roughly bounded by RR tracks, Fox River, Stevens and W. State Sts., Geneva, 3/25/82, A,C,a, 82002549

OAKLAWN FARM, Army Trail and Dunham Rds., Wayne, 7/26/79, A,C, 79000848

OLD SECOND NATIONAL BANK, 37 S. River St., Aurora, 5/08/79, C, 79000840

PARAMOUNT THEATRE, 23 E. Galena Blvd., Aurora, 3/18/80, A,C,g, 80001371

PELTON, ORA, HOUSE, 214 S. State St., Elgin, C: 82002548

SMITH EHRAIM, HOUSE, NE of Sugar Grove, Sugar Grove vicinity, 6/06/80, C,b, 80001377

STEARNS-WADSWORTH HOUSE, 1 S. 570 Bliss Rd., Batavia vicinity, 3/19/82, A,C, 82002547

STOLP ISLAND HISTORIC DISTRICT, Stolp Island, Aurora, 9/10/86, A,C, 86001487

STOLP WOOLEN MILL STORE, 2 W. Downer Pl., Aurora, 9/01/83, A,B, 83000319

TANNER, WILLIAM A., HOUSE, 304 Oak Ave., Aurora, 8/19/76, C, 76000711

TEEPLE BARN, NW of Elgin on Randall Rd., Elgin vicinity, 12/10/79, A,C, 79000844

UNITED METHODIST CHURCH OF BATAVIA, 8 N. Batavia Ave., Batavia, 7/28/83, C,a, 83000320

WEISEL, ANDREW, HOUSE, 312 N. 2nd Ave., St. Charles, 2/26/82, C, 82002550

WEST SIDE HISTORIC DISTRICT, Roughly bounded by W. Downer Pl., Lake St., Garfield Ave and S. Highland St., Aurora, 8/13/86, A,C 86001484

WHITE, LOUISE, SCHOOL, Washington Ave., Batavia, 11/07/80, A,C, 80001373

WILSON, JUDGE ISAAC, HOUSE, 406 E. Wilson St., Batavia, 5/09/85, B,C, 85000978

KANKAKEE COUNTY

HICKOX, WARREN, HOUSE, 687 S. Harrison Ave., Kankakee, 1/03/78, C, 78001158

MILK, LEMUEL, CARRIAGE HOUSE, 165 N. Indiana Ave. Kankakee, 6/04/79 B,C, 79000849

RIVERVIEW HISTORIC DISTRICT, Roughly bounded by River and Eagle Sts., Wildwood Ave., and the Kankakee River, Kankakee, 8/22/86, A,C, 86001488

SWANNELL, CHARLES E., HOUSE, 901 S. Chicago, Kankakee, 6/03/82, C, 82002551

KENDALL COUNTY

EVELYN SITE, Address Restricted, Newark vicinity, 12/19/78, D, 78001159

SEARS, ALBERT H., HOUSE, 603 E. North St., Plano, 1/29/87, B,C, 86003720

KNOX COUNTY

CONGER, J. NEWTON, HOUSE, 334 N. Knox St., Oneida, 4/20/79, C, 79003111

GALESBURG HISTORIC DISTRICT, Roughly bounded by Berrien, Clark, Pearl, and Sanborn Sts. Galesburg, 11/21/76, A,C,a, 76000715

MEETING HOUSE OF THE CENTRAL CONGREGATIONAL CHURCH, Central Sq., Galesburg, 9/30/76, C,a, 76000716

OLD MAIN, KNOX COLLEGE, Knox College campus, Galesburg, 10/15/66, B, NHL, 66000323

WOLF COVERED BRIDGE, NV of Yates City, on CR 17 over Spoon River, Yates City vicinity, 12/04/74, A, 74000763

LA SALLE COUNTY

HOSSACK, JOHN, HOUSE, 210 W. Prospect St., Otta, 3/16/72 BC 72000462

HOTEL KASKASKIA, 217 Marquette St., LaSalle, 11/03/88, A,C, 88002229

LASALLE CITY BUILDING, 745 2nd St., LaSalle, 8/29/85, A, 85001909

OLD KASKASKIA VILLAGE, Address Restricted, Ottawa vicinity, 10/15/66, D, NHL, 66000324

SPRING VALLEY HOUSE-SULFUR SPRINGS HOTEL, Dee Bennett Rd., Utica, 11/20/87, A,C, 87002055

STARVED ROCK, 6 mi. from Ottawa on IL 71, Starved Rock State Park, Ottawa vicinity, 10/15/66, D, NHL, 66000325

STARVED ROCK LODGE AND CABINS, {Illinois State Parks Lodges and Cabins TR}, Box 116, Utica, LaSalle-Peru vicinity, 5/08/85, A,C, 85002702

WASHINGTON PARK HISTORIC DISTRICT, Bounded by Jackson, LaSalle, Lafayette, and Columbus Sts., Ottawa, 4/11/73, A,C, 73000710

WILLIAMS, SILAS, HOUSE, 702 E. Broadway, Streator, 6/23/76, C, 76002146

LAKE COUNTY

ADAMS, MARY W., HOUSE, {Highland Park MRA}, 1923 Lake Ave., Highland Park, 9/29/82, C, 82002552

ARMOUR, J. OGDEN, HOUSE, 1500 W Kennedy Rd., Lake Forest, 6/28/82, B,C, 82002578

ARMOUR, LESTER, HOUSE, Sheridan Rd., Lake Bluff, 5/03/84, C, 84001131

BEATTY, ROSS J., HOUSE, (Highland Park MRA}, 344 Ravine Dr., Highland Park, 9/29/82, B,C, 82002553

BEATTY, ROSS, HOUSE, {Highland Park MRA}, 1499 Sheridan Rd., Highland Park, 9/29/82, B,C, 82002554

BECKER, A. G., PROPERTY, 405 Sheridan Rd., Highland Park, 11/15/84, C, 84000343

BOWEN, JOSEPH T., COUNTRY CLUB, 1917 N. Sheridan Rd., Braeside School Waukegan, 11/30/78, A, 78003400

BRAESIDE SCHOOL, {Highland Park MRA}, 124 Pierce Rd., Highland Park, 9/29/82, A,C, 82002555

CAMPBELL, ALBERT, HOUSE, {Highland Park MRA}, 434 Marsh man, Highland Park, 9/29/8 2,C, 82002556

CHURCH OF THE ST. SAVA SERBIAN ORTHODOX MONASTERY, N of Libertyville on N. Milwaukee Ave, Libertyv ille vicinity, 9/06/79, C,a, 79000850

CHURCHILL, RICHARD, HOUSE, {Highland Park MRA}, 1214 Green Bay Rd., Highland Park, 9/29/82, C, 82002557

DEWEY HOUSE, Veterans Administration Medical Center, North Chicago, 5/08/85, B,C, 85001008

DUBIN, HENRY, HOUSE, {Highland Park MRA}, 441 Cedar, Highland Park, 9/29/82, C, 82002558

EVERT HOUSE, Highland Park MRA, 2687 Logan, Highland Park, 9/29/82, C, 82002559

FLORSHEIM, HAROLD, HOUSE, {Highland Park MRA}, 650 Sheridan Rd., Highland Park, 9/29/82, B,C, 82002560

FORT SHERIDAN HISTORIC DISTRICT, Off IL 22, Fort Sheridan, 9/29/80, A,C, NHL, 80001379

GEYSO, MRS. FRANK, HOUSES, {Highland Park MRA}, 450 and 456 Woodland Rd., Highland Park, 9/29/82, C, 82002561

GRANVILLE-MOTT HOUSE, (Highland Park MRA}, 80 Laurel Ave., Highland Park, 9/29/82, C, 82002562

GREAT LAKES NAVAL TRAINING STATION, Bounded by Cluverius Ave., Lake Michigan, G St., and Sheridan Rd., Waukegan vicinity, 9/15/86, A,C, 86002890

GRIGSBY ESTATE, 125 Buckley Rd., Barrington Hills, 5/12/87, C, 87000649

HAZEL AVENUE PROSPECT AVENUE HISTORIC DISTRICT, {Highland Park MRA}, St. Johns, Hazel, Dale, Forest, and Prospect Aves., Highland Park, 9/29/82, C, 82002563

HIGHLAND PARK WATER TOWER, (Highland Park MRA}, N of Central Green Bay Rd., Highland Park, 9/29/82, C, 82002564

HOLMES, SAMUEL, HOUSE, {Highland Park MRA}, 2693 Sheridan Rd., Highland Park, 9/29/82, C, 82002565

HUMER BUILDING, (Highland Park MRA}, 1894 Sheridan Rd., Highland Park, 9/29/82, C, 82002566

JAMES, JEAN BUTZ, Museum of the Highland Park Historical Society {Highland Park MRA}, 326 Central Ave., Highland Park, 9/29/82, C, 82002567

LAKE FOREST HISTORIC DISTRICT, Roughly bounded by Western, Westleigh, Lake Michigan, and N city limits, Lake Forest, 1/26/78, C, 78001161

LANZL, HAERMAN, HOUSE, {Highland Park MRA}, 1635 Linden, Highland Park, 9/29/82, C, 82002568

LEWIS, LLOYD, HOUSE, 153 Little St. Mary, Libertyville, 6/15/82, C,g, 82002579

LICHTSTERN HOUSE, (Highland Park MRA}, 105 S. Deere Park Dr., Highland Park, 9/29/82, C, 82002569

LINDEN PARK PLACE-BELLE AVENUE HISTORIC DISTRICT, (Highland Park MRA}, Roughly bounded by Sheridan Rd., Elm Pl., Linden, Park, and Central Aves., Highland Park, 12/13/83, C, 83003580

LOEB, ERNEST, HOUSE, {Highland Park MRA}, 1425 Waverly, Highland Park, 5/18/83, A,C, 83000321

MAPLE AVENUE MAPLE LANE HISTORIC DISTRICT, {Highland Park MRA}, Maple Ave. and Maple Lane between St. Johns Ave. and Sheridan Rd., Highland Park, 9/29/82, C, 82002570

MILLARD, GEORGE MADISON, HOUSE, {Highland Park MRA}, 1689 Lake Ave., Highland Park, 9/29/82, C, 82002571

MILLARD, SYLVESTER, HOUSE, {Highland Park MRA}, 1623 Sylvester Pl., Highland Park, 9/29/82, A,C, 82002572

MILLBURN HISTORIC DISTRICT, U.S. 45, Millburn and Grass Lake Rds., Millburn, 9/18/79, A,C, 79000851

MINEOLA HOTEL, 91 N. Cora St., Fox Lake, 7/29/79, A,C, 79003785

NEAR NORTH HISTORIC DISTRICT, Roughly bounded by Ash St., RR. tracks, Glen Flora Ave., Waukegan, 5/03/78, C, 78001162

NORTH SHORE SANITARY DISTRICT TOWER, {Highland Park MRA}, Cary Ave., Highland Park, 6/30/83, C, 83000322

OBEE HOUSE, (Highland Park MRA}, 1642 Green Bay Rd., Highland Park, 9/29/82, C, 82002573

PICK, GEORGE, HOUSE, (Highland Park MRA}, 970 Sheridan Rd., Highland Park, 9/29/82, C, 82002574

PUBLIC SERVICE BUILDING, 344-354 N. Milwaukee Ave., Libertyville, 12/08/83, B,C, 83003581

RAGDALE, 1230 N. Green Bay Rd., Lake Forest, 6/03/76, C, 76000717

RAVINIA PARK HISTORIC DISTRICT, (Highland Park MRA}, Roughly bounded by Lambert Tree Ave., Sheridan Rd., St. Johns Ave., Rambler Lane, and Ravinia Park Ave., Highland Park, 9/29/82, C, 82002575

ROSEWOOD PARK, (Highland Park MRA}, Roger Williams Ave., Highland Park, 9/29/82, C, 82002576

SHILOH HOUSE, 1300 Shiloh Blvd., Zion, 5/12/77, B,C,a, 77000488

SOULE, C. S., HOUSE, {Highland Park MRA}, 304 Laurel Ave., Highland Park, 9/29/82, C, 82002577

VINE-OAKWOOD-GREEN BAY ROAD HISTORIC DISTRICT, Green Bay Rd., E. Vine and N. Oakwood Aves., Lake Forest, 3/28/80, A,C, 80001381

WATER TOWER, Building 49, Leonard Wood Ave., Fort Sheridan, 12/04/74, C, 74000764

WILLITS, WARD WINFIELD, HOUSE, 1445 Sheridan Rd., Highland Park, C, 80001380

ZION CHAPTER HOUSE, (American Woman s League Chapter Houses TR}, 2715 Emmaus Ave., Zion, 11/28/80, A,C, 80001382

LEE COUNTY

BROCKNER, CHRISTOPHER, HOUSE, 222 N. Dixon Ave., Dixon, 11/13/84, C, 84000319

ILLINOIS CENTRAL STONE ARCH RAILROAD BRIDGES, W. First, W. Second, & W. Third Sts. between Monroe & College Aves., Dixon, 12/02/87, A, 87002048

NACHUSA HOUSE, 215 S. Galena Ave., Dixon, 2/10/83, A,C, 83000323

REAGAN'S, RONALD, BOYHOOD HOME, 816 S. Hennepin Ave., Dixon, 3/26/82, B ,c, 82002580

VAN EPPS, WILLIAM H., HOUSE, 212 S. Ottawa Ave., Dixon, 2/11/82, C, 82002581

LIVINGSTON COUNTY

BEACH, THOMAS A., HOUSE, 402 E. Hickory St., Fairbury, 7/28/83, B,C, 8300032

DWIGHT CHICAGO AND ALTON RAILROAD DEPOT, East St., Dwight, 12/27/82, A,C, 82000398

JONES HOUSE, 314 E. Madison St., Pontiac, 5/05/78, B,C, 78001163

LIVINGSTON COUNTY COURT-HOUSE, 112 W. Madison, Pontiac, 11/19/86, A,C, 86003165

OUGHTON, JOHN R., HOUSE, 101 W. South St., Dwight, 9/23/80, B,C, 80001383

PIONEER GOTHIC CHURCH, 201 N. Franklin St., Dwight, 7/28/83, C,a, 83000325

SCHULTZ, RAYMOND, Round Barn {Round Barns in Illinois TR}, S of Pontiac off US 66, Pontiac vicinity, 8/26/82, A, 82002582

LOGAN COUNTY

ATLANTA PUBLIC LIBRARY, Race and Arch Sts., Atlanta, 12/11/79, C, 79000852

BUCKLES, ROBERT, Barn {Round Barns in Illinois TR}, SE of Mt. Pulaski, Mount Pulaski vicinity, 2/10/83, A,C, 83000326

FOLEY, STEPHAN A., HOUSE, 427 Tremont St., Lincoln, 5/03/84, B,C, 84001141

LINCOLN COURTHOUSE SQUARE HISTORIC DISTRICT, Roughly bounded by Sangamon, Pekin, Chicago, Delaware, Broadway, and Pulaski Sts., Lincoln, 12/24/85, A,C, 85003166

LINCOLN PUBLIC LIBRARY, 725 Pekin St., Lincoln, 9/12/80, A,C 80001384

MOUNT PULASKI COURTHOUSE, Public Sq., Mount Pulaski, 8/03/78, A,C, 78001164

UNIVERSITY HALL, 300 Keokuk St., Lincoln, 4/24/73, C, 73000711

MACON COUNTY

DECATUR DOWNTOWN HISTORIC DISTRICT, Merchant St. roughly bounded by North, Water, Wood, and Church Sts., Decatur, 5/09/85, A,C, 85001011

DECATUR HISTORIC DISTRICT, Roughly bounded by Hayward, El Dorado, and Church, and Lincoln Park Dr., Decatur, 11/07/76, C, 76000719

MILLIKIN, JAMES, HOUSE, 125 N. Pine St., Decatur, 12/03/74, B,C, 74000765

ULERY, ELI, HOUSE., E of Mount Zion on SR 60, Mount Zion vicinity, 10/01/79, B, 79000854

MACOUPIN COUNTY

CARLINVILLE CHAPTER HOUSE, (American Woman's League Chapter Houses TR}, 111 S. Charles St., Carlinville, 11/28/80, A,C, 80001385

CARLINVILLE HISTORIC DISTRICT, Roughly-bounded by Oak, Mulberry, Morgan, and E. city limits, Carlinville, 5/17/76, C, 76000721

ROBINSON, J. L., GENERAL STORE, Off IL 108, Hagaman, 9/12/80, A, 80001386

SHRIVER FARMSTEAD, NW of Virden, Virden vicinity, 9/29/80, A,C, 80001387

UNION MINERS CEMETERY, 0.5 mi. N of Mount Olive city park, Mount Olive, 10/18/72, A,d,f, 72000463

MADISON COUNTY

ALTON CHAPTER HOUSE, {American Woman's League Chapter Houses TR}, 509 Beacon St., Alton, 11/28/80, A,C, 80001388

ALTON MILITARY PRISON SITE, Address Restricted, Alton vicinity, 12/31/74, D, 74000766

BERLEMAN HOUSE, 1155. Main St., Edwardsville, 3/27/80, C, 80001391

BETHALTO VILLAGE HALL, 124 Main St., Bethalto, 12/02/87, A, 87002049

CARNEY, JOHN, HOUSE, 306 E. Market St., Troy, 7/28/83, C, 83000327

CHRISTIAN HILL HISTORIC DISTRICT, Roughly bounded by Broadway, Belle, 7th, Cliff, Bluff, and State Sts., Alton, 5/22/78, A,B,C,a, 78001165

EDWARDSVILLE CHAPTER HOUSE, {American Woman's League Chapter Houses TR}, 515 W. High St., Edwardsville, 11/28/80, A,C,80001392

GODFREY, BENJAMIN, MEMORIAL CHAPEL, Godfrey Rd., Godfrey, 5/10/79, A,C,a, 79000856

GUERTLER HOUSE, 101 Blair St., Alton, 7/30/74, A,C, 74000767

HASKELL PLAYHOUSE, Henry St. in Haskell Park, Alton, 7/30/74, C, 74000768

HORSESHOE LAKE MOUND AND VILLAGE SITE, Address Restricted, Granite City vicinity, 11/26/80, D, 80001396

JARVIS, WILLIAM W., HOUSE, 317 E. Center St., Troy, 2/03/88, C, 87002514

KUHN STATION SITE, Address Restricted, Edwardsville vicinity, 11/25/80, D, 80001393

LECLAIRE HISTORIC DISTRICT, Roughly bounded by RR tracks, Wolf St., Hadley and Madison, Edwardsville, 8/08/79, A, 79000855

MADISON COUNTY SHERIFF'S MAIN ST., Edwardsville, 5/31/80, C, 80001394

MARINE CHAPTER HOUSE, (American Woman's League Chapter Houses TR}, Silver St., Marine 11/28/80, A,C, 80001397

MIDDLETOWN HISTORIC DISTRICT, Roughly bounded by Broadway, Market, Alton, Franklin, Common, Liberty, Humboldt, and Plum Sts., Alton, 7/11/78, C, 78001166

MIDDLETOWN HISTORIC DISTRICT, (Boundary Increase), 3rd St. between Market and Piasa St., Alton 9/16/82, C, 82002583

MINERS' INSTITUTE BUILDING, 204 W. Main, Collinsville, 8/29/85, A, 85001913

MITCHELL ARCHEOLOGICAL SITE, Address Restricted Mitchell vicinity, 2/07/78, D, 78001168

MOUNT LOOKOUT, 2018 Alby St., Alton, 6/17/80, B,C, 80001389 Post House, 1516 State St., Alton, 5/28/80, B,C, 80001390

RUTHERFORD HOUSE, 1006 Pearl St., Alton, 3/19/82, A,C, 82002584

ST. LOUIS STREET HISTORIC DISTRICT, 603-1306 St. Louis St., Edwardsville, 5/09/83, C, 83000328

STEPHENSON, BENJAMIN, HOUSE, 4095. Buchanan St., Edwardsville, 5/31/80, B,C, 80001395

TRUMBULL, LYMAN, HOUSE, 1105 Henry St., Alton, 5/15/75, B, NHL, 75000667

UPPER ALTON HISTORIC DISTRICT, Seminary St., College, Leverett, and Evergreen Aves., Alton, 5/02/78, A,C, 78001167

WEIR, JOHN, HOUSE, 715 N. Main St., Edwardsville, 5/09/83, A,C, 83000329

YAKEL HOUSE AND UNION BREWERY, 1421-1431 Pearl St., Alton, 5/11/82, A,C, 82002585

MARION COUNTY

BRYAN, WILLIAM JENNINGS, BOYHOOD HOME, 408 S. Broadway, Salem, 2/18/75, B,b, 75000668

ROHRBOUGH, CALENDAR, HOUSE, 3rd and Madison Sts., Kinmundy, 9/06/79, B,C, 79000857

SENTINEL BUILDING, 232 E. Broadway, Centralia, 4/15/78, C, 78001169

MARSHALL COUNTY

WAUGH, ROBERT, HOUSE, 202 School St., Sparland, 10/04/78, C, 78001170

MASON COUNTY

CLEAR LAKE SITE, AddressRestricted, ManitoVicinity, 11/28/78, D, 78001171

ROCKWELL MOUND, ADDRESS RESTRICTED, HavanaVicinity, 12/10/87, C,D, 87000679

MASSAC COUNTY

CURTIS, ELIJAH P., HOUSE, 405 Market St., Metropolis, B,C, 78001172

FORT MASSAC SITE, SE of Metropolis on the Ohio River, Metropolis vicinity, 7/14/71, D, 71000293

KINCAID SITE, Address Restricted, Brookport vicinity, 10/15/66, D, NHL, 66000326

MCCARTNEY, R. W., MUSIC HALL, 116-120 E. Fourth St., Metropolis, 8/13/86, C, 86001490

MCDONOUGH COUNTY

KLEINKOPF, CLARENCE, Round Barn {Round Barns in Illinois TR}, N of Colchester, Colchester vicinity, 8/26/82, A, 8200286

MCDONOUGH COUNTY COURTHOUSE, Public Sq., Macomb, 10/30/72, C, 72001448

WELLING-EVERLY HORSE BARN, Off US 136, Adair vicinity, 8/29/85, A,C, 85001911

MCHENRY COUNTY

COUNI'S HOUSE, 3803 Waukegan, McHenry, 6/03/82, C, 82002587

HIBBARD, CHARLES H., HOUSE, 413 W. Grant Hwy., Marengo, 2/14/79, C, 79003113

OLD MCHENRY COUNTY COURTHOUSE, City 5q., Woodstock, 11/01/74, C, 74002183

PALMER, COL. GUSTAVIUS A., HOUSE, 5516 Terra Cotta Rd., Crystal Lake, 5/24/85, C, 85001127

ROGERS, ORSON, HOUSE, E of Marengo at 19621 E. Grant St., Marengo vicinity, 6/22/79, B,C, 79003114

STICKNEY, GEORGE, HOUSE, NE of Woodstock at 1904 Cherry Valley Rd., Woodstock vicinity, 5/14/79, B,C, 79003115

TERWILLIGER HOUSE, E of Woodstock at Mason Hill and Cherry Valley Rds., Woodstock vicinity, 5/14/79, B,C, 79003116

WOODSTOCK OPERA HOUSE, 119 Van Buren St., Woodstock, 7/17/74, C, 74002184

WOODSTOCK SQUARE HISTORIC DISTRICT, Roughly bounded by Calhoun, Throop, Cass, Main, C and NW RR Tracks, and Jefferson Sts., Woodstock, 11/12/82, C, 82000399

MCLEAN COUNTY

BANE, WARREN, SITE, Address Restricted, Ellsworth vicinity, 3/19/82, D, 82002588

BENJAMIN, RUBEN M., HOUSE, 510 E. Grove St., Bloomington, 8/30/78, B, 78003109

BENJAMINVILLE FRIENDS MEETING HOUSE AND BURIAL GROUND, N of Holder, Holder vicinity, 12/13/83, A,C,a,d, 83003584

BLOOMINGTON CENTRAL BUSINESS DISTRICT, Roughly bounded by Main, Center and Front Sts., Bloomington, 2/28/85, A,C, 85000363

CLOVER LAWN, 1000 E. Monroe Dr., Bloomington, 10/18/72, B,C, NHL, 72001479

COOK, JOHN W., HALL, Illinois State University, US 51, Normal, 2/20/86, A,C, 86000268

COX, GEORGE H., HOUSE, 701 E. Grove St., Bloomington, 11/14/85, C, 85002838

DAVIS, DAYID, III & IV, House, 1005 E. Jefferson, Bloomington 11/12/82, C, 82000400

DUNCAN MANOR, SW of Towanda off IL 4, Towanda vicinity, 2/09/79, B,C, 79003164

EAST GROVE STREET DISTRICT-BLOOMINGTON, 400-700 E. Grove St., Bloomington, 2/26/87, C, 86003176

FRANKLIN SQUARE, 300 and 400 blocks of E. Chestnut and E. Walnut Sts., 900 block of N. Prairie and N. McLean Sts., Bloomington, 1/11/76, A,C, 76002164

GILDERSLEEVE HOUSE, 108 Broadway, Hudson, 7/28/77, A, 77001517

HAMILTON JOHN M., HOUSE, 502 S. Clayton St., Bloomington, 9/06/78, B, 78003110

HOLY TRINITY CHURCH RECTORY AND CONVENT, 704 N. Main and 106 W. Chestnut Sts., Bloomington, 12/08/83, A,C,a, 83003585

HUBBARD HOUSE, 310 Broadway, Hudson, 2/01/79, B, 79003163

MCLEAN COUNTY COURTHOUSE AND SQUARE, Main, Washington, Center, and Jefferson Sts., Bloomington, 2/06/73, C, 73002160

MILLER, GEORGE H., HOUSE, 405 W. Market St Bloomington, 7/20/78, B,C, 78003111

MILLER-DAVIS LAW BUILDINGS, 101-103 N. Main St. and 102-104 E. Front St., Bloomington, 4/27/79, B, 79003162

PATTON, JOHN, LOG CABIN, Lexington Park District Park, Lexington, 8/01/86, A,b,e, 86002008

SCOTT, MATTHEW T., HOUSE, 2271st Ave., Chenoa, 2/10/83, A,C, 83000331

SCOTT-VROOMAN HOUSE, 701 E. Taylor St., Bloomington, 8/18/83, A,C,g, 83000330

STEVENSON HOUSE, 1316 E. Washington St., Bloomington, 5/24/74, B, 74002196

WHITE PLACE HISTORIC DIS-TRICT, White Pl., Clinton Blvd., and E side of Fell Ave. between Empire and Emerson Sts., Bloomington, 8/12/88, A,C, 88001230

MENARD COUNTY

LINCOLN'S NEW SALEM VIL-LAGE, S of Petersburg in New Salem State Park, Petersburg vicinity, 6/19/72, B,b,e,g, 72000464

NORTH SANGAMON UNITED PRESBYTERIAN CHURCH, N of Athens on SR 2, Athens vicinity, 3/23/79, C,a, 79000858

PETERSBURG HISTORIC DIS-TRICT, IL 97, Petersburg, 6/17/76, A,C,d, 76000722

PETERSBURG HISTORIC DIS-TRICT, (Boundary Increase), Smoot Hotel, corner of Sixth and Douglas, Petersburg, 1/31/86, A,C, 86000138

MERCER COUNTY

COMMERICAL HOUSE, 4th and Main St., Keithsburg, 5/09/83, A, 83000332

KEITHSBURG HISTORIC DIS-TRICT, Roughly bounded by Jackson, Fifth, Washington, and Third Sts., Keithsburg, 5/08/86, A, 86001004

MERCER COUNTY COURT-HOUSE, SE 3rd St. (IL 17), Aledo, 6/17/82, A, 82002589

MONROE COUNTY

FOUNTAIN CREEK BRIDGE, Off IL 156, Waterloo vicinity, 12/22/78, C, 78001176

GUNDLACH GROSSE HOUSE, 625 N. Main St., Columbia, 12/18/78, C, 78001173

LUNSFORD-PULCHER ARCHE-OLICAL SITE, Adress Restricted, Columbia vicinity, 7/23/73 C,D, 73000712

MAEYSTOWN HISTORIC DIS-TRICT, SR 7, Maeystown, 6/23/78, A,C,78001174

PETERSTOWN HOUSE, 275 N. Main St., Waterloo, 11/16/77, A, 77000489

WATERLOO HISTORIC DIS-TRICT, 5175. Main St., Waterloo, 12/01/78, C, 78001177

MONTGOMERY COUNTY

BLACKMAN, GEORGE, HOUSE, 904 S. Main St., Hillsboro, 11/06/86, C, 86003180

HAYWARD-HILL HOUSC, 5405. Main St., Hillsboro, 5/08/80, B,C, 80001399

THOMAS, LEWIS H., HOUSE, N. Virden Rd., Virden vicinity, 12/07/83, A,C, 83003586

MORGAN COUNTY

AYERS BANK BUILDING, 200 W. State St., Jacksonville, 11/20/86, A, 86003178

BEECHER HALL, Illinois College, Illinois College campus, Jacksonville, 4/08/74, A ,C, 74000769

DUNCAN, JOSEPH, HOUSE, 4 Duncan Pl., Jacksonville, 11/05/71, B,C, 71000294

GRIERSON, GEN. BENJAMIN HENRY, HOUSE, 852 E. State St., Jacksonville, 11/20/80, B, 80001400

JACKSONVILLE HISTORIC DIS-TRICT, Roughly bounded by Anna, Mound, Finley, Dayton, Lafayette and Church Sts., Jacksonville, 6/09/78, A,B,C, 78001178

JACKSONVILLE LABOR TEMPLE, 2285. Mauvaisterre St., Jacksonville, 11/13/80, A, 80004524

MORGAN COUNTY COURT-HOUSE, 300 W. State St., Jackson-ville, 11/19/86, A,C, 86003167

OGLE COUNTY

BARBER, HENRY D., HOUSE, 410 W. Mason St., Polo, 3/28/74, C, 74000770

DEERE, JOHN, HOUSE AND SHOP, Illinois and Clinton Sts., Grand Detour, 10/15/66, B, NHL, 66000327

FLAGG TOWNSHIP PUBLIC LI-BRARY, NE corner 7th St. at 4th Ave. Rochelle, 10/25/73, C, 73000713

HITT, SAMUEL M., HOUSE, 7782 IL 64 W, Mount Morris, 11/14/85, C, 85002841

HOLCOMB, WILLIAM H., HOUSE, 526 N. 7th St., Rochelle, 10/25/73, C, 73000714

MOATS, WILLIAM, FARM, Wood Rd., Ashton vicinity, 2/12/87, A,C, 86003724

OGLE COUNTY COURTHOUSE, Courthouse Sg., Oregon, 9/10/81, C, 81000222

PINEHILL,400 Mix St., Oregon, 7/24/78, C, 78001179

SOLDIER'S MONUMENT, Chestnut and 2nd Sts., Byron, 2/14/85, A,f, 85000268

STILLMANS RUN BATTLE SITE, Roosevelt and Spruce Sts., Stillman Valley, 12/08/83, A,f, 83003587

WHITE PINES STATE PARK LODGE AND CABINS, {Illinois State Parks Lodges and Cabins TR}, RR #1, Mount Morris, 3/04/85, C,g, 85002404

PEORIA COUNTY

CENTRAL NATIONAL PARK BUILDING, 103 SW Adams St., Peoria, 12/18/78, C, 78003450

CHRIST CHURCH OF LOWER KICKAPOO, W of Norwood Park on Christ Church Rd., Norwood Park vicinity, 2/10/83, A,C,a, 83000333

CUMBERLAND PRESBYTERIAN CHURCH, 405 N. Monson St., Peoria, 3/18/80, A,C,a, 80001401

FLANAGAN, JUDGE, RESIDENCE, 942 NE Glen Oak Ave., Peoria, 9/05/75, C, 75000670

GALE, JUDGE JACOB, HOUSE, 403 NE Jefferson St., Peoria, 3/19/82, B,C, 82002591

GRAND ARMY OF THE REPUB-LIC MEMORIAL HALL, 416 Hamilton Blvd., Peoria, 7/13/76, C, 76000723

JUBILEE COLLEGE, NW of Kick-apoo on U.S. 150 and 1-74, Kick-apoo vicinity, 1/04/72, A,C,a,

MADISON THEATRE, 502 Main St., Peoria, 11/21/80, A,C, 80001402

NORTH SIDE HISTORIC DIS-TRICT, Roughly bounded by Perry, Caroline, Madison and Fayette Sts., Peoria, 11/21/83, A,C, 83003588

PEACE AND HARVEST, Jefferson and Hamilton Sts., Peoria, 1/25/88, C,b,g, 87002527

PEORIA CITY HALL, 419 Fulton St., Peoria, 2/06/73, C, 73000715

PEORIA CORDAGE COMPANY, Address Restricted, Peoria vicinity, 3/19/82, A,C, 82002592

PEORIA MINERAL SPRINGS, 701 W. 7th Ave., Peoria, 3/05/82, A,C 82002593

PEORIA STATE HOSPITAL, Ricketts Ave. and U.S. 24, Bartonville, 2/17/82, A,C, 82002590

PEORIA WATERWORKS, Lorentz Ave., Peoria, 3/18/80, A,C, 80001403

PEREMARQUETTE HOTEL, 501 Main St., Peoria, 8/12/82, A,C, 82002594

PETTINGILL-MORRON HOUSE, 1212 W. Moss Ave., Peoria, 4/02/76, C, 76000724

PROCTOR, JOHN C., RECREATION CENTER, 300 S. Allen St, Peoria, 9/06/79, A,C, 79000860

ROCK ISLAND DEPOT AND FREIGHT HOUSE, 32 Liberty St., Peoria, 12/22/78: A,C, 78001180

WEST BLUFF HISTORIC DISTRICT, Randolph, High and Moss Sts., E of Western St., Peoria, 12/17/76, B,C, 76000725

PIATT COUNTY

VOORHIES CASTLE, S of Bement, Bement vicinity, 6/20/79, C, 79000861

PIKE COUNTY

BARRY HISTORIC DISTRICT, U.S. 36, Barry, 3/13/79, C, 790 00862

GRIGGSVILLE HISTORIC DISTRICT, Irregular pattern along Corey, Stanford, Quincy and Liberty Sts., Griggsville, 1/17/79, C, 79000863

MCWORTER, FREE FRANK, GRAVE SITE, Off US 36, 4 mi. E of Barry, Barry vicinity, 4/19/88, B,c, 87002533

NAPLES MOUND 8, Address Restricted, Griggsville vicinity, 10/14/75, B,D,a, 75000671

PITTSFIELD EAST SCHOOL, 400 E. Jefferson St., Pittsfield, 2/12/71, A,C, 71000295

PITTSFIELD HISTORIC DISTRICT, Roughly bounded by Washington Ct., Sycamore, Morrison and Griggsville Sts., Pittsfield, 6/04/80, C,a, 80001404

SCOTT, LYMAN, HOUSE, U.S. 54, Summer Hill, 2/10/83, A, 83000334

POPE COUNTY

GOLCONDA HISTORIC DISTRICT, IL 146, Golconda, 10/22/76, A,B,C, 76000726

MILLSTONE BLUFF, Address Restricted, Glendale vicinity, 10/15/73, D, 73000716

PULASKI COUNTY

MOUND CITY CIVIL WAR NAVAL HOSPITAL, Commercial Ave. and Central St., Mound City, 10/09/74, A, 74002285

PUTNAM COUNTY

CONDIT, CORTLAND, HOUSE, Off IL 29, Putman, 9/16/83, A,C, 83000335

PULSIFER, EDWARD, HOUSE, IL 71, Hennepin, 9/04/79, B,C, 79000864

PUTNAM COUNTY COURTHOUSE, 4th St., Hennepin, 3/04/75, A,C, 75000672

RANDOLPH COUNTY

CHARTER OAK SCHOOLHOUSE, W of Schuline, Schuline vicinity, 10/11/78, C, 78001181

CREOLE HOUSE, Market St., Prairie du Rocher, 4/03/73, C, 73000717

FORT DE CHARTRES, Terminus of IL 155, W of Prairie du Rocher, Fort Chartres, Prairie du Rocher vicinity, 10/15/66, A, NHL, 66000329

FRENCH COLONIAL HISTORIC DISTRICT, From Fort Chartres State Park to Kaskasia Island, Prairie du Rocher, 4/03/74 A,C,D,a 74000772

KOLMER SITE, Address Restricted, Prairie du Rocher vicinity, 5/01/74, D, 74000773

MARY'S RIVER COVERED BRIDGE, About 4 mi. NE of Chester on IL 150, Chester vicinity, 12/31/74, A,C, 74000771

MENARD, PIERRE, HOUSE, Fort Kaskaskia State Park, Ellis Grove vicinity, 4/15/70, B,C, NHL, 70000245

MODOC ROCK SHELTER, Address Restricted, Modoc vicinity, 10/15/66 D, NHL, 66000328

RED BUD HISTORIC DISTRICT, Irregular pattern along Main and Market Sts., Red Bud, 12/29/79, B,C, 79000865

SPARTA HISTORIC DISTRICT, 5. St. Louis, W. 3rd and 5. James Sts., Sparta, 6/03/82, C, 82002595

RICHLAND COUNTY

ELLIOTT STREET HISTORIC DISTRICT, S. Elliott St. between Chestnut St. and South Ave., Olney, 11/26/80, A,C,a,g, 80001405

LARCHMOUND, 1030 S. Morgan St., Olney, 1/03/80, B, 80001406

ROCK ISLAND COUNTY

BLACK HAWK MUSEUM AND LODGE, {Illinois State Parks Lodges and Cabins TR}, 1510 46th Ave., Rock Island vicinity, 3/04/85, C,g, 85002402

BLACK'S STORE, 1st Ave., Hampton, 5/28/76, A,B, 76000727

CONNOR HOUSE, 702 Twentieth St., Rock Island, 8/11/88, A, 88001227

DENKMANN-HAUBERG HOUSE, 130024th St., Rock Island, 12/26/72, B,C, 72000466

FORT ARMSTRONG HOTEL, 3rd Ave. and 19th St., Rock Island, 11/13/84, A,C, 84000327

FORT ARMSTRONG THEATRE, 1826 3rd Ave., Rock Island, 5/23/80, A,C, 80001407

LINCOLN SCHOOL, 7th Ave. and 22nd St., Rock Is-land, 8/29/85, A,C, 85001910

OLD MAIN, AUGUSTANA COLLEGE, 7th Ave. between 35th and 38th Sts., Rock Island, 9/11/75, A,C,a, 75000673

ROCK ISLAND ARSENAL, Rock Island in Mississippi River, Rock Island, 9/30/69, A,B,C,D,d,g, NHL, 69000057

ROCK ISLAND LINES PASSENGER STATION, 3029 5th Ave., Rock Island, 6/03/82, A, 82002596

STAUDUHAR HOUSE, 1609 21st St., Rock Island, 3/05/82, C, 82002597

WEYERHAEUSER HOUSE, 3052 10th Ave., Rock Island, 9/11/75, A,B, 75000674

SALINE COUNTY

CARRIER MILLS ARCHEOLOGICAL DISTRICT, Address Restricted, Carrier Mills vicinity, 8/25/78, D, 78001184

SANGAMON COUNTY

BOULT, H. P., HOUSE, 11235. 2nd St., Springfield, 6/03/82, C, 82002598

BRESSMER-BAKER HOUSE, 913 6th St., Springfield, 6/29/82, C, 82002599

BRINKERHOFF, GEORGE M., HOUSE, 1500 N. 5th St., Springfield, 12/18/78, C, 78001186

CALDWELL FARMSTEAD, IL 4 Chatham vicinity, 8/16/84, B,C, 84001145

CAMP LINCOLN COMMISSARY BUILDING, 1301 N. Central Springfield Historic District (Boundary Increase), Sixth St. from Capitol to Monroe St., Springfield, 11/19/86, A,C, 86003184

CHRIST EPISCOPAL CHURCH, 611 E. Jackson St., Springfield, 9/12/80, C,a, 80001410

CLAYVILLE TAVERN, 0.5 mi. SE of Pleasant Plains on IL 125, Pleasant Plains vicinity, 5/08/73, A,C, 73000718

DANA, SUSAN LAWRENCE, HOUSE, 301 Lawrence Ave., Springfield, 7/30/74, C, NHL, 74000774

EDWARDS PLACE, 700 N. 4th St., Springfield, 12/17/69, C, 69000058 Executive Mansion, 4th and Jackson Sts., Springfield, 7/19/76, A,g, 76000728

FREEMAN, CLARKSON W., HOUSE, 704 W. Monroe St., Springfield, 9/29/80, C, 80001411

GOTTSCHALK, FRED, GROCERY STORE, 301 W. Edwards St., Springfield, 3/18/85, C, 85000607

HICKOX APARTMENTS, 4th and Cook Sts., Springfield, 11/13/84, A,C, 84000337

HICKOX, VIRGIL, HOUSE, 518 E. Capitol Ave., Springfield, 3/05/82, B, 82002600

ILES, ELIJAH, HOUSE, 1825 S. 5th St., Springfield, 2/23/78, A,B,C,b, 78001188

ILLINOIS DEPARTMENT OF MINES AND MINERALS, Springfield Mine Rescue Station, 609 Princeton Ave., Springfield, 7/05/85, A, 85001481

ILLINOIS STATE CAPITOL, Capitol Ave. and Second St., Springfield, 11/21/85, C, 85003178

LEWIS, JOHN L., HOUSE, 1132 W. Lawrence Ave., Springfield, 9/10/79, B,g, 79000867

LINCOLN HOME NATIONAL HISTORIC SITE, 8th and Jackson Sts., Springfield, 8/18/71, B, NHL, 71000076

LINCOLN TOMB, Oak Ridge Cemetery, Springfield, 10/15/66, B,c,f, NHL, 66000330

LINDSAY, VACHEL, HOUSE, 603 S. 5th St., Springfield, 11/11/71, B, NHL, 71000297

MAID-RITE SANDWICH SHOP, 118 N. Pasfield St., Springfield, 8/16/84, A, 84001146

MILLER, JOSEPH, HOUSE, Buckhart Rd., Rochester vicinity, 11/24/80, B,C, 80001408

OLD STATE CAPITOL, Bounded by 5th, 6th, Adams, and Washington Sts., Springfield, 10/15/66, A,B, NHL, 66000331

PRICE/WHEELER HOUSE, 618 S. 7th St., Springfield, 2/14/85, C, 85000269

ST. NICHOLAS HOTEL, 400 E. Jefferson St., Springfield, 2/10/83, A,C, 83000336

SUGAR CREEK COVERED BRIDGE, SE of Chatham off 155, Chatham vicinity, 1/09/78, A,C, 78001185

TAFT FARMSTEAD, SR 3, Rochester, 11/20/80, B, 80001409

TIGER ANDERSON HOUSE, CR 3 N, Springfield vicinity, 6/11/86, C, 86001316

UNION STATION, Madison St., Springfield, 11/27/78, A,C, 78001189

WEBER, HOWARD K., HOUSE, 925 S. 7th St., Springfield, 10/01/79, C, 79000868

WHEELAND HAVEN, E of Riverton on 1-72 Riverton vicinity, 3/12/85, B,C, 85000557

YATES, GOV. RICHARD, HOUSE, 1190 Williams Blvd., Springfield, 3/01/84, C, 84001148

SCHUYLER COUNTY

PHOENIX OPERA HOUSE BLOCK, 112-122 W. Lafayette St., Rushville, 5/09/85, A,C, 85001010

SCOTT COUNTY

NAPLES ARCHEOLOGICAL DISTRICT, Address Restricted, Naples vicinity, 12/22/79, A,C,D,a, 79000869

WINCHESTER HISTORIC DISTRICT, IL 106, Winchester, 2/14/79, A,C,a, 79000870

SHELBY COUNTY

CHATAUQUA AUDITORIUM, Forest Park and NE 9th St., Shelbyville, 1/30/78, A,C, 78001190

SHELBYVILLE HISTORIC DISTRICT, Roughly bound by the railroad tracks, Will, N. 8th, and S. 6th Sts., Shelbyville, 12/22/76, A,B,C, 76000729

TALLMAN, HORACE M., HOUSE, 816 W. Main, Shelbyville, 5/06/88, A, 88000470

THOMPSON MILL COVERED BRIDGE, 0.5 mi. NE of Cowden over Kaskaskia River, Cowden vicinity, 3/13/75, A,C, 75000675

ST. CIAIR COUNTY

BELLEVILLE HISTORIC DISTRICT, Between E, S. Belt, Illinois, and Forest Sts., Belleville, 11/07/76, C, 76002165

CAHOKIA MOUNDS, 7850 Collinsville Rd., Cahokia Mounds State Park, Collinsville vicinity, 10/15/66, D, NHL, 66000899

CHURCH OF THE HOLY FAMILY, E. 1st St., Cahokia, 4/15/70, C,a, NHL, 70000851

EADS BRIDGE, Spanning the Mississippi River at Washington St., East St. Louis, 10/15/66, A,C, NHL, 66000946

EMERALD MOUND AND VILLAGE SITE, Address Restricted, Lebanon vicinity, 10/26/71, D, 71001026

JARROT, NICHOLAS, HOUSE, 1st St., Cahokia, 11/19/74, BC, 74002197

KNOBELOCH & SIEBERT FARM, Address Restricted, Belleville vicinity, 5/09/83, A, 83004186

LEBANON HISTORIC DISTRICT, Irregular pattern centered along St. Louis and Belleville Sts., Lebanon, 10/04/78, A,B,C,D, 78003113

MAJESTIC THEATRE, 240 246 Collinsville Ave., East St. Louis, 5/09/85, A,C, 85000977

MERMAID HOUSE HOTEL, 114 E. St. Louis St., Lebanon, 12/04/75, B,C, 75002078

OLD CAHOKIA COURTHOUSE, Corner of W. 1st and Elm Sts., Cahokia, 11/09/72, A,C,b,e, 72001480

PENNSYLVANIA AVENUE HISTORIC DISTRICT, Pennsylvania Ave., East St. Louis, 7/27/79, B,C, 79003166

STARK COUNTY

CHICAGO, BURLINGTON & QUINCY RAILROAD DEPOT, Williams St., Wyoming, 4/30/87, 87000650

STEPHENSON COUNTY

ADDAMS, JOHN H., HOMESTEAD, 425 N. Mill St., Cedarville, 4/17/79, A,B,c, 79000871

BRUCE, JAMES, Round Barn {Round Barns in Illinois TR}, S of Freeport, Freeport vicinity, 2/23/84, A,C, 84001157

FEHR, CHARLES, Round Barn {Round Barns in Illinois TR}, NE of Orangeville, Orangeville vicinity, 2/23/84, AC, 84001152

HARBACH, GERALD, Round Barn {Round Barns in Illinois TR}, US 20, Eleroy vicinity, 2/23/84, A,C, 84001155

JENSEN, CHRIS, Round Barn {Round Barns in Illinois TR}, 11723 W. Galena Rd., Lena vicinity, 2/23/84, A,C, 84001150

KELLOGG'S GROVE, SE of Kent, Kent vicinity, 6/23/78, AD, 78001191

LEEK, CLYDE, Round Barn {Round Barns in Ilinois TR}, N. Dakota Rd., Dakota, 2/23/84, A,C,84001161

OTTE, DENNIS, Round Barn {Round Barns in Illinois TR}, E of Eleroy, Eleroy vicinity, 2/23/84, A,C, 84001164

STEPHENSON COUNTY COURTHOUSE, Courthouse Sq., Freeport, 1/17/74, C, 74002284

TAYLOR, OSCAR, HOUSE, 14405. Carroll Ave., Freeport, 5/11/84, B,C, 84001165

TAZEWELL COUNTY

ALLENTOWN UNION HALL, 2 mi. E of IL 121, Allentown, 8/12/88 A, 88001228

ILLINOIS TRACTION SYSTEM MACKINAW DEPOT, N. Main St., Mackinaw, 11/30/78, A,C, 78001192

PEKIN FEDERAL BUILDING, 334 Elizabeth St., Pekin, 10/09/80, C, 80001412

TAZEWELL COUNTY COURTHOUSE, Court St. between Capitol and Fourth Sts., Pekin, 11/14/85, C, 85002837

UNION COUNTY

ST. PAULUS EVANGELISCH LUTHERISCHEN GEMEINDE, S of Jonseboro off IL 127, Jonesboro vicinity, 11/24/80, A,C,a, 80001413

STINSON MEMORIAL LIBRARY, 409 S. Main St., Anna, 6/09/78, C, 78001193

WARE MOUNDS AND VILLAGE SITE, Address Re stricted, Ware vicinity, 10/18/77, D, 77000490

VERMILION COUNTY

COLLINS ARCHEOLOGICAL DISTRICT, Address Restricted, Danville vicinity, 8/03/79, D, 79000872

DANVILLE PUBLIC LIBRARY, 307 N. Vermillion St., Danville, 11/30/78, A,C, 78003064

FITHIAN HOUSE, 116 N. Gilbert St., Danville, 5/01/75, A,B,C, 75002060

HOLLAND APARTMENTS, 324-326 N. Vermillion St., Danville, 11/16/88, C, 88002232

HOOPES-CUNNINGHAM MANSION, 424 E. Penn St., Hoopeston, 9/11/85, B,C, 85002307

WARREN COUNTY

ALEXIS OPERA HOUSE, 101-105 N. Main St., Alexis, 7/30/87, A, 87001267

CARR HOUSE, 416 E. Broadway, Monmouth, 8/11/88, C, 88001229

MARTIN, SARAH, HOUSE, 310 E. Broadway, Monmouth, 10/09/80, A,C, 80001414

QUINBY, IVORY, HOUSE, 605 N. 6th St., Monmouth, 11/20/80, B,C, 80001415

WASHINGTON COUNTY

LOUISVILLE AND NASHVILLE DEPOT, 101 E. Railroad St. Nashville, 3/01/85, A,C, 85000496

ORIGINAL SPRINGS HOTEL AND BATHHOUSE, 301 E. Walnut St., Okawville, 12/22/78, A,C, 78001194

SCHLOSSER, FRANK, COMPLEX, W. Walnut St., Okawville, 8/15/83, A,C, 83000337

WAYNE COUNTY

MAYBERRY MOUND AND VILLAGE SITE, Address Restricted, Sims vicinity, 11/21/78, D, 78001195

WHITE COUNTY

BIEKER-WILSON VILLAGE SITE, Address Restricted, New Haven vicinity, 11/21/78, D, 78001197

CARMI CHAPTER HOUSE, {American Woman's League Chapter Houses TR}, 604 W. Main St., Carmi, 11/28/80, A,9. 80001416

HUBELE MOUNDS AND VILLAGE SITE, Address Restricted, Maunie vicinity, 8/25/78, D, 78001196

OLD MORRISON MILL, Off Liberty Rd., Burnt Prairie, 7/11/84, A, 84001169

RATCLIFF INN, 214 E. Main St., Carmi, 6/04/73, B, 73000719

ROBINSON STEWART HOUSE, 1105. Main Cross St., Carmi, 8/17/73, B,C, 73000720

WILLIAMS, JAMES ROBERT, HOUSE, 310 E. Main St., Carmi, 1/29/87, B,C, 86003716

WILSON MOUNDS AND VILLAGE SITE, Address Restricted, Maunie vicinity, 11/16/77, D, 77000491

WHITESIDE COUNTY

ALBANY MOUNDS SITE, Addrss Restricted, Albany vicinity, 10/09/74, D, 74000775

KIRK, COL. EDWARD N., HOUSE, 1005 E. 3rd St., Sterling, 10/09/80, B, 80001417

MAIN STREET HISTORIC DISTRICT, 5. Main St., Tampico, 6/03/82, A,B,C,c, 82002602

MCCUNE MOUND AND VILLAGE SITE, Address Restricted, Sterling vicinity, 8/16/79, D, 79000873

SINNISSIPPI SITE, Address Restricted, Sterling vicinity, 5/14/79, D, 79000874

WILL COUNTY

BRISCOE MOUNDS, Address Restricted, Channahon vicinity, 12/22/78, D, 78001198

CHRIST EPISCOPAL CHURCH, 75 W. Van Buren St., Joliet, 8/12/82, C,a, 82002603

FITZPATRICK HOUSE, IL 53, Lockport vicinity, 2/09/84, B,C,

GEORGE, RON, ROUND BARN, {Round Barns in Illinois TR}, NE of Romeoville off US 66,

Romeoville vicinity, 12/07/82, C, 82000401

HENRY, JACOB H., HOUSE, 205. Eastern Ave., Joliet, 5/14/79, C, 79000875

ILLINOIS AND MICHIGAN CANAL, 7 mi. SW of Joliet on U.S. 6, in Channahon State Park, Joliet vicinity, 10/15/66, A,C, NHL, 66000332

JOLIET EAST SIDE HISTORIC DISTRICT, Roughly bounded by Washington and Union Sts., 4th and Eastern Aves., Joliet, 8/15/80, A,C, 80001418

JOLIET MUNICIPAL AIRPORT, 4000 W. Jefferson St., Joliet, 12/10/80, A, 80001419

JOLIET TOWNSHIP HIGH SCHOOL, 201 E. Jefferson St., Joliet, 8/12/82, A,C, 82002604

LOCKPORT HISTORIC DIS-TRICT, Area between 7th and 11th Sts.
and Canal and Washington Sts., Lockport, 5/12/75, A,C, 75000676
MILNE, ROBERT, HOUSE, 535 E. 7th St., Lockport, 12/17/79, B,C, 79000876

PLAINFIELD HALFWAY HOUSE, 503 Main St., Plain-field, 9/29/80, A, 80001421

RATHJE, H. A., MILL, 433 W. Corning Ave., Peotone, 3/19/82, A,C, 82002605

RUBENS RIALTO SQUARE THEATER, 102 N. Chicago St Joliet, 7/24/78, A,C, 78001199

STANDARD OIL GASOLINE STA-TION, 600 W. Lockport St., Plain-fleld, 11/13/84, A,C, 84000340

STONE MANOR, SE of Lockport, Lockport vicinity, 11/26/80, C, 80001420

U.S. POST OFFICE, 150 N. Scott St., Joliet, 8/20/81, C, 81000223

UNION STATION, 50 E. Jefferson St., Joliet, 8/01/78, A,C, 78001200

WILL COUNTY HISTORICAL SOCIETY HEADQUARTERS, 803 S. State St., Lockport, 5/17/72, A,C, 72000467

WILLIAMSON COUNTY

ALLEN, WILLIS, HOUSE, 514 S. Market St., Marion, 2/11/82, B, 82002606

GODDARD CHAPEL, Rose Hill Cemetery, IL 37 N, Marion, 11/06/86, C,a, 86003157

WINNEBAGO COUNTY

CORONADO, 312-324 N. Main St, Rockford, 9/06/79, A,C, 79000878

EAST ROCKFORD HISTORIC DISTRICT, U.S. 20 and U.S. 51, Rockford, 3/20/80, A,C, 80001422

GRAHAM-CINESTRA HOUSE, 1115 S. Main St., Rockford, 6/11/79, B,C, 79000879

HAIGHT VILLAGE HISTORIC DISTRICT, Roughly bounded by Walnut & Kishwaukee Sts., Chicago Northwestern RR tracks & Madison St., Rockford, 11/20/87, A,C, 87002044

HERRICK COBBLESTONE, 2127 Broadway, Rockford, 5/14/80, A,C, 80001423

JACOBY, LYSANDER, HOUSE, 2 Jacoby Pl., Rockford, 3/05/82, C, 82002607

LAKE-PETERSON HOUSE, 1313 E. State St., Rockford, 6/25/80, B,C, 80001424

LIMESTONES, THE, 118-122 S. Main, Rockford, 8/22/86, A, 86001491

MACKTOWN HISTORIC DIS-TRICT, W of Rockton on Pecaton-ica River, Rockton vicinity, 1/05/78, A,B,C, 78001201

ROBERTS, WILLIAM H., HOUSE, 523 Main St., Pecatonica, 9/06/79, C, 79000877

ROCKTON HISTORIC DISTRICT, Roughly bounded by River, Warren, Cherry, and West Sts., Rockton, 5/02/78, B,C, 78001202

SOLDIERS AND SAILORS MEMORIAL HALL, 211-215 N. Main St., Rockford, 1/31/76, A,f, 76000731

SPAFFORD, AMOS CATLIN, HOUSE, 501 N. Prospect St., Rockford, 2/20/80, B,C, 80001425

SVEA MUSIC HALL, 326 7th St., Rockford, 3/19/82, A, 82002608

TINKER SWISS COTTAGE, 411 Kent St., Rockford, 12/27/72, C, 72000468

WEBER, ROBERT, Round Barn {Round Barns in Illinois TR}, E of Durand, Durand vicinity, 2/23/84, A,C, 84001172

WOODFORD COUNTY

BENSON WATER TOWER, Clayton St. between Front & Pleasant Sts., Benson, 11/20/87. A, 87002034

EUREKA COLLEGE ADMINIS-TRATION AND CHAPEL, 300 College Ave., Eureka, 5/31/80, A,C,a, 80001426

METAMORA COURTHOUSE, 113 E. Partridge St., Metamora, 3/30/78, B,C, 78001203

STEVENSON, ADLAI E., 1, HOUSE, 104 W. Walnut St., Metamora, 3/18/80, B,C, 80001427

ALPHABETICAL LISTING
OF HISTORIC PLACES

Alphabetical List of Historic Places

Alphabetical List of Historic Places

Alphabetical List of Historic Places

Alphabetical List of Historic Places

Alphabetical List of Historic Places

Alphabetical List of Historic Places

Alphabetical List of Historic Places

PICTORIAL SCENES
OF
ILLINOIS

Old State Capitol Building, Springfield

New State Capitol Building, Springfield

Abraham Lincoln Law Office, Springfield

Neo-Gothic Chicago Water Tower, built in 1869

Twin Towers of Marina City, on the Chicago River

Pictorial   Scenes

Downtown Dundee

Algonquin Library, Algonquin

Downtown Peoria

Peoria Civic Center

Blackhawk Statue in Louden State Park

Lincoln's Tomb

Lincoln's Home in Springfield

Fort Massac State Park

Egyptian   Theatre   in De Kalb

Sears Tower in Chicago

Scenery of Quincy

Frank Lloyd Wright Home

Prarie Park, Peoria

Mary's Covered Bridge in Chester

Garden of the Gods, Shawnee National Forest

Ulysses S. Grant Home, Galena

New Salem State Park

Pettengill-Morron House, Peoria

CONSTITUTION OF ILLINOIS

Adopted in Convention at Springfield, September 3, 1970. Ratified
by the People, December 15, 1970. In force July 1, 1971.

PREAMBLE

We, the People of the State of Illinois — grateful to Almighty God for the
civil, political and religious liberty which He has permitted us to enjoy and
seeking His blessing upon our endeavors — in order to provide for the health,
safety and welfare of the people; maintain a representative and orderly government; eliminate poverty and inequality; assure legal, social and economic
justice; provide opportunity for the fullest development of the individual;
insure domestic tranquility; provide for the common defense; and secure the
blessings of freedom and liberty to ourselves and our posterity — do ordain
and establish this Constitution for the State of Illinois.

ARTICLE I — Bill of Rights

Section 1. INHERENT AND INALIENABLE RIGHTS

All men are by nature free and independent and have certain inherent
and inalienable rights among which are life, liberty and the pursuit of happi-
ness. To secure these rights and the protection of property, governments are
instituted among men, deriving their just powers from the consent of the governed.

Section 2. DUE PROCESS AND EQUAL PROTECTION

No person shall be deprived of life, liberty or property without due
process of law nor be denied the equal protection of the laws.

Section 3. RELIGIOUS FREEDOM

The free exercise and enjoyment of religious profession and worship,
without discrimination, shall forever be guaranteed, and no person shall be
denied any civil or political right, privilege or capacity, on account of his religious opinions; but the liberty of conscience hereby secured shall not be construed to dispense with oaths or affirmations, excuse acts of licentiousness, or
justify practices inconsistent with the peace or safety of the State. No person
shall be required to attend or support any ministry or place of worship
against his consent, nor shall any preference be given by law to any religious
denomination or mode of worship.

Section 4. FREEDOM OF SPEECH

All persons may speak, write and publish freely, being responsible for the
abuse of that liberty. In trials for libel, both civil and criminal, the truth, when
published with good motives and for justifiable ends, shall be a sufficient
defense.

Section 5. RIGHT TO ASSEMBLE AND PETITION

The people have the right to assemble in a peaceable manner, to consult
for the common good, to make known their opinions to their representatives
and to apply for redress of grievances.

Section 6. SEARCHES, SEIZURES, PRIVACY AND INTERCEPTIONS

The people shall have the right to be secure in their persons, houses, papers and other possessions against unreasonable searches, seizures, invasions of privacy or interceptions of communications by eavesdropping devices or other means. No warrant shall issue without probable cause, supported by affidavit particularly describing the place to be searched and the persons or things to be seized.

Section 7. INDICTMENT AND PRELIMINARY HEARING

No person shall be held to answer for a criminal offense unless on indictment of a grand jury, except in cases in which the punishment is by fine or by imprisonment other than in the penitentiary, in cases of impeachment, and in cases arising in the militia when in actual service in time of war or public danger. The General Assembly by law may abolish the grand jury or further limit its use.

No person shall be held to answer for a crime punishable by death or by imprisonment in the penitentiary unless either the initial charge has been brought by indictment of a grand jury or the person has been given a prompt preliminary hearing to establish probable cause.

Section 8. RIGHTS AFTER INDICTMENT

In criminal prosecutions, the accused shall have the right to appear and defend in person and by counsel; to demand the nature and cause of the accusation and have a copy thereof; to meet the witnesses face to face and to have process to compel the attendance of witnesses in his behalf; and to have a speedy public trial by an impartial jury of the county in which the offense is alleged to have been committed.

Section 8.1. CRIME VICTIM'S RIGHTS

(a) Crime victims, as defined by law, shall have the following rights as provided by law:

(1) The right to be treated with fairness and respect for their dignity and privacy throughout the criminal justice process.

(2) The right to notification of court proceedings.

(3) The right to communicate with the prosecution.

(4) The right to make a statement to the court at sentencing.

(5) The right to information about the conviction, sentence, imprisonment, and release of the accused.

(6) The right to timely disposition of the case following the arrest of the accused.

(7) The right to be reasonably protected from the accused throughout the criminal justice process.

(8) The right to be present at the trial and all other court proceedings on the same basis as the accused, unless the victim is to testify and the court determines that the victim's testimony would be materially affected if the victim hears other testimony at the trial.

(9) The right to have present at all court proceedings, subject to the rules of evidence, an advocate or other support person of the victim's choice.

(10) The right to restitution.

(b) The General Assembly may provide by law for the enforcement of this Section.

(c) The General Assembly may provide for an assessment against convicted defendants to pay for crime victims' rights.

(d) Nothing in this Section or in any law enacted under this Section shall be construed as creating a basis for vacating a conviction or a ground for appellate relief in any criminal case.

Section 9. BAIL AND HABEAS CORPUS

All persons shall be bailable by sufficient sureties, except for the following offenses where the proof is evident or the presumption great: capital offenses; offenses for which a sentence of life imprisonment may be imposed as a consequence of conviction; and felony offenses for which a sentence of imprisonment, without conditional and revocable release, shall be imposed by law as a consequence of conviction, when the court, after a hearing, determines that release of the offender would pose a real and present threat to the physical safety of any person. The privilege of the writ of habeas corpus shall not be suspended except in cases of rebellion or invasion when the public safety may require it.

Any costs accruing to a unit of local government as a result of the denial of bail pursuant to the 1986 Amendment to this Section shall be reimbursed by the State to the unit of local government. (As amended by the Fourth Amendment to the Constitution. Approved November 4, 1986, effective November 25, 1986.)

Section 10. SELF-INCRIMINATION AND DOUBLE JEOPARDY

No person shall be compelled in a criminal case to give evidence against himself nor be twice put in jeopardy for the same offense.

Section 11. LIMITATION OF PENALTIES AFTER CONVICTION

All penalties shall be determined both according to the seriousness of the offense and with the objective of restoring the offender to useful citizenship. No conviction shall work corruption of blood or forfeiture of estate. No person shall be transported out of the State for an offense committed within the State.

Section 12. RIGHT TO REMEDY AND JUSTICE

Every person shall find a certain remedy in the laws for all injuries and wrongs which he receives to his person, privacy, property or reputation. He shall obtain justice by law, freely, completely, and promptly.

Section 13. TRIAL BY JURY

The right of trial by jury as heretofore enjoyed shall remain inviolate.

Section 14. IMPRISONMENT FOR DEBT

No person shall be imprisoned for debt unless he refuses to deliver up his estate for the benefit of his creditors as provided by law or unless there is a strong presumption of fraud. No person shall be imprisoned for failure to pay a fine in a criminal case unless he has been afforded adequate time to make payment, in installments if necessary, and has willfully failed to make payment.

Section 15. RIGHT OF EMINENT DOMAIN

Private property shall not be taken or damaged for public use without just compensation as provided by law. Such compensation shall be determined by a jury as provided by law.

Section 16. EX POST FACTO LAWS AND IMPAIRING CONTRACTS

No ex post facto law, or law impairing the obligation of contracts or making an irrevocable grant of special privileges or immunities, shall be passed.

Section 17. NO DISCRIMINATION IN EMPLOYMENT AND THE SALE OR RENTAL OF PROPERTY

All persons shall have the right to be free from discrimination on the basis of race, color, creed, national ancestry and sex in the hiring and promotion practices of any employer or in the sale or rental of property.

These rights are enforceable without action by the General Assembly, but the General Assembly by law may establish reasonable exemptions relating to these rights and provide additional remedies for their violation.

Section 18. NO DISCRIMINATION ON THE BASIS OF SEX

The equal protection of the laws shall not be denied or abridged on account of sex by the State or its units of local government and school districts.

Section 19. NO DISCRIMINATION AGAINST THE HANDICAPPED

All persons with a physical or mental handicap shall be free from discrimination in the sale or rental of property and shall be free from discrimination unrelated to ability in the hiring and promotion practices of any employer.

Section 20. INDIVIDUAL DIGNITY

To promote individual dignity, communications that portray criminality, depravity or lack of virtue in, or that incite violence, hatred, abuse or hostility toward, a person or group of persons by reason of or by reference to religious, racial, ethnic, national or regional affiliation are condemned.

Section 21. QUARTERING OF SOLDIERS

No soldier in time of peace shall be quartered in a house without the consent of the owner; nor in time of war except as provided by law.

Section 22. RIGHT TO ARMS

Subject only to the police power, the right of the individual citizen to keep and bear arms shall not be infringed.

Section 23. FUNDAMENTAL PRINCIPLES

A frequent recurrence to the fundamental principles of civil government is necessary to preserve the blessings of liberty. These blessings cannot endure unless the people recognize their corresponding individual obligations and responsibilities.

Section 24. RIGHTS RETAINED

The enumeration in this Constitution of certain rights shall not be construed to deny or disparage others retained by the individual citizens of the State.

ARTICLE II — The Powers of the State

Section 1. SEPARATION OF POWERS

The legislative, executive and judicial branches are separate. No branch shall exercise powers properly belonging to another.

Section 2. POWERS OF GOVERNMENT

The enumeration in this Constitution of specified powers and functions shall not be construed as a limitation of powers of state government.

ARTICLE III — Suffrage and Elections

Section 1. VOTING QUALIFICATIONS

Every United States citizen who has attained the age of 18 or any other voting age required by the United States for voting in State elections and who has been a permanent resident of this State for at least 30 days next preceding any election shall have the right to vote at such election. The General Assembly by law may establish registration requirements and require permanent residence in an election district not to exceed thirty days prior to an election. The General Assembly by law may establish shorter residence requirements for voting for President and Vice-President of the United States. (As amended by the Fifth Amendment to the Constitution. Approved November 8, 1988, effective November 28, 1988.)

Section 2. VOTING DISQUALIFICATIONS

A person convicted of a felony, or otherwise under sentence in a correctional institution or jail, shall lose the right to vote, which right shall be restored not later than upon completion of his sentence.

Section 3. ELECTIONS

All elections shall be free and equal.

Section 4. ELECTION LAWS

The General Assembly by law shall define permanent residence for voting purposes, insure secrecy of voting and the integrity of the election process, and facilitate registration and voting by all qualified persons. Laws governing voter registration and conduct of elections shall be general and uniform.

Section 5. BOARD OF ELECTIONS

A State Board of Elections shall have general supervision over the administration of the registration and election laws throughout the State. The General Assembly by law shall determine the size, manner of selection and compensation of the Board. No political party shall have a majority of members of the Board.

Section 6. GENERAL ELECTION

As used in all articles of this Constitution except Article VII, "general election" means the biennial election at which members of the General Assembly are elected. Such election shall be held on the Tuesday following the first Monday of November in even-numbered years or on such other day as provided by law.

ARTICLE IV
The Legislature

Section 1. LEGISLATURE — POWER AND STRUCTURE

The legislative power is vested in a General Assembly consisting of a Senate and a House of Representatives, elected by the electors from 59

Legislative Districts and 118 Representative Districts. (As amended by the First Amendment to the Constitution. Approved November 4, 1980, effective November 26, 1980.)

Section 2. LEGISLATIVE COMPOSITION

(a)   One Senator shall be elected from each Legislative District. Immediately following each decennial redistricting, the General Assembly by law shall divide the Legislative Districts as equally as possible into three groups. Senators from one group shall be elected for terms of four years, four years and two years; Senators from the second group, for terms of four years, two years and four years; and Senators from the third group, for terms of two years, four years and four years. The Legislative Districts in each group shall be distributed substantially equally over the State.

(b)   Each Legislative District shall be divided into two Representative Districts. In 1982 and every two years thereafter one Representative shall be elected from each Representative District for a term of two years.

(c)   To be eligible to serve as a member of the General Assembly, a person must be a United States citizen, at least 21 years old, and for the two years preceding his election or appointment a resident of the district which he is to represent. In the general election following a redistricting, a candidate for the General Assembly may be elected from any district which contains a part of the district in which he resided at the time of the redistricting and reelected if a resident of the new district he represents for 18 months prior to reelection.

(d)   Within thirty days after a vacancy occurs, it shall be filled by appointment as provided by law. If the vacancy is in a Senatorial office with more than twenty-eight months remaining in the term, the appointed Senator shall serve until the next general election, at which time a Senator shall be elected to serve for the remainder of the term. If the vacancy is in a Representative office or in any other Senatorial office, the appointment shall be for the remainder of the term. An appointee to fill a vacancy shall be a member of the same political party as the person he succeeds.

(e)   No member of the General Assembly shall receive compensation as a public officer or employee from any other governmental entity for time during which he is in attendance as a member of the General Assembly.

No member of the General Assembly during the term for which he was elected or appointed shall be appointed to a public office which shall have been created or the compensation for which shall have been increased by the General Assembly during that term. (As amended by the First Amendment to the Constitution. Approved November 4, 1980, effective November 26, 1980.)

Section 3. LEGISLATIVE REDISTRICTING

(a)   Legislative Districts shall be compact, contiguous and substantially equal in population. Representative Districts shall be compact, contiguous, and substantially equal in population.

(b)   In the year following each Federal decennial census year, the General Assembly by law shall redistrict the Legislative Districts and the Representative Districts.

If no redistricting plan becomes effective by June 30 of that year, a Legislative Redistricting Commission shall be constituted not later than July 10. The Commission shall consist of eight members, no more than four of whom shall be members of the same political party.

The Speaker and Minority Leader of the House of Representatives shall each appoint to the Commission one Representative and one person who is not a member of the General Assembly. The President and Minority Leader of the Senate shall each appoint to the Commission one Senator and one person who is not a member of the General Assembly.

The members shall be certified to the Secretary of State by the appointing authorities. A vacancy on the Commission shall be filled within five days by the authority that made the original appointment. A Chairman and Vice Chairman shall be chosen by a majority of all members of the Commission.

Not later than August 10, the Commission shall file with the Secretary of State a redistricting plan approved by at least five members.

If the Commission fails to file an approved redistricting plan, the Supreme Court shall submit the names of two persons, not of the same political party, to the Secretary of State not later than September 1.

Not later than September 5, the Secretary of State publicly shall draw by random selection the name of one of the two persons to serve as the ninth member of the Commission.

Not later than October 5, the Commission shall file with the Secretary of State a redistricting plan approved by at least five members.

An approved redistricting plan filed with the Secretary of State shall be presumed valid, shall have the force and effect of law and shall be published promptly by the Secretary of State.

The Supreme Court shall have the original and exclusive jurisdiction over actions concerning redistricting the House and Senate, which shall be initiated in the name of the People of the State by the Attorney General. (As amended by the First Amendment to the Constitution. Approved November 4, 1980, effective November 26, 1980.)

Section 4. ELECTION

Members of the General Assembly shall be elected at the general election in even-numbered years.

Section 5. SESSIONS

(a) The General Assembly shall convene each year on the second Wednesday of January. The General Assembly shall be a continuous body during the term for which members of the House of Representatives are elected.

(b) The Governor may convene the General Assembly or the Senate alone in special session by a proclamation stating the purpose of the session; and only business encompassed by such purpose, together with any impeachments or confirmation of appointments shall be transacted. Special sessions of the General Assembly may also be convened by joint proclamation of the presiding officers of both houses, issued as provided by law.

(c) Sessions of each house of the General Assembly and meetings of committees, joint committees and legislative commissions shall be open to the public. Sessions and committee meetings of a house may be closed to the public if two-thirds of the members elected to that house determine that the public interest so requires; and meetings of joint committees and legislative commissions may be so closed if two-thirds of the members elected to each house so determine.

Section 6. ORGANIZATION

(a) A majority of the members elected to each house constitutes a quorum.

(b) On the first day of the January session of the General Assembly in odd-numbered years, the Secretary of State shall convene the House of Representatives to elect from its membership a Speaker of the House of Representatives as presiding officer, and the Governor shall convene the Senate to elect from its membership a President of the Senate as presiding officer.

(c) For purposes of powers of appointment conferred by this Constitution, the Minority Leader of either house is a member of the numerically strongest political party other than the party to which the Speaker or the President belongs, as the case may be.

(d) Each house shall determine the rules of its proceedings, judge the elections, returns and qualifications of its members and choose its officers. No member shall be expelled by either house, except by a vote of two-thirds of the members elected to that house. A member may be expelled only once for the same offense. Each house may punish by imprisonment any person, not a member, guilty of disrespect to the house by disorderly or contemptuous behavior in its presence. Imprisonment shall not extend beyond twenty-four hours at one time unless the person persists in disorderly or contemptuous behavior.

Section 7. TRANSACTION OF BUSINESS

(a) Committees of each house, joint committees of the two houses and legislative commissions shall give reasonable public notice of meetings, including a statement of subjects to be considered.

(b) Each house shall keep a journal of its proceedings and a transcript of its debates. The journal shall be published and the transcript shall be available to the public.

(c) Either house or any committee thereof as provided by law may compel by subpoena the attendance and testimony of witnesses and the production of books, records and papers.

Section 8. PASSAGE OF BILLS

(a) The enacting clause of the laws of this State shall be: "Be it enacted by the People of the State of Illinois, represented in the General Assembly."

(b) The General Assembly shall enact laws only by bill. Bills may originate in either house, but may be amended or rejected by the other.

(c) No bill shall become a law without the concurrence of a majority of the members elected to each house. Final passage of a bill shall be by record vote. In the Senate at the request of two members, and in the House at the request of five members, a record vote may be taken on any other occasion. A record vote is a vote by yeas and nays entered on the journal.

(d) A bill shall be read by title on three different days in each house. A bill and each amendment thereto shall be reproduced and placed on the desk of each member before final passage.

Bills, except bills for appropriations and for the codification, revision or rearrangement of laws, shall be confined to one subject. Appropriation bills shall be limited to the subject of appropriations.

A bill expressly amending a law shall set forth completely the sections amended.

The Speaker of the House of Representatives and the President of the Senate shall sign each bill that passes both houses to certify that the procedural requirements for passage have been met.

Section 9. VETO PROCEDURE

(a) Every bill passed by the General Assembly shall be presented to the Governor within 30 calendar days after its passage. The foregoing requirement shall be judicially enforceable. If the Governor approves the bill, he shall sign it and it shall become law.

(b) If the Governor does not approve the bill, he shall veto it by returning it with his objections to the house in which it originated. Any bill not so returned by the Governor within 60 calendar days after it is presented to him shall become law. If recess or adjournment of the General Assembly prevents the return of a bill, the bill and the Governor's objections shall be filed with the Secretary of State within such 60 calendar days. The Secretary of State shall return the bill and objections to the originating house promptly upon the next meeting of the same General Assembly at which the bill can be considered.

(c) The house to which a bill is returned shall immediately enter the Governor's objections upon its journal. If within 15 calendar days after such entry that house by a record vote of three-fifths of the members elected passes the bill, it shall be delivered immediately to the second house. If within 15 calendar days after such delivery the second house by a record vote of three-fifths of the members elected passes the bill, it shall become law.

(d) The Governor may reduce or veto any item of appropriations in a bill presented to him. Portions of a bill not reduced or vetoed shall become law. An item vetoed shall be returned to the house in which it originated and may become law in the same manner as a vetoed bill. An item reduced in amount shall be returned to the house in which it originated and may be restored to its original amount in the same manner as a vetoed bill except that the required record vote shall be a majority of the members elected to each house. If a reduced item is not so restored, it shall become law in the reduced amount.

(e) The Governor may return a bill together with specific recommendations for change to the house in which it originated. The bill shall be considered in the same manner as a vetoed bill but the specific recommendations may be accepted by a record vote of a majority of the members elected to each house. Such bill shall be presented again to the Governor and if he certifies that such acceptance conforms to his specific recommendations, the bill shall become law. If he does not so certify, he shall return it as a vetoed bill to the house in which it originated.

Section 10. EFFECTIVE DATE OF LAWS

The General Assembly shall provide by law for a uniform effective date for laws passed prior to July 1 of a calendar year. The General Assembly may provide for a different effective date in any law passed prior to July 1. A bill passed after June 30 shall not become effective prior to July 1 of the next calendar year unless the General Assembly by the vote of three-fifths of the members elected to each house provides for an earlier effective date.

Section 11. COMPENSATION AND ALLOWANCES

A member shall receive a salary and allowances as provided by law, but changes in the salary of a member shall not take effect during the term for which he has been elected.

Section 12. LEGISLATIVE IMMUNITY

Except in cases of treason, felony or breach of peace, a member shall be privileged from arrest going to, during, and returning from sessions of the General Assembly. A member shall not be held to answer before any other tribunal for any speech or debate, written or oral, in either house. These immunities shall apply to committee and legislative commission proceedings.

Section 13. SPECIAL LEGISLATION

The General Assembly shall pass no special or local law when a general law is or can be made applicable. Whether a general law is or can be made applicable shall be a matter for judicial determination.

Section 14. IMPEACHMENT

The House of Representatives has the sole power to conduct legislative investigations to determine the existence of cause for impeachment and, by the vote of a majority of the members elected, to impeach Executive and Judicial officers. Impeachments shall be tried by the Senate. When sitting for that purpose, Senators shall be upon oath, or affirmation, to do justice according to law. If the Governor is tried, the Chief Justice of the Supreme Court shall preside. No person shall be convicted without the concurrence of two-thirds of the Senators elected. Judgment shall not extend beyond removal from office and disqualification to hold any public office of this State. An impeached officer, whether convicted or acquitted, shall be liable to prosecution, trial, judgment and punishment according to law.

Section 15. ADJOURNMENT

(a) When the General Assembly is in session, neither house without the consent of the other shall adjourn for more than three days or to a place other than where the two houses are sitting.

(b) If either house certifies that a disagreement exists between the houses as to the time for adjourning a session, the Governor may adjourn the General Assembly to a time not later than the first day of the next annual session.

ARTICLE V
The Executive

Section 1. OFFICERS

The Executive Branch shall include a Governor, Lieutenant Governor, Attorney General, Secretary of State, Comptroller and Treasurer elected by the electors of the State. They shall keep the public records and maintain a residence at the seat of government during their terms of office.

Section 2. TERMS

These elected officers of the Executive Branch shall hold office for four years beginning on the second Monday of January after their election and, except in the case of the Lieutenant Governor, until their successors are qualified. They shall be elected at the general election in 1978 and every four years thereafter.

Section 3. ELIGIBILITY

To be eligible to hold the office of Governor, Lieutenant Governor, Attorney General, Secretary of State, Comptroller or Treasurer, a person must be a United States citizen, at least 25 years old, and a resident of this State for the three years preceding his election.

Section 4. JOINT ELECTION

In the general election for Governor and Lieutenant Governor, one vote shall be cast jointly for the candidates nominated by the same political party or petition. The General Assembly may provide by law for the joint nomination of candidates for Governor and Lieutenant Governor.

Section 5. CANVASS — CONTESTS

The election returns for executive offices shall be sealed and transmitted to the Secretary of State, or other person or body provided by law, who shall examine and consolidate the returns. The person having the highest number of votes for an office shall be declared elected. If two or more persons have an equal and the highest number of votes for an office, they shall draw lots to determine which of them shall be declared elected. Election contests shall be decided by the courts in a manner provided by law.

Section 6. GUBERNATORIAL SUCCESSION

(a) In the event of a vacancy, the order of succession to the office of Governor or to the position of Acting Governor shall be the Lieutenant Governor, the elected Attorney General, the elected Secretary of State, and then as provided by law.

(b) If the Governor is unable to serve because of death, conviction on impeachment, failure to qualify, resignation or other disability, the office of Governor shall be filled by the officer next in line of succession for the remainder of the term or until the disability is removed.

(c) Whenever the Governor determines that he may be seriously impeded in the exercise of his powers, he shall so notify the Secretary of State and the officer next in line of succession. The latter shall thereafter become Acting Governor with the duties and powers of Governor. When the Governor is prepared to resume office, he shall do so by notifying the Secretary of State and the Acting Governor.

(d) The General Assembly by law shall specify by whom and by what procedures the ability of the Governor to serve or to resume office may be questioned and determined. The Supreme Court shall have original and exclusive jurisdiction to review such a law and any such determination and, in the absence of such a law, shall make the determination under such rules as it may adopt.

Section 7. VACANCIES IN OTHER ELECTIVE OFFICES

If the Attorney General, Secretary of State, Comptroller or Treasurer fails to qualify or if his office becomes vacant, the Governor shall fill the office by appointment. The appointee shall hold office until the elected officer qualifies or until a successor is elected and qualified as may be provided by law and shall not be subject to removal by the Governor. If the Lieutenant Governor fails to qualify or if his office becomes vacant, it shall remain vacant until the end of the term.

Section 8. GOVERNOR — SUPREME EXECUTIVE POWER

The Governor shall have the supreme executive power, and shall be responsible for the faithful execution of the laws.

Section 9. GOVERNOR — APPOINTING POWER

(a)   The Governor shall nominate and, by and with the advice and consent of the Senate, a majority of the members elected concurring by record vote, shall appoint all officers whose election or appointment is not otherwise provided for. Any nomination not acted upon by the Senate within 60 session days after the receipt thereof shall be deemed to have received the advice and consent of the Senate. The General Assembly shall have no power to elect or appoint officers of the Executive Branch.

(b)   If, during a recess of the Senate, there is a vacancy in an office filled by appointment by the Governor by and with the advice and consent of the Senate, the Governor shall make a temporary appointment until the next meeting of the Senate, when he shall make a nomination to fill such office.

(c)   No person rejected by the Senate for an office shall, except at the Senate's request, be nominated again for that office at the same session or be appointed to that office during a recess of that Senate.

Section 10. GOVERNOR — REMOVALS

The Governor may remove for incompetence, neglect of duty, or malfeasance in office any officer who may be appointed by the Governor.

Section 11. GOVERNOR — AGENCY REORGANIZATION

The Governor, by Executive Order, may reassign functions among or reorganize executive agencies which are directly responsible to him. If such a reassignment or reorganization would contravene a statute, the Executive Order shall be delivered to the General Assembly. If the General Assembly is in annual session and if the Executive Order is delivered on or before April 1, the General Assembly shall consider the Executive Order at that annual session. If the General Assembly is not in annual session or if the Executive Order is delivered after April 1, the General Assembly shall consider the Executive Order at its next annual session, in which case the Executive Order shall be deemed to have been delivered on the first day of that annual session. Such an Executive Order shall not become effective if, within 60 calendar days after its delivery to the General Assembly, either house disapproves the Executive Order by the record vote of a majority of the members elected. An Executive Order not so disapproved shall become effective by its terms but not less than 60 calendar days after its delivery to the General Assembly.

Section 12. GOVERNOR — PARDONS

The Governor may grant reprieves, commutations and pardons, after conviction, for all offenses on such terms as he thinks proper. The manner of applying therefore may be regulated by law.

Section 13. GOVERNOR — LEGISLATIVE MESSAGES

The Governor, at the beginning of each annual session of the General Assembly and at the close of his term of office, shall report to the General Assembly on the Condition of the State and recommend such measures as he deems desirable.

Section 14. LIEUTENANT GOVERNOR — DUTIES

The Lieutenant Governor shall perform the duties and exercise the powers in the Executive Branch that may be delegated to him by the Governor and that may be prescribed by law.

Constitution

Section 15. ATTORNEY GENERAL — DUTIES
The Attorney General shall be the legal officer of the State, and shall have the duties and powers that may be prescribed by law.

Section 16. SECRETARY OF STATE — DUTIES
The Secretary of State shall maintain the official records of the acts of the General Assembly and such official records of the Executive Branch as provided by law. Such official records shall be available for inspection by the public. He shall keep the Great Seal of the State of Illinois and perform other duties that may be prescribed by law.

Section 17. COMPTROLLER — DUTIES
The Comptroller, in accordance with law, shall maintain the State's central fiscal accounts, and order payments into and out of the funds held by the Treasurer.

Section 18. TREASURER — DUTIES
The Treasurer, in accordance with law, shall be responsible for the safekeeping and investment of monies and securities deposited with him, and for their disbursement upon order of the Comptroller.

Section 19. RECORDS — REPORTS
All officers of the Executive Branch shall keep accounts and shall make such reports as may be required by law. They shall provide the Governor with information relating to their respective offices, either in writing under oath, or otherwise, as the Governor may require.

Section 20. BOND
Civil officers of the Executive Branch may be required by law to give reasonable bond or other security for the faithful performance of their duties. If any officer is in default of such a requirement, his office shall be deemed vacant.

Section 21. COMPENSATION
Officers of the Executive Branch shall be paid salaries established by law and shall receive no other compensation for their services. Changes in the salaries of these officers elected or appointed for stated terms shall not take effect during the stated terms.

ARTICLE VI
The Judiciary

Section 1. COURTS
The judicial power is vested in a Supreme Court, an Appellate Court and Circuit Courts.

Section 2. JUDICIAL DISTRICTS
The State is divided into five Judicial Districts for the selection of Supreme and Appellate Court Judges. The First Judicial District consists of Cook County. The remainder of the State shall be divided by law into four Judicial Districts of substantially equal population, each of which shall be compact and composed of contiguous counties.

447

Encyclopedia of Illinois

Section 3. SUPREME COURT — ORGANIZATION

The Supreme Court shall consist of seven Judges. Three shall be selected from the First Judicial District and one from each of the other Judicial Districts. Four Judges constitute a quorum and the concurrence of four is necessary for a decision. Supreme Court Judges shall select a Chief Justice from their number to serve for a term of three years.

Section 4. SUPREME COURT — JURISDICTION

(a) The Supreme Court may exercise original jurisdiction in cases relating to revenue, mandamus, prohibition or habeas corpus and as may be necessary to the complete determination of any case on review.

(b) Appeals from judgments of Circuit Courts imposing a sentence of death shall be directly to the Supreme Court as a matter of right. The Supreme Court shall provide by rule for direct appeal in other cases.

(c) Appeals from the Appellate Court to the Supreme Court are a matter of right if a question under the Constitution of the United States or of this State arises for the first time in and as a result of the action of the Appellate Court, or if a division of the Appellate Court certifies that a case decided by it involves a question of such importance that the case should be decided by the Supreme Court. The Supreme Court may provide by rule for appeals from the Appellate Court in other cases.

Section 5. APPELLATE COURT — ORGANIZATION

The number of Appellate Judges to be selected from each Judicial District shall be provided by law. The Supreme Court shall prescribe by rule the number of Appellate divisions in each Judicial District. Each Appellate division shall have at least three Judges. Assignments to divisions shall be made by the Supreme Court. A majority of a division constitutes a quorum and the concurrence of a majority of the division is necessary for a decision. There shall be at least one division in each Judicial District and each division shall sit at times and places prescribed by rules of the Supreme Court.

Section 6. APPELLATE COURT — JURISDICTION

Appeals from final judgments of a Circuit Court are a matter of right to the Appellate Court in the Judicial District in which the Circuit Court is located except in cases appealable directly to the Supreme Court and except that after a trial on the merits in a criminal case, there shall be no appeal from a judgment of acquittal. The Supreme Court may provide by rule for appeals to the Appellate Court from other than final judgments of Circuit Courts. The Appellate Court may exercise original jurisdiction when necessary to the complete determination of any case on review. The Appellate Court shall have such powers of direct review of administrative action as provided by law.

Section 7. JUDICIAL CIRCUITS

(a) The State shall be divided into Judicial Circuits consisting of one or more counties. The First Judicial District shall constitute a Judicial Circuit. The Judicial Circuits within the other Judicial Districts shall be as provided by law. Circuits composed of more than one county shall be compact and of contiguous counties. The General Assembly by law may provide for the division of a circuit for the purpose of selection of Circuit Judges and for the selection of Circuit Judges from the circuit at large.

(b)   Each Judicial Circuit shall have one Circuit Court with such number of Circuit Judges as provided by law. Unless otherwise provided by law, there shall be at least one Circuit Judge from each county. In the First Judicial District, unless otherwise provided by law, Cook County, Chicago, and the area outside Chicago shall be separate units for the selection of Circuit Judges, with at least twelve chosen at large from the area outside Chicago and at least thirty-six chosen at large from Chicago.

(c)   Circuit Judges in each circuit shall select by secret ballot a Chief Judge from their number to serve at their pleasure. Subject to the authority of the Supreme Court, the Chief Judge shall have general administrative authority over his court, including authority to provide for divisions, general or specialized, and for appropriate times and places of holding court.

Section 8. ASSOCIATE JUDGES

Each Circuit Court shall have such number of Associate Judges as provided by law. Associate Judges shall be appointed by the Circuit Judges in each circuit as the Supreme Court shall provide by rule. In the First Judicial District, unless otherwise provided by law, at least one-fourth of the Associate Judges shall be appointed from, and reside, outside Chicago. The Supreme Court shall provide by rule for matters to be assigned to Associate Judges.

Section 9. CIRCUIT COURTS — JURISDICTION

Circuit Courts shall have original jurisdiction of all justiciable matters except when the Supreme Court has original and exclusive jurisdiction relating to redistricting of the General Assembly and to the ability of the Governor to serve or resume office. Circuit Courts shall have such power to review administrative action as provided by law.

Section 10. TERMS OF OFFICE

The terms of office of Supreme and Appellate Court Judges shall be ten years; of Circuit Judges, six years; and of Associate Judges, four years.

Section 11. ELIGIBILITY FOR OFFICE

No person shall be eligible to be a Judge or Associate Judge unless he is a United States citizen, a licensed attorney-at-law of this State, and a resident of the unit which selects him. No change in the boundaries of a unit shall affect the tenure in office of a Judge or Associate Judge incumbent at the time of such change.

Section 12. ELECTION AND RETENTION

(a)   Supreme, Appellate and Circuit Judges shall be nominated at primary elections or by petition. Judges shall be elected at general or judicial elections as the General Assembly shall provide by law. A person eligible for the office of Judge may cause his name to appear on the ballot as a candidate for Judge at the primary and at the general or judicial elections by submitting petitions. The General Assembly shall prescribe by law the requirements for petitions.

(b)   The office of a Judge shall be vacant upon his death, resignation, retirement, removal, or upon the conclusion of his term without retention in office. Whenever an additional Appellate or Circuit Judge is authorized by law, the office shall be filled in the manner provided for filling a vacancy in that office.

(c)   A vacancy occurring in the office of Supreme, Appellate or Circuit Judge shall be filled as the General Assembly may provide by law. In the absence of a law, vacancies may be filled by appointment by the Supreme Court. A person appointed to fill a vacancy 60 or more days prior to the next primary election to nominate Judges shall serve until the vacancy is filled for a term at the next general or judicial election. A person appointed to fill a vacancy less than 60 days prior to the next primary election to nominate Judges shall serve until the vacancy is filled at the second general or judicial election following such appointment.

(d)   Not less than six months before the general election preceding the expiration of his term of office, a Supreme, Appellate or Circuit Judge who has been elected to that office may file in the office of the Secretary of State a declaration of candidacy to succeed himself. The Secretary of State, not less than 63 days before the election, shall certify the Judge's candidacy to the proper election officials. The names of Judges seeking retention shall be submitted to the electors, separately and without party designation, on the sole question whether each Judge shall be retained in office for another term. The retention elections shall be conducted at general elections in the appropriate Judicial District, for Supreme and Appellate Judges, and in the circuit for Circuit Judges. The affirmative vote of three-fifths of the electors voting on the question shall elect the Judge to the office for a term commencing on the first Monday in December following his election.

(e)   A law reducing the number of Appellate or Circuit Judges shall be without prejudice to the right of the Judges affected to seek retention in office. A reduction shall become effective when a vacancy occurs in the affected unit.

Section 13. PROHIBITED ACTIVITIES
(a)   The Supreme Court shall adopt rules of conduct for Judges and Associate Judges.

(b)   Judges and Associate Judges shall devote full time to judicial duties. They shall not practice law, hold a position of profit, hold office under the United States or this State or unit of local government or school district or in a political party. Service in the State militia or armed forces of the United States for periods of time permitted by rule of the Supreme Court shall not disqualify a person from serving as a Judge or Associate Judge.

Section 14. JUDICIAL SALARIES AND EXPENSES — FEE OFFICERS ELIMINATED
Judges shall receive salaries provided by law which shall not be diminished to take effect during their terms of office. All salaries and such expenses as may be provided by law shall be paid by the State, except that Appellate, Circuit and Associate Judges shall receive such additional compensation from counties within their district or circuit as may be provided by law. There shall be no fee officers in the judicial system.

Section 15. RETIREMENT — DISCIPLINE
(a)   The General Assembly may provide by law for the retirement of Judges and Associate Judges at a prescribed age. Any retired Judge or Associate Judge, with his consent may be assigned by the Supreme Court to judicial service for which he shall receive the applicable compensation in lieu of retirement benefits. A retired Associate Judge may be assigned only as an Associate Judge.

(b)   A Judicial Inquiry Board is created. The Supreme Court shall select two Circuit Judges as members and the Governor shall appoint four persons who are not lawyers and three lawyers as members of the Board. No more than two of the lawyers and two of the non-lawyers appointed by the Governor shall be members of the same political party. The terms of Board members shall be four years. A vacancy on the Board shall be filled for a full term in the manner the original appointment was made. No member may serve on the Board more than eight years.

(c)   The Board shall be convened permanently, with authority to conduct investigations, receive or initiate complaints concerning a Judge or Associate Judge, and file complaints with the Courts Commission. The Board shall not file a complaint unless five members believe that a reasonable basis exists (1) to charge the Judge or Associate Judge with willful misconduct in office, persistent failure to perform his duties, or other conduct that is prejudicial to the administration of justice or that brings the judicial office into disrepute, or (2) to charge that the Judge or Associate Judge is physically or mentally unable to perform his duties. All proceedings of the Board shall be confidential except the filing of a complaint with the Courts Commission. The Board shall prosecute the complaint.

(d)   The Board shall adopt rules governing its procedures. It shall have subpoena power and authority to appoint and direct its staff. Members of the Board who are not Judges shall receive per diem compensation and necessary expenses; members who are Judges shall receive necessary expenses only. The General Assembly by law shall appropriate funds for the operation of the Board.

(e)   A Courts Commission is created consisting of one Supreme Court Judge selected by that Court, who shall be its chairman, two Appellate Court Judges selected by that Court and two Circuit Judges selected by the Supreme Court. The Commission shall be convened permanently to hear complaints filed by the Judicial Inquiry Board. The Commission shall have authority after notice and public hearing, (1) to remove from office, suspend without pay, censure or reprimand a Judge or Associate Judge for willful misconduct in Office, persistent failure to perform his duties, or other conduct that is prejudicial to the administration of justice or that brings the judicial office into disrepute, or (2) to suspend, with or without pay, or retire a Judge or Associate Judge who is physically or mentally unable to perform his duties.

(f)   The concurrence of three members of the Commission shall be necessary for a decision. The decision of the Commission shall be final.

(g)   The Commission shall adopt rules governing its procedures and shall have power to issue subpoenas. The General Assembly shall provide by law for the expenses of the Commission.

Section 16. ADMINISTRATION

General administrative and supervisory authority over all courts is vested in the Supreme Court and shall be exercised by the Chief Justice in accordance with its rules. The Supreme Court shall appoint an administrative director and staff, who shall serve at its pleasure, to assist the Chief Justice in his duties. The Supreme Court may assign a Judge temporarily to any court and an Associate Judge to serve temporarily as an Associate Judge on any Circuit Court. The Supreme Court shall provide by rule for expeditious and inexpensive appeals.

Section 17. JUDICIAL CONFERENCE
The Supreme Court shall provide by rule for an annual judicial conference to consider the work of the courts and to suggest improvements in the administration of justice and shall report thereon annually in writing to the General Assembly not later than January 31.

Section 18. CLERKS OF COURTS
(a) The Supreme Court and the Appellate Court Judges of each Judicial District, respectively, shall appoint a clerk and other non-judicial officers for their Court or District.

(b) The General Assembly shall provide by law for the election, or for the appointment by Circuit Judges, of clerks and other non-judicial officers of the Circuit Courts and for their terms of office and removal for cause.

(c) The salaries of clerks and other non-judicial officers shall be as provided by law.

Section 19. STATE'S ATTORNEYS — SELECTION, SALARY
A State's Attorney shall be elected in each county in 1972 and every fourth year thereafter for a four year term. One State's Attorney may be elected to serve two or more counties if the governing boards of such counties so provide and a majority of the electors of each county voting on the issue approve. A person shall not be eligible for the office of State's Attorney unless he is a United States citizen and a licensed attorney-at-law of this State. His salary shall be provided by law.

ARTICLE VII
Local Government

Section 1. MUNICIPALITIES AND UNITS OF LOCAL GOVERNMENT
"Municipalities" means cities, villages and incorporated towns. "Units of local government" means counties, municipalities, townships, special districts, and units, designated as units of local government by law, which exercise limited governmental powers or powers in respect to limited governmental subjects, but does not include school districts.

Section 2. COUNTY TERRITORY, BOUNDARIES AND SEATS
(a) The General Assembly shall provide by law for the formation, consolidation, merger, division, and dissolution of counties, and for the transfer of territory between counties.

(b) County boundaries shall not be changed unless approved by referendum in each county affected.

(c) County seats shall not be changed unless approved by three-fifths of those voting on the question in a county-wide referendum.

Section 3. COUNTY BOARDS
(a) A county board shall be elected in each county. The number of members of the county board shall be fixed by ordinance in each county within limitations provided by law.

(b) The General Assembly by law shall provide methods available to all counties for the election of county board members. No county, other than Cook County, may change its method of electing board members except as approved by county-wide referendum.

(c) Members of the Cook County Board shall be elected from two districts, Chicago and that part of Cook County outside Chicago, unless (1) a different method of election is approved by a majority of votes cast in each of the two districts in a county-wide referendum or (2) the Cook County Board by ordinance divides the county into single member districts from which members of the County Board resident in each district are elected. If a different method of election is adopted pursuant to option (1) the method of election may thereafter be altered only pursuant to option (2) or by county-wide referendum. A different method of election may be adopted pursuant to option (2) only once and the method of election may thereafter be altered only by county-wide referendum.

Section 4. COUNTY OFFICERS

(a) Any county may elect a chief executive officer as provided by law. He shall have those duties and powers provided by law and those provided by county ordinance.

(b) The President of the Cook County Board shall be elected from the County at large and shall be the chief executive officer of the County. If authorized by county ordinance, a person seeking election as President of the Cook County Board may also seek election as a member of the Board.

(c) Each county shall elect a sheriff, county clerk and treasurer and may elect or appoint a coroner, recorder, assessor, auditor and such other officers as provided by law or by county ordinance. Except as changed pursuant to this Section, elected county officers shall be elected for terms of four years at general elections as provided by law. Any office may be created or eliminated and the terms of office and manner of selection changed by county-wide referendum. Offices other than sheriff, county clerk and treasurer may be eliminated and the terms of office and manner of selection changed by law. Offices other than sheriff, county clerk, treasurer, coroner, recorder, assessor and auditor may be eliminated and the terms of office and manner of selection changed by county ordinance.

(d) County officers shall have those duties, powers and functions provided by law and those provided by county ordinance. County officers shall have the duties, powers or functions derived from common law or historical precedent unless altered by law or county ordinance.

(e) The county treasurer or the person designated to perform his functions may act as treasurer of any unit of local government and any school district in his county when requested by any such unit or school district and shall so act when required to do so by law.

Section 5. TOWNSHIPS

The General Assembly shall provide by law for the formation of townships in any county when approved by county-wide referendum. Townships may be consolidated or merged, and one or more townships may be dissolved or divided, when approved by referendum in each township affected. All townships in a county may be dissolved when approved by a referendum in the total area in which township officers are elected.

Section 6. POWERS OF HOME RULE UNITS

(a) A County which has a chief executive officer elected by the electors of the county and any municipality which has a population of more than

25,000 are home rule units. Other municipalities may elect by referendum to become home rule units. Except as limited by this Section, a home rule unit may exercise any power and perform any function pertaining to its government and affairs including, but not limited to, the power to regulate for the protection of the public health, safety, morals and welfare; to license; to tax; and to incur debt.

(b) A home rule unit by referendum may elect not to be a home rule unit.

(c) If a home rule county ordinance conflicts with an ordinance of a municipality, the municipal ordinance shall prevail within its jurisdiction.

(d) A home rule unit does not have the power (1) to incur debt payable from ad valorem property tax receipts maturing more than 40 years from the time it is incurred or (2) to define and provide for the punishment of a felony.

(e) A home rule unit shall have only the power that the General Assembly may provide by law (1) to punish by imprisonment for more than six months or (2) to license for revenue or impose taxes upon or measured by income or earnings or upon occupations.

(f) A home rule unit shall have the power subject to approval by referendum to adopt, alter or repeal a form of government provided by law, except that the form of government of Cook County shall be subject to the provisions of Section 3 of this Article. A home rule municipality shall have the power to provide for its officers, their manner of selection and terms of office only as approved by referendum or as otherwise authorized by law. A home rule county shall have the power to provide for its officers, their manner of selection and terms of office in the manner set forth in Section 4 of this Article.

(g) The General Assembly by a law approved by the vote of three-fifths of the members elected to each house may deny or limit the power to tax and any other power or function of a home rule unit not exercised or performed by the State other than a power or function specified in subsection (I) of this section.

(h) The General Assembly may provide specifically by law for the exclusive exercise by the State of any power or function of a home rule unit other than a taxing power or a power or function specified in subsection (I) of this Section.

(i) Home rule units may exercise and perform concurrently with the State any power or function of a home rule unit to the extent that the General Assembly by law does not specifically limit the concurrent exercise or specifically declare the State's exercise to be exclusive.

(j) The General Assembly may limit by law the amount of debt which home rule counties may incur and may limit by law approved by three-fifths of the members elected to each house the amount of debt, other than debt payable from ad valorem property tax receipts, which home rule municipalities may incur.

(k) The General Assembly may limit by law the amount and require referendum approval of debt to be incurred by home rule municipalities, payable from ad valorem property tax receipts, only in excess of the following percentages of the assessed value of its taxable property: (1) if its population is 500,000 or more, an aggregate of three percent; (2) if its population is more than 25,000 and less than 500,000, an aggregate of one percent; and (3) if its population is 25,000 or less, an aggregate of one-half percent. Indebtedness which is outstanding on the effective date of this Constitution or which is thereafter approved by referendum or assumed from another unit of local government shall not be included in the foregoing percentage amounts.

(l)   The General Assembly may not deny or limit the power of home rule units (1) to make local improvements by special assessment and to exercise this power jointly with other counties and municipalities, and other classes of units of local government having that power on the effective date of this Constitution unless that power is subsequently denied by law to any such other units of local government or (2) to levy or impose additional taxes upon areas within their boundaries in the manner provided by law for the provision of special services to those areas and for the payment of debt incurred in order to provide those special services.

(m)   Powers and functions of home rule units shall be construed liberally.

Section 7. COUNTIES AND MUNICIPALITIES OTHER THAN HOME RULE UNITS

Counties and municipalities which are not home rule units shall have only powers granted to them by law and the powers (1) to make local improvements by special assessment and to exercise this power jointly with other counties and municipalities, and other classes of units of local government having that power on the effective date of this Constitution unless that power is subsequently denied by law to any such other units of local government; (2) by referendum, to adopt, alter or repeal their forms of government provided by law; (3) in the case of municipalities, to provide by referendum for their officers, manner of selection and terms of office; (4) in the case of counties, to provide for their officers, manner of selection and terms of office as provided in Section 4 of this Article; (5) to incur debt except as limited by law and except that debt payable from ad valorem property tax receipts shall mature within 40 years from the time it is incurred; and (6) to levy or impose additional taxes upon areas within their boundaries in the manner provided by law for the provision of special services to those areas and for the payment of debt incurred in order to provide those special services.

Section 8. POWERS AND OFFICERS OF SCHOOL DISTRICTS AND UNITS OF LOCAL GOVERNMENT OTHER THAN COUNTIES AND MUNICIPALITIES

Townships, school districts, special districts and units, designated by law as units of local government, which exercise limited governmental powers or powers in respect to limited governmental subjects shall have only powers granted by law. No law shall grant the power (1) to any of the foregoing units to incur debt payable from ad valorem property tax receipts maturing more than 40 years from the time it is incurred, or (2) to make improvements by special assessments to any of the foregoing classes of units which do not have that power on the effective date of this Constitution. The General Assembly shall provide by law for the selection of officers of the foregoing units, but the officers shall not be appointed by any person in the Judicial Branch.

Section 9. SALARIES AND FEES

(a)   Compensation of officers and employees and the office expenses of units of local government shall not be paid from fees collected. Fees may be collected as provided by law and by ordinance and shall be deposited upon receipt with the treasurer of the unit. Fees shall not be based upon funds disbursed or collected, nor upon the levy or extension of taxes.

(b) An increase or decrease in the salary of an elected officer of any unit of local government shall not take effect during the term for which that officer is elected.

Section 10. INTERGOVERNMENTAL COOPERATION

(a) Units of local government and school districts may contract or otherwise associate among themselves, with the State, with other states and their units of local government and school districts, and with the United States to obtain or share services and to exercise, combine, or transfer any power or function, in any manner not prohibited by law or by ordinance. Units of local government and school districts may contract and otherwise associate with individuals, associations, and corporations in any manner not prohibited by law or by ordinance. Participating units of government may use their credit, revenues, and other resources to pay costs and to service debt related to intergovernmental activities.

(b) Officers and employees of units of local government and school districts may participate in intergovernmental activities authorized by their units of government without relinquishing their offices or positions.

(c) The State shall encourage intergovernmental cooperation and use its technical and financial resources to assist intergovernmental activities.

Section 11. INITIATIVE AND REFERENDUM

(a) Proposals for actions which are authorized by this Article or by law and which require approval by referendum may be initiated and submitted to the electors by resolution of the governing board of a unit of local government or by petition of electors in the manner provided by law.

(b) Referenda required by this Article shall be held at general elections, except as otherwise provided by law. Questions submitted to referendum shall be adopted if approved by a majority of those voting on the question unless a different requirement is specified in this Article.

Section 12. IMPLEMENTATION OF GOVERNMENTAL CHANGES

The General Assembly shall provide by law for the transfer of assets, powers and functions, and for the payment of outstanding debt in connection with the formation, consolidation, merger, division, dissolution and change in the boundaries of units of local government.

ARTICLE VIII
Finance

Section 1. GENERAL PROVISIONS

(a) Public funds, property or credit shall be used only for public purposes.

(b) The State, units of local government and school districts shall incur obligations for payment or make payments from public funds only as authorized by law or ordinance.

(c) Reports and records of the obligation, receipt and use of public funds of the State, units of local government and school districts are public records available for inspection by the public according to law.

Section 2. STATE FINANCE

(a) The Governor shall prepare and submit to the General Assembly, at a time prescribed by law, a State budget for the ensuing fiscal year. The budget shall set forth the estimated balance of funds available for appropriation at the beginning of the fiscal year, the estimated receipts, and a plan for expenditures and obligations during the fiscal year of every department, authority, public corporation and quasi-public corporation of the State, every State college and university, and every other public agency created by the State, but not of units of local government or school districts. The budget shall also set forth the indebtedness and contingent liabilities of the State and such other information as may be required by law. Proposed expenditures shall not exceed funds estimated to be available for the fiscal year as shown in the budget.

(b)   The General Assembly by law shall make appropriations for all expenditures of public funds by the State. Appropriations for a fiscal year shall not exceed funds estimated by the General Assembly to be available during that year.

Section 3. STATE AUDIT AND AUDITOR GENERAL

(a)   The General Assembly shall provide by law for the audit of the obligation, receipt and use of public funds of the State. The General Assembly, by a vote of three-fifths of the members elected to each house, shall appoint an Auditor General and may remove him for cause by a similar vote. The Auditor General shall serve for a term of ten years. His compensation shall be established by law and shall not be diminished, but may be increased, to take effect during his term.

(b)   The Auditor General shall conduct the audit of public funds of the State. He shall make additional reports and investigations as directed by the General Assembly. He shall report his findings and recommendations to the General Assembly and to the Governor.

Section 4. SYSTEMS OF ACCOUNTING, AUDITING AND REPORTING

The General Assembly by law shall provide systems of accounting, auditing and reporting of the obligation, receipt and use of public funds. These systems shall be used by all units of local government and school districts.

ARTICLE IX
Revenue

Section 1. STATE REVENUE POWER

The General Assembly has the exclusive power to raise revenue by law except as limited or otherwise provided in this Constitution. The power of taxation shall not be surrendered, suspended, or contracted away.

Section 2. NON-PROPERTY TAXES — CLASSIFICATION, EXEMP-TIONS, DEDUCTIONS, ALLOWANCES AND CREDITS

In any law classifying the subjects or objects of non-property taxes or fees, the classes shall be reasonable and the subjects and objects within each class shall be taxed uniformly. Exemptions, deductions, credits, refunds and other allowances shall be reasonable.

Section 3. LIMITATIONS ON INCOME TAXATION

(a)   A tax on or measured by income shall be at a non-graduated rate. At any one time there may be no more than one such tax imposed by the State for State purposes on individuals and one such tax so imposed on corporations. In any such tax imposed upon corporations the rate shall not exceed the rate imposed in individuals by more than a ratio of 8 to 5.

(b)   Laws imposing taxes on or measured by income may adopt by reference provisions of the laws and regulations of the United States, as they then exist or thereafter may be changed, for the purpose of arriving at the amount of income upon which the tax is imposed.

Section 4. REAL PROPERTY TAXATION

(a)   Except as otherwise provided in this Section, taxes upon real property shall be levied uniformly by valuation ascertained as the General Assembly shall provide by law.

(b)   Subject to such limitations as the General Assembly may hereafter prescribe by law, counties with a population of more than 200,000 may classify or to continue to classify real property for purposes of taxation. Any such classification shall be reasonable and assessments shall be uniform within each class. The level of assessment or rate of tax of the highest class in a county shall not exceed two and one-half times the level of assessment or rate of tax of the lowest class in that county. Real property used in farming in a county shall not be assessed at a higher level of assessment than single family residential real property in that county.

(c)   Any depreciation in the value of real estate occasioned by a public easement may be deducted in assessing such property.

Section 5. PERSONAL PROPERTY TAXATION

(a)   The General Assembly by law may classify personal property for purposes of taxation by valuation, abolish such taxes on any or all classes and authorize the levy of taxes in lieu of the taxation of personal property by valuation.

(b)   Any ad valorem personal property tax abolished on or before the effective date of this Constitution shall not be reinstated.

(c)   On or before January 1, 1979, the General Assembly by law shall abolish all ad valorem personal property taxes and concurrently therewith and thereafter shall replace all revenue lost by units of local government and school districts as a result of the abolition of ad valorem personal property taxes subsequent to January 2, 1971. Such revenue shall be replaced by imposing statewide taxes, other than ad valorem taxes on real estate, solely on those classes relieved of the burden of paying ad valorem personal property taxes because of the abolition of such taxes subsequent to January 2, 1971. If any taxes imposed for such replacement purposes are taxes on or measured by income, such replacement taxes shall not be considered for purposes of the limitations of one tax and the ratio of 8 to 5 set forth in Section 3 (a) of this Article.

Section 6. EXEMPTIONS FROM PROPERTY TAXATION

The General Assembly by law may exempt from taxation only the property of the State, units of local government and school districts and property used exclusively for agricultural and horticultural societies, and for school, religious, cemetery and charitable purposes. The General Assembly by law may grant homestead exemptions or rent credits.

Constitution

Section 7. OVERLAPPING TAXING DISTRICTS

The General Assembly may provide by law for fair apportionment of the burden of taxation of property situated in taxing districts that lie in more than one county.

Section 8. TAX SALES

(a) Real property shall not be sold for the nonpayment of taxes or special assessments without judicial proceedings.

(b) The right of redemption from all sales of real estate for the nonpayment of taxes or special assessments, except as provided in subsections (c) and (d), shall exist in favor of owners and persons interested in such real estate for not less than 2 years following such sales.

(c) The right of redemption from the sale for nonpayment of taxes or special assessments of a parcel of real estate which: (1) is vacant non-farm real estate or (2) contains an improvement consisting of a structure or structures each of which contains 7 or more residential units or (3) is commercial or industrial property; shall exist in favor of owners and persons interested in such real estate for not less than one year following such sales.

(d) The right of redemption from the sale for nonpayment of taxes or special assessments of a parcel real estate which: (1) is vacant non-farm real estate or (2) contains an improvement consisting of a structure or structures each of which contains 7 or more residential units or (3) is commercial or industrial property; and upon which all or a part of the general taxes for each of 2 or more years are delinquent shall exist in favor of owners and persons interested in such real estate for not less than 6 months following such sales.

(e) Owners, occupants and parties interested shall be given reasonable notice of the sale and the date of expiration of the period of redemption as the General Assembly provides by law. (As amended by the Sixth Amendment to the Constitution. Approved November 6, 1990, effective November 26, 1990.)

Section 9. STATE DEBT

(a) No State debt shall be incurred except as provided in this Section. For the purpose of this Section, "State debt" means bonds or other evidences of indebtedness which are secured by the full faith and credit of the State or are required to be repaid, directly or indirectly, from tax revenue and which are incurred by the State, any department, authority, public corporation or quasi-public corporation of the State, any State college or university, or any other public agency created by the State, but not by units of local government, or school districts.

(b) State debt for specific purposes may be incurred or the payment of State or other debt guaranteed in such amounts as may be provided either in a law passed by the vote of three-fifths of the members elected to each house of the General Assembly or in a law approved by a majority of the electors voting on the question at the next general election following passage. Any law providing for the incurring or guaranteeing of debt shall set forth the specific purposes and the manner of repayment.

(c) State debt in anticipation of revenues to be collected in a fiscal year may be incurred by law in an amount not exceeding 5% of the State's appropriations for that fiscal year. Such debt shall be retired from the revenues realized in that fiscal year.

(d) State debt may be incurred by law in an amount not exceeding 15%

459

of the State's appropriations for that fiscal year to meet deficits caused by emergencies or failures of revenue. Such law shall provide that the debt be repaid within one year of the date it is incurred.

(e) State debt may be incurred by law to refund outstanding State debt if the refunding debt matures within the term of the outstanding State debt.

(f) The State, departments, authorities, public corporations and quasi-public corporations of the State, the State colleges and universities and other public agencies created by the State, may issue bonds or other evidences of indebtedness which are not secured by the full faith and credit or tax revenue of the State nor required to be repaid, directly or indirectly, from tax revenue, for such purposes and in such amounts as may be authorized by law.

Section 10. REVENUE ARTICLE NOT LIMITED

This Article is not qualified or limited by the provisions of Article VII of this Constitution concerning the size of the majorities in the General Assembly necessary to deny or limit the power to tax granted to units of local government.

ARTICLE X
Education

Section 1. GOAL — FREE SCHOOLS

A fundamental goal of the People of the State is the educational development of all persons to the limits of their capacities.

The State shall provide for an efficient system of high quality public educational institutions and services. Education in public schools through the secondary level shall be free. There may be such other free education as the General Assembly provides by law.

The State has the primary responsibility for financing the system of public education.

Section 2. STATE BOARD OF EDUCATION — CHIEF STATE EDUCATIONAL OFFICER

(a) There is created a State Board of Education to be elected or selected on a regional basis. The number of members, their qualifications, terms of office and manner of election or selection shall be provided by law. The Board, except as limited by law, may establish goals, determine policies, provide for planning and evaluating education programs and recommend financing. The Board shall have such other duties and powers as provided by law.

(b) The State Board of Education shall appoint a chief state educational officer.

Section 3. PUBLIC FUNDS FOR SECTARIAN PURPOSES FORBIDDEN

Neither the General Assembly nor any county, city, town, township, school district, or other public corporation, shall ever make any appropriation or pay from any public fund whatever, anything in aid of any church or sectarian purpose, or to help support or sustain any school, academy, seminary, college, university or other literary or scientific institution, controlled by any church or sectarian denomination whatever; nor shall any grant or donation of land, money, or other personal property ever be made by the State, or any such public corporation, to any church, or for any sectarian purpose.

Constitution

ARTICLE XI
Environment

Section 1. PUBLIC POLICY — LEGISLATIVE RESPONSIBILITY
The public policy of the State and the duty of each person is to provide and maintain a healthful environment for the benefit of this and future generations. The General Assembly shall provide by law for the implementation and enforcement of this public policy.

Section 2. RIGHTS OF INDIVIDUALS
Each person has the right to a healthful environment. Each person may enforce this right against any party, governmental or private, through appropriate legal proceedings subject to reasonable limitation and regulation as the General Assembly may provide by law.

ARTICLE XII
Militia

Section 1. MEMBERSHIP
The State militia consists of all able-bodied persons residing in the State except those exempted by law.

Section 2. SUBORDINATION OF MILITARY POWER
The military shall be in strict subordination to the civil power.

Section 3. ORGANIZATION, EQUIPMENT AND DISCIPLINE
The General Assembly shall provide by law for the organization, equipment and discipline of the militia in conformity with the laws governing the armed forces of the United States.

Section 4. COMMANDER-IN-CHIEF AND OFFICERS
(a)   The Governor is commander-in-chief of the organized militia, except when they are in the service of the United States. He may call them out to enforce the laws, suppress insurrection or repel invasion.

(b)   The Governor shall commission militia officers who shall hold their commissions for such time as may be provided by law.

Section 5. PRIVILEGE FROM ARREST
Except in cases of treason, felony or breach of peace, persons going to, returning from or on militia duty are privileged from arrest.

ARTICLE XIII
General Provisions

Section 1. DISQUALIFICATION FOR PUBLIC OFFICE
A person convicted of a felony, bribery, perjury or other infamous crime shall be ineligible to hold an office created by this Constitution. Eligibility may be restored as provided by law.

Section 2. STATEMENT OF ECONOMIC INTERESTS
All candidates for or holders of state offices and all members of a

461

Commission or Board created by this Constitution shall file a verified statement of their economic interests, as provided by law. The General Assembly by law may impose a similar requirement upon candidates for, or holders of, offices in units of local government and school districts. Statements shall be filed annually with the Secretary of State and shall be available for inspection by the public. The General Assembly by law shall prescribe a reasonable time for filing the statement. Failure to file a statement within the time prescribed shall result in ineligibility for, or forfeiture of, office. This Section shall not be construed as limiting the authority of any branch of government to establish and enforce ethical standards for that branch.

Section 3. OATH OR AFFIRMATION OF OFFICE

Each prospective holder of a State office or other State position created by this Constitution, before taking office, shall take and subscribe to the following oath or affirmation:

"I do solemnly swear (affirm) that I will support the Constitution of the United States, and the Constitution of the State of Illinois, and that I will faithfully discharge the duties of the office of .... to the best of my ability."

Section 4. SOVEREIGN IMMUNITY ABOLISHED

Except as the General Assembly may provide by law, sovereign immunity in this State is abolished.

Section 5. PENSION AND RETIREMENT RIGHTS

Membership in any pension or retirement system of the State, any unit of local government or school district, or any agency or instrumentality thereof, shall be an enforceable contractual relationship, the benefits of which shall not be diminished or impaired.

Section 6. CORPORATIONS

Corporate charters shall be granted, amended, dissolved, or extended only pursuant to general laws.

Section 7. PUBLIC TRANSPORTATION

Public transportation is an essential public purpose for which public funds may be expended. The General Assembly by law may provide for, aid, and assist public transportation, including the granting of public funds or credit to any corporation or public authority authorized to provide public transportation within the State.

Section 8. BRANCH BANKING

Branch banking shall be authorized only by law approved by three-fifths of the members voting on the question or a majority of the members elected, whichever is greater, in each house of the General Assembly.

ARTICLE XIV
Constitutional Revision

Section 1. CONSTITUTIONAL CONVENTION

(a) Whenever three-fifths of the members elected to each house of the General Assembly so direct, the question of whether a Constitutional Convention should be called shall be submitted to the electors at the general election next occurring at least six months after such legislative direction.

(b)   If the question of whether a Convention should be called is not submitted during any twenty-year period, the Secretary of State shall submit such question at the general election in the twentieth year following the last submission.

(c)   The vote on whether to call a Convention shall be on a separate ballot. A Convention shall be called if approved by three-fifths of those voting on the question or a majority of those voting in the election.

(d)   The General Assembly, at the session following approval by the electors, by law shall provide for the Convention and for the election of two delegates from each Senatorial District; designate the time and place of the Convention's first meeting which shall be within three months after the election of delegates; fix and provide for the pay of delegates and officers; and provide for expenses necessarily incurred by the Convention.

(e)   To be eligible to be a delegate a person must meet the same eligibility requirements as a member of the General Assembly. Vacancies shall be filled as provided by law.

(f)   The Convention shall prepare such revision of or amendments to the Constitution as it deems necessary. Any proposed revision or amendments approved by a majority of the delegates elected shall be submitted to the electors in such manner as the Convention determines, at an election designated or called by the Convention occurring not less than two nor more than six months after the Convention's adjournment. Any revision or amendments proposed by the Convention shall be published with explanations, as the Convention provides, at least one month preceding the election.

(g)   The vote on the proposed revision or amendments shall be on a separate ballot. Any proposed revision or amendments shall become effective, as the Convention provides, if approved by a majority of those voting on the question.

Section 2. AMENDMENTS BY GENERAL ASSEMBLY

(a)   Amendments to this Constitution may be initiated in either house of the General Assembly. Amendments shall be read in full on three different days in each house and reproduced before the vote is taken on final passage. Amendments approved by the vote of three-fifths of the members elected to each house shall be submitted to the electors at the general election next occurring at least six months after such legislative approval, unless withdrawn by a vote of a majority of the members elected to each house.

(b)   Amendments proposed by the General Assembly shall be published with explanations, as provided by law, at least one month preceding the vote thereon by the electors. The vote on the proposed amendment or amendments shall be on a separate ballot. A proposed amendment shall become effective as the amendment provides if approved by either three-fifths of those voting on the question or a majority of those voting in the election.

(c)   The General Assembly shall not submit proposed amendments to more than three Articles of the Constitution at any one election. No amendment shall be proposed or submitted under this Section from the time a Convention is called until after the electors have voted on the revision or amendments, if any, proposed by such Convention.

Section 3. CONSTITUTIONAL INITIATIVE FOR LEGISLATIVE ARTICLE

Amendments to Article IV of this Constitution may be proposed by a petition signed by a number of electors equal in number to at least eight per-cent of the total votes cast for candidates for Governor in the preceding guber-natorial election. Amendments shall be limited to structural and procedural subjects contained in Article IV. A petition shall contain the text of the pro-posed amendment and the date of the general election at which the proposed amendment is to be submitted, shall have been signed by the petitioning elec-tors not more than twenty-four months preceding that general election and shall be filed with the Secretary of State at least six months before that general election. The procedure for determining the validity and sufficiency of a peti-tion shall be provided by law. If the petition is valid and sufficient, the pro-posed amendment shall be submitted to the electors at that general election and shall become effective if approved by either three-fifths of those voting on the amendment or a majority of those voting in the election.

Section 4. AMENDMENTS TO THE CONSTITUTION OF THE UNITED STATES

The affirmative vote of three-fifths of the members elected to each house of the General Assembly shall be required to request Congress to call a Federal Constitutional Convention, to ratify a proposed amendment to the Constitution of the United States, or to call a State Convention to ratify a pro-posed amendment to the Constitution of the United States. The General Assembly shall not take action on any proposed amendment to the Constitution of the United States submitted for ratification by legislatures unless a majority of the members of the General Assembly shall have been elected after the proposed amendment has been submitted for ratification. The requirements of this Section shall govern to the extent that they are not incon-sistent with requirements by the United States.

TRANSITION SCHEDULE

The following Schedule Provisions shall remain part of this Constitution until their terms have been executed. Once each year the Attorney General shall review the following provisions and certify to the Secretary of State which, if any, have been executed. Any provisions so certified shall thereafter be removed from the Schedule and no longer published as part of this Constitution.

Section 1. (Removed)
Section 2. Prospective Operation of Bill of Rights.
Section 3. (Removed)
Section 4. Judicial Offices.
Section 5. Local Government.
Section 6. Authorized Bonds.
Section 7. (Removed)
Section 8. Cumulative Voting for Directors.
Section 9. General Transition.
Section 10. (Removed)

Section 2. PROSPECTIVE OPERATION OF BILL OF RIGHTS

Any rights, procedural or substantive, created for the first time by Article I shall be prospective and not retroactive.

Section 4. JUDICIAL OFFICES

(a) On the effective date of this Constitution, Associate Judges and mag-

Constitution

istrates shall become Circuit Judges and Associate Judges, respectively, of their Circuit Courts. All laws and rules of court theretofore applicable to Associate Judges and magistrates shall remain in force and be applicable to the persons in their new offices until changed by the General Assembly or the Supreme Court, as the case may be.

(b) (Removed)

(c) (Removed)

(d) Until otherwise provided by law and except to the extent that the authority is inconsistent with Section 8 of Article VII, the Circuit Courts shall continue to exercise the non-judicial functions vested by law as of December 31, 1963, in county courts or the judges thereof.

Section 5. LOCAL GOVERNMENT

(a) The number of members of a county board in a county which, as of the effective date of this Constitution, elects three members at large may be changed only as approved by county-wide referendum. If the number of members of such a county board is changed by county-wide referendum, the provisions of Section 3(a) of Article VII relating to the number of members of a county board shall govern thereafter.

(b) In Cook County, until (1) a method of election of county board members different from the method in existence on the effective date of this Constitution is approved by a majority of votes cast both in Chicago and in the area outside Chicago in a county-wide referendum or (2) the Cook County Board by ordinance divides the county into single member districts from which members of the County Board resident in each district are elected, the number of members of the Cook County Board shall be fifteen except that the county board may increase the number if necessary to comply with apportionment requirements. If either of the foregoing changes is made, the provisions of Section 3(a) of Article VII shall apply thereafter to Cook County.

(c) Townships in existence on the effective date of this Constitution are continued until consolidated, merged, divided or dissolved in accordance with Section 5 of Article VII.

Section 6. AUTHORIZED BONDS

Nothing in Section 9 of Article IX shall be construed to limit or impair the power to issue bonds or other evidences of indebtedness authorized but unissued on the effective date of this Constitution.

Section 8. CUMULATIVE VOTING FOR DIRECTORS

Shareholders of all corporations heretofore organized under any law of this State which requires cumulative voting of shares for corporate directors shall retain their right to vote cumulatively for such directors.

Section 9. GENERAL TRANSITION

The rights and duties of all public bodies shall remain as if this Constitution had not been adopted with the exception of such changes as are contained in this Constitution. All laws, ordinances, regulations and rules of court not contrary to, or inconsistent with, the provisions of this Constitution shall remain in force, until they shall expire by their own limitation or shall be altered or repealed pursuant to this Constitution. The validity of all public and private bonds, debts and contracts, and of all suits, actions and rights of action, shall continue as if no change had taken place. All officers filling any

465

office by election or appointment shall continue to exercise the duties thereof, until their offices shall have been abolished or their successors selected and qualified in accordance with this Constitution or laws enacted pursuant thereto.

(ATTESTATION)

Done in Convention at the Old State Capitol, in the City of Springfield, on the third day of September, in the year of our Lord one thousand nine hundred and seventy, of the Independence of the United States of America the one hundred and ninety-fifth, and of the Statehood of Illinois the one hundred and fifty-second.

AMENDMENTS PROPOSED

(A proposed amendment shall become effective if approved by either three-fifths of those voting on the question or a majority of those voting in the election.)

1974—Governor's Amendatory Veto. Amends Article IV, Section 9, Paragraph (e). Failed. Total vote, 3,047,822. For, 1,302,313; Against, 1,329,719.

1978—Personal Property Tax. Amends Article IX, Section 5. Failed. Total vote, 3,342,985. For, 952,416; Against, 733,845.

1978—Veterans Organizations' Post Homes Exemption. Amends Article IX, Section 6. Failed. Total vote, 3,342,985. For, 747,907; Against, 806,579.

1980—Cutback Amendment. Amends Article IV, Sections 1, 2 and 3. Approved. First Amendment to the Constitution. Total vote, 4, 868,623. For, 2,112,224; Against, 962,325.

1980—Delinquent Tax Sales. Amends Article IX, Section 8. Approved. Second Amendment to the Constitution. Total vote, 4,868,623. For, 1,857,985; Against, 798,422.

1982—Bail and Habeas Corpus. Amends Article I, Section 9. Approved. Total vote, 3,856,875. For, 1,389,796; Against, 239,380.

1984—Veterans' Property Tax Exemption. Amends Article IX, Section 6. Failed. Total vote, 4,969,330. For, 1,147,864. Against, 1,042,481.

1986—Bail and Habeas Corpus. Amends Article I, Section 9. Approved. Total vote, 3,322,657. For, 1,368,242. Against, 402,891.

1986—Veterans' Property Tax Exemption. Amends Article IX, Section 6. Failed. Total vote, 3,322,657. For, 860,609. Against, 727,737.

1988—Voting Qualifications. Amends Article III, Section 1. Approved. Total vote, 4,697,192. For, 2,086,744. Against, 1,162,258.

1988—Delinquent Tax Sales. Amends Article IX, Section 8. Failed. Total vote, 4,697,192. For, 1,497,885. Against, 1,035,190.

1990—Delinquent Tax Sales. Amends Article IX, Section 8. Approved. Total vote, 1,390,318. For, 1,004,546. Against, 385,772.

1992—Crime Victim's Rights. Adds Section 8.1 to Article I. Approved. Total vote, 5,164,357. For, 2,964,592. Against, 715,602.

1992—Education. Amends Article X, Section 1. Failed. Total vote, 5,164,357. For, 1,882,569. Against, 1,417,520.

PROPOSED CONSTITUTIONAL CONVENTION

1988—Proposed call for a Constitutional Convention. Failed. Total vote, 4,697,192. For, 900,109. Against, 2,727,144.

BOOKS ABOUT ILLINOIS

Adair, Anna B. *Indian Trails to Tollways,* 1968.

Adams, James N. *Illinois Place Names,* 1969.

Addams, Jane. *Twenty Years at Hull House* and *The Second Twenty Years at Hull House.* 1910, 1930.

Allen, John W. *Legends & Love of Southern Illinois,* 1963.

Alvord, Clarence W. and C.E. Carter *The Illinois Country,* 1673-1818, 1917-1920. (1965).

Andreas, A. T. *History of Chicago,* 3 vols. 1884-86.

Angle, Paul M. *Here I Have Lived,* 1935.

Angle, Paul M. *Prairie State,* 1968.

Ayars, James Sterling. *The Illinois River,* 1968.

Bale, Florence Gratiot. *Galena's Old Stockade,* 1932.

Bateman, Newton and Paul Selby, *Historical Encyclopedia of Illinois, With Commemorative Biographies,* 1915.

Beardsley, Harry M. *Joseph Smith and his Mormon Empire,* 1931.

Beckner, Earl R. *A History of Illinois Labor Legislation,* 1929.

Beveridge, Albert J. *Abraham Lincoln,* 1809-1858. 2 vols. 1928. *Blue Book of the State of Illinois,* edited by the Secretary of State. Published by authority of the State of Illinois, 1903-1907 to date. A biennial synthesis of the administrative program and record of all the major departments of the State.

Bogart, Ernest L. and Charles M. Thompson. *The Industrial State,* 1870-1893, 1917-1920. *The Modern Commonwealth,* 1893-1918, 1917-1920.

Buck, Solon J. *Illinois in 1818.* 1917-1920.

Burton, W.L. *The Trembling Land, Illinois in the Age of Exploration,* (1966).

Bussan, Carol. *Grant and Galena* 1964.

Calkins, Ernest Elmo. *They Broke the Prairie,* 1937.

Carpenter, John Allan. *Illinois, from its glorious past to present.* 1963. *Land of Lincoln,* 1968.

Clark, George Rogers. *The Conquest of Illinois,* 1920.

Casson, Herbert N *The Romance of Reaper,* 1908.

Clayton, John. *The Illinois Fact Book and Historical Almanac, 1673-1968.* 1970.

Clemen, R. A. *The American Livestock and Meat Industry,* 1923.

Cole, Arthur C. *The Era of the Civil War, 1848-1870.* 1917-20.

Cole, Cyrenus. *I Am A Man, The Indian Black Hawk,* 1938.

Cole, Fay-Cooper and Thorne Duel. *Re-Discovering Illinois,* 1937.

Cromie, Robert Allen. *The Great Chicago Fire,* 1963.

Dedmon, Emmett. *Fabulous Chicago,* 1953.

DeLove, Sidney. *Cook County and Daniel Pope Cook; their story,* 1968.

Drury, John. *Old Illinois Houses* 1977.

Duis, Perry. *Chicago, Creating New Traditions,* 1976. *Early Narratives of the Northwest, 1634-1699,* edited by Louise Phelps Kellogg. 1917.

Faragher, J.M. *Sugar Creek, Life on the Illinois Prairie,* 1988.

Farr, Finis. *Chicago; a Personal History of America's Most American City,* 1973.

Federal Writers' Project. *Illinois; A Descriptive & Historical Guide,* 1939. Reprinted 1971.

Ford, Thomas. *A History of Illinois,* 1854.

Foster, Olive S. *Illinois; A Student's Guide to Localized History,* 1968.

Fradin, Dennis. *Illinois; in Words and Pictures,* 1976.

Gilbert, Paul and Charles Lee Bryson. *Chicago and its Makers,* 1929.

Bibliography

Goodspeed, Thomas Wakefield. *The Story of the University of Chicago*, 1925.

Gray, James. *The Illinois*, 1940.

Hansen, Harry. *Midwest Portraits*, 1923. *A History of Illinois in Paintings, Historical Illustrator:* Robert A. Thom. 1968.

Havighurst, Walter. *The Heartland*, 1962.

Horsley, A.D. *Geography of Illinois*, 1988.

Howard, Robert P. *Illinois; a History of the Prairie State*, 1972.

Humphrey, Grace. *Illinois*, 1917. *Illinois Calendar of Events Illinois* Division of Tourism, 1974-1975. *Illinois Department of Conservation Recreational Areas*, Illinois, Division of Instruction. *Illinois Architecture*, 1974. *Illinois Guide & Gazetter*, Illinois Sespuicentennia Commission 1969. *Illinois: Resources — Development — Possibilities*, Illinois Chamber of Commerce, 1930.

James, Alton James *The Life of George Rogers Clark*, 1928.

Jensen, Richard J. *Illinois Government*, revised, edited 1974. *Illinois A History*, 1978.

Johnson, Charles B. *Growth of Cook County*, 1960.

Keiser, John H. *Building for the Centuries: Illinois*, 1865-1998, 1977.

Kenney, David. *Basic Illinois Government*, Revised and edited. 1974.

King, Martha Bennett. *The Key to Chicago*, 1961.

Kinzie, Mrs. Juliette A. *Wau-Bun, The "Early Days,"* 1933.

Koerner, Gustave. *Memoirs of Gustave Koerner*, 1809-1896. 2 vols. 1908.

Lathrop, Ann. *Illinois, Its People and Culture*, 1975.

Lewis, Lloyd and Henry Justin Smith. *Chicago: The History of its Reputation*, 1929.

MacFarland, Lanning Jr. *Chicagoland's Community Guide*, 1976-1977.

MacFall, Russell P. *Gem Hunter's Guide,* 1963.

Masters, Edgar Lee. *The Sangamon,* 1942.

Masters, Edgar Lee. *The Tale of Chicago,* 1933.

Milton, George Fort. *The Eve of Conflict,* 1934.

Nardulli, P.F. edited, *Diversity, Conflict and State Politics, Regionalism in Illinois Conflict and State Politics. Regionalism in Illinois,* 1989.

Nelson, Ronald E., edited *Illinois, Land and Life in the Prairie State,* 1978.

Nevins, Allan *Illinois.*

Pease, Theodore C. *The Frontier State* 1818-1848. 1917-1920.

Pease, Theodore C. *The Story of Illinois,* 3d. edited. 1965.

Phalen, James M. *Sinnissippi, A Valley under a Spell,* 1942. *The Prairie State, A Documentary History of Illinois,* edited by Robert P. Sutton. 1976.

Putnam, James William. *The Illinois and Michigan Canal* 1918. Quaife, Milo M. *Checagou, From Indian Wigwam to Modern City,* 1933.

Reyonlds, John. *My own Times; Embracing Also a History of My Life,* 1879.. *Parks & Memorials of the State of Illinois,* C.M. Service. 1920.

Reynolds, John. *The Pioneer History of Illinois,* 1887.

Ridgley, Douglas C. *The Geography of Illinois,* 1887.

Sandburg, Carl. *Abraham Lincoln, the Prairie Years,* 1926.

Schlarman, J.H. *From Quebec to New Orleans,* 1929.

Shertone, Henry Clyde. *The Mound Builders,* 1931.

Smith, Henry Justin. *Chicago, A Portrait,* 1931.

Sparks, Edwin Erle, (Ed..) *The Lincoln-Douglas Debates of 1958.*

Staley, Eugene. *History of the Illinois State Federation of Labor,* 1930. *Starved Rock Land,* Department of Business & Economy Development Division of Tourism. 1970.

Suggested Readings in Illinois History,
complied by Paul M. Angle.

Thomas, Benjamin P. *Lincoln's New Salem,* 1934.

Tingley, Donald F. *Essays in Illinois History,* 1968.
Twenty Scenic Motor Tours to Take in Illinois,
State of Illinois Division of Tourism, 1977. U.S.
Department of Commerce, Illinois, 1972 Census of
Manufactures U.S. Government Printing Office.

Walton, Clyde C. *An Illinois Reader,* edited 1970.

Ward, Estelle Francis. *The Story of Northwestern
University,* 1924.

Watters, Mary. *Illinois in the Second World War,*
1951-52.

Wheeler, Adade, with Wortman, Marlene S., *The Roads
They Made, Women in Illinois History,* 1977.

Wilson, Howard E. *Mary McDowell, Neighbor,* 1928.

Wolfe, Anya. *It Happened in Illinois,* 1974.

Wollin, J.C. *The Mazon Creek Fossils,* Earth Science
Magazine, Published 1965.

INDEX

(see page 403 for Alphabetical Listing to Historic Places)

Index

Index

Index

Index

Index

Index

Index

Index

Index

Index

Index

Index

Index

Index

MacMurray
  Fred, 290
Macomb, 303
Macomb
  Alexander, 303
Macon, 303
Macon County
  Museum Complex, 230
Madison, 303, 351
Madison County
  Historical Museum, 243
Madison
  James, 95, 96
Madlener
  Albert F., House, 215
Maeystown, 304
Magnolia Manor, 197
Makanda, 304
Malaria, 34
Malden, 304
Mallinckrodt College, 357
Manchester, 304
Manhattan, 304
Manito, 304
Manlius, 304
Mann Act, 267
Mann
  James Robert, 267
Manny
  John H., 160
Mansfield, 304
Manteno, 304
Manufacturing, 39, 228
Maquon, 305
Marathon Electric Manufacturing
  Corporation, 238
Marcus
  L., 72
Marcy
  Pasquale (Pat), 76
Marina City, 213, 422
Marine, 305
Marion Hills, 305
Marissa, 305
Market House, 263
Markham, 305
Marley, 305
Maroa, 305
Marquette, 131
Marquette Building, 215
Marquette
  Father Jacques, 1, 19,

    29, 58, 156, 195, 251,
    260, 271, 274, 283,
    288, 291, 295, 302, 345
Marquis
  A.N., 251
Marseilles, 305
Marshall, 306
Marshall County, 306
Marshall Field's, 213
Marshall
  John, 306
Martin
  Joseph, 306
Martin-Mitchell Museum, 319
Martinsville, 306
Martinton, 306
Mary's Covered Bridge, 432
Mary's River Covered, 212
Maryville, 306
Mascoutah, 306
Mason, 306
Mason City, 307
Mason County, 307
Mason State Forest, 304
Mass Transit Division, 86
Mass Transit Program, 129
Massac Ccounty, 307
Massasoit
  Chief, 310
Masters
  Edgar Lee, 343
Material Service
  Corporation, 255
Matteson, 307
Matteson
  Elnathan, 102
  Joel A., 307
Matthiessen State Park, 331
Matthiesson, 330
Mattoon, 307
Mattoon Fish Hatchery, 328
Mattoon
  William, 307
Mayenard
  John, 281
Maywood, 308
Mazon, 308
Mazon Creek, 188
McBane
  William A., 310

Index

Index

Index

Index

Index

Index

Index

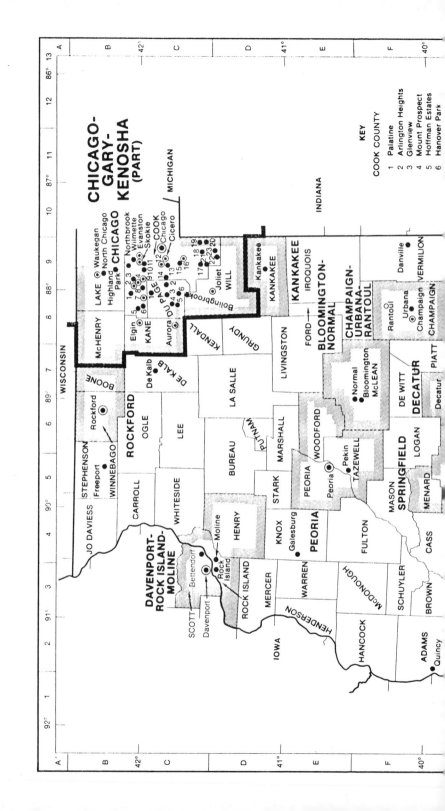

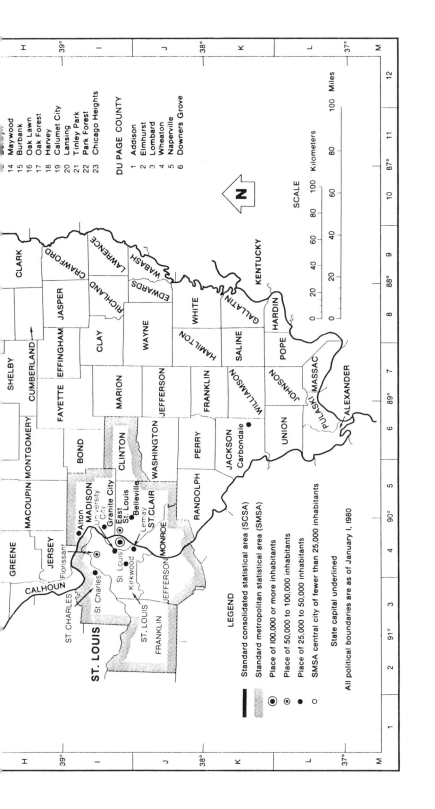

14 Maywood
15 Burbank
16 Oak Lawn
17 Oak Forest
18 Harvey
19 Calumet City
20 Lansing
21 Tinley Park
22 Park Forest
23 Chicago Heights

DU PAGE COUNTY

1 Addison
2 Elmhurst
3 Lombard
4 Wheaton
5 Naperville
6 Downers Grove

N

SCALE

Kilometers

0   20   40   60   80   100

0   20   40   60   80   100 Miles

CLARK
CRAWFORD
LAWRENCE
WABASH
EDWARDS
RICHLAND
JASPER
CLAY
WAYNE
WHITE
HAMILTON
GALLATIN
SALINE
HARDIN
POPE
JOHNSON
MASSAC
PULASKI
ALEXANDER
UNION
WILLIAMSON
FRANKLIN
JEFFERSON
MARION
WASHINGTON
PERRY
JACKSON
  Carbondale
RANDOLPH
CLINTON
ST.CLAIR
MONROE
BOND
MADISON
  Alton
  University City
  Granite City
  Belleville
  East St. Louis
  Lemay
  St. Louis
  Kirkwood
JEFFERSON
FRANKLIN
ST. LOUIS
St. Charles
ST. CHARLES
  Florissant
CALHOUN
JERSEY
GREENE
MACOUPIN MONTGOMERY
FAYETTE EFFINGHAM
CUMBERLAND
SHELBY

ST. LOUIS

KENTUCKY

SHELBY

H 39° I 38° J 38° K L 37° M

1   2   3   4   5   6   7   8   9   10   11   12

91° 90° 89° 88° 87°

37°
38°
39°